A History of Jazz in Britain
1950–70

Other Quartet titles by the same author

A History of Jazz in Britain 1919–50
All This and Many a Dog (*autobiography*)

A History of Jazz in Britain 1950–70

Jim Godbolt

Quartet Books
London   New York

For Al, Alex, Bruce, George (two of these), Humph, Mick, Pete, Ronnie, Sandy and Wally

First published by Quartet Books Limited 1989

A Member of the Namara Group
27/29 Goodge Street, London W1P 1FD

Copyright © 1989 by Jim Godbolt

British Library Cataloguing in Publication Data
Godbolt, Jim, *1922–*
   A History of Jazz in Britain 1950–70
   1. Great Britain. Jazz, 1950–1970
   I. Title
   785.42'0941

ISBN 0-7043-2526-8

Typeset by MC Typeset Ltd, Gillingham, Kent
Reproduced, printed and bound in Great Britain by
BPCC Hazell Books Ltd
Member of BPCC Ltd
Aylesbury, Bucks, England

Contents

	Introduction and Acknowledgements	vii
1	New Orleans to Barnehurst to Royal Festival Hall	1
2	On the Boats and Up at Carlo's	26
3	He Played as He Pleased	48
4	Traditionalism Rampant	67
5	Bop on the Road	93
6	The Condon Connection, the Three Bs and Traddy-pop	121
7	Towards the Centre	148
8	The Ban is Breached	166
9	First of the Giants	189
10	The Invasion Mounts	209
11	Entry of the Soloists and Coals to Alabama	231
12	Jazz City	247
13	A Flood of Literature	271
14	Twenty Extraordinary Years	296
	Discography and Bibliography by Alun Morgan	300
	Index	320

Introduction and Acknowledgements

In my *A History of Jazz in Britain 1919–50*, published in 1984, I wrote a lengthy introduction in which I explained why I ended my narrative in 1950. Briefly, I offered two reasons for what some critics later referred to as an 'arbitrary' termination. The first was that to embrace sixty-five years of jazz in Britain up to 1984 would have been an extremely punishing task, and had I been brave or foolish enough to tackle such a span it would inevitably have resulted in loss of essential detail – or the production of a book twice the size and prohibitively expensive. The second part of the explanation revolved around my considered view that the post-1950 scene was markedly different in many respects from the years that preceded it. Among the many new circumstances, the most notable was that, in 1950, British musicians could actually earn some sort of a living playing jazz; previously, such activity took place mainly in recording studios or unpaid 'after hours' jam sessions for professionals and, in pub back rooms, for amateurs and semi-professionals. There was also to be a flood of records on both major and independent labels (on 78s and microgroove) and the introduction of the long-playing record, enabling 'modern jazz' musicians to extend themselves infinitely more than their counterparts in the twenties, thirties and forties, these having been limited to the approximate three-minute duration of the 78-rpm disc.

In addition, in 1956, the Musicians' Union ban on American musicians appearing in Britain was lifted, and the steady stream of players from the country of the music's birth added a new dimension to the general picture, by enabling British musicians to stand alongside their mentors on the club and concert stage, as well as delighting the jazz public.

The music itself was to move in many directions and what had once (in the main) been described simply as 'jazz' was henceforth to be referred to by a variety of designations: New Orleans, dixieland, revivalism, traditionalism, mainstream, bebop, cool, free-form, avant-garde etc, all testimony to the completely different nature of events after 1950, although, of course, many of the stylistic classifications had their roots in previous decades. There was also a spate of books covering all aspects of jazz – musical, historical, biographical, autobiographical and discographical – and, generally, the media were to provide more and better-informed coverage of the music.

These changed circumstances clearly deserved a separate volume, here presented, but again, in my preparation, I was confronted with the problem of where to end the tale and, after due consideration of the enormous amount of data upon which I could draw, I decided to set this date at 1970. I thus find myself once again constrained to offer an explanation as to why I have set my sights on this particular span of years.

In my view events after 1970 were a continuation of prior trends, except in the case of the avant-garde (free form), embracing musicians such as Joe Harriott – in his abstract-improvisation phase – Keith Tippett, John Stevens and Trevor Watts. Many of the musicians involved in this commenced their activities in the timespan covered in this volume, but since their careers flourished through the period 1970–90, and as Charles Fox – a writer infinitely more sympathetic to, and knowledgeable about, this development than myself – is at present engaged in preparing the jazz history of these two decades, editor Chris Parker and myself agreed that these musicians could be comprehensively dealt with in his volume: *A History of Jazz in Britain 1970–90*. Fox's book will also include studies of such musicians as Mike Westbrook, Ian Carr, John Surman, Kenny Wheeler and Chris McGregor, as it was thought that these significant artists, having stylistic affinities with the music of the subsequent decades, would be more suitably accommodated within Fox's volume.

I must add an unashamed note regarding my own attitudes. The question was once asked of a music historian: 'Are you writing history or criticism? Make up your mind!' Pre-empting such a question, this volume is *both*. I was heavily involved as a manager, agent, club promoter and occasional writer in that eventful generation and cannot help but pass observations on the personalities and events that were an integral part of my life. I trust that my opinions are not overly intrusive, and I also ask the reader's indulgence in respect of some material already covered in my first volume. A little repetition and some overlapping is inevitable, and will, I hope, prove useful to those who have not read this history's predecessor.

It must also be pointed out that the quotes from critiques (of performances, records, books and actions) have been selected for their historical relevance and therefore reflect thinking prevalent at the time, whether musical, racial, moral or sociological. Nowadays, many of these opinions quoted will seem comical, often asinine, sometimes unbelievable. But as one of the aims of this book is to reflect the ethos of the twenty years covered, they have been included.

Some of the historical facts – the origins of bebop at Minton's, or the meaning of the term 'tailgate', for example – will be very well known to the jazz buff, but since I nurture the hope that this book will be read by a good number of those not conversant with jazz history and terminology, I have inserted these explanations for their benefit.

A note on phraseology: writing on events after their time means, inevitably, that many terms may no longer have the meanings they once had (although most are still used in contemporary jazz journalism). I refer especially to words like 'traditional', 'mainstream' and 'modern'. Brian Priestley's note on this last category, in *Jazz: The Essential Companion* by Ian Carr, Digby Fairweather and Brian Priestley, is highly relevant in this connection:

> A description whose built-in obsolescence did not prevent it gaining currency in the 1950s to describe bebop and post-bop. Chiefly used at the time by writers and fans who found the onomatopoeic word 'bebop' sounded childish and demeaning, 'modern jazz' is now mainly heard from diehard followers of swing and New Orleans; in their opinion, the term 'modernists' sounds equally demeaning, and covers indiscriminately anyone who arrived on the scene after 1940.

Concerning the overall balance of this volume: that a considerable part of it is devoted to traditional/mainstream jazz in various manifestations is due entirely to the incontrovertible fact that the sheer extent of that activity in the number of bands, clubs and recordings and associated literature compelled this attention. To have minimized this category for the sake of an artificial equality of stylistic coverage would not have been faithful to my intention of presenting an account, as accurate as possible, of jazz happenings in this country during the period covered.

I hope that any British musicians who read this volume will forgive my repeated mentions of their American inspirations. Even those who have developed an individual style started with a model and, anyway, it is a fact of British jazz (and, of course, all non-American jazz) that it is largely emulative. I do make it clear in my narrative, however, that I see nothing intrinsically wrong in absorbing and adapting the language of another culture, especially a language as rich as jazz.

The ability to describe music in words is a blessing given only to a few and, freely admitting to not possessing this gift, I have kept my attempts at such description to a minimum – in any case, the records speak far more eloquently than any words.

Lastly, while the author acknowledges that jazz activity between 1950 and 1970 was nationwide, the metropolis was, inevitably, the hub of such activity and has therefore received the lion's share of his attention.

I wish to thank the following for their help in providing me with information and/or memorabilia. Without assistance of this kind a book of this nature would never see completion. I am therefore truly grateful to Jim Asman, Chris Barber, John and Pat Barnes, Acker Bilk, Colin Bowden, Terry Brown, Glyn Callingham, Ian Carr, Chris Clark (of the National Sound Archive), Mike Collier, Bill Colyer, Roy Crimmins, Tom Crow, John Dankworth, Brian Davis, Jack Docherty, Mike Doyle, Mickey Eaves, Jeff Ellison, Al Fairweather, Digby Fairweather, Wally Fawkes, Charles Fox, Rob Froud (of the National Jazz Foundation Archive), Bob Gardiner, Bob Glass, Benny Green, Joe Green, Stan Greig, Kitty Grime,

Introduction and Acknowledgements xi

Eddie Harvey, Harry Hayes, Clarrie Henley, Mike Hennessey, Kevin Henriques, Fred Hunt, Jack Hutton, John Jack, Eric Jackson, Max Jones, Pete King, Bill Le Sage, Bill Lewington, Frank Liniger, Alf Lumby, Humphrey Lyttelton, Barry McRae, Jack Massarik, David Meeker, George Melly, Tony Middleton, Laurie Morgan, Peter Newbrook, John Postgate, Steve Race, David Redfern, Don Rendell, Ronnie Scott, Ray Smith (two of these), Don Sollash, Alf Summers, Monty Sunshine, Dave Trett, Noel Wain, George Webb, Bert Wilcox, Al Woodrow, Fred Wright and Matthew Wright.

Above all, my undying gratitude goes to Alun Morgan, whose unstinting help went far beyond the call of discographical duty.

Regarding printed material, my thanks to Alan Jones, editor of the *Melody Maker*, Eddie Cook, editor of *Jazz Journal*; Bert Wilcox, proprietor of *Jazz Illustrated*; Harold Pendleton, publisher of *Jazz News*; and posthumous thanks to the late Albert McCarthy, editor of *Jazz Monthly*.

Again, I thankfully acknowledge the reference books, without which anyone attempting a history would be utterly lost: *Who's Who of Jazz* by John Chilton; *The Illustrated Encyclopedia of Jazz* by Stan Britt, Brian Case and Chrissie Murray; *The Encyclopedia of Jazz* by Leonard Feather; *Jazz, the Essential Companion* by Ian Carr, Digby Fairweather and Brian Priestley; *The New Grove Dictionary of Jazz* edited by Barry Kernfeld and *Jazz Records 1942–65* by Jorgen Grunet Jepsen.

Other books into which I have dipped are the *PLY Year Book of Jazz* edited by Albert McCarthy, the autobiographical *I Play as I Please* and *Second Chorus* by Humphrey Lyttelton, *Owning Up* by George Melly, *Some of My Best Friends are Blues* by Ronnie Scott (with Mike Hennessey), the compilation of quotes and photographs, *Jazz at Ronnie Scott's*, by Kitty Grime, and the collected criticisms of Philip Larkin, *All What Jazz*.

Once again, I express my gratitude to my editor at Quartet, Chris Parker, for his patience and hard work sorting through the various tangles I got myself into during the years I was preparing this volume. Anyone attempting a work of this kind requires a sympathetic editor and I was lucky to have such in Chris.

Thanks, also to the ladies who sat at the typewriter making

sense of my appalling handwriting and inept typing: Susi Hines, Anne Piombino, and Ginny Tapley.

Photographs courtesy of: General News Features, Simpson's Photographic Service, Photo-Records Ltd, Rex Harris, Colour Features, Denis Rose, Bill Colyer, P. Scotford, Jeff Ellison, Don Rendell, Terry Cryer, Trevor Glenroy, *Melody Maker*, Ron Cohen, Bert Wilcox, Photography 33, Bob Gardiner, Jack Sharpe, Peter Symes, *Jazz Scene*, Nigel Bowles; line illustrations courtesy of: Bill Colyer, Bert Wilcox, Humphrey Lyttelton, *Melody Maker*, Wally Fawkes, Acker Bilk, Dick Jordan, *Record Changer*, Jazz Book Club.

Jim Godbolt
London, 1989

1
New Orleans to Barnehurst to Royal Festival Hall

The saga of jazz in Britain, begun with this country's first experience of a brash new music by exposure to the Original Dixieland Jazz Band in April 1919, saw the emergence of many styles called jazz, but one of these – the traditional kind, which had affinities with the ODJB, but was more inspired by that band's black contemporaries in New Orleans – became a significant part of the British entertainment business during the fifties and sixties and remains popular to a lesser but still significant extent up to the present day.

In the fifties the 'revivalist' phenomenon induced up to two or three thousand young Britishers to play in this style, all of them initially amateurs, but eventually providing a considerable financial turnover for clubs, concert halls and recording studios. Irrespective of its disputed musical validity, the enormous proliferation of this music compelled attention.

When this form of jazz first attracted the public's attention to any considerable degree, in the late forties and early fifties, it took the entertainment establishment completely by surprise. A new dimension to popular music had grown furtively from rank amateurism; five years previously, when the first murmurings of the explosion to come were heard, no one, particularly the music's early exponents, would have believed that it would ever meet with such general public acceptance.

After all, it was 'old-fashioned' music; its day was surely over, except as a 'novelty'. Yet the music was reborn, its innate vitality and fundamental simplicity facilitating an astonishing resurgence and, ironically, one instigated and conducted entirely by whites. The race of these musicians and that of the critics who supported them is highly relevant. A relatively small number of middle-aged black American musicians, a hundred or so, who had first played the music at the turn of the century, some even starting a little later, were indeed brought out of retirement in their forties and fifties, but these pioneers were considerably outnumbered by teenaged whites in Australia, Europe, Scandinavia and, most tellingly, in Britain. A few British bands with roots in this revival, those of Humphrey Lyttelton, Chris Barber, Acker Bilk, Ken Colyer and Kenny Ball, have since gained a secure international reputation.

The traditional way of playing jazz, with trumpet, trombone, clarinet and rhythm section (sometimes with tenor saxophone), had suffered a decline in the thirties, but interest was sustained by the gramophone records of a handful of musicians: Wingy Manone from 1934 (using, initially, members of the Bob Crosby band); the Crosby band itself, which from 1935 onwards played 'arranged Dixieland' with a plenitude of solos; and, from 1937, the Bobcats (a contingent from the large orchestra), Tommy Dorsey's Clambake Seven (from the large Dorsey band) and Eddie Condon's various units.

But 'revivalism', the emulation of, principally, King Oliver's Creole Jazz Band, Jelly Roll Morton's Red Hot Peppers, and Louis Armstrong's Hot Five and Seven, was a forties amateur phenomenon. It is an intriguing fact that not *one* of America's vast black population was involved, not even merely for financial reasons, in playing a music that was regaining so much prominence and which, in essence, was a bow to the unique musicality of the older black musicians, many of them deceased, but still revered for their recordings. The reason was simple: this 'old' music was redolent of the social and economic deprivation of their race, particularly in the racist South where it had originated, and they, understandably, wanted none of it. It is unlikely that young blacks ever listened to the recordings of their forebears, still less wanted to play in this 'Dixieland' style. Young white men had no such unhappy sociological heritage. The young black musician of that period was to play a different kind of jazz called bop, or re-bop, and this style came to stand rebelliously in opposition to revivalism, and was soon to manifest itself in Britain via another group of young white men, with a sprinkling of resident blacks, West Indian and West African.

It gives a further ironic twist to this extraordinary situation to note that a great number of white Americans played jazz in the twenties and made many recordings, but in this exercise called revivalism the white trumpeters emulated Louis Armstrong not Bix Beiderbecke; trombonists Kid Ory, not Tommy Dorsey; clarinettists Johnny Dodds, not Benny Goodman; pianists Ferdinand 'Jelly Roll' Morton, not Joe Sullivan; drummers Baby Dodds, not Gene Krupa.

The second names in these couplings are all white, but none is from New Orleans, the city in Louisiana which had become the revivalists' centre of interest. The exciting music of another race and another generation was profoundly affecting the musical activities of teenagers in the forties playing at home, to the distraction of parents and neighbours, in places as far removed from New Orleans as, say, Barnehurst, Kent.

An especially dreary example of thirties speculative building, Barnehurst consists of row upon row of semi-detached houses with neo-Tudor pointed and timbered gables, occupied by the middle working class who had moved from the inner suburbs of Lambeth, Southwark and Camberwell. It was a subtopia of the dullest kind on what had once been orchard and pasture land, just a few more thousands of acres of home-counties countryside succumbing to bricks and mortar in an era of rapid urban expansion.

At a public house called the Red Barn, near Barnehurst Station, on what was then the Southern Railway, a band – George Webb's Dixielanders, all, with one exception, musically unread – spearheaded the 'New Orleans' revival in Britain. It was perhaps incongruous that such a rumbustious sound, springing originally from the cross-fertilization of the music of many cultures in a multi-racial and cosmopolitan city with a notorious reputation for crime, corruption, gambling and, above all, prostitution, should have found itself being resuscitated in a lacklustre and eminently respectable outer London suburb.

There was no Barnehurst *Blue Book* listing the addresses of brothels and providing details of the girls' charms and hints of their special proclivities; neither did the local paper, the *Bexleyheath and Welling Observer*, carry news of the comings and goings of these ladies. Barnehurst's architecture did not match the grace and style of the French Quarter, with its filigree wrought-iron balconies, nor did the fragrant smell of magnolia waft from the suburb's gardens. The restaurants did not offer Creole fries, oyster patties, red beans and rice, crawfish boule, jambalaya and frogs' legs. For the surrender of your food coupon in austerity-bound Britain the fare would be spam and chips, off-white bread and barely sweetened tea.

But these incongruities did not occur to the young enthusiasts. The author, for one, was totally overwhelmed by the Dixielanders as they belted out 'Panama', 'High Society', 'Muskrat Ramble' and 'Dippermouth Blues', no doubt to the anguish of those occupying 'Mon Repos', 'Chez Nous', 'Theydon' and 'Thistledome' nearby, especially on summer nights, when the windows of the basement in which they played were opened. It was a heady experience, and one little devalued by the fact that the records the band made at the time tend, on re-examination, to destroy the illusions so readily nurtured in those halcyon days.*

The band was first formed in 1943 and, after undergoing a few changes and additions, in 1945 comprised Reg Rigden (trumpet), Owen Bryce (cornet, the band's only 'school' musician), Wally Fawkes (clarinet), Eddie Harvey (trombone), Buddy Vallis (banjo), Roy Wykes (drums), Art Streatfield (tuba) and George Webb (piano). Other British bands laid claim to being the first to play in the style but, indisputably, it was George Webb's Dixielanders, resident band of the Bexleyheath and District Rhythm Club, meeting every Monday at the Red Barn, who made the most impact. Their enthusiasm was dramatically infectious and jazz enthusiasts travelled from all over the country to hear a group whose intransigent dedication to their music was to be the foundation of the (relatively) big business to come in the 'trad' boom.

Apart from their regular Monday-night appearances at the Red Barn they also presented the first series of traditional-jazz concerts

---

*See Discography.

New Orleans to Barnehurst to Royal Festival Hall

CRANE RIVER JAZZ CLUB

Name _____
Address _____
No. _____

W. J. Colyer   TEM 2315

EASTBOURNE JAZZ SUPPORTERS
Present
THE CRANE RIVER JAZZ BAND
A dance to be held at
SEASIDE LIBRARY
on
Saturday, 16th December, 1950
7.30-11.30 p.m.

Admission 3/-   No. 80

NEW ORLEANS
COMES TO EALING

The
Crane River Jazz Band

Every Monday at 8 p.m.

West Ealing Club, Mervyn Road, W.13

Dancing, Bar and Refreshments

Crane River Jazz Club Membership

2/- per year.   Entrance 2/6.   Guests 3/-

On the door or S.A.E.—
    JAMES BRYNING,
        9, Piccadilly Arcade S.W.1.

in England, at the King George's Hall, Tottenham Court Road, under the name of the Hot Club of London. They were to be the inspiration for many bands of similar calibre that soon multiplied up and down the country and it was an irony that their enlistment in April 1947 of a young trumpet player, one Humphrey Lyttelton (replacing Rigden), newly discharged from the army with the rank of captain, quickly accelerated their fame but effectively also signed the band's death warrant. For Lyttelton left in November the same year, taking with him Wally Fawkes and Harry Brown (who had replaced Harvey when the latter joined the RAF). The Dixielanders had played a tremendous part in spreading the gospel, but it was almost as though their role was to clear the ground for a man of destiny who would provide true leadership, not in the disciplinarian sense – Webb amply provided that – but musically, for the band was undoubtedly improved immeasurably by Lyttelton's presence, especially when the second trumpet dropped out, leaving him to project a strong, jutting lead that imparted the lift and momentum they had previously lacked.

On his departure, in November 1947, the band virtually folded, but played the last Hot Club of London concert, with Lyttelton, Fawkes and Brown, on 31 January 1948, with Graeme Bell's Australian Jazz Band. Valedictory speeches were made by Rex Harris, George Webb, the Marquis of Donegall and the author. The Lyttelton band played their first engagement at Cooks Ferry Inn, Edmonton, in north London, on 8 February.

Lyttelton's first band consisted of the leader himself, Fawkes and Brown, Pat Hawes (piano), Nevil Skrimshire (guitar), Les Rawlings (bass) and John Robinson (drums), occasionally joined by Pip Gaskell (clarinet). Attention was soon concentrated upon this tall figure with the Eton and Brigade of Guards background; the press seized upon the apparent contradiction of an aristocrat leading a jazz band, but the band's success within its first year of existence was also consolidated by its being a part of the 'dancing to jazz' policy of the Leicester Square Jazz Club, which met every Monday at the Café de l'Europe, Leicester Square, run by three jazz enthusiasts, Ken Lindsay, Pete Martin and Ray Jackson.

Lyttelton alternated with Graeme Bell's Australian Jazz Band, the instigators of the dancing policy, who made a big feature of this in their advertising. These breezy Australians were appalled by the stuffily formal 'rhythm club' practice whereby club members would sit gravely nodding their heads to records played by an erudite recitalist/commentator who would occasionally cede the floor to a 'jam session', during which the audience remained firmly seated. Their innovation proved to be another and very crucial step towards the popularization of traditional jazz, the dancing policy attracting people not in the least interested in the music's history and its stylistic categorizations, but rather in physically reacting to its lively rhythms.

The Bell band played in a very 'white' Dixieland manner, but had a remarkable multi-instrumentalist in Ade Monsbourgh who displayed a ferocious, highly individual style on alto saxophone. During Bell's second trip to England Lyttelton offered him a job. Lyttelton was studying at the Camberwell School of Art and students from there, particularly, turned up at his gigs to leap about in a highly extrovert manner. They were joined by dancers who could really 'jive', an extremely animated but, properly executed, very disciplined co-ordination of movements originally learned in dancehalls from visiting US servicemen. This combination of spirited jazz music and creative dancing made for a unique atmosphere infinitely healthier than the previous solemnity of rhythm-club procedure.

The purists were alarmed by this new dimension to jazz music, as noted by Humphrey Lyttelton in *I Play as I Please*:

> Some of the old guard from the peaceful, beer-drinking, pipe-smoking Hot Club of London days turned up as well, determined to make the worst of a bad job and hoping perhaps for the day when the floor would give in, plummeting the dancers into the restaurant below and leaving them perched round the walls to enjoy their jazz in peace.

Lyttelton was referring to the wildly exhibitionistic dancing. At first the management tolerated these antics and contented themselves with a notice that read:

> THE MANAGEMENT EARNESTLY REQUEST THAT OUR PATRONS REFRAIN FROM SUCH DANCES THAT INCLUDE STAMPING AND JUMPING. THERE IS A RESTAURANT BELOW AND THE DISCOMFORT THEREBY CAUSED IS VERY GREAT.
> THANK YOU.

But press reports of the high kicking and frenzied whirling eventually blew the promoters' cover. The *Leader* magazine commented:

> It's gala night at the Jazz Club. New looks swirl, shirt tails fly. Feet stamp, hands flutter, hair-dos tumble in ruins. Youths close their eyes and twitch to the savage rhythms. A naval officer throws his head back and howls like a wolf. Solicitors, art students and barrow boys sway to the beat. A bearded artist hurls his partner halfway across the room.

The report, and photographs of the antics, alarmed the landlords of the premises and one Monday evening when the band and fans arrived they found the entrance chained and padlocked.

Such an eager band and equally eager followers were quick to find a new home, at Mac's Rehearsal Rooms, Great Windmill Street, near Piccadilly, run by two shopkeepers, Bert and Stan Wilcox, under the banner of the London Jazz Club and meeting on Mondays and Saturdays. By the examples of these clubs, the economic basis of jazz promotions was drastically changed. Hundreds of young people attended the clubs to dance, paying at the door, their numbers multiplying as dozens of similar clubs opened throughout the country.

The Lyttelton band in its early stages was purely traditional, their repertoire including 'Ory's Creole Trombone', 'Tailgate', 'Canal Street Blues', 'When the Saints Go Marching In', 'Melancholy Blues', 'Panama', 'Working Man Blues', 'Weary Blues' and others previously recorded by the New Orleans giants, plus many of Lyttelton's own compositions. He was the first traditionalist to write his own material, presaging increased activity of this nature later in his career.

In the autumn of 1948, George Webb joined the band, to be followed by Buddy Vallis and Bernard Saward (drummer Wykes's successor in the Webb band) the following year. Vallis played banjo, replacing Nevil Skrimshire on guitar, thus at once strengthening Lyttelton's associations with his immediate past and, in the now total use of the banjo, endearing himself more strongly to the devout purists, who swore by that instrument as being superior to the 'effete' guitar. The non-conformist in his social life was now a fully conforming traditionalist in his musical career.

Cartoon strip from the *Daily Sketch* purporting to represent a conversation between anxious parents, promoter Bert Wilcox and Lyttelton clarinettist Ian Christie, at the London Jazz Club, Mac's Rehearsal Rooms, Great Windmill Street

It would be impossible to catalogue all those following the example of Webb and Lyttelton in London and the provinces, but certainly every town could boast a traditional-jazz band – several in the large conurbations – and the following list, by no means comprehensive and limited to those formed in the late forties and early fifties, indicates the extent to which a music, of low-life origins, played largely by second-class citizens in the United States of America, took such a hold on young white men of all classes in the United Kingdom. Most of the bands listed made records:

LONDON: Freddy Randall and his band, Humphrey Lyttelton and his band, John Haim's Jelly Roll Kings, Mike Daniels Delta Jazz Band, Chris Barber's New Orleans Jazz Band, Roy Vaughan's Chicagoans, Russell–Wickham Hot Six, Alan Kirby's Dixielanders, Mick Mulligan's Magnolia Jazz Band with George Melly, Crane River Jazz Band, Ken Colyer's Jazzmen, Cy Laurie and his band, Charles Galbraith Jazzmen, Eric Silk's Southern Jazz Band, Mike Collier and his band, Steve Lane's Southern Stompers, Bill Brunskill and his band, Commodore Jazz Band, Christie Brothers Stompers, the Original Dixielanders and Doug Whitton's Jazz Band.
PROVINCES: Yorkshire Jazz Band (Leeds); Merseyssippi Jazz Band (Liverpool);

Delta Rhythm Kings, Zenith Six, Saints Jazz Band, Eric Batty's Jazz Aces, Smoky City Stompers, Dizzy Burton's Jazz Aces (Manchester); Wall City Jazz Band (Chester); George Jackson's Jazz Band (Macclesfield); Tony Short's Original Varsity Sack Droppers (Cambridge); Ray Foxley's Levee Loungers, Ken Rattenbury and his band, Second City Jazzmen (Birmingham); Sonny Monk and his band, Mick Gill's Imperial Jazz Band, Roy Cooper's Stompers (Nottingham); Leicester Jazz Band (Leicester); Ken Grinyer's Wolverines (Southampton) and Avon Cities Jazz Band (Bristol).

SCOTLAND: Clyde Valley Stompers (Glasgow); Sandy Brown and his band, Archie Semple's Capitol Jazzmen (Edinburgh).

The instrumentation was invariably trumpet, trombone, clarinet, piano, bass, drums and banjo (sometimes guitar, but the banjo predominated). Occasionally, as with pre-Lyttelton Webb, some bands like Chris Barber, the Merseysippi Jazz Band and the Original Dixielanders (several of the George Webb band led by Owen Bryce) carried two trumpets.

Probably the most influential of the mentors of these bands was King Oliver's Creole Jazz Band, who first recorded in 1923 and made forty-three sides in their relatively brief existence. While the acoustic process used in their recordings could not possibly reflect their true sound, they were obviously a band that must have been exhilarating to hear in the flesh. The sheer force of their ensemble drive, generated almost entirely by the two cornettists King Oliver and Louis Armstrong, and clarinettist Johnny Dodds, made a considerable impact on the neo-New Orleanians in Barnehurst, Edinburgh, Manchester, Birmingham and elsewhere. The Oliver records were not issued in this country until 1936 (no previous press mention had been made of them) and these were not pressings from original masters, but dubbings of existing 78s, a process that muddied the sound even further. Despite this, the inventive thrust of the two cornets, along with Dodds's interweaving clarinet, was highly impressive. They were favourably reviewed by the few critics of the time, but were seen primarily as historical pieces on which subsequent developments were an 'improvement'. The local jazz musicians of that period, first and foremost dance-band players, regarded them as no more than dated curiosities, and would never have dreamed of attempting to play in such an 'old-fashioned' manner.

It was the jazz renaissance that brought these recordings, along with those by Morton, and Armstrong as a leader, into sharp focus and inspired so many, beginning with the white Yerba Buena Band in Los Angeles in the early forties, to emulate them.

Oliver himself died in poverty-stricken obscurity in 1938, and it is another of the many ironies of jazz history that had he survived and not played another note in all his life he would (or should have) received a substantial income from the royalties on his compositions played the world over from the forties up to the present day. He would surely have been astonished by this reversal in his fortunes.

Morton, too, died in reduced circumstances, but the revival gave Louis Armstrong a new lease of life with his All-Stars. Other New Orleans musicians to enjoy increased fame included the clarinettists Ed Hall, Albert Nicholas and Omer Simeon, the trombonist Kid Ory and the trumpeter Mutt Carey. Others were rescued from near obscurity. Ed Hall, for instance, was barely known as an occasional soloist with Claude Hopkins's fourteen-piece band, and it was the revival that made jazz record collectors aware that he was a remarkable solo and ensemble player in the classic tradition.

This upsurge of interest in the older forms of jazz was responsible for bringing into prominence and providing an acceptable living for these fairly well-known veterans, but it was to have yet another success: that of bringing to public notice and into the recording studios many New Orleans musicians who had not previously recorded, those who had stayed in their native city when their contemporaries had moved north to find work and to make the records that eventually assured them of their places in the jazz pantheon. Foremost among the veterans about which virtually *nothing* had previously been heard were the trumpeter William 'Bunk' Johnson and the clarinettist George Lewis. Johnson was either sixty-three or ten years younger, according to which source you believe, when he first recorded, and Lewis forty-two. Both emerged very suddenly from total obscurity to international status. Lewis made global tours up to 1961 and continued to work up to his death in 1968, at the age of sixty-eight. The belated success of both musicians was almost entirely attributable to the book *Jazzmen* by Frederic Ramsey and Charles Edward Smith, published in New York in 1939. Some US copies were initially imported into Britain, but it was not published here until 1940 and reprinted in 1949. In this fascinating book, the authors published correspondence from Johnson in reply to a letter addressed to him by Ramsey addressed merely 'c/o the Postmaster, New Iberia, Louisiana'. Subsequently Johnson was recorded with fellow New Orleanians, including George Lewis, for the Jazzman and Jazz Information labels, on portable equipment in New Orleans. It was the beginning of a romantic saga that gripped the imagination of hundreds of young whites and when, in 1945, the HMV company issued recordings of Bunk Johnson and Lewis in Britain they were to prove as influential as the Oliver recordings made twenty-two years earlier.

Controversy swiftly followed: one of bebop's earliest and most persuasive supporters was the English, but US resident, critic Leonard Feather, and in his massive *Encyclopedia of Jazz* (1960 and subsequent revisions) he included an extensive biography of Johnson, but was, in the eyes of the new fundamentalists, bent on denigrating the old man's playing and his memory of past events. He referred to the team of collectors that travelled to New Orleans to make those first Johnson recordings in June 1942 as 'well-meaning but misguided amateurs', and eagerly quoted New Orleans jazz historian Samuel Charters's uncomplimentary references to Johnson in his *Jazz New Orleans*; a bonus for a modernist.

Feather was as a result reviled by the traditionalists in America and Britain and his condemnation of revivalism in general, and Bunk and his colleagues in particular, was to rally the old guard and result in much abuse being heaped on the expatriate's head. This was a phase of the bitter war that was raging between the traditionalists, who by now had acquired the uncomplimentary epithet of 'mouldy fygges', and the modernists, who were unkindly referred to as the 'dark glasses, goatee beard and beret brigade', among many more offensive terms.

To many collectors, these revivalist recordings of Bunk Johnson, and those made by Lewis under his own name with other of his kinsmen (who had also never recorded previously), were 'archaic', not to be compared with the relative sophistication of Armstrong, Bechet and Morton. To many others, however, such obscurity and total identification with the city of their birth lent enchantment to the sound they produced.

Johnson and Lewis's success led to many other unknowns entering the studios, with variable results, but the fundamentalists were rarely critical of the occasionally faltering, indifferently recorded performances. The romance of this renaissance often clouded their judgement, such was their fervent belief that these musicians were unquestionably the 'genuine' jazzmen, for had they not stayed at home playing the real thing and been shamefully ignored by the record companies in the twenties? Moreover, their records were attacked by the propagandists for bebop, a sound that was anathema to the ears of the revivalists, as they rallied clamorously to defend the 'primitives', as the modernists dubbed them. The Johnson records undoubtedly directly influenced many British musicians. Wally Fawkes in the Webb band emulated the mannerisms of Lewis for a while and the prolonged 'tailgate' slurs of Johnson's trombonist, Jim Robinson (the one man in the Johnson band who had been on record previously, bassist Alcide Pavageau having taken part in a rejected Magee String Band 1928 session), were copied by Ed Harvey. Fawkes, however, later returned to Bechet for his inspiration and Harvey developed 'modern' tastes that earned him the condemnation of his colleagues.

The first British band wholly to embrace the spirit and style and certainly the guts of the New Orleans stay-at-homes emerged in 1949. This was the Crane River Jazz Band, based at Cranford, then a semi-rural town in Middlesex. The 'Crane's' following owed much to their belligerent projection of a chosen style of jazz and to their constant proselytizing about its sociological, racial and historical background, this supposedly contrasting with the aristocratic Lyttelton. Their own proletarian background was heavily emphasized (despite the fact that two of their members, John and Julian Davies, were decidedly middle-class) and much of this class angle fervently promulgated by the band's manager and washboard player, Bill Colyer.

Absurd as these extra-musical considerations may now appear, they were nurtured at a time when ideological feelings about jazz ran passionately high, when harsh words exchanged in print and in person were commonplace. The release of many historic records, and the publication of home-produced magazines spreading the gospel of jazz according to New Orleans aroused considerable interest and much play was made of 'sincerity'. The Aunt Sallies of the traditionalists were bop, the big swing bands and the efforts of the dance band-cum-jazz musician, contemptuously dubbed 'Archer Street jazz'. Collectively they were branded as 'slick', 'mechanical' or 'insincere', and even the Lyttelton band was castigated by the extreme left of jazz thought in those turbulent days.

To many collectors and critics only the music of Johnson and Lewis and their confrères was pure and sincere. The Crane River Jazz Band represented the very embodiment of these virtues and there could not have been a more fiercely purist duo than the founder members, trumpeter Ken Colyer and his brother Bill. Both would be prepared to put up their fists to emphasize a point and frequently did.

The manner in which the band rehearsed further emphasized their dedication. Often this was in open fields, sometimes, strange to relate, in a roadmender's hut. They were chased off these meadows by a Mr Wild, landowner, and rehearsals in their parents' front room understandably caused the neighbours to complain. The style itself was rumbustious enough but, badly performed by unread amateurs, it must have been a gruelling ordeal for any non-believers in earshot.

The hostility they encountered was supposedly parallelled by the oppression of their black mentors over three thousand miles away, and this identification was much protested by the fanatically zealous Bill Colyer. It was rehearsing on the banks of the Crane River that inspired the band's name. This river, nothing more than a muddy, polluted trickle running into the Grand Union Canal, was hardly the mighty, rolling Mississippi, so much a part of American jazz lore, but it was a river nevertheless and its name was accordingly adopted.

Eventually, they rehearsed in a bleak hall alongside the White

Hart Inn, Southall and originally described themselves as the Crane River Brass Band, a further emulation of the brass bands famed for their participation in the New Orleans parades. The original personnel was Ken Colyer, Sonny Morris (second trumpet), Bill Colyer (washboard), Ben Marshall (guitar, later changing to banjo) and Ron Bowden (drums). Later came their first trombonist, Ray Orpwood. Later still, they were joined by the Davies brothers, Julian on sousaphone and John, who played most instruments, but replaced Orpwood on trombone. In November 1949 they were joined by clarinettist Monty Sunshine, just out of the RAF. A few weeks later, they made their first records, recorded by John Davies, who has since achieved an international reputation reprocessing 78s for LP compilations. The White Hart became the band's regular venue – admission one shilling.

In *Music Fare*, March 1950, an anonymous writer reviewed the band's appearance at a club called Greenwich Village, meeting at Mac's Rehearsal Rooms.

> Bill Colyer went to great pains to tell us that the group doesn't play Dixieland, or two-beat . . . it's New Orleans, that's what it is! Well, let's take that as read. Mr C also pointed out that his boys just played basic raw jazz . . . The group has many fine points . . . chiefly its virile heartiness . . . but their trouble, as with other groups appearing at the club, is little knowledge of the chords. A pity, and something should be sorted out quickly. Because of its heartiness and beat – which is literally thrust down one's throat – one can well understand why the band is so popular.

A feature on the band in *Jazz Journal*, December 1950, also unsigned, included the following comment:

> The band stick to a New Orleans four-beat pattern, finding that this is the only method of becoming really relaxed. Curiously perhaps, the opinions of the members of the band do not vary on the belief that no Europeans, or anyone outside New Orleans for that matter, will ever re-create New Orleans music. Before New Orleans music can be played, a complete relaxation and unself-consciousness, not normally an attribute of the white man, must be attained. All this may take twenty years, or a lifetime, but the boys are still hoping.

(This report at least revealed an awareness that they had much to learn, an attitude rather different from that of one bandleader, who solemnly assured the author that his version of a certain tune, 'Irish Black Bottom', previously recorded by Louis Armstrong's Hot Seven, was 'tidier' than Armstrong's!)

Maybe because of Bill Colyer's heavy emphasis on the proletarian occupations of the New Orleans musicians before they were discovered – Johnson working as a truck and tractor driver, Lewis as a stevedore – and the Cranes being largely of the working class, the band was invited to appear at the Third World Festival of Youth and Students for Peace in East Berlin in May 1951. This engagement was reported in the *Daily Worker*. The writer, Peter Fryer, omitted the word 'East' as his paper and party did not recognize the 'West' part of divided Berlin, and he also took the opportunity for a sideswipe at America with:

> Britain's leading jazz group, the Crane River Band, is going to the festival. The average age of these young workers is twenty-two-and-a-half. The improvised jazz they produce with such vigour and single-mindedness is going to rock Berlin solid, as the jazz fans would say. This sort of popular music has nothing in common with the canned American dance music of which the BBC is so fond.

They were not averse, however, to performing for an organization of a somewhat different political persuasion, the Heston and Isleworth Young Liberal Association, at Bulstrode Schools, Holloway Street, Hounslow in January 1951. The programme notes were characteristically pontifical and, very likely, from the pen of Bill Colyer:

> PURIST JAZZ MUSIC
> Its meaning and history
> 7.45 p.m. An Illustrated History of Jazz Music
> 8.45–9.00 p.m. Interval
> 9.00 p.m. Spontaneous Improvised Counterpoint
> 10.00 p.m. Curtain

An introductory note read:

> 'Playing jazz is talking from the heart – you don't lie' (W.G. Johnson – seventy-year-old pioneer jazzman).

New Orleans to Barnehurst to Royal Festival Hall

The conception of Hounslow's first jazz concert, fifty years after the inception of the music, must necessarily be historical. And yet, if music is to be a vital and significant force – something more than a mere game of juxtaposing suitable harmonies, of mathematical formulae and melodic lines – then a contemporary element must be introduced.

The Crane River Jazz Band, with its insistence upon English, as well as negro folk art, does, therefore, fulfil this dual purpose. Their repertoire bears adequate testimony to the internationality of jazz. As the only major folk music extant, its value, in these days of national disquiet, cannot be over-emphasized.

'English folk art' was probably a reference to tunes in their repertoire like 'The Miner's Dream of Home' and 'Crane River Woman' (with an emotive vocal by Bill Colyer), alongside the 'negro folk art', New Orleans compositions such as 'Bucket's Got a Hole in It', 'Ice Cream' and 'All the Whores Love the Way I Ride'.

The band inspired many others throughout the country to play in a similarly earthy manner, and was the blueprint for the bands Ken Colyer was later to lead. Their records stand up well these many years later, exhibiting a genuine lift, a rolling momentum characteristic of the best in jazz. The earnest study of their mentors and the resultant assimilation of their stylistic essence by these (then) fanatical young men effectively transcends their technical limitations and the poor recording quality.

There was another category of revivalist band in Britain in the late forties, and one such was led by trumpeter Freddy Randall, who was resident at the Cleveland Rhythm Club, Cooks Ferry Inn, Edmonton, every Sunday. This band was largely influenced by the white groups of Muggsy Spanier, Eddie Condon and Bob Crosby. Claims have been made that Randall, older than most revivalists (he was born in 1920) was playing 'traditional' jazz as far back as 1939 with his St Louis Four. He certainly recorded with Freddy Mirfield's Garbage Men in 1943, but the results should never have been issued, so poor is the conception and performance. He started his regular band, playing mostly in North London in 1943, about the same time as the Dixielanders, south of the Thames.

Ernest Borneman, the Austrian-born anthropologist, filmmaker and author (now a sexologist in his native country), was one of the most perceptive of critics surveying the British scene at the time and wrote a lengthy article on it in the *Record Changer*. This was an American publication noted both for its high standard of writing and extremely funny, superbly drawn cartoons of Gene Deitch affectionately mocking the super-serious jazz enthusiast. Borneman wrote:

> Lyttelton is the most literate and conscientious musician playing New Orleans jazz in Britain today. He knows exactly what he is after and he is pursuing his ideas with a single-mindedness which seems awe-inspiring and, in fact, rather frightening to many of his competitors. And though Humph's band is not always on top of the world, it has a felicity that can only be compared to Claude Luter's among the Europeans. And as for musicianship Humphrey has it all over Luter. There is a certain monotony about his rhythm section having a clanging banjo-cum-woodblocks sound which I find objectionable but then I'm sure that's exactly what Humphrey is after.
>
> Freddy Randall's band is much less coherent as a group, but paradoxically enough, much more accomplished as a team of soloists . . .
>
> The Crane River Band is a case on its own. While Humphrey's band is semi-pro and Freddy's is professional, the Crane River Boys are amateurs, but they are the most determined, fervent and driving amateurs I ever heard play New Orleans jazz anywhere. They wear athletic sweaters with the words Crane River embroidered across; and they all play louder, weirder and more unpredictably than I would have ever thought possible. They are, in short, England's sole uninhibited jazz band. To evaluate them in terms of musicianship might also be a little unfair in view of the fact that most members of the group are entirely self-trained. But it is precisely this lack of training which makes for unexpected and sometimes genuinely original effects.
>
> I hope I am not romanticizing when I say that the band seems closer than any other to the sound of the band-before-Buddy-Bolden's as I can imagine. There is a feeling of anything-can-happen, a complete disregard for the rules (or more probably, a complete ignorance of the fact that there was ever such a thing as a rule), an absence of the facsimile aspect which mars so much of today's New Orleans jazz, and a sheer joy in playing for the public. It had, for this writer at any rate, a strongly therapeutic effect . . .
>
> I felt for the first time that such joy was not doomed to be missing from today's jazz when I listened to the Crane River Jazz Band. And that, after a year away from all but African music, was a very pleasant feeling.

Maurice Burman, in the *Melody Maker*, 10 February 1951, reviewing a broadcast made on BBC's 'Jazz Club', was less impressed: 'A farce of New Orleans music. The boys in the band suffered from bad intonation, very poor time and lack of technique. All they had was a primordial sense of jazz. The general sound of the band, to be kind, was very sour. It's a mystery how they ever passed the BBC test.'

Bands of all styles, testifying to the enormous enthusiasm of that period, rushed into the recording studios. Tyros were eager to commit their efforts to wax for posterity. Apart from the Decca recordings of the Garbage Men and Webb's Dixielanders, only Parlophone of the major record companies showed any interest in traditional jazz and this not until November 1949* with the Lyttelton band, and with Randall, and with a concert at the Royal Festival Hall in 1951. The rest fought shy of the amateur bands, but a handful of independent labels run by enthusiasts welcomed the neo-New Orleanians. They were Jazz, run by Midlands collectors Jim Asman and Bill Kinnell, followed by Jazz Collector (Colin Pomeroy), Melodisc (Emil Shalit), Tempo (Jimmy Bryning), Esquire (Carlo Krahmer) and 77 (Doug Dobell). Provincial labels included Decibel in Manchester, Tailgate in Sheffield, Riverside in Liverpool, S & M in Scotland and Beltona in Scotland and Ireland.

While it was to the credit of these independent companies that a part of British jazz history was captured on vinyl, sadly the musical content on most records is negligible. The bands' entry into the studios was all too premature; throughout the resultant recordings, examples of technical immaturity abound, and without the despised proficiency no amount of 'feeling' and 'sincerity' could compensate for their blatant inadequacies. The most striking examples are John Haim's Jelly Roll Kings on Delta and Doug Whitton's Jazz Band on the Tempo label. The latter was included in a scathing round-up of these tyro bands by Sinclair Traill in *Jazz Journal*, January 1950. Other bands sternly reprimanded were the Smoky City Stompers from Manchester, Ray Foxley's Levee Loungers from Birmingham and Shamus O'Brien, the pianist with Whitton.

---

*Parlophone recorded the Vic Lewis–Jack Parnell Jazzmen, all 'professional' musicians, in 1944.

> Now look here you kids, this won't do! It's all very well for 'revivalist' groups to play in front of their own friends and club members, but such stuff should never be put on sale to the general public. Frankly, these sides are horrible and will do nothing but give jazz a bad name. Before coming out into the open such bands must at least learn how to play in tune; it might also be a good idea if the musicians involved learned to play their instruments.

Some of the recordings made by the young and eager at that time have re-emerged in LP compilations to haunt their now middle-aged performers who, no doubt, fervently wish that they had repressed their youthful enthusiasm to be immortalized. But their sincerity and vitality could not be denied and won them support that amazed and upset many professional dance-band musicians, some of them proficient if only occasional jazzmen, if, in the eyes of emerging traditionalists – musicians and fans – lacking in 'true' jazz feeling.

The specialist magazines, notably *Jazz Music*, edited by Max Jones and Albert McCarthy; *Jazz Record*, edited by James Asman and Bill Kinnell; *Jazz Journal*, edited by Sinclair Traill, and the same writer's column in the *Melody Maker* were generally supportive of traditional jazz, but most of their praise was for the Lyttelton band. In much of the appraisal of British revival bands the words 'improved' or 'improving' appeared regularly. It was accepted that all the musicians concerned were apprentices and, furthermore, had been denied, because of the Musicians' Union's restrictive practices, the opportunity to hear their mentors in the flesh. It was an apprenticeship where the gramophone record was the tutor, with all the limitations imposed by that impersonal method of learning.

In the June 1951 issue of the *MM*, Sinclair Traill reviewed the records of five bands, under the heading of 'HOW BRITISH JAZZ IS PROGRESSING!' The bands were Chris Barber and his New Orleans Jazz Band, the Crane River Jazz Band, Mike Daniels's Delta Jazz Band, Freddy Randall and his band and the Saints Jazz Band. He prefaced his generally favourable reviews with:

> From the standard displayed on this selection of records by our local bands it would appear that a definite and steady improvement has been made in the past months. To prove it I took the trouble to rake out from my dusty

cupboard of discards some records by British bands of twelve months ago.

Imposing upon myself a sort of self-inflicted blindfold test, accomplished by screwing up the eye and groping for the gramophone, I played a few of these sides without looking at the labels. It was merely the sound of British jazz I wanted without knowing who was playing. I then went back to playing the records under review; the relief was enormous.

Many of the crudities and wrinkles of twelve months ago have now disappeared. The general standard of playing has improved, and – dare I say it? – British jazz has progressed immeasurably.

But there were others less charitably disposed towards the concept of the revival and less so towards its technically inept practitioners, these dubbed the 'blow and hope boys'. Pianist Ralph Sharon, a pioneer British bebop player, wrote in the *NME*, 16 May 1952:

After listening to many of our so-called 'traditional' outfits during the last few months, I have come to the rather frightening conclusion that ninety-nine per cent of the stuff these boys turn out is just an excuse for wrong notes and bad musicianship. That's quite a bold statement and I know it, but after hearing the cacophony of blatant howls and squeals emitting from a group of fellows with enough gall to call themselves a 'band' last week my back is up.

Who are these musical morons trying to kid, anyway? Real musicians laugh at them, jazz critics scorn them, and the jazz fan knows the music turned out just isn't! Or do they? I very much doubt it. Just because some character takes to wearing his sideboards long, sports dirty corduroys and lets his feet get the air through open-top sandals should he therefore be able to distinguish between good jazz and bad? Certainly not! ...

Don't think I'm prejudiced against two-beat music – I love the real thing. In common with many musician friends of mine, I term New Orleans, Chicago, collective or what-have-you jazz as two-beat ...

'The boys are improving,' I've been told. 'They're slowly learning.' Now that's nice for us, isn't it, but why don't they practise at home, not on the stand?

What's even more infuriating: these characters laugh at the modern musicians and try to belittle them. What right have they got to do this? Practically all the modern boys who play jazz in the clubs can sit in with any band in the country and read and interpret their parts perfectly. At least the modern school have sat down and studied their instruments. Come on, you traditionalist hounds, where are your men that can compare in musicianship with, say, Ronnie Scott or Johnny Dankworth?

I grant you one exception in the ranks. Trombonist Keith Christie has my utmost admiration. At a recent recording session surrounded by modernists he acquitted himself admirably – the guy read his parts like a trouper, blew fine solos on the right chords and proved to all present that he is entitled to be called a musician, and a fine one at that.

Ernest Borneman, in the *Melody Maker*, 10 May 1950, wrote at length on the validity of the revival, his article headed: 'Loyalty to tradition is all very well . . . BUT THE REVIVAL HASN'T GIVEN US ONE JAZZMAN OF GENIUS!' Borneman's plangent observation was correct, but this particular renaissance was to produce many fine musicians, particularly in Britain.

The music that was originally nurtured in the lowlife culture of whorehouses, drinking palaces and street parades had moved into the US concert hall by the late thirties, and in its imitative form into England from 1946 when Webb's Dixielanders pioneered traditional-jazz concerts. These took place initially under the aegis of *Challenge*, the organ of the Young Communist League, at the Memorial Hall, Farringdon Street, but were subsequently put on by the band themselves under the name of the Hot Club of London.

From the late forties the Wilcox Brothers continued the presentation of traditional concerts, the most notable of which was the 'illegal' appearance of Sidney Bechet with Humphrey Lyttelton's band at the Winter Garden Theatre, Covent Garden in November 1949. The National Federation of Jazz Organizations continued in this role in the early fifties and thereafter, but the success of these attracted 'outsiders' – astute entrepreneurs who, unlike the Webb band (myself its functionary), the Wilcoxes and the NFJO, were not in the least interested in jazz, only in its commercial potential.

In June 1948 a group of enthusiasts, journalists and musicians formed an organization called the National Federation of Jazz Organizations of Great Britain and Northern Ireland. Nearly a hundred delegates from jazz clubs all over the country attended the inaugural meeting at the Lizbeth Hall, Soho Square, notables present including clarinettist Robert Feldman, his father Joe, writers Rex Harris, Sinclair Traill, producer Mark White, *Melody*

Maker editor Ray Sonin, and promoters Bert Wilcox and Ken Lindsay.

The NFJO was to be active in the promotion of concerts on a non-sectarian and non-profit-making basis, and its committee was to change several times during its life, elected members including Humphrey Lyttelton, Steve Race, Ernest Borneman, Peter Leslie, Stan Wilcox, the Honourable Gerald Lascelles, the Marquis of Donegall, Cecil 'Flash' Winston, Laurie Gold, Pete Payne, James Asman and Harold Pendleton.

This succession of ill-assorted committees were inescapably doomed to fall out, and did. In 1956 the federation became a private company under Harold Pendleton and continued intensive promotions, many with visiting musicians.

An early opportunist was agent Maurice Kinn, who started what became known as Mammoth Concerts with as many as fifteen bands and soloists/singers. A typical Kinn production, at the Royal Albert Hall, 2 June 1952, was the 'JAZZ BIG SHOW' – seventeen star attractions in the greatest programme ever staged in Great Britain: Sid Phillips, Freddy Randall, Freddy Clayton, Mick Mulligan, Crane River, Ken Rattenbury, Sandy Brown, Yorkshire Jazz Band, Eric Silk, Charles Galbraith, the Jimmy Walker Quintet, Galleon and Mike Collier Bands, with guest singers George Melly, Beryl Bryden, Lonnie Donegan and Denny Dennis – compere Michael Black.

Each band was paid a nominal sum, sometimes as little as fifteen pounds, and each, within the few minutes it was allotted, played its own rabble-rousing numbers. There was a total absence of presentation. These huge bills were unanimously attacked in the musical press as being a disservice to jazz. Ernest Borneman savaged the Albert Hall concert in the *Melody Maker*, 6 June 1952. He condemned the mammoth conception, Sid Phillips's 'pretty Bob Crosby-styled music' and the Jimmy Walker Quintet as a 'second-rate modernist band playing dull arrangements'. He also complained that the concert had overrun.

Kinn replied in the 13 June issue, alleging that the criticism was 'unfair', that the inconsiderate behaviour of the bands was the reason for the programme not keeping to schedule, and was particularly unhappy that Sandy Brown, allocated nine minutes, exceeded this by all of five and a half minutes.

When booking Brown as just another traditional-style band, Kinn would not have realized that the forceful Alexander Brown was not the sort of leader to have his band's performance restricted to a mere nine minutes. Kinn denied that there had been any *concerted* (his italics) booing for the Phillips band, but the promoter's inclusion of Phillips's Archer Street Dixie and the modernist Jimmy Walker group showed just how badly he had misjudged the mood and temper of the audience at which his concert was aimed.

The more respected (if internally fractious) NFJO promoted a traditional-jazz concert at the newly-completed Royal Festival Hall, South Bank, on 14 July 1951 in the presence of Her Royal Highness Princess Elizabeth. The bands playing on this auspicious occasion were Humphrey Lyttelton and his band, the Saints Jazz Band, Joe Daniels and his band, the Crane River Jazz Band, Mick Mulligan and his Magnolia Jazz Band with George Melly and Graeme Bell's Australian Jazz Band. The Saints were the hit of the show.

The appearance of a royal, next in line to the throne, was due to the influence of the Marquis of Donegall and the Honourable Gerald Lascelles, first cousin to HRH Princess Elizabeth. The Marquis introduced Her Royal Highness to members of the bands and to the NFJO committee. The latter included two hard-line Communists who, nevertheless, were eager for the honour of shaking the lady's hand. There was much ribald amusement among the less reverent members of the jazz fraternity when photographs of the occasion were published that showed these fervent anti-establishmentarians, decked out in their Moss Bros best, bowing before this symbol of upper-class privilege and inherited wealth.

The press was overwhelmed by this royal patronage of a *jazz* event. Long accustomed to looking upon jazz musicians of all persuasions as degenerate drug addicts, they had to accept that the music of the bordello was now 'respectable'. Had they known – and few did – these wide-eyed journalists could also have mentioned that such patronage commenced with the Princess's grandfather having the Original Dixieland Jazz Band and the

Southern Syncopated Orchestra at Buckingham Palace in 1919/20. They could also have reported that her uncle, the Duke of Windsor, as Prince of Wales, had patronized Duke Ellington's shows at the London Palladium in 1933 and had attended a party in press baron Lord Beaverbrook's palatial London home, Stornoway House, behind St James's Street, where he played Sonny Greer's drums.

Given that the nature of all revivalist jazz was essentially derivative, there was, nevertheless, a considerable variety of styles to be heard, particularly in the London area. By the early fifties, many of the bands had turned professional, their activities reported, as a matter of course, in the musical press. Traditional jazz had truly arrived. But at the same time it was making this unexpected impact, another school of musicians had commenced playing in a style so utterly different that the jazz world was soon split into two mutually antagonistic camps.

2
On the Boats and Up at Carlo's

Founded in 1926, the *Melody Maker* devoted considerable space to jazz, from the paper's inception until the late seventies. This was perhaps surprising, considering that the *MM* was essentially a trade paper concerned mainly with conventional dance music, and that the main body of its readers were musicians who manned the bands playing in the dancehalls, hotels, restaurants, holiday camps and 'swank niteries', this last being a vulgarism copied from the US *Down Beat*, as one of that paper's favourite terms for expensive nightspots.

This workforce was rather grandly named in the *Melody Maker* 'The Profession' ('Bombshell Hits the Profession' was one of its favourite headlines) and its central meeting-place was Archer Street, a little thoroughfare, not more than eighty yards long, connecting Rupert Street and Great Windmill Street, near Piccadilly. It was known simply as 'The Street' and as it was virtually an open-air employment bureau, the *Melody Maker* often jocularly called it 'The Street of Hope'. On Mondays in particular 'The Street' was thronged with musicians and often the police charged individuals with 'loitering', the guilty appearing before the Great Marlborough Street Court magistrate and fined ten or twenty shillings, an absurdity against which the *Melody Maker* duly and quite properly railed.

A sprinkling of the profession played jazz when the opportunity arose: in the recording studios with specially assembled groups; in 'after-hours' sessions, often in rather shady 'joints'; occasionally in rhythm clubs attended by serious buffs; but not to make a living. Until the late forties, the economic and artistic climate was not right for such a luxury, but then the profession was severely jolted by the astonishing success of the amateur bands playing in the 'old-fashioned' style ('Dixie' or 'two-beat' as they dismissively called it) and was chagrined by the revivalists' criticisms of their own occasional jazz efforts.

Members of the profession initially reacted by condemning the traditional musicians' limited techniques but, ironically, that same profession was shortly itself to be fragmented by a cadre of young musicians playing in a manner that defied the conventions. The headquarters of these rebels was a grubby, tattily furnished basement, Mac's Rehearsal Rooms, only yards from Archer Street. They called themselves the Club Eleven and the music they played was termed 'rebop', a gibberish, onomatopoeic term that reflected the phrasing employed by the horns and the drum patterns. The term was reasonably familiar to the long-standing collector, who had heard it, for instance, on New Orleans clarinettist Tony Parenti's 'In the Dungeon', made in 1927; the Three Ts' (Jack and Charlie Teagarden and Frankie Trumbauer) version of 'I's a Muggin' made in 1936; and by Ella Fitzgerald with her band (formerly Chick Webb's) playing 'A-tisket, A-tasket' in 1940, but somehow it had become attached to the experiments of a group of black musicians operating, almost clandestinely, at Minton's Playhouse, West 118th Street, Harlem, New York, from the early forties. Those now fabled names included alto saxophonist Charlie Parker, trumpeter Dizzy Gillespie, pianist Thelonious Monk and drummers Kenny Clarke and Max Roach.

The innovations of these pioneers, most of whom had played in big bands, sprang from boredom with formal chord sequences and the unremitting four-beats-in-a-bar rhythm of 'conventional' jazz. Gillespie, for instance, had played with Teddy Hill's Orchestra as far back as 1937, and Parker with Jay McShann's Orchestra in 1940. They introduced substitutions and inversions in the chords, the drummers played infinitely more intricate patterns to accentuate the improvisational flights of the soloists; the tonality changed from the broad, open tone of the pre-war horn players (on trumpet, trombone or saxophone) to a sound seemingly pinched and sour. It was as much an expression of black discontent as it was musical experimentation. Some tunes were played at a breakneck tempo both to test the technical facility of the performers and to confuse the eavesdropping white musicians dropping in to see, in their time-honoured fashion, what they could 'borrow' from the innovative blacks. There was no disputing that they were attempting to break away completely from the established rules, but the essential pulse of the music was retained. It was still dance music.

Like all revolutionary movements, bop was savagely attacked, but this did not deter the experimenters and they made historic recordings, initially on independent labels, that marked the beginning of a new era in jazz. The music's adventurousness and its overtones of rebellion appealed to many young British musicians; it was in accord with their own irreverent attitudes to authority in the prevailing turmoil of post-war social and economic change.

Like the traditionalists, the modernists relied upon records for inspiration and guidance, but unlike their counterparts on the other side of the ideological fence, they had few records at their disposal to study and emulate. Nor were there any examples of bop to be heard live. Since 1933, the Ministry of Labour, bowing to the demands of the British Musicians' Union, had placed an almost total ban on Americans playing in this country.

It was a particular category of employment that led to the first bop records being listened to with reverential awe in various enclaves, and a most unlikely figure was to play a role in the traffic from America of these strange-sounding records. This was Gerald Bright, pianist, accordionist, bandleader and impresario, better known as Geraldo. Born in 1904, he had been active in the dance-band industry since the late twenties, becoming nationally famous with his Gaucho Tango Orchestra playing at, and broadcasting from, the Savoy Hotel in the Strand, and making hundreds of records. In the late thirties, he formed a highly polished conventional dance orchestra of brass, reeds and rhythm, three vocalists and often a battery of strings. Immaculately attired in a splendidly cut tailcoat, his black hair shiny with massive amounts of brilliantine, he 'conducted' his orchestra in the (totally superfluous) fashion of the time, for the public then expected the personal appearance of the bandleader waving his baton, and dance- and concert-hall managements made this a firm contractual stipulation.

During the Second World War, Geraldo maintained a full quota of first-class musicians due, in part at least, to a quite unofficial connection with the Guards barracks in Kensington where so many dance-band musicians in uniform found themselves, thus able to play civilian engagements at night. From Geraldo's 'Guards', it was a short step at the end of hostilities to the founding of his 'Navy'. A less likely figure to have his 'Guards' and 'Navy' would be difficult to imagine, but his 'Navy' consisted of Cunard's luxury liners, for which he was musical director. In this capacity he was, albeit unawares, responsible for bop becoming an established musical form in Britain. Berths in his Navy were eagerly sought by aspirant boppers who had no particular yen for the sea, but who realized that such employment was a golden opportunity to be paid to travel to New York to see and hear their idols and bring back precious gramophone records.

The New York jazz scene, then centred mainly on 52nd Street, was an almost round-the-clock affair with the established giants rubbing shoulders, sometimes in a harmonious spirit, sometimes not, with the Minton alumni – a riot of divergent activity avidly lapped up by the British sailor-musicians.

Drummer Laurie Morgan, one of the first 'on the boats' to bring back the educative records, recalled his experiences in *Jazz at Ronnie Scott's*, a photo-book edited by Kitty Grime:

> There was Charlie Parker, Max Roach, Bud Powell in one club; the relief band was Mary Lou Williams's. Next door – I mean one wall thickness – was Dizzy's band – Ray Brown, Milt Jackson, absolutely amazing power-control. It sounded like a *spaceship*. They played 'Things to Come' three times a night. Each time it was faster until it was one. I picked up a lot of records at Ray Nance's record shop – Ray Nance's House of Note – motto 'Let Us Put Good Wax In Your Ears'. All the Dials and Savoys, Boyd Raeburn, Thelonious Monk, things no one had *heard*. I went round to all my friends back home and played them and Carlo Krahmer made some dubs. This was *years* before they were released, so it must have been quite an important event in London. I mean, when I played these records to Don Rendell one night, he was a different man the next day. And he never thought about music the same afterwards.

Another of Geraldo's sailors was alto saxophonist Johnny Dankworth, and his recollections were quoted in 'The Growth of

Modern Jazz in Britain' by Tony Hall in the *Decca Blue Book of Jazz*.

> 'We would listen to Parker for hours. I remember one trip when Lester Young was at a club next door to where Bird was playing. We listened to Pres for only ten minutes; then we went back and heard Bird for about five hours. I think at the time we looked upon Lester as a great jazz player, but almost a "has been".' Johnny makes the important observation on the effect Parker's music had on British musicians: 'At that time, only a few of us realized that the new music was a complete alteration harmonically and not just a stylization or way of phrasing. That's where some British musicians fell down, for instance, the leading saxophonists of the time. They tried hard to assimilate Parker into their playing, but fell into the trap of merely incorporating what you would call "bebop phrases", almost clichés.'

Another who found a berth in 'Gerry's Mob' was drummer Tony Crombie: 'It's not so much hearing it live as *seeing* it live. You got a funny idea what the bebop drummers were doing from the records because of the bad balance. You could hear the bass-drum punctuations but the cymbals sounded like surface noise. When you saw the people in action it was a great lesson.'

Had Geraldo been aware of the applicants' true motives for wanting berths in his Navy there are a few he would certainly not have signed on and, more frequently than was reported to him, those he booked to play sweet dance music engaged in boppish exercises not always to the shipboard dancers' taste.

Once past the Customs (along with a few other items not easily obtainable in post-war Britain) the records inevitably found their way to an address in literary Bloomsbury, 39 Bedford Court Mansions, Bedford Avenue, the flat of drummer/bandleader/collector and record producer Carlo Krahmer. He was an extraordinary man. Only partially sighted, a jazz-record collector from the early thirties (he once owned over a hundred versions of 'Tiger Rag'), he, unlike most other collectors of the late forties, displayed unusually catholic taste. He was also the first to record British bop musicians on his Esquire label, the first independent to issue American bop records. Understanding of the new idiom owed much to Carlo Krahmer.

Every Sunday afternoon at his flat he held record sessions,

attended by young musicians keen to hear the new jazz. The interest aroused at these sessions, and at the Charing Cross flat of two guitarists, Peter Chilver and Dave Goldberg, led to attempts at playing the bop idiom at various sessions. Older Archer Street jazz musicians became increasingly aware of angular phrases creeping into the horn players' solos, unexpected chords from bassists, guitarists and pianists and disturbing 'bombs' being dropped by drummers, the offenders (as they were often regarded) inevitably the younger element who had been 'on the boats' or 'up at Carlo's', or both.

As with the corresponding situation in America, the new jostled with the old and the juxtaposition was not always a happy experience for either, but the new, as in all the arts, must perforce thrust itself forward whenever the opportunity arises, bandstand or audience disfavour notwithstanding. The most favoured and easily accessible jam-session spot for the young lions to infiltrate was the Feldman Swing Club at 100 Oxford Street, London W1, founded in 1941 by furrier Joseph Feldman as a showcase for his sons, Robert on clarinet, Monty on accordion and Victor, a child prodigy, on drums. Their Sunday-night sessions featured all the established Archer Street jazz musicians and a few semi-professionals. Occasionally musicians from the visiting US service bands dropped in, one of these being the alto saxophonist Art Pepper, previously with Stan Kenton.

Another club, the Fullado, 6 New Compton Street (a street which no longer exists), was a meeting-place for those wholly preoccupied with the new mode. It was a bare, grimy basement but the decor and amenities were of scant interest to the young bloods keen to put into practice what they had heard on the records that had come over on the boats.

Don Rendell, tenor saxophonist, recalls:

> The fountainhead of 'modern' jazz in this country is usually said to be the Club Eleven. Actually, the music was fermenting earlier in the Fullado Club where sessions took place from 3 p.m. to midnight. I spent most of my spare hours there while working with Duncan Whyte's band at the Astoria, Charing Cross Road. Other musicians always around then were Ronnie Scott, Tommy Whittle, Johnny Dankworth, Terry Brown, Hank Shaw, Dave Goldberg, Tommy Pollard, Jack Parnell, Laurie Morgan, Tony Crombie and many

others. And Denis Rose, undoubtedly the most progressive-thinking of all the jazz musicians at that time. He practically lived in Archer Street, but then a lot of us did. In fact, just prior to joining Duncan Whyte I had been out of work for thirteen weeks, which was mainly spent drinking tea in Archer Street cafes. Denis ran a rehearsal band at the Fullado. We'd do things like the Dizzy Gillespie arrangements of 'That's Earl, Brother' and 'Cubana Be, Cubana Bop'. He hadn't a particularly strong tone on trumpet but he had a very thorough understanding of what bop was all about. He had an exceptional ear for chords. When Denis was about there was always some sort of action. We would troop off to Stepney and play in those enormous school halls. Afterwards we would go to someone's house and have a blow, Denis always the organizer.

Since those exploratory days there has been consistent and unanimous praise for Rose as the teacher, the inspirer; he was a veritable guru; musicians now in their middle years clearly recall his influence. Born in 1922, he was a few years older than those he so successfully coached, and he is best remembered for his analytical brain and his tuition.

Ronnie Scott: 'I got most of my theory from Denis, but then so did everyone else.'

Jeff Ellison: 'Denis was a brilliant teacher, a hard taskmaster, but he gave all us youngsters tremendous encouragement.'

Johnny Dankworth: 'A brilliant mind.'

Tony Crombie: 'In the early days it was Denis who took the lid off the music we were trying to understand.'

Laurie Morgan: 'Socially, Denis was reticent, aloof. But when it came to music he was the most generous and outgoing man I have ever known. If he was teaching you something you would have to plead with him to let you go – he was that much of a perfectionist.'

His reputation was enhanced by an unusual lifestyle. Although not a criminal, he liked to be among villains. During the war he played in a number of Soho clubs where jazz flourished among black-market racketeering, prostitution, gambling and violence. In this social substratum he developed a sardonic, streetwise persona. Although due for conscription in 1941, he evaded military service until 1944. The constraints of service life, however, were entirely antipathetic to such a free spirit and he soon deserted, spending the following six years on the run, though rarely venturing further than the confines of Soho, a relatively closed community always ready to shelter in its warrens a nonconformist.*

Had Rose been so disposed, he could have been financially secure arranging for big commercial dance orchestras, but this would not have been the style of a roving non-comformist who preferred the ambience of jazz clubs and pubs. In an interview with trumpeter Digby Fairweather in the *Melody Maker*, he stressed that he wanted freedom and, by inference, expressed sympathy for his old colleague, Ronnie Scott, for *having* to be at his club every night. If Rose found that whatever he was doing proved uncongenial he upped and left.

He was scrupulously honest about himself. In a conversation with the author only a year before his death on 22 November 1984, I referred to the plaudits he had received for his singular contribution to British bop. With a characteristic shrug of the shoulders he replied, 'Whatever any of us were doing then, it was all second-hand.' Then, spotting a song copy of 'Sometimes', a waltz by Fred Elizalde, he picked it up and though he had never heard, or heard of, the tune before, immediately sight-read it. It struck me as odd that this rather sinister-looking figure, who had been the wild young man of bebop, was now humming a pretty waltz, at exactly the tempo on a record made in 1928 by Van Phillips's band.

In 1947 Rose played in Britain's first regular bop-influenced band, the Tito Burns Sextet, broadcasting regularly on 'Accordion Club' for the BBC's Light Programme. Also in the band were Ronnie Scott, Peter Chilver, Joe Muddel, Tony Crombie and Ray Ellington. It is one of the many ironies attending the history of jazz in Britain that a band containing a representative number of the young revolutionaries should be a group led by an accordionist, appearing weekly in a radio programme devoted to that instrument. For it was probably the most reviled of all instruments by jazz buffs, second only to the harmonica in its unacceptability. Although a keyboard instrument, it is a hybrid, and does not possess the articulation and resonance of the piano, spinet or

---

*He wasn't on the phone, even in the 1980s, and was reluctant to give me his address. I asked Joe Green, one of Ronnie Scott's staff, who had known Rose for years, if he was still on the run. 'No,' replied Green, 'but he's always careful in case he *might* be.'

harpsichord. The mechanics of playing it involve the sucking of wind into its bellows, producing a muddy, wheezy tone. Even during the twenties when much rooty-tooty ephemera was produced in the name of jazz, it was rarely used. Entrepreneur Irving Mills (who managed both an accordionist named Cornell Smeltzer and Duke Ellington) foisted the former on the latter for a few recordings and on a white band called Irving Mills's Hotsy Totsy Gang. The instrument also appeared, surprisingly, on records made by Bennie Moten's band, the precursors of Count Basie's orchestra, in Kansas City in the late twenties, and in the late forties a blind musician, Joe Mooney, effectively handled it on many recordings. Generally, however, it was an instrument wholly shunned by jazz musicians.

Tito Burns was rated by his fellow musicians as a good jazz player, even, but as Don Rendell pointed out in an article for *Crescendo* it must have been something of a shock for lovers of the accordion to hear the seemingly nervy rhythms and staccato phrasing of bebop from the Burns band. They were more accustomed to dance music by Primo Scala and his Accordion Band or light classics such as Albert Ketelbey's 'In a Monastery Garden' played by accordion virtuoso Tollefson, a skilled technician on that instrument.

The producer of 'Accordion Club' was Charles Chilton, one of the first BBC staffmen in the thirties to persuade the planners to allow jazz on to the air. The programmes were introduced by the late Roy Plomley, a keen jazz enthusiast, later famous for his 'Desert Island Discs'. It was Chilton who produced the first programme the BBC devoted entirely to bop, on 27 May 1947, with Reg Arnold (trumpet), Wally Stuart (tenor saxophone), Denis Rose (tenor horn), Ralph Sharon (piano), Pete Chilver (guitar) and Russ Allen (bass).

When Tito Burns went out on the road in 1947/8 he employed Ronnie Scott, Johnny Dankworth, Tommy Pollard, Denis Rose, Tony Crombie and Pete Chilver. In his *Some of My Best Friends are Blues*, co-written with Mike Hennessey, Scott recalls that a band comprised of such musicians played 'a summer season in exotic Cliftonville', a Kent seaside resort. Bop was beginning to appear in the most unlikely places.

But the young lions were not satisfied. Scott wrote:

> Even in the best of bands the professional life of a musician represented a constant artistic compromise because the music that we had to play in order to live wasn't the music we lived to play.
>
> So, the incorrigible jazzmen among us would congregate whenever the opportunity arose and play unadulterated unrelenting jazz. To make it easier, a group of us in December 1948 got together and rented a room at Mac's Rehearsal Rooms. There were ten musicians: Hank Shaw, Lennie Bush, Joe Muddel, Bernie Fenton, Tommy Pollard, Tony Crombie, Laurie Morgan, Johnny Dankworth, Johnny Rogers, myself and a manager, Harry Morris, hence the Club Eleven.

Two main bands, one led by Ronnie Scott and the other by Johnny Dankworth, regularly took the stand, although they were frequently joined by others attracted to the idiom.

Actually bebop jazz had been the sole policy, as Rendell asserts, at the Fullado Club before the opening of the Club Eleven, but prior to the Club Eleven opening, in December 1948, another club, the Metropolitan Bopera House, at 6 New Compton Street, the same premises which the Fullado had occupied, was opened on 31 October 1948. Their advertisement in the *Melody Maker*, 5 November 1948, read:

> Metropolitan Bopera House, a new swing club, which opened on 31 October meets again this Sunday, 7 November, at 6 New Compton Street when tenorist Ronnie Scott is bringing along his quartet comprised of himself, Tommy Pollard (piano), Lennie Bush (bass) and Tony Crombie (drums).
>
> Bop fans! Alf Summers and Harry Morris are responsible for this new club.

Scanning this advertisement now, it almost appears as if the promoters were offering an admission of guilt.

Instead of drifting in disorganized fashion from one club to another, musicians soon found that the Club Eleven was the most positive step towards the grouping of kindred spirits to play together constantly, to formalize their activities. Virtually no music of this kind was played outside of London, and that dingy basement in Great Windmill Street became the temple of British bebop, the musicians acquiring an exotic aura, due in no small part to the highly eccentric behaviour of some of the principals.

Since the club had been opened to provide an opportunity to those interested in bop to rehearse, Laurie Morgan recalls that they did their best to keep non-musicians out but, as Don Rendell recollects: 'Once payment for admission was established it was one of the first instances ever of being paid to play bop!'

Drummer Jeff Ellison recalls:

> I was a regular visitor to the Club Eleven, and played whenever Tony or Laurie couldn't make it. The Club Eleven was magic; just magical, all those guys together just at the right time. We all played with such *enthusiasm*. We had a terrific bond between us. We were a brotherhood, probably because we were such a minority, playing to so few people. We couldn't understand why the young people at the time preferred traditional jazz rather than something that was contemporary, the jazz of the time. I admit that we were put out that the traditional-style bands did so much better business than we did.
>
> The gathering at the club was as much a reassurance of our faith rather than for financial gain. In fact we played there primarily for our own pleasure and to *learn* from each other and although Great Windmill Street was the centre of bop activity, we would go *anywhere* for a blow. Any distance. We were all that mad keen.

The Club Eleven staged several concerts in London, and one in Birmingham. One of their promotions, at King George's Hall, Adeline Place, Tottenham Court Road, on 9 April 1949, was recorded by Carlo Krahmer. In October of the same year, the club promoted another concert at the Central Hall, Westminster. Mike Nevard, one of the early champions of bop, wrote a scathing review in the *Melody Maker*, 5 November 1949 issue, complaining bitterly about 'circus-like antics'. It was headed 'GOOD BOP BUT POOR BUFFOONERY AT THE CENTRAL HALL':

> FROM BOP TO SCHMIP
>
> The 1,200 people packing the hall were there, I imagine, to hear the music – not to listen to bawdy buffoonery and watch the antics of an athletic type in austerity shorts, named, for some reason 'Mr Bebop 1949'.
>
> If only Tony Crombie had taken the acoustics into account when playing with the Ronnie Scott group. His cymbals echoed so much I had the idea that an atom-bomb explosion in a china-shop would have been less shattering. Through the incessant clatter of Tony's ironmongery I managed to pick out some fine tenor from Ronnie himself – though only just. Trumpeter Henry Shaw played well. Pianist Bernie Fenton and bassist Lennie Bush were

practically inaudible in the ensembles, but the former produced a couple of good solos.

The concert, arranged by the Club Eleven musicians who comprise the club and secretary Harry Morris, was to mark the first anniversary of that famous bop spot. Needless to say, the club and the boys who run it have done a lot for the cause of modern music in the establishment of a regular rendezvous where bop can be heard in its pure form. There is very little comedy at the club. Why was it introduced into what should have been a serious concert? It is said that opportunity knocks but once; let's keep our fingers crossed and hope that it knocks again.

The Scott group was preceded by a big band comprising most of the Club Eleven's two resident bands, plus Dave Wilkins (trumpet and vocal), Pete Pitterson (trumpet), Aubrey Frank (tenor saxophone), Oscar Birch (baritone), Harry Klein (alto) and Mac Minshull, Fred Woods and Eddie Harvey (trombone). In the conglomeration of sound produced by so much echo, it was impossible to review the band's performance. The audience, however, lapped it up.

Melody Maker radio critic Maurice Burman was another of the unproductive workers, though to a lesser extent. His lecture on modern trends was more in the way of being a string of amusing anecdotes, punctuated by interesting observations on the future of bop and its successor – schmip, or whatever it may be called. Let it suffice to say that Maurice is a good radio critic.

What Nevard did not report was the abrupt cessation of Burman's address. Burman, then in his mid-thirties, was an enthusiastic convert to bop and tended to proselytize at length about it, in much the same way Bill Colyer shouted hosannas for traditionalism. On this occasion the musicians in the wings were becoming increasingly restive as Burman went on and on until, eventually, Scott marched on to the stage loudly clapping his hands and addressing the audience with a very positive: 'Thank *you*, Maurice Burman. Thank you, thank you *very* much! Now, ladies and gentlemen, a *big* hand for Maurice Burman! *Thank you*, Maurice . . .' and a peeved Burman retired from the stage.

Gutter-press sensationalism apart, it was nevertheless a fact that many bebop musicians, both in America and the UK, indulged in illegal stimulants, usually marijuana, but occasionally becoming addicted to more dangerous substances. Sadly, four of Britain's greatest jazzmen, Phil Seamen, Dave Goldberg, Tommy Pollard and, later, Tubby Hayes, died as a result. Another victim was the drummer Dickie Devere.

The case for legalizing marijuana has been strongly argued, but since it was (and still is) illegal to possess or trade in such, the boppers' well-known indulgence in the substance led to the much-publicized raid on the Club Eleven at their new premises in Carnaby Street in April 1951. Serious as the matter was, the incidents on the night and during the defendants' time in custody had an extremely comic side, particularly when Flash Winston, on bended knee in the cell, as though he were the Count of Monte Cristo at the Château d'If, cried, 'Water, water, for God's sake – *water*!'

The *Melody Maker*, however, was not amused and in its 29 April 1950 issue thundered against the offenders, heading the condemnation with – 'FIVE FOOLISH YOUNG MEN'.

> Thus have five foolish young men dealt the profession, their music and their followers a blow, the effects of which may be incalculable.
>
> Now, what are the facts? Out of the twelve men arrested, less than half that number were musicians. Among those charged, three were American seamen. Did the newspapers come out with headlines to the effect that American ships were hotbeds of vice, that American sailors needed drugs so that they might be 'stimulated into an ecstasy which allowed them to climb the rigging with complete abandonment'? Of course not. Dance music has been the Aunt Sally of mudslingers in this country for years and this case has given them a heaven-sent opportunity.
>
> The total number of drug addicts in the whole of Great Britain was given in 1949 as 383 out of a population of 48,000,000! If all these were 'bop addicts' the proportion to the total number of musicians in the country would be infinitesimal. And it was explained in court that the five were not addicts. But the fact is that ninety-nine per cent of musicians and fans are decent, clean-living individuals, playing or studying their music in places that are decently run. The general public is, alas, only too eager to think otherwise, and five foolish young men have now given them the concrete cause for so doing. To place the affair in its proper perspective, the *Melody Maker* has asked one of the country's premier exponents of bebop, Tito Burns, and the man who introduced it into this country in 1946, to state his point of view below.

Burns, one-time employer of most of the offenders, wrote a strongly moralizing piece about the iniquities of the habit. He commenced his article by saying that writing it was the most heartbreaking and difficult thing for him to do: 'Had I ever thought back in 1946 that I would see headlines such as have been appearing in the national press coupled with the word "bebop" I would never have considered introducing it on the air in "Accordion Club".' He ended by expressing the fear that parents 'would prevent their children participating in enjoyment of the music; thus in turn musically-minded youngsters – the vanguard of musical progress in this country – may be denied the right to further their interest and, indirectly, ours because of this stigma that has been placed on modern music'. It is difficult to believe that Burns was unaware that his former sidemen were partial to a 'smoke'.

Considering the decidedly sporadic appearance of American bebop records in the UK the assimilation of the form by a handful of musicians was pretty rapid, if patchy, given that (trips with Geraldo's Navy apart) their apprenticeship was not served on the bandstand alongside their idols.

During 1947 the first British recordings indicating the influence of bop were issued. On 21 April, Jack Parnell and his quartet – Jack Parnell (drums), Tommy Whittle (tenor saxophone), Norman Stenfalt (piano), Charlie Short (bass) and Dave Goldberg (guitar), drawn from the Ted Heath Orchestra, recorded 'Sweet Lorraine' and 'Old Man Rebop'. The latter had been recorded by Dizzy Gillespie in New York in February 1946, but it was not issued in Britain until 1949, although clearly one of the records must have been imported via the boats. Later, the Parnell group recorded 'Hide Parker', an obvious reference to Charlie Parker, but this was not issued. From 1947, however, the Heath orchestra performed and recorded more material by bop writers, including 'Euphoria' by the pianist Tadd Dameron, one of the first arrangers to make full use of bop devices.

Parnell's 'Old Man Rebop' could not reasonably be described as more than a bop-tinged recording and while it is debatable what constituted bop, the claim could be made that the first positive example of the idiom played by British musicians was by a pick-up group led by a veteran 'sideman', the alto saxophonist Harry Hayes.

In June 1947, the *Melody Maker*, in collaboration with Columbia Records, promoted a concert at the EMI Studios, Abbey Road, North London, calling it the 'Melody Maker/Columbia Jazz Rally 1947'. In December the same year a much-edited selection was released on the Columbia label on two ten-inch and one twelve-inch 78-rpm records. Before the event it was announced that the aim of the rally was to make recordings for distribution not only in Britain but in the United States as well, to show how well British jazz musicians had developed since their faltering attempts at essaying the jazz idiom in the early twenties.

First-class musicians were selected, all of whom had revealed their abilities on other recordings. Furthermore, the assemblage was interesting in that both the old and new guard were represented. The established musicians were Reg Arnold, Dave Wilkins (trumpet); Woolf Phillips, George Chisholm, Lad Busby (trombone); Reggie Dare (tenor saxophone); Carl Barriteau, Frank Weir, Harry Parry, Cliff Townshend (clarinet); Jack Collier (bass); Jock Cummings, George Fierstone (drums); Frank Deniz (guitar). The new school was represented by Ronnie Scott, Tommy Whittle (tenor saxophone); Ralph Sharon, Norman Stenfalt, George Shearing (piano); Charlie Short, Jack Fallon (bass); Pete Chilver and Dave Goldberg (guitar).

It turned out to be a tatterdemalion jam-session affair, some players even palpably out of tune. Outstanding, however, is an excerpt from the aforementioned Harry Hayes group playing Charlie Parker's 'Thrivin' on a Riff'. It is notable not only for the quality of the solos, by Hayes and Goldberg, but for its conception, entirely different from the rest of the offerings.

Clearly, the Parker record, made in November 1945 for the Savoy label but not issued in Britain until 1952, was the model. It is thus yet another example of a significant record finding its way to Britain via Geraldo's Navy, or via Laurie Morgan, who mentions the Savoy records as part of his haul from Ray Nance's shop.

Hayes's playing reveals how thoroughly he had assimilated the Parker line, albeit in emulation and, understandably, lacking the power and clarity of the original, but Goldberg's construction, no doubt influenced by long hours of listening to Charlie Christian, one of the Minton alumni, was exceptional, especially since there was no guitar solo on the original record for him to copy or adapt. Unfortunately, a full version of this Columbia session no longer exists. The other members of the group were trombonist Lad Busby, trumpeter Dave Wilkins, baritone saxophonist Bill Lewington, pianist Norman Stenfalt, bassist Charlie Short and drummer George Fierstone.

Harry Hayes remembers:

> I can't honestly recall where I first heard 'Thrivin' on a Riff'. I think Dave Goldberg had the record and worked out the chords. What I do remember is being totally overcome the first time I heard a Parker record – 'Cool Blues' – in 1946. Before then few knew what he played like, until I met someone who told me he was a very technical player, someone moving up and down the scales. I wasn't really interested until one day: that day I heard 'Cool Blues'. [Not issued until January 1949 – clearly another 'boat' record.] I couldn't eat or sleep for a week! I just couldn't believe that anyone could play the saxophone like that. It was absolutely incredible. *Incredible.* I-N-C-R-E-D-I-B-L-E. His playing was so beautiful; so logical.
>
> I remember discussing the experience with an old friend and colleague of mine, Phil Cardew, another member of Elizalde's Anglo-American Band, and he too couldn't figure out how Parker played the way he did. It was a revelation. No wonder Parker was such an influence.
>
> I had to have a go myself, I didn't want to be left behind! But I never really considered myself a bop man. I used to visit the Club Eleven to hear the young players who were really grasping the idiom.
>
> As for my contribution to 'Thrivin' on a Riff' that afternoon at EMI – well, I'd heard the Parker. I'm almost certain that Dave Wilkins and Norman Stenfalt took solos. It's a shame they were cut . . .

It is odd, more than a shade ironic, that in an assembly including so many emergent boppers it was a veteran who showed the young lions that the bop idiom could be successfully tackled. Hayes's 'Thrivin' on a Riff' vindicated the determination of the original boppers to get away from the free-for-all jam session which, as these Columbia records reveal, actually obtained throughout the rest of the concert.

Hayes had commenced his career as far back as 1926 and at the age of seventeen, in 1928, was a member of Fred Elizalde's Anglo-American Band seated just behind multi-instrumentalist (but specializing on the bass saxophone) Adrian Rollini. In 1931 he was a member of Spike Hughes's Orchestra, the first continuously recording jazz orchestra in Britain, and in 1932 was in Louis Armstrong's only British band. He spent most of his career, however, in dance bands like Geraldo's, enlivening many an otherwise dull performance with his graceful solos.

In the same year as he made 'Thrivin' on a Riff' he recorded 'Ol' Man Rebop', with boppish overtones, and on 22 July that year made his final record in an HMV series that started in 1944, 'The Be-Bop'. This contained dire 'bopalese' by vocalist Lawrence Jackson, and was the last record Hayes made under his own name.

A few other Archer Street jazz musicians flirted with the bop idiom. One of these, surprisingly in the light of his long emulation and championship of Louis Armstrong, was Nat Gonella. Indeed, there exists a photograph of him at the Club Eleven in the company of West Indian trumpeter Pete Pitterson, Johnny Rogers, Tommy Pollard, Ronnie Scott and an unknown vocalist.

In an excerpt from an 'Arena' programme shown during the Club Eleven reunion on BBC TV, Gonella told how he took his bop band to the dancehalls and got a hostile reception from the proprietors and public. In this interview, Gonella wryly recalled conversations with ballroom managers who remembered him with his Georgians. ' "What's this?" they asked. "It's bop, the new thing," I replied "Is it?" they said. "You can take it away and don't come back with it." ' The records he made at that time, however, show little evidence of bop.

Gonella was by no means an isolated case. Another old hand who dabbled was the multi-saxophonist Derek Neville, who often sat in at the Club Eleven. His style of alto saxophone playing was unusual – so much so that Humphrey Lyttelton, on his 'Best of Jazz' on Radio 2 in 1984, referred to Neville's phrasing on records (made with Harry Parry in 1942) as uncannily prefiguring Parker's.

Another highly respected veteran who became attracted to the new jazz was tenor saxophonist Buddy Featherstonehaugh – also a member of Spike Hughes's Decca Band and Louis Armstrong's British band – but it was not until the fifties, when he changed to

---

*See *A History of Jazz in Britain 1919–50* (HJB1).

baritone saxophone, that he made recordings firmly in the bop mould, with the much younger Bobby Wellins (tenor saxophone) and Kenny Wheeler (trumpet).

Generally, however, the older musicians who tried to keep up with the times were not successful in the attempt. It usually required the malleability of youth to make the transition effectively. Musicians like Scott, Stenfalt, Pollard and Dankworth did not start their careers as bop players, but they had not been around long enough for their ways to become set, and they swiftly assimilated the new idiom.

Furthermore, the slowly increasing audience for bop was just as purist, in its fashion, as the traditionalists, and it was equally suspicious of players who seemed to be jumping on a bandwagon. It was as quick to sniff out the spurious as the traditionalist who rejected the 'Archer Street Dixie' in the bands led by Harry Gold, Sid Phillips and Joe Daniels, all pre-war dance-band musicians.

The traditionalists, of course, savaged the new jazz at every opportunity. One of its more stringent critics was the chief propagandist for white jazz, Ralph Goodwin Vaughan Venables who, reviewing records on the Commodore label (not then available in Britain) in the *Melody Maker*, 25 November 1950, harped upon the sartorial eccentricities of the American bebop players: 'What a good thing there are so many of these Commodores. There's not a bop in the bucketful and the volume of wholesome sound banishes all thoughts of goatee beards, horn-rimmed glasses, droop drapes and similar transitory nonsense.'

Peter Tanner, reviewing recordings by Keith Bird's Esquire Six on the Esquire label in *Jazz Journal*, January 1950, wrote, 'Tuneful music played with impeccable musicianship, but not to be confused with jazz.'

Brian Rust in the same paper, in an article on his methods of discographical research, ended: 'Note to Steve Race: I haven't the least desire to know who played third – or any other sax – on a Gillespie record. Why, because I study jazz from a historical viewpoint and that, you will admit, must involve knowledge of records that deserve to be called jazz.'

Criticism also came from a denizen of Archer Street. In the 10 July 1947 issue of the *Melody Maker* an article by Harry Singer was headed: 'REBOP – AN INSPIRED PUBLICITY STUNT?'

> As you know it is the current vogue to talk and write about bebop. I'll allow that it has weird and wonderful harmonies and a terrific beat. I also grant it has a distinctive and refreshing novel idiom, but it has left me with the impression that Gillespie or his recording company has somebody with a brilliant flair for publicity working for them. For other bandleaders have formulated their own musical idioms, such as Duke Ellington, Django Reinhardt and Hindu Shar, leader of the Hindu hand drummers who toured America inspiring people like Gene Krupa. However, they lack that little word (bebop) so easy to utter which, because a couple of quavers phrased with a rim-shot then on a bass drum, is not sufficiently onomatopoeic for accurate description.
>
> Musicians as great as the above three are intelligent enough though to realize that it is their music alone which has got them talked about and not publicity catchwords like rebop, which because of the way musicians like to hear themselves talk, now induce a greater association of ideas than the music itself. I'm sure that any honest disciple of rebop will honestly admit this after the spate of pretentious nonsense it has aroused.

In the same issue of the *Melody Maker*, Edgar Jackson reviewed 'Scuttlebut', 'Ol' Man Rebop', 'Dubonnet' and 'Lucky Number' by Harry Hayes and his band on HMV.

Many were surprised that an old hand like Jackson, reviewing jazz records as far back as 1926, should have been a supporter of this new jazz but then again, perhaps it wasn't so surprising given the man's wildly inconsistent pronouncements in the past.* It was, however, hard to determine the sincerity of someone so chimerical in his approval. Perhaps he was hedging his bets, in case this departure from the norm became the norm.

Whatever his motives, it was assuredly the same Jackson in his writing style; this was as puzzling as ever. In his references to bop phrasing creeping into the work of British jazzmen, though, his observations were pertinent. Under the heading 'BEAU BRUMMEL OF THE ALTO SAX', he wrote:

---

*See HJB1.

Harry Hayes, always the immaculate Beau Brummel of the alto, is even better on these records than usual. For all their fascinating line, his phrases still sound rather formal because he fits them so rigidly to set two- or four-bar patterns instead of cutting them across the measure. But this is to some extent offset by the greater drive with which he plays. You will notice this, even in 'Dubonnet', although as a composition this is just another of the maestro's charming little tunes with the accent mainly on the melodic appeal . . . Maybe it's because the playing is so much cleaner now that there is no longer the least ground for criticism on this point, or maybe because the scoring is better, or maybe because there is less in the way of uninterrupted chunks of block scoring for the whole front line.

Also quite a few people in the band seem to have been bitten by the rebop bug. Drummer Norman Burns shows the most inflamed spots but the rash is to a greater or lesser extent discernible on most others.

You need not expect rebop to break out suddenly in full force in any British band, because British musicians are not made that way. But, like all jazz and swing modes, it will gradually infiltrate into our more advanced dance combinations and it seems that Harry Hayes has been the first to introduce the trend on records.

More shots were to be fired in this war. In July 1948 the BBC staged an outside broadcast that combined both a bop band and that of Humphrey Lyttelton, at the Leicester Square Jazz Club, the home of the latter and Graeme Bell's Australian Jazz Band. The venue and 'pairing' of stylistically antipathetic bands was a grave error of judgement. The bop band was heartily booed by the traditionalists present. Casual listeners must have wondered at this unmannerly reaction. Anyone in the jazz world, of course, could have told them that this unfavourable reaction to bop was symptomatic of the traditional versus modern war. This partisan vilification has long ceased, but the jazz community is still, broadly speaking, divided into two camps.

Such was the climate that the *Melody Maker*, 12 August 1950, reported what was tantamount to an ideological pronouncement, and a confession of his views on jazz generally, from BBC producer John Foreman, due to take over as producer of the BBC's half-hour allocation of jazz – 'Jazz Club': ' "There will be no modernists on 'Jazz Club'," says Mr Foreman. "The music I know as jazz comes from the heart, not the mind. I intend 'Jazz Club' to present the real thing, music with a real beat. There will be no bop and no progressive music . . ." ' The *Melody Maker* received literally hundreds of letters in protest. As passions ran high about jazz, partisan feelings were vehemently expressed. In those disputative days it was a matter of great import. One of those to register his objections was the present author:

> John Foreman's statement is a startling declaration of faith and intention from one employed by an organization that consistently, if unconvincingly, protests strict impartiality in matters ideological, theological and artistic.
>
> Frankly, I think that Foreman is going to have a hard time filling a 'live' programme each week with our traditional-style bands and not to lose his job for creating a public nuisance.
>
> There are not more than three such bands proficient enough to broadcast, and to have sessions with semi-pros who have little to offer but slickness could make the BBC's contribution to 'true' jazz look ridiculous.
>
> Further, speaking as a fig mouldy to the point of decomposition, I take a poor view of the intention to exclude modern jazz. Not that I'd miss the stuff in a thousand years, but there are many who appreciate it, and are as much entitled to their tastes as the mouldy fig is entitled to his 'true' jazz.
>
> This viewpoint is prompted not so much by big-heartedness, but more for fear that any rigid exclusion of certain styles could be applied to traditional jazz if the programme changed hands.

During this ideological war, and as early as 1948, Krahmer produced 'Bopping at Esquire' with Ronnie Scott, Ralph Sharon and Pete Chilver; in May of the same year, he issued records by the Victor Feldman Quartet with Johnny Dankworth and Eddie Thompson; and in September 1948 he released a recording of the Club Eleven unit, 'Buzzy', parts one and two, made by the band at the Birmingham Town Hall.

In the same year, a major company, Parlophone, showed interest, issuing their first bop records, by Dizzy Gillespie. By the early fifties there were enough of the genre to be studied, and enough trips had been made to the source of the music via the boats for British musicians to have more than just grasped the idiom. In a few short years the face of jazz in Britain had changed immensely.

In September 1985 the BBC made two films that were part of their 'Jazz Week', running in December that year, both instigated by the author. One was 'Club Eleven Reunion', a gathering of the Club Eleven pioneers (all had survived excepting Tommy Pollard), and the other 'The Street', a compilation of clips from Denis Rose's collection of silent films, shot with a 16mm camera, mainly using Archer Street and its characters as his subjects. As Laurie Morgan succinctly put it in the 'Club Eleven Reunion' programme: 'The war was just over and this music reflected the new thinking. It was aggressive, vibrant; it wasn't apologetic. Dizzy, Bird put it down. We just had to take it up. It seemed the natural thing to do – good or bad – we *had* to do it.'

Against all odds and every kind of opposition, this is exactly what the young British boppers did.

3
He Played as He Pleased

Like their 'mouldy fygge' counterparts on the other side of the ideological divide, the modernists were unwavering in their beliefs about the validity of 'their' jazz, although they must have entertained grave doubts about ever making a living from such endeavours. They watched, with perhaps more than a degree of envy and no doubt considerable surprise, the traditional bands attracting crowds at clubs and concerts and occupying, far more than themselves, the ground once held by the conventional dance band, in the dance and concert halls.

By the early 1950s traditional jazz had indeed become a commercial proposition and the man who played the most influential part in establishing its popularity was Humphrey Lyttelton. Following his rapid and total conversion to the verities of New Orleans jazz, the combination of his talents, panache and social background gelled to make him a spectacular success.

This success was not obtained without attracting adverse comment, such criticism inevitably dwelling on much-publicized extra-musical details concerning his background. What, certain members of the profession acidly enquired, had all this to do with being a musician? Did his blue blood make him a better player?

Dance-band-cum-jazz musicians who also wrote record reviews – trombonist Jack Bentley, drummer Maurice Burman and trumpeter Max Goldberg – were critical of his technical limitations, but there was more than a trace of sour grapes in their strictures. The Archer Street jazzmen were being usurped by amateurs, and one of these of aristocratic lineage, apparently cashing in on his upper-crust background.

Lyttelton did not actively encourage this sort of publicity but, sensibly, neither did he discourage it. In his *Second Chorus*, he acknowledged that talent and artistry had to be promoted, and that he had no objection to receiving publicity on account of his class. He cited the example of a band, Johnny Dankworth's, widely reported upon in the national papers as well as the musical press, after their coach had been fired at. Photographs were shown of the bullet hole in the coach window and it was said the occupants had been showered with glass. It turned out to be a publicity stunt, arranged by publicist Les Perrin. Lyttelton comments laconically: 'I was lucky in not having to search for angles. The papers have found the Old Etonian and Ex-Guards angles inexhaustible and in so far as it saves me the expense and bother of cooking up new ones, I don't complain.'

If jazz was to be given a boost because one of its executants had been to Eton, so be it and, as his records (even the very early ones) proved, he sounded a lot more convincing in the jazz role than most of his dance-band-musician critics to whom jazz was only a part-time activity. Paradoxically though, his first playing experience of any note was with Archer Street jazzmen. In his *I Play as I Please*, he relates that his first gigs were with Carlo Krahmer at the Nuthouse, a nightclub in Regent Street. This was a favourite haunt of American servicemen and mixed in with the clientele were a number of slumming Guards and Cavalry officers and a floating population of socially dubious night owls.

> On one of my first visits to the Nuthouse I took my trumpet along and asked to sit in. There passed over the musicians' faces an expression which, in later years, I have come to know very well. It is a special look, registering consent with the minimum degree of encouragement such musicians reserve for society types who ask if they can have a go with the band. I was never a society type, but on this occasion I was in the uniform of a Grenadier Captain which to them amounted to much the same thing . . .
>
> Some of the musicians have told me since that when I first appeared in front of them with my trumpet their hearts sank and they nodded glumly to my request. I won't say that my playing brought them to their feet cheering and applauding but it was certainly better than what they expected and from that time on I was allowed – invited, even – to sit in regularly.

It could reasonably be supposed that these hardened professionals were surprised at such a talent from such an unlikely 'sitter-in', for here was no aristo ineffectually 'having a go on the trumpet', but it is an equally reasonable supposition that the same musicians were astonished when this young trumpeter started making such a name for himself a few years later.

His original band played their first engagements on a purely semi-professional basis from February 1948. After several years of revivalism, attitudes had hardened in support of the 'proper' instrumentation (trombone, trumpet, clarinet, piano, banjo, bass and drums) and collective improvisation. The purists' convictions as to what constituted 'true' jazz had become firmly established and few were more convinced about the righteousness of these component parts than Humphrey Lyttelton in his early days as a bandleader.

The author can recall a conversation with him in the Blue Posts, a pub in Eastcastle Street now known as the Rose and Crown, used by the band and members of the London Jazz Club. Lyttelton was passionately declaiming his admiration for the Creole Jazz Band, even going so far as to praise the 'warmth' of drummer Baby Dodds's woodblocks – just about the only part of Dodds's kit the primitive recording processes in 1923 registered on the shellac.

Dave Carey's use of woodblocks on Lyttelton's early records on the Tempo and London Jazz labels clearly indicates his leader's instructions, and on some of these recordings Nevil Skrimshire plays banjo. Skrimshire, in a liner note for a compilation of Lyttelton's London Jazz recordings (*Delving Back with Humph*, Esquire 310), claims that: 'Humph had finally talked me into playing banjo on a few numbers and I bought a cheap second-hand one. This is evident on some of the next titles on this record!' In the same note he wrote of his dismissal from the band because, 'among other things, Humph wanted more banjo . . .'

Obviously, Lyttelton had become a convinced traditionalist, a different posture from the one he had held when he first burst upon the scene in early 1947.

In *I Play as I Please*, he wrote:

> When I first discovered jazz at Eton there had been no such thing as the New Orleans revival and jazz appreciation was a simple and haphazard affair amounting to just 'knowing what one liked'. My earliest record collection ranged over jazz styles, without rhyme or reason.

By pure coincidence it contained a lot of jazz by such as Louis Armstrong, Johnny Dodds and Sidney Bechet, later to be regarded as the High Priests of Revivalism. The beginnings of the movement – the critical crying in the wilderness and attacks on current taste – went right over my head and by the time I reached Camberwell School of Art and began to look around the jazz world I was by no means a purist.

And from his *Second Chorus*:

I took up with the revivalists for several reasons. The great era of swing music, during which I had been attracted to jazz, was over. The general trend was towards modern jazz – a new, complex, uneasy music that did not appeal to me. The old style of jazz had more in common with the music of Louis Armstrong, Fats Waller, Teddy Wilson and Count Basie on which I had been bred. Furthermore, New Orleans jazz is a group music with emphasis on collective rather than solo playing. It had especial appeal for one who had been freelance, sitting in here and there wherever the opportunity presented itself but never settling for long with one group. And lastly, it seemed a good plan, at a stage when jazz music in general was groping around for some sense of direction, to go back to the beginning and learn the fundamentals. With all the optimism and arrogance of youth, we even thought we might be playing a part in putting jazz back on the rails.

This is wholly consistent with his remarks to the author on the first occasion that I met him, at a Hot Club of London meeting in January 1947. It was his first ever concert appearance and at the end of the show he said: 'I'm no purist, Jim, but I sincerely hope George and the boys keep going.' But, in a later conversation with the author (again in the Blue Posts), he berated the 'sterile' arrangements common to most 'swing' bands and the 'isolation of the solo', citing a Benny Carter big-band record as an example. This was at the very height of his revivalist fervour. It was his brief association with the Dixielanders and his catching up on recordings of New Orleans musicians that led him to such a pronounced traditionalist stance.

In October 1948 the London Jazz Club moved to the basement of 100 Oxford Street, a nondescript restaurant called Mack's during the day but exploding into life on Monday and Saturday evenings, the small dancefloor becoming a seething, teeming mass of twirling and swirling bodies – in high summer a heat haze hung below the low ceiling. As many as a hundred couples or more jived in this area and, as most had learned the art by now, miraculously avoided each other in the mêlée – until, that is, an unexpected influx of maladroit Hooray Henrys joined the proceedings.

Lyttelton's band was now riding high on a quite remarkable wave of popularity and press attention. It was the first truly successful British jazz band. Harry Brown had been replaced by a brilliant seventeen-year-old trombonist, Keith Christie, whom Lyttelton had first heard when Keith and his brother Ian, a clarinettist, made pilgrimages from Blackpool to the Red Barn to sit in with the Dixielanders. With Lyttelton, Fawkes and Christie there was a formidable front line not, however, matched by the rhythm section, but the limitations here, like the Creole Jazz Band's (and this is no comparison between the bands) were, in part at least, overcome by the heat generated by the horns.

In October 1949, Ian Christie joined the band. He was inspired by Albert Nicholas and, in addition to contributing gracile solos, he joined with Fawkes for pleasant two-part unison passages which lent further orchestral colour to the ensemble.

On 30 November 1949, only seventeen days after the band made historic recordings with the great New Orleans soprano saxophonist Sidney Bechet (a cloak-and-dagger affair, put on to circumvent the Musicians' Union ban), they made their first records for a major label, Parlophone, the company that, in 1927, had issued their famous 'Rhythm-Style' series introducing the British public to Louis Armstrong, Duke Ellington, Bix Beiderbecke and many other giants of jazz.

The first Parlophone release sold over four thousand copies in the first month of its issue and when Oscar Preuss, the company's A&R man, sent Lyttelton his first royalty cheque he scrawled across the statement – 'Who would have thought it?' Indeed! Such a sale for a jazz record! George Webb very likely entertained wry thoughts when he heard the news.

The author wrote, in *Jazz Illustrated*, a highly fulsome review of the first Lyttelton Parlophone coupling, 'Maple Leaf Rag'/ 'Memphis Blues', and all these years later still holds the same warm sentiments towards a significant release. Both sides had class, but what one did not recognize in those heady days of youthful enthusiasm was the rhythm section's ponderousness, with the banjo clunkily dominating it. But this was very much a characteristic sound of the time, one that was to be associated with British traditionalism for many years to come.

But on these Parlophones at least the rhythm section was steady. Certainly the banjo is over-recorded, but there is, mercifully, no clatter of woodblocks. If Bernard Saward (Carey's replacement) had been given instructions that they be used (assuming he had them in his kit) he obviously disobeyed them and – pure conjecture – perhaps the leader, on listening to the playbacks where rimshots and use of the ride cymbal were the predominant features of the drumming, was glad that his instructions had been ignored.

In January 1951, Ian Christie left the band. He and Fawkes carefully worked out their roles, especially on records, so as not to clash, but generally it was an uneasy situation for both. In December of the same year, Keith Christie also departed, and they formed the Christie Brothers Stompers.

Stylistic factors and financial machinations were both involved in this development. During Lyttelton's preoccupation with the ensemble sound, his instructions to Keith Christie were to keep to the simple 'tailgate' role.* This was at a time when the young and highly talented trombonist was extending his horizons, a scanning of the vista that led to him joining the first Johnny Dankworth Big Band in 1953.

It was ironic that a leader who a few months afterwards savagely attacked parochialism in jazz, was, in this instance, curtailing adventurousness in a youthful and swollen-headed sideman, but in the light of the band's policy, he undoubtedly had every justification for doing so. These disagreements and the offer of more money led Keith Christie to toe the traditional line, but not with Lyttelton.

It was known at the time by many that there were differences between this teenager from Blackpool and his much older leader and this was confirmed years later when Lyttelton, reviewing an

---

*A term originating from New Orleans street parades, where the band often played on an open cart. To facilitate free use of his slide the trombonist was seated at the rear, i.e. the 'tailgate'.

Eddie Condon record in the *New Musical Express*, slammed the trombonist, Lou McGarity, and made appositely critical remarks about Keith Christie.

During Keith Christie's and brother Ian's stint with Lyttelton they had recorded eighteen sides under the name of the Christie Brothers Stompers with arch-purist Ken Colyer on trumpet. These were strictly in the 'old' New Orleans style with Keith coming in strongly in a Jim Robinson manner, employing the broad sweeps of the New Orleans 'primitive'.

Their earthy approach was undoubtedly due to the strong personality of Ken Colyer imposing rigidly orthodox views on ensemble playing, and in these recordings rarely is there a solo without the *sotto-voce* counter-improvisations from the other horns, very much a characteristic of the New Orleans stay-at-homes.

Meanwhile, Lyttelton was becoming increasingly dissatisfied with the money he was getting – allegedly thirty pounds a session inclusive – for packing out the London Jazz Club twice weekly, and in February 1951 Lyttelton's manager, Lyn Dutton, negotiated with the lessee of the premises for their hire on Wednesday nights. Thus the London Jazz Club operated on Mondays and Saturdays and Lyttelton, in opposition, on Wednesdays. The Wilcoxes had to find another regular band and agreed terms with the Christie Brothers, it being firmly understood that they were to play in the 'traditional' manner. The Christies engaged trumpeter Dickie Hawdon, formerly with the Yorkshire Jazz Band, and the rest of the band was comprised of Pat Hawes (piano), Ben Marshall (banjo), Denny Coffee (bass) and Bernard Saward (drums), George Hopkinson replacing Saward in the Lyttelton band.

Lyttelton did not replace Keith Christie, although the trombone was an instrument thought to be vital to a jazz band of their kind, and its omission a matter of concern. Initially, however, Lyttelton carried the day without the instrument, continuing quite successfully with only a six-piece, packing the 2,000-seater Empire Theatre, Liverpool, for instance. So few attracting so many people! Only one or two of the fourteen- to sixteen-strong orchestras touring at the time could have played to such houses, and the band's drawing power remained generally strong despite the lack of the pumping, rorty trombone.

Although the acknowledged leader of the traditionalists, Lyttelton had already displayed indications of his desire to move outside the strict confines of the New Orleans model. In 1951, he combined with members of Graeme Bell's Australian Jazz Band to record four sides, two under the name of the Bell–Lyttelton Jazz Nine, and two as the Bell–Lyttelton Jazz Twelve, the instrumentation involving the saxophones of Don 'Pixie' Roberts and Ade Monsbourgh with arrangements by Graeme Bell.

It was in the December 1952 issue of *Jazz Journal* that, in an article of two thousand words headed 'OPEN UP THOSE WINDOWS', Lyttelton disturbed many of his followers with a searing attack on the New Orleans Revival. This is a pithy, beautifully written appraisal which warrants quotation in its entirety.

> 'Open up those windows and let the bad air out!' This legendary command, attributed to Buddy Bolden, should be embroidered in coloured wools and framed above the bed of every jazz enthusiast the world over, whatever his denomination. For there can be few departments of intellectual activity which need such frequent ventilation as the noble art of jazz-loving. Witness the unhygienic fug which we still call the New Orleans Revival. This began as a critical movement aimed at discovering the real roots of jazz and establishing in their rightful place the pioneers of the New Orleans era. When we remember that, as late as 1928, it was quite generally accepted that jazz began with the Original Dixieland Jazz Band, and that Jelly Roll Morton was a legendary figure of obscure origin whose music was practically unknown, we can appreciate the value of the movement. For many, it was not so much a revival as a revelation – an era of excitement in which a whole treasury of music was discovered, hitherto buried in history.
>
> All of which should have been an unqualified blessing to jazz as a whole, straightening out its story and enlarging its boundaries. But what has happened? The cries of excitement have turned to stale parrot-cries, the exploration has become a witch-hunt, and the territories of jazz have dwindled almost to a pinpoint. And why? Because the writings inspired by the Revival – notably Blesh's *Shining Trumpets* and Rex Harris's Pelican *Jazz* – have established a rule-of-thumb which is as strict and unyielding as anything laid down by the Politburo. And this purist party line, reflected in a whole mass of small articles and reviews, has virtually replaced the human ear as the medium of jazz appreciation.

ACROBATICS

The effect of Bleshmanship and Pelicanism upon contemporary criticism, both professional and amateur, has come near to being disastrous, because it is based upon a process of analysis which is fundamentally false. The technique, stated quite simply, is to start with the basic assumption that New Orleans jazz, in all its manifestations, is 'true jazz', and to build upon this a great network of rules and principles by which subsequent jazz can be judged. Most jazz fans have gone through the stage in which they have tried to rationalize their own likes and dislikes into some sort of set standard of judgement, but in books which are published as serious 'histories' of the music, it really won't do. One has only to witness the evasive contortions performed by Mr Blesh and Mr Harris to grasp the absurdity of rigid purism. See how they twist and turn to ward off Coleman Hawkins with one hand and embrace Fats Waller with the other! And how precariously they balance on their heads in accepting Sidney Bechet, whose present-day style is no nearer to old New Orleans than that of any other swing saxophonist! Listen to Rudi Blesh explaining away the tendency of Bunk Johnson and his band to stray occasionally from the chords. 'The harmony, while felt, is never in focus of consciousness: this polyphony veers continuously into heterophony.' Now, if this mumbo-jumbo means anything it is that the habit of veering into heterophony is a characteristic of New Orleans jazz. In which case, one might expect to find a corresponding accusation of decadence levelled against those bands – Kid Ory's for instance, or King Oliver's or the Hot Five – which observe the more orthodox European rules of harmony. But no, one of the beauties of Bleshmanship is that you can have it both ways.

When George Lewis plays out of tune, he does so on purpose. And when, after a little more practice, he starts to play in tune, we all look the other way and pretend not to notice. In Rex Harris, we find the same happy facility for turning the blind eye to awkward conclusions. Hear what he says of the large swing bands. 'Conscious arrangement, when it reaches the stage in which the structure of the performance is controlled in its entirety by a preconceived design, can only be detrimental to good jazz.' In view of this sweeping pronouncement, we turn to the section on Jelly Roll Morton, expecting to find some pretty pungent criticism of the 'preconceived' piano solos and the band performances which, by careful comparison with the piano music, we know to have been almost entirely arranged. Not a word. Not a syllable to explain the discrepancy. And what has Mr Harris to say about those Armstrong solos which have been played almost note for note the same for thirty years? Absolutely nothing. The point is blandly ignored. For the simple reason that it makes nonsense of the whole chapter about swing music. You must either accept 'arrangement' and find some other more profound charges to level against swing, or you must stick to the rather embarrassing conclusion that almost the entire output of Morton and Armstrong, to name only two, is not 'good jazz'. Or, on the other hand, you can be a Pelican and have it both ways.

BOGUS PURISM

Now let nobody think that I am rounding on the New Orleans Revival, or attacking the purists, or even panning two publications simply because I disagree with the views which they express. What does concern me more is the appalling amount of shoddy, dishonest criticism which is bandied about in the name of the Revival, and which threatens to kill the whole thing stone dead. My postbag is full of evidence of the extent to which bogus purism has become the yardstick of contemporary jazz appreciation. There are the one-time fans who tell me that they have not thought it worthwhile to listen to my band since we dropped the trombone. There are the serious jazz students, all aglow with the spirit of purism, who write to warn me that I'm going the same way as Louis Armstrong! And there is the most frightening example of the man who came up to me after Ade Monsbourgh had sat in at our club, and said, 'Yes, it was certainly a wonderful noise ... I must admit Ade's great ... but I still don't like the saxophone.'

Now, it's my firm, but perhaps misguided, belief that jazz lovers really want to break away from the shackles of Orthodox Revivalism (looks frightening, doesn't it? – and brother, it is!) and follow their own ears for a change. Indeed, there is a certain amount of evidence of this. Those who were at our show at the Royal Festival Hall will remember, perhaps with shame, the spontaneous burst of applause given to a modernish alto saxophone solo by Bertie King. No doubt many of the clappers, after due reflection and a hurried glance at Pelican *Jazz*, resolved the very next day never to go again to see a show which was quite obviously given over to decadent, impure swing. But the point is they clapped! And who knows what they will clap in the future if only they will open up the windows and chuck out their bogus principles and prejudices. This doesn't mean throwing away their right to criticize. On the contrary, it will give them the power, perhaps for the first time, to use their own judgement, apply their own knowledge and jump to their own conclusions. If this leads to the elevation of Johnny Hodges over Stomp Evans, of a good Basie record which swings over a bad Morton which doesn't, and of Coleman Hawkins (four lines in Pelican *Jazz*) over Humphrey Lyttelton (two pages and sundry quotes) – then at least the New Orleans Revival will have meant something.

And given a corresponding spring-clean in the modernist household, where the atmosphere is just as foul, we might even reach a Utopian state of affairs in which musicians are once again allowed to play as they feel, and fans can look each other straight in the eye and say, 'I know what I like' instead of, 'I know what I ought to like.'

Powerful stuff! The fact that he was singled out for considerable praise in Rex Harris's book (examined later in this volume) did not deter him from criticizing the more suspect of Harris's tenets. His strictures were seen, however, as rocking the ideological boat. That same year he had been on tour, and recorded with a combination of himself, Fawkes and West Indian musicians, called the Grant/Lyttelton Paseo Band. It came of the Lyttelton band playing a Mardi Gras celebration at a Holborn hotel in February 1952 with a calypso band. Towards the end of the evening the bands merged and in the ensuing free-for-all anyone who could shake a maracca or strike a bottle joined in.

In his *Second Chorus* Lyttelton wrote:

> The result was sensational. Some of the simpler New Orleans tunes we played came vividly to life in the clattering rhythmic surroundings. After the rugged four-to-a-bar of the conventional 'traditional' rhythm section of that time the shifting rhythms were highly stimulating. And the evening rose to a climax with everyone, including some of the serious jazz students who had come along to give the proceedings their critical appraisal, coiling round the floor in a long, hilarious procession. The upshot was that I felt the urge to do something more along the same lines – and, as before, my mind turned to gramophone records.
>
> In collaboration with record supervisor Denis Preston, who was then handling most of the West Indian recording artists in London, plans were laid for a recording session. And the Grant–Lyttelton Paseo Band came into being. The word 'Paseo', a Trinidad dance, was chosen to distinguish the group from my regular band.

The groups that recorded comprised Lyttelton, Fawkes, Freddy Grant (clarinet), Mike McKenzie (piano), Fitzroy Coleman (guitar), Norman Boucarat (bass), Donaldo, Leslie Weeks (bongo), George Roberts, George Walker (maraccas), George Brown (conga) and Brylo Ford (quatro). They recorded New Orleans tunes and calypsos and while they lacked the thrust of the conventional rhythms they were notable for the miscellaneous nature of their effects, including parts for three clarinets, played by Grant, Lyttelton and Fawkes, the last on the bass clarinet.

In October 1952, Lyttelton, with Mike McKenzie, Denny Wright (guitar) and Jack Fallon (bass), accompanied the black US singer, Marie Bryant, who had starred in the classic jazz short *Jammin' the Blues* with Lester Young. On these four tracks Lyttelton demonstrates his ability to play the discreet but complementary obbligato to the vocal line.

These 'experiments' were accepted by most of his followers without complaint, but in January 1953, a year after Keith Christie's departure, Lyttelton engaged Bruce Turner to play clarinet and saxophone. Significantly and crucially, however, the newcomer concentrated mostly on the latter instrument.

This was violently to disturb many of Lyttelton's fans. In the climate of purist fervour, the misconceptions which Lyttelton had railed against in his *Jazz Journal* article, the saxophone was reviled (the sole exception being the soprano played by Sidney Bechet from New Orleans) as the serpent sliding in to besmirch the purity of the trumpet, clarinet and trombone line-up (although there was no trombone in this instance).

And if Sidney Bechet from New Orleans was acceptable, Bruce Turner, born in Saltburn, Yorkshire, was not (although Turner did occasionally play the soprano). In the minds of certain die-hards Lyttelton embracing such an instrument was nothing more than abandonment of vital first principles; an inexcusable deviation from the faith.

A bizarre event, much discussed both at the time and since, occurred when the band played at the Town Hall, Birmingham (one of the first strongholds of traditional jazz in the country, George Webb's Dixielanders having made a sensationally successful appearance there in 1946). After the first number the band saw a banner erected, stretching across several seats, with the words 'Go Home Dirty Bopper' emblazoned across it. The message was unambiguously directed at Turner.

This exhortation exemplified blinkered purists at their very worst and one wonders these many years later how many of those involved in this gratuitous insult to a fine player would care now to admit complicity?

Turner was not a 'bop' player, even though he had studied with the pioneer white bop alto saxophonist Lee Konitz in New York. Turner had looked at bebop, but elected to play in the tradition of Benny Carter, Charlie Holmes and Johnny Hodges, alto saxophonists who had played in the greatest of the pre-war big black bands. But the purists were not to know this – few would have heard of these players. They were a new breed of enthusiast who knew only British traditional jazz. While this was a testimony to the overwhelming impact of the home product it sadly reflected its followers' narrow vision. What would those who conceived and executed this stupid and insulting action have thought had they

Humph's own illustration of his 1953 band: Johnny Parker (p), Micky Ashman (b), Freddy Legon (bjo), George Hopkinson (d), Wally Fawkes (clt), Bruce Turner (as) and Humphrey Lyttelton (tpt)

known that in a few short years there were to be *three* saxophones in Lyttelton's band! Some, surely, would have expired on the spot at the very idea!

But, irrational objections to the instrument *per se* apart, the purists had a valid point against the instrument in the classic ensemble pattern. This is demonstrated in an album called *Humph at the Conway*, twelve titles recorded by Parlophone at the Conway Hall, Red Lion Square, Holborn on 2 September 1954. One title in particular, 'Bucket's Got a Hole in It', illustrates the reasons for the purists' objections. This is a lengthy track with the band virtually playing ensemble throughout. The only solo emphasis is on Fawkes for a chorus, but even this is supported by Lyttelton's trumpet, *à la* Lewis and Johnson recordings, and in such a setting the alto saxophone is totally ineffective. Its tone is too soft; it cannot compete with the strong trumpet and piercing clarinet. A tenor saxophone can cope in this company, as proved by Bud Freeman in numerous Condon recordings, but not the alto. Intelligently, self-effacingly, Turner contents himself with a few timid interpolations. The style cries out for aggressive tailgate trombone.

Bearing in mind the year, 1954, these tracks reveal how much Lyttelton was still playing in the traditional mould despite the inclusion of an 'unacceptable' instrument, but (again ironically) it was the choice of Keith Christie's eventual replacement (three years after his departure) that took Lyttelton further along the renegade's path.

This was John Picard, previously with Cy Laurie's band. His playing was clumsy and it seemed a surprising choice for Lyttelton to make, but the leader's keen ear had perceived a strong potential and Picard developed into an agile and impassioned player, becoming one of the finest jazz trombonists Britain has ever produced. His change of approach was to be consistent with the drastic policy changes in the band as a whole.

In April 1956, the Lyttelton band recorded two sides for Parlophone, 'Waiting for Picard' and 'Sugar Rose', and having studio time to fill Lyttelton recorded a medium-fast blues with himself and the rhythm section only – pianist Johnny Parker, drummer Stan Greig and bassist Jim Bray. They called it 'Bad Penny Blues'; it was issued as any other Lyttelton record, with no more than the standard promotion.

At that time Lyttelton wrote a weekly column for *Reynolds News*, a newspaper published by the Co-operative Society, and in the issue dated 14 July 1956, he wrote: 'You'll never find any good music in the hit parade', this written and received by the paper's editor before 'Bad Penny Blues' suddenly appeared, at number 20, in the *New Musical Express* and *Melody Maker* charts dated 13 July. A week later it rose to number 18.

In the *NME*, 20 July 1956, Mike Butcher wrote:

> So why have the pop fans flipped over 'Penny' – an ungimmicked twelve-bar blues with slicked-up Cripple Clarence Lofton piano figures and a preaching muted trumpet as its main ingredients?
>
> I wish I knew. But I'm delighted it's so! Because proof lies here for the looking and hearing that sheer jazz of no specially defined category can be more saleable on records than Ruby Murray in Great Britain, 1956...
>
> The band, formed in 1948, built up a local following in a matter of weeks. And it soon commenced a series of continental jaunts which have continued

regularly to include the Paris 'New Orleans Jazz Festival' this March and dates again in France, Holland, Germany, and Switzerland the following month.

Mention of a 'New Orleans Jazz Festival' looks at first sight as if Humph's musical ideals have remained unchanged over the years. Nevertheless, he's the first to admit that they haven't.

I was recently a co-speaker with him at Pendley Manor, Tring, but was unfortunately prevented from hearing the Lyttelton lecture by other work in London. However, I was much less surprised than most of the audience at the line he is reported to have taken.

'Humph says he repudiates revivalism in jazz.' 'He thinks the purists have wasted their time, done more harm than good.' 'You should have heard him, how he put down the kids at the Armstrong concerts for not knowing what jazz is.' 'I won't be surprised if he goes modern.'

Which looks like the evidence of a startling turn-about-face . . . unless you've spoken to Humph since about 1952, or read his *NME* reviews at all regularly.

True enough, he's not likely to 'go modern' in the sense of improvising like Miles Davis or Thad Jones. Yet Humphrey Lyttelton's Chelsea-style clothes, bearing and haircut, his informal kind of showmanship and genuine mistrusting of the entertainment business as a whole, are no longer the outward aspects of a nostalgia for 'jazz as it was'.

Most jazzmen of all eras and factions similarly reject the get-rich-quick kind of commercialism, and Humph has long abandoned the ambition to be a 'traditional' jazzman, a 'modern' jazzman, or anything else which needs to be printed in quotes.

He'd rather Play as He Pleases – not as the bigots of any faddist persuasion might prefer.

The unexpected success of 'Bad Penny Blues' helped re-establish faith with remaining purist fans, but events were soon to put an unbearable strain on their loyalty, for Lyttelton continued to play as he pleased, whether or not his followers were equally pleased.

In April 1956, Wally Fawkes left the band after eight years' continuous association, from its very inception, and made his last recording, 'Close Your Eyes', on 26 March that year. Stories abounded as to why, as to how both parties viewed the separation. There was a time-honoured tradition in the jazz world relating to departures, voluntary or enforced. Disappointingly bland announcements that the separation was 'amicable' were customary; in the case of dance-band musicians, the *Melody Maker* invariably reported that so-and-so left X to 'pursue his extensive freelance connections in town', which usually meant that this player would be seen in Archer Street a lot more frequently than previously.

Far more enjoyable were the privately (and, often, not so privately) expressed views of the bandleader and the departing sideman. The bandleader: 'X's presence has long been a big pain. His departure is like a boil being lanced. His replacement has improved the sound of the band beyond recognition.' The departing sideman: 'I stayed with the band because I didn't want to let them down with the number of important gigs they had, but it's a great relief to be allowed to express myself in my own way. I left of my own accord.' There were occasional variations of the theme.*

One story is that Lyttelton was visibly upset and disturbed when he made the announcement to the rest of the band in their dressing-room. If this was so it didn't show in his public countenance. Fawkes was interviewed by Max Jones in the *Melody Maker* and gave a very light-hearted and genial account of his reasons but then, he was the one that had elected to depart.

Fawkes was from a totally different background to Lyttelton, but in terms of his abilities, he too was born with a silver spoon in his mouth. He possessed enormous talent, whether on the cricket field, playing clarinet or drawing – his cartoons earning him an international reputation. A practised lifeman, a master of one-upmanship, he perfectly complemented Lyttelton, musically and temperamentally, and was always a match for his somewhat imperious boss. Indeed, it was a pairing of considerable egos and while it was Lyttelton's name and presence that propelled the band to fame, he relied more on Fawkes than Fawkes on him – the latter being a cartoonist first and musician second – and although Lyttelton had many other strings to his bow and could easily have earned a good living out of almost all of them, leading a band clearly took precedence.

Both possessed the advantage of height; Lyttelton was six feet three, Fawkes an inch shorter; both were heavyweights in every

---

*The classic example was banjoist Paddy Lightfoot getting the sack from Kenny Ball. Ball's comment was alleged to be: 'It's not working out, Paddy.' Lightfoot had been with the band for twelve years.

sense. Lyttelton, like all Titans, recognized another when he saw one and trod carefully in his dealings with Fawkes, but it was the interaction of two strong and talented personalities that played so great a part in triggering off the enormous popularity of revivalist jazz in the fifties.

A remarkable pair; 'Humphanwally' was the combined nomenclature that rolled easily and often off the tongue when talking about these heroes of the period. Spring 1956 saw the end of that union and there being no satisfactory replacement to hand Lyttelton continued without a clarinettist. It was not only the end of a memorable partnership, but one of the last links with Lyttelton's revivalist past. True, he now had a trombonist in the ranks, one with acceptable traditional associations, but he was soon to be playing a role different from the tailgate function Lyttelton had urged upon Keith Christie a few years earlier.

In the May 1982 issue of *100 Club News*, columnist 'Earwigger', in a tribute to Lyttelton on his sixty-second birthday, wrote:

> This nod to one of Britain's senior statesmen of jazz takes me back three decades when the band played regularly at 100 Oxford Street, with Wally Fawkes on clarinet and the late Keith Christie on trombone. Humph and Wally were lofty fellows, in height and demeanour. Veritable Gods in those halcyon days of early revivalism. They knew it, too. And what with being positioned on the dais above the dancefloor, it enabled them to look down on the rest of us with quite devastating effect.
>
> When one went up to make a request one made obeisant noises on touching the hems of *those* robes. Only the foolhardy would dare to criticize and for their effrontery get the Humph fisheye and scathing tongue. Fawkes would tilt his considerable chin and that didn't bode well for the impertinent either.
>
> Their unity of thought went back to their first acquaintanceship in the Red Barn. They took to each other immediately. On one occasion their musical rapport was demonstrated when Lyttelton, with his flair for the dramatic, suddenly produced a clarinet and played a dazzling duet with Fawkes. Before that moment we had no idea that he played clarinet as well. At the end of this *tour de force* George Webb got up from the piano and quipped: 'Why don't you two get married?!'

Webb was not always that amiable. At another rehearsal Lyttelton and Fawkes suddenly went into corny 'cod' Dixieland phrasing. Webb, short of stature, leapt from the piano stool, confronted the offenders and, gripping his braces, seething with fury, lashed them for frivolously wasting time. The giants, shamefaced, nervously shuffled their feet before the diminutive Webb's onslaught, didn't utter a word and serious rehearsal commenced. It is the only time I've seen either Lyttelton or Fawkes put down – and together!

In 1983 they reunited to record an album titled *Humphanwally – It Seems Like Only Yesterday* and again in 1985, under Fawkes's name, they made an album called *October Song*, a wry allusion to the years that had passed since these two young blades were the Titans of traditionalism.

In the *Melody Maker*, 13 October 1956, Lyttelton wrote an article headed 'I'M NO TRADITIONALIST' in which, typically, he defended his changes in musical policy, seemingly forgetting the days when he insisted upon Neville Skrimshire strumming the banjo, Dave Carey clattering on the woodblocks and Keith Christie playing rorty tailgate.

George Melly commented, in his *Owning Up*:

> One of Humph's characteristics is to believe that what he wanted to play at any given moment is what he always wanted to play. He rewrites his musical history like a one-man Ministry of Truth in *1984*, but the files of the musical press remain as they were. Only the other day I came across a description of Humph listening to a modern jazz record and then when it had finished, turning away with the remark, 'Back to 1926 and sanity.'
>
> Even Humph, although he always denied it, was affected by Ken Colyer's ideas. Every month or so he tended to look over his shoulder. The ghost of Mutt Carey whispered in his ear. Then he turned away and swam slowly into the mainstream.

This was regarded by many as fair comment (although Lyttelton never held it against Melly). Equally, it could be said that consistency, the hobgoblin of the petty mind, was an imp that never settled on those broad shoulders, but it was inevitable that for someone so much in the public eye and not the least reticent in unequivocally expressing his views, inconsistencies should have been noted.

Nor were his conceits overlooked. Examples of Lyttelton's confidence and integrity abound. Quite unperturbed by an action he knew would be greeted with hostility, he once engaged an Archer Street jazzman in drummer Max Abrams, teacher, among others, of the infant Vic Feldman, to replace Bernard Saward. Abrams's first recordings were made as early as 1931. The association didn't last long. Although highly proficient (he had played with Jack Hylton among others) his style was incompatible with the band and he *looked* uncomfortable and out of place.

On another occasion, Lyttelton and his band were offered a part in a Herbert Wilcox film starring Anna Neagle. The payment and the publicity would have been considerable, but Lyttelton objected to the overt racialism and the emphasis on drugs in jazz clubs in the script and turned it down. (In any case, banned substances in traditional clubs were unknown, nor did traditional musicians indulge in them.) Denizens of Archer Street must have thought him mad, or possessed of a fortune – which wasn't the case – to indulge such a conscience. The musical direction was eventually given to Jack Miranda, veteran Archer Street professional, who also played clarinet on the soundtrack.

Lyttelton also once withdrew from a concert at the Albert Hall staged by the BBC on discovering that the main body of the bill was composed of rock and roll bands. There was also the famous occasion when, sitting on a BBC 'Brains Trust', the answer to a question was slipped to him. He quickly and loudly denounced the deception over the air.

An extraordinarily active man, he has made full use of his considerable talents. He once met up with one of his old schoolmasters who enquired what he was doing. Lyttelton replied that he was drawing a strip cartoon, doing freelance journalism, general cartooning, playing trumpet, leading a band and writing a book. The master replied, 'I suppose you'll give all that up one day and start thinking about a career.' At the time of writing (1989) he is celebrating his forty-first anniversary as a bandleader; in his long career he has been involved in a great deal of controversy, taking ever more radical steps in his aim to play as he pleased.

4
Traditionalism Rampant

Lyttelton's 'defection' was emulated by other traditionalists, but there was one musician in particular, a man of messianic fervour, who tenaciously clung to the tenets of fundamentalism, not to be shaken from his rigid beliefs that true jazz was played only by the New Orleans stay-at-home musician. He did not even rate those who had left the city to play and record in New York and Chicago. Not for him the 'deviationism' of a Lyttelton! This intransigent character was Ken Colyer. He was born in Great Yarmouth on 18 April 1928, and spent his childhood in Soho, his family moving to Cranford, Middlesex, in 1936. He left school at the age of fourteen, tried to join the Merchant Navy when submarine attacks on merchant shipping were at their height, but was far too young to be accepted. He did a variety of labouring jobs and ran a milk round before joining a ship at Glasgow in June 1945. Before signing on, he became interested in jazz, listening to brother Bill's collection when the latter was in the army.

He started playing harmonica, then changed to trumpet, teaching himself and taking his instrument to sea. He spent three years in various ships, roughing it on many an unstable vessel in violent North Atlantic storms. Had it not been for his jazz interest, he might have stayed with the Merchant Navy, but it was difficult to play gramophone records on a heaving ship and there was no chance of playing in, or forming, a jazz band aboard. Later, he was joined at sea by Bill Colyer, who, playing suitcase or any other flat surface, provided him with rhythmic accompaniment. Their last trip ended on 23 November 1948 and they returned to Cranford to work in various 'hard graft' jobs, including a spell on a construction site. The gritty, down-to-earth nature of both was shaped by this succession of 'dirty' occupations on land and sea.

No dilettantes with lily-white hands they!

In 1949, trumpeter John Haim, leader of the Jelly Roll Kings, died suddenly at the age of twenty. Colyer auditioned to take his place, but failed to get the job. From then on, he played with the Crane River Jazz Band, a period during which he was for some time a railway-carriage cleaner with the London Transport Board. He stayed with the band for approximately two and half years, leaving in July 1951 (Sonny Morris taking over the leadership) to join the Christie Brothers Stompers, a decision he was to regret bitterly.

The musical differences between him and the Christies soon reached boiling point. Steadfastly preoccupied with the 'pure' New Orleans style, Colyer was at odds with Keith, whose interest in modern jazz could not help but show, even in the traditional context of the Stompers; and also with Ian, who favoured the 'Chicago' style of Eddie Condon, with whom his idol, Albert Nicholas, had played and recorded. The association that had begun in the recording studio in March 1951 lasted barely six months.

In November of the same year, Colyer rejoined the Merchant Navy, his motive being to reach New Orleans, the traditionalists' Mecca. For whereas the aspirant bopper in Geraldo's Navy had a situation ready-made for him, the luxury liners' destination being New York, the hub of modern jazz activity, and the boat berthing for twenty-four hours, sufficient time to visit many clubs, the traditionalist had no such opportunity. Even had he possessed the technical ability to pass Geraldo's audition, his arrival in New York would still have entailed a further journey to New Orleans – and back – and inevitably missing the re-embarkation schedule.

But Colyer was determined to make the pilgrimage. It took him over a year, via Cape Town, Port Sudan, Zanzibar, St Helena, the Pitcairn Islands, Auckland and Panama. He jumped ship, the *Empire Patria*, at Mobile, 175 miles east of his goal. Travelling this distance by bus, he arrived in New Orleans on 10 October 1952. It must have been a tremendously exciting moment for one so dedicated. Colyer wrote letters to his brother and these despatches, edited by Bill, appeared in the *Melody Maker*, *New Musical Express* and *Jazz Journal*. In the December 1952 issue of

A LETTER FROM NEW ORLEANS

British cornettist KEN COLYER sends this first-hand account of life today in the Crescent City

This impression of George Lewis was drawn by Monty Sunshine—artist-jazzman—who once played with Ken Colyer in the Crane River Band.

IT was Tuesday midnight when I got into New Orleans. Leaving my gear at the bus station, I grabbed a cab to the Paddock Bar.

When the band "Octave Crosby's" finished the set, I went into the back room with them.

After some odd chatter with Bill Matthews, the trombonist, Happy "Black" Goldston (drummer), bassist Maclean Broux and old man Picou, Alvin Alcorn (trumpet) said: "The George Lewis band is at the Mardi Gras tonight.

"As I'm getting late, I should get down there if you want to hear them."

I said goodnight and floated down to the M.G. The band was playing as I walked in. I sat down, ordered a beer, and almost went into a trance.

I was near Marrero

Marrero was playing about five feet from me, with Drag just behind him and Alton Purnell, on piano, just to the right facing the band.

Drummer Joe Watkins was in front, to Marrero's left. George Lewis, Percy Humphries and Jim Robinson made a line just behind and to the left of Joe Watkins.

Marrero plays beautiful solos on most numbers, and lifts like a dream when he comes back to that soft yet biting tour. All the musicians in the band play unpretentiously and so wonderfully.

At the end of their set, I met them. They all shook hands—but were rather quiet and didn't seem to want to talk much.

A fellow came in and talked to the dozen about Bix and Gillette and so on—I think he was an ex-Whiteman drummer.

"Do you use any of So-and-so's arrangements?" he asked. "We don't use no arrangements," says Joe Watkins. "We just play."

Lizzie Miles came in as the band went to go on again. She does the intermission spots, with Joe Robishaux on piano. She is a wonderful person who has helped me considerably. She found me a room here on Bourbon-street, over the Mardi Gras.

A disc session

About noon next day I saw Doctor Souchon at his surgery in the Pan-American Insurance building on Canal-street. After a talk, we drove to his home and had a great record session and general confab.

I learned that the famous Bunk talking records are about to be issued, also some more Wooden Joes and Eureka Brass Band sides.

The Thursday evening I spent with Dick Allen, a young fellow here who works for Mercury Records and knows just about every musician and everything that goes on.

When I got back here I heard the Fred Kohlman Dixieland Band. They are the resident group at the M.G., and George

Lewis just does the Tuesdays. They are workmanlike but not more, I'm afraid.

After hearing them a while I dropped down to the Paddock to catch an hour of the Crosby band over a long beer. This may not be the greatest band ever, but it's still pretty good.

Alvin plays some lyrical horn and boasts a fine tone. Matthew's style is known to some collectors from records. He punches it out all the time, and is fine to watch.

Picou sits with his head down most of the time when not playing. He sang the vocal on "Eh, La Bas" with animation, and with verses aimed at the crowd.

What Picou said

One was about a dame who was with a fellow at the bar. She must have taken offence, because when I went into the back room Picou was being told off about it. "I wish I could tell you what he replied."

The Dukes of Dixieland are pounding and screaming away while I write this. Once in a while they play something decent, but on the whole they are not for me.

On Friday I went with Dick Allen to see Emile Barnes, who we spent a couple of interesting hours with him.

He brought up many names unknown to me of men he played with in the old days. Apparently he started on a tin flute.

He remembers one night he made a mess of money gambling and stayed up the rest of the night drinking with Bunk Johnson.

Bunk, he says, was really good in those days, but was a "gone man" when he came back to music. They used to call him "Willie the Pleaser," and it seems he was just that; people always came flocking in wherever he played.

Emile's favourite

It was Bunk who bought Emile his first clarinet (for $9), and then the latter started playing and working straight away. The first tune he played was a piece that goes something like the main theme of "Black Cat."

Emile, by the way, is a mattress maker by trade.

His all-time favourite on cornet was Chris Kelly, who he says was a very fine leader. Barnes stresses the importance of every man knowing his exact part in a band, and says no matter how good a man thinks he is, he's always got to be "chastised from the outside."

Today, Barnes doesn't like playing the blues—though he was once crowned king of the blues at a contest in New Orleans—and admits he is a little corroded now, as he has not been playing much these past few years.

Charles Love he speaks of as a great ragtime man who knows most of the old tunes and has the music of a lot of rags as well. I think Barnes is rehearsing a band with Love on piano, Brazely on tram and possibly Albert Glenny on bass.

"I am hoping to meet Love and some of the others next week. So I'll sign off for now and tell the rest in my next letter.

Mid-century New Orleans—St. Ann Street, looking towards Jackson Square, in the heart of the French Quarter. In such surroundings, K. Colyer wrote the letter on this page.

Collectors' Christmas Corner
Edited by MAX JONES and SINCLAIR TRAILL

ONCE again it is time to wish readers all the best for Christmas, and to thank many of them for writing letters, articles and so on for these columns.

In particular, our thanks are due to regular contributors Albert McCarthy, Harold Grut, John Jorgensen, Hugues Panassié, Jonny Simmen, Brian Rust, Erik Wiedemann and Dave Mylne.

Jonny Simmen writes this week to report that Jimmy Archey's band, after its disastrous German tour, arrived in Switzerland eight days earlier than planned.

Archey and the band met with considerable success there, we are glad to hear, and Simmen will review the Swiss concerts in next week's issue.

He tells us that at Archey's Zurich concert (November 26), it was announced that Lee Collins' New Orleans Jazz Band would not appear in Europe for the moment, "due to the illness of two of the musicians."

But Jonny has received two letters from Collins which indicate that nobody is sick in his band, but that he (Collins) is upset about a telegram telling him that the tour has been postponed.

At the time of writing, the mystery remains. In a recent letter to us, Lee Collins wrote: "I will be in Zurich on the first of December. We will tour Germany, and end our tour on December 22.

"I have Al Wynn on trombone, Don Ewell on piano, Herbert Jeep Robinson on clarinet and sax, Baby Dodds on drums. I thought that if I could get in touch with any promoters in England, I could get a chance to play there, which is what I want to do.

"There hasn't been time to hear again from Lee Collins. But we were able to tell him that, under the present MU administration, he doesn't stand a dog's chance.

Thinking of foreign jazzmen reminds us that one British player, Ken Colyer, is now in the USA.

About a fortnight ago, he got immigration clearance and went into New Orleans. He has been there ever since living at Bourbon-street. His first newsletter appears this week.

How do you sound?

Listen! Here is the Grundig "Reporter" Tape Recorder — the finest in the world. So versatile, such perfect reproduction that it revolutionises the recording and reproducing of music, voices, sounds of every sort.

SINGERS — INSTRUMENTALISTS — BANDS — ORCHESTRAS

Know how you sound! Record your voice, your music, with the wonderful "Reporter." The "Reporter" is an invaluable part of every singer's and musician's equipment; it records exactly what it hears and reproduces it perfectly at the touch of a button. It's the way to perfection before the performance!

MAKE YOUR OWN RECORDINGS of solos, whole bands, singers, in your own home, or from stage or radio. Sing and play duets, etc., yourself. Record whole programmes of your favourite musicians with your own introductions or commentaries.

NOTE THESE 6 SENSATIONAL FEATURES

(1) Compact and completely portable. Where there's power there's your "Reporter" ready!

(2) Immediate play-back of your recordings at the touch of a button.

(3) Tape can be used again and again or the recording can be kept for a lifetime.

(4) Push button controls give quick, simple operation.

(5) One whole hour of perfect recording and reproduction per spool.

(6) Unique condenser microphone as sensitive as the human ear.

SPECIFICATION: Push button controls; revolutionary design of plug-in recording reproducing and erasure heads, giving a reconstruction in cost from sp-10,000 c.p.s.; silent fast forward and rewind; twin track recording giving over one hour's recording from one reel of tape; separate sockets for microphone, radio, recording from disc and resume tuner; provision for monitoring; tone and volume controls. Suitable for A.C. operation only, 195 to 250 volts; 50 cycles single phase. Housed in a loudspeaker coloured reposing covered panel and belt hook. Weight 14 lb. 4½ Output, 3½ at 30.

★ *Your dealer has details about the "Reporter"*

GRUNDIG "Reporter"

GRUNDIG (GT. BRITAIN) LTD., Kidbrooke

SEE YOUR RADIO DEALER —

Jazz Journal the report was headed 'CRANE RIVER TO CRESCENT CITY' and Bill Colyer commences the article in characteristically dramatic fashion: 'When Ken Colyer stepped across the threshold of the International House, Common Street, New Orleans, on 11 October 1952, nearly eight years of frustration and longing were finally over.'

Bill, fervent propagandist for the 'true jazz', and not one to let a close blood tie inhibit his idolatry in word or print, continued:

> Using letters from Dr Edmond Souchon and Ken himself, I'd like to set down the first chapter of his New Orleans story but, first, a brief preamble.
>
> Some time ago, Steve Race, eminent musician and scribe, mentioned three British musicians whom he considered to be jazzmen. Three men only able to immerse and express themselves in the jazz idiom. If memory serves me right they were all modernists.
>
> In the traditional field I know of two, possibly three. Two are clarinettists. The third, who is by far and away the best, is Ken Colyer. [Bill did not name the clarinettists.]
>
> As Ken's playing matured I knew his one aim was to find out whether he was capable of playing with the men he most admired. Knowing, too, how different his approach is, in comparison to nearly every British instrumentalist I knew or have heard, I believe his story is of some importance, particularly to those very few who are making the right approach.

The last sentence leaves the reader in no doubt that in Bill Colyer's mind there was only *one* approach; nor did he believe that it had to be defined. It was typical of the very likable but very intense Bill not to entertain the least doubt about his convictions.*

The article continues:

> Let's hear from Dr Souchon first: 'Ken phoned me from Mobile to tell me he was heading this way. I gave him the address of the International House where the New Orleans Jazz Club had been asked to gather at a special meeting in honour of representatives of the NAJO (England, France, Italy, Denmark, Sweden, Norway and Germany). The club had given the "all out" signal to its members and many people of importance showed up with bells on.
>
> 'Paul Barbarin's band was there in full force; all of Johnny Wiggs's band;

---

*During these heady days I, and many others, often bore the full weight of his verbiage on these matters! Fond of a word, he was dubbed 'Spout' and Bill 'Hear-Me-Talkin'-To-Ya' Colyer.

Papa Celestin; old Papa Jack Laine, the father of white jazz, and dozens of other local celebrities in the music world.

'Ken arrived at about 8.15 p.m. The Wiggs group had just finished their set and Paul Barbarin was getting ready to take the stand for half an hour.'

Now over to Ken Colyer: 'The Barbarin band was lined up and being presented to people. I promptly joined in and made with the handshakes like an octopus. I nearly dropped when I met Kid Howard. You can imagine my emotions on meeting so many "greats" at once.

'The set-up was very informal, fine and friendly. People recognized one like an old friend the second time you saw them and Doc proved to be one of the finest guys I've met for a long time.

'The band kicked off with "Weary Blues" with Howard on trumpet. He played "under wraps" and muted all the time, which is just as well or I might have passed out from happiness!

'Al Burbank was playing some really wound-up clarinet. Great stuff! But the bass player, Maclean, was the man who really knocked me out. Heavens! What power and tone. He rocked the band and then some.'

Back to Dr Souchon: 'This was followed by a mixed session, with both bands playing together and this is where Ken couldn't stand it a moment longer and borrowed a trumpet from one of the Barbarin men.' Ken says: 'I was batting with Kid Howard and he urged me to get up and blow with the boys. I had my mouthpiece with me, so he lent me his horn. Doc Souchon introduced me to Buglin' Sam Kemel on stage and I joined the group in backing Sam on "How'm I Doing, Hey, Hey?" '

Dr Souchon: 'I can't recall all the numbers that we played, but recollect a spiritual and "Jelly Roll". Ken was quite equal to anyone there or better – what I heard was enough to make me want more, and this we shall have at a later date, I'm sure. Lizzie Miles was present in all her glory and really put the heat on for your boy, Ken. I'd like to say that I enjoyed meeting Ken so very much and am looking forward to hearing him play in the sanctity of my own living-room and to record him with some of us backing him up.'

Ken Colyer was the first British musician to make the pilgrimage to the fountainhead of jazz. In the same issue of *Jazz Journal*, however, Humphrey Lyttelton wrote that long, powerful argument against what he described as 'the unhygienic fug which we still call the New Orleans Revival'.

Colyer spent three months in the city, nightly listening to his heroes; including such legendary figures as clarinettist Alphonse Picou (then seventy-four), creator of the famous clarinet chorus on 'High Society' played by hundreds of clarinettists since; and bassist Albert Glenny, who had played with that most fabled of jazz names, trumpeter Buddy Bolden, who had led and played in bands that saw the beginning of jazz, who played his last musical engagement in 1906, and who, it is rumoured, made cylinder recordings whose survival would have revealed how jazz sounded at the turn of the century.

Colyer sat in with the George Lewis band and sufficiently impressed the leader to be offered a tour, Lewis's own trumpeter, Percy Humphrey, being unwilling to travel, but labour regulations prevented a once-in-a-lifetime experience for the young English trumpeter.

The same official hindrance was experienced when recordings with local musicians were mooted, but on 23 and 24 February 1953 he recorded with a band of New Orleanians on very inferior equipment in the home of clarinettist Emile Barnes. With Colyer were Barnes (sixty), trombonist Harrison Brazlee (sixty-five), drummer Albert Jiles (forty-six), bassist Albert Gleny (eighty-three!), all black musicians, and banjoist Billy Huntington, a white youth only fifteen years of age.

The experiences of this fifties musical Odysseus were stirring enough: the time it took him to reach Mobile; breaking his contract with the ship-owners by jumping the *Empire Patria*; the bus journey to New Orleans; the offer by George Lewis and the recording with honoured veterans were already the stuff of legend, but all this was to be capped by another drama that guaranteed Colyer's entry into the jazz pantheon.

While he had undoubtedly broken the social code by playing with black musicians (and was acting against the dictates of the local branch of the American Federation of Musicians, there being at this time separate unions for whites and blacks), this was not sufficient to warrant any legal action against him; but overstaying his visitor's permit was, and he was summarily clapped into the notorious New Orleans Parish Jail, where he stayed for thirty-eight days.

This imprisonment was reported in the *New Orleans Item*, 15 February 1953, by a sympathetic journalist, Ralston Crawford. The headline ran: 'BRITISH SEAMAN HELD THIRTY-EIGHT DAYS – WHY? N.O. JAZZ', and below was a photograph of a pensive-looking Colyer.

Traditionalism Rampant 73

On 29 December, four days after his visitor's permit had expired, Colyer turned himself in to Immigration. He told Immigration the reason he hadn't come in earlier was because the permit expired on Christmas Eve and he didn't get around to turning himself in right away. Under Immigration regulations he was arrested immediately and a $5,000 bond set.

Three times between the date of his arrest and his release, a friend, John Bernard, went to Immigration and offered to put up the money. Each time he was refused. Each time he was told, 'There's no point in releasing Colyer. He'll be sent to New York to be deported in a few more days.'

Edward Ahrens, immigration officer in charge, said, 'We wanted to make his steamship company pay his passage home and we ran into a lot of delay.'

Was there any other reason for not releasing Colyer on bond?

'Yes,' said Ahrens. 'He told us he would like to stay in New Orleans to study jazz. He wanted an extension. He practically admitted the only reason he came here was to study New Orleans jazz. We were afraid he would try to stay here illegally.'

During his thirty-eight-day stay in Parish Jail, Colyer was kept locked in a cell or in a prison dayroom. He said he would like to stay here but that he had no intention of doing so illegally.

When the news of these events reached Britain the faithful were stirred. Here was a man of fierce integrity, jailed for his beliefs, punished because he had played with black musicians who had not 'deserted' to the north, who were still playing 'true' jazz. Colyer's reputation in Britain had grown substantially in his absence and what could be more fitting for his triumphant return to Britain than to find a band ready and waiting for him to lead? On the surface, this appeared to be the case and it did no harm to those concerned to let the story ride. It had considerable publicity value, but the truth was that in his absence, trombonist Chris Barber had formed a co-operative band that included Monty Sunshine (clarinet), Jim Bray (bass), Lonnie Donegan (banjo) and Ron Bowden (drums). Trumpeter Pat Halcox, playing in a semi-professional capacity with the Albemarle Jazz Band based in Southall, had been approached to join, but Halcox, studying to be a research chemist, declined, and it was decided, in view of his New Orleans saga, to offer Colyer the job.

They took up residency at Bert Wilcox's London Jazz Club, operating by now in the vaults of a church in Bryanston Street, near Marble Arch – until the commissioners decided that jazz was not suitable for premises on holy ground.

The band had an enthusiastic following, making a highly successful tour of Denmark, and on their return they recorded an album suitably entitled *New Orleans to London* which included a thirties British pop song called 'Isle of Capri'. Oddly, it caught the attention of Jack Payne, famous bandleader in the twenties and thirties turned disc jockey, who played it on his BBC 'Pick of the Pops' programme. When released as a single it fleetingly appeared at the tail of the best-seller charts in the musical papers.

It was the first British jazz record ever to appear in such a listing, even if its stay was brief.

Colyer, however, had ideas incompatible with a co-operative set-up and it was not long before he was imposing his dominant personality on the band, or attempting to do so. There was bitter discord, on and off the stand, and although the band lasted for nine months, matters came to a head with Colyer protesting that some of the musicians were not in agreement with his strict fundamental beliefs and demanding their dismissal. He was particularly unhappy with Donegan and accused Bowden of being a 'bebop drummer' which, for Colyer, was the supreme derogatory epithet. It was pointed out to him that he was part of a co-operative, that he had no right to sack anyone. His dissatisfaction with the situation affected his playing, he was drinking heavily and, in the event, left the band in May 1954. As intolerant as he was fervent, his bitterness about the band's decision to let him go, rather than agreeing to mould itself to his wishes, continued long after the break-up.

In September 1954, the second Ken Colyer band came into being, with a young man from Somerset, Bernard 'Acker' Bilk, on clarinet; Eddie O'Donnell (trombone) and William 'Diz' Disley (banjo), both from the Yorkshire Jazz Band; Dick Smith (bass) and Stan Greig (drums) from Sandy Brown's Edinburgh band. They played regularly at the Studio 51, Great Newport Street, later to be the venue of the Ken Colyer Club, but although he was a legend in his own lifetime and signed to the Lyn Dutton Agency, which handled all the top traditional names, the band had to scuffle. Like many others of this calibre, they had to work abroad, notably in Dusseldorf and Hamburg in Germany, and in Scandinavia. The enthusiasm for traditional jazz was very strong in those countries and proved to be a life-saver for many British bands.

John Reddihough, in a monograph on Colyer published by *Jazz News*, wrote:

> Through great persistence Colyer achieved his big ambition in life, to make New Orleans jazz his living and a vital thing of the present. The integrity of his efforts to achieve this is beyond question and the measure of success he has been accorded is more than fully deserved.
>
> It is difficult to pin down the precise elements in Ken's playing that give it its distinctive quality. One notices, however, his inherent feel for a suitable tempo, the use of tonal changes, the rhythmic effectiveness of his phrasing and his ability to develop a number logically, using the full range and capabilities of his instrument. These qualities perhaps come out more clearly in his muted playing, in particular when he is using his bowler-hat mute, which frequently provides his hottest moments.

Although he gave up bandleading in May 1971 because of illness, he soon returned to the leader's role and almost until his death in March 1988 was working regularly with a band that in essence was not very different from the first he organized in 1954. When he 'retired' he was interviewed for the *Melody Maker* by veteran critic Max Jones:

> Our band sound was bound to change slightly. You have the freedom within the idiom, the freedom of individuality within the confines of the New Orleans style. There's no end of variety possible and make no mistake ... nobody outside New Orleans has mastered the idiom yet, not by what we know of the best examples of New Orleans jazz music. That's all I've tried to do and there are not many doing that, here or over there.
>
> I'm not belly-aching at all. Looking back, I'd do it again. There's no other life I prefer. The music has been a way of life to me and playing full-time you learn to take the bad times with the good.

Colyer's intransigence and blunt demeanour made him a cult figure. Wherever he played his audiences were composed largely of people who would not go to hear anyone else. To them he was the 'Guv'nor'. They were his faithful flock, rallying to Gabriel's call.

The stories that accumulated around this rugged character are legion. Although Humphrey Lyttelton twice threatened physical violence in print he never, as far as is known, actually carried out his threats, but Colyer did. When some misguided fan of his injudiciously told him that he thought Colyer's band better than George Lewis's, Colyer thumped him for his heresy!

This incident took place some years back. At the end of his life the Guv'nor mellowed a little, although he was still messianic in his beliefs, still extremely serious about his role, still making pungent comments, all eagerly lapped up by the traditional-jazz community. For all his dogmatism and acerbity Colyer was a much-loved figure.

He once played an engagement in Cambridge in 1985, and something or other annoyed him during the session. On its completion, he strode up to the food-and-drinks counter. The organizer, who was eating fish and chips, saw all was not well with the Guv'nor, and enquired: 'Anything wrong, Ken?' Colyer growled: 'Anything *wrong*? Here we are playing music born of anguish and suffering and all you can do is to eat fucking fish and chips!'

In August 1953, Colyer's New Orleans recordings were issued on the Decca label. The musicians were not of the highest calibre, Emile Barnes being the most adept, but the recording quality was the biggest disappointment. It was sad that such a pilgrimage should not have resulted in mementoes better than these, the efforts of the Decca engineers to clean them up notwithstanding.

Sinclair Traill reviewed these recordings in *Jazz Journal* (temporarily called *Jazz Journal and Popular Music Review*), in September 1953.

> Had this LP not been fairly advertised as a special limited edition available to subscribers only, I should have said it was not worth issuing. The recording and balance are awful and the music suffers in consequence. In places something worthwhile peeps through the fog but for the most part the proceedings are dominated by a vastly over-recorded banjo.
>
> The session was probably worth hearing in the flesh, for now and again one can hear bits of good music, as in 'That's a Plenty' with its shouting trombone, and 'Frankie and Johnny' on which one can hear good trumpet by Colyer.
>
> This LP is probably the realization of a British musician's ambition and as such I am sorry to have to be so rude about it, but in all fairness one can't say nice things about music one can't hear.

From the dissolution of the Colyer band came the Chris Barber band. It was not Barber's first stab at bandleading; he had led a band as far back as 1949. The author was the band's agent and it was hardly a productive time for either of us, Barber being inexperienced at bandleading and I a novice in the jungle of the agency business. The band worked for as little as £15 an engagement and not many of these were to be found. At that time, it would never have occurred to me, or to anybody else, that Donald Christopher Barber, born in London on 17 April 1930, the son of a statistician and a schoolmistress and educated at St Paul's School, would ever be a success at bandleading and become an internationally famed figure.

The author first met him in 1946 when he was a member of a 'Brains Trust' at a Hot Club of London concert. Just sixteen, he won the prize, a 78-rpm record, for providing the largest number of correct answers in a quiz. His enthusiasm and knowledge were undeniable, but as a bandleader in 1949/50, he was totally ineffectual.

After Colyer departed in high dudgeon, Pat Halcox decided to abandon his studies and joined the band, commencing an association with Barber that has lasted, continuously, until the present day, a record in the history of jazz in Britain. The Barber band was to have a much cleaner sound than the Colyer group. Halcox's technique was superior to Colyer's and his style nearer to the sophistication of Louis Armstrong than that of the 'primitive' Bunk Johnson and Kid Howard. Unlike the wayward and fractious Colyer, he was a sober young man with a pleasant manner. Immediately there was a harmony in Halcox and Barber's personalities as well as in their music, but the new sophistication in the sound was unfavourably compared in some quarters with the down-to-earth ruggedness it had replaced.

George Melly, in his *Owning Up*, commented on the stylistic differences between the Colyer and the Barber bands:

> Modern jazz was of course outside this dispute. Modern jazz was like the Roman Catholic Church at the time of the Reformation. It had developed historically from the origins of jazz but had, in the eyes of the revivalists, become decadent and it was time to return to the source. The revivalists represent in this parallel the Church of England. Later, the traditionalists arose, like the non-conformist sects, to accuse the revivalists themselves of decadence,

of meaningless ritual, of elaboration. Back to the Bible-jazz from New Orleans: 'Away with Cope and Mitre – solos and arrangements; Down with the Bishops – Armstrong and Oliver.'

Ken Colyer was initially responsible for this revolution. It was he who established the totems and taboos of traditional jazz, the piano-less rhythm section, the relentless four-to-the-bar banjo, the loud but soggy thump of the bass drum. Even so, Ken by himself would never have effected the trad boom. He was too uncompromising, too much of a purist. Picasso, accused of ugliness, pointed out that the inventor is always ugly because he has to make something which wasn't there before, but that afterwards others can come along and make what he had invented beautiful.

It was rather like this. Ken invented British traditional jazz: It wasn't exactly ugly; on the contrary it was quite often touchingly beautiful, but it was clumsy. It needed prettifying before it could catch on. Chris Barber was there to perform this function.

He was converted to fundamentalism by Ken Colyer when the holy fool returned from New Orleans ... the formation of the Barber band in 1954 seemed to us at the time of only parochial interest.

Later it proved to have been a watershed.

Melly mentioned Barber's will to succeed, and succeed he did, despite an unprepossessing stage personality and a penchant for interminably long and unbearably unfunny announcements delivered with a slight stammer. A non-smoking teetotaller, and a truly dedicated and conscientious figure with a clear idea of what he wanted from his band, he developed into a first-class ensemble player in the great tailgate tradition established by Kid Ory, George Brunies and Jim Robinson. He would probably have made a success of anything he did. Two 'freak' hit-parade entries then catapulted his band to international fame.

The first of these hits was 'Rock Island Line', recorded on 13 July 1954 with a small contingent from the band as part of an LP called *New Orleans Joys*. The personnel comprised Lonnie Donegan (banjo), Chris Barber (bass), Ron Bowden (drums) and, guesting on washboard, singer Beryl Bryden. It was issued as by Lonnie Donegan's Skiffle Group. Each member of the band (and guest) received a straight fee of £2/10s. The album sold 10,000 copies. 'Rock Island Line' was issued as a single in America and the UK in 1956 and became a big hit on both sides of the Atlantic. Attendances for the Barber band shot up and Donegan left to pursue a solo career. By 1961 'Rock Island Line' had sold a million

Traditionalism Rampant 79

and Donegan received a gold disc.

In both the previous and present volumes of this *History* the author has felt compelled to refer to the number of ironies attending the history of jazz in Britain and the success of 'Rock Island Line' is surely one of the most striking of these. It was not, of course, a jazz record, but it had been made by members of a jazz band and appeared on an album otherwise dedicated to jazz. The band were to benefit enormously by the association. The tune was composed by a black US convict, Huddie 'Leadbelly' Ledbetter, and recorded by him first in 1934 and again in 1942 and 1944, the last version issued on the English Capitol label, and inspiring the Donegan/Barber version. Ledbetter died in 1949 and there are no figures available as to how many copies of any version of his records of this tune sold, but certainly they were nowhere, not by hundreds of thousands, near the numbers sold of the version by a Glasgow-born Cockney banjo player.

The total sales for a unit of a band not long from amateur status astonished the business generally and the record industry in particular. Considering the vast profits Decca made from the

Guitarist Diz Disley was also a fine draughtsman and contributed many pithy drawings to the 1950s *Melody Maker*

combined sales of the album and the single, all for the payment of £2/10s per man (and woman), they might have shown a little prudent generosity to the players and paid them something extra even though they were not, within the terms of the contract, bound to do so. Conversely, of course, when recording companies paid all-out fees for records that didn't sell at all, it was not known for musicians, sympathizing with the company's plight, to offer a recompense . . .

The band was induced by astute record producer Denis Preston to record at Lansdowne Studios, Notting Hill Gate, West London, and Preston then profitably released the tapes to Columbia. The story goes that when this news reached Decca a distraught executive went to Sir Edward ('Ted') Lewis, founder and managing director of the company, with the bad news. Sir Edward, puzzled at Barber's dissatisfaction, is alleged to have said, 'Well, then, give the boy a radiogram', to which the disbelieving executive replied, 'I think he's already got one, sir.'

Donegan's inevitable departure to embark upon a lucrative solo career did not impair the band's progress. They had the substance to succeed on their own account, and later another contingent from the band was to have a massive hit that rocketed them to even greater popularity.

In a monograph on the Barber band published by the National Jazz Federation, Humphrey Lyttelton wrote:

> Chris and the band have achieved many things, but retaining their own strong and instantly recognizable sound identity. Jazz pundits who for years have complained that British jazzmen are imitative have been known to speak disparagingly about the band's 'British sound'. This does little justice to the great variety of contemporary British jazz and even less to Chris Barber. For it is the Chris Barber sound which has attracted such a huge international following over the years, and long may it continue.

Lyttelton's reference to a 'British sound' was pertinent. For British jazz musicians were constantly faced with the implied criticism that their sound had a 'British' flavour, but if they imitated Americans they were merely copyists: a no-win situation.

In Lyttelton's piece there was more than a hint that the dilemma applied equally to himself.

Traditionalism Rampant   81

Johnny Dodds and George Lewis were undoubtedly the foremost inspirations for British traditional clarinettists, and one Dodds man in particular made a strong impact on the critics: Alexander ('Sandy') Brown, born Izatnagar, India, 25 February 1929. He grew up in Edinburgh from the age of six, attending the Royal High School and playing in bands with fellow students, including trumpeter Al Fairweather and drummer/pianist Stan Greig.

Al Fairweather recalls:

We got copies of the home-produced magazines. I can't remember us reading them much, but they must have been an influence. We talked a lot about New Orleans jazz. Just before I was called up in 1945 the Brunswick record of King Oliver's Creole Jazz Band playing 'Riverside Blues' and 'Mabel's Dream' was issued and immediately we were hooked. We played it over and over again. We decided to play in a like manner, but call-up intervened just as we got going.

We, like other cities, had our own rhythm club with raincoated enthusiasts sitting listening to a talk illustrated by records. There was barely any live jazz. We heard anything that was available at the time – Bechet, Morton, Bix, any small-group jazz and often big bands too, such as Benny Goodman, Woody Herman and Count Basie. We were lucky that one or two collectors had really rare stuff and one guy had a large collection of blues records which had a profound effect on us, particularly Sandy. In Dave Mylne we also had the country's leading collector of Sidney Bechet records.

After Sandy came out of the army we re-formed, using Rob Craig on trombone and various guys dragooned into playing banjo, drums, etc. We had a wonderful stroke of luck in finding, right on our doorstep, in the same school, a pianist who knew his jazz and also played drums, Stan Greig.

We settled down to reproduce the sounds of Oliver and Morton, playing the same arrangements and solos note for note. We ran our own Jazz Band Ball at the Oddfellows Hall: Tom Connery, later known as Sean Connery, was one of the bouncers, and we infiltrated university and rugby-club dances and private parties.

Stan Greig had a sympathetic mother and we rehearsed regularly in her front room. We made one or two trips 'down south', appearing in (often mammoth) concerts with other bands. We did one or two trips with the Mick Mulligan band, which then had George Melly, and a former acquaintance from Edinburgh, Archie Semple.

During a trip to Paris, Sandy became very interested in 'African' music and rhythms. When he returned we introduced one or two of these African-based tunes into the repertoire. Generally speaking, we stuck pretty rigidly to Hot Five and Seven and Oliver tunes, mostly because we were so enthralled by them and couldn't imagine there could be jazz that was anywhere near so good. Sandy had much wider, more tolerant views and his taste ranged from rural blues singers to Woody Herman. Providing there were a few bars of jazz to be found on a record he was not concerned whose band it was.

After one of the trips to London, Fairweather and Greig settled there, Fairweather playing with Cy Laurie's band and working in the International Bookshop,* Charing Cross Road by day, and Stan Greig joining Ken Colyer's band. Brown remained in Edinburgh to complete his architectural studies.

In 1955 Brown came to live in London and joined up with Fairweather. The first London-based Sandy Brown band was formed, the line-up completed by John R.T. Davies (trombone), Alan Thomas (piano), Mo Umansky (banjo), Brian Parker (bass) and Graham Burbridge (drums). It was a characteristically traditional-style band, but the differences from the usual run of such were soon noticeable, particularly the stark force of Brown's clarinet.

His solos commanded attention by the sheer force of their urgent projection. He interweaved between, and soared over, the brass in the collective improvisation, in the grand manner of a Dodds, Bechet, Simeon, Nicholas and Hall. He was a dominating player, and Fairweather's sparse line was a perfect foil for the bravura of his partner. Both also wrote memorable tunes.

The two of them, once reunited, quickly challenged the existing boss trumpet/clarinet partnership of Lyttelton and Fawkes. Indeed, the latter, in private conversation, acknowledged Brown's superiority, but Lyttelton in his *New Musical Express* column was also quick to praise:

> If all that you require of a jazz band is that it should play in tune, should avoid making mistakes and should lilt along in an unquestionable fashion like the village band accompanying the maypole dance, then Sandy Brown's band is not for you. Nor are the Armstrong Hot Five, the King Oliver Creole Jazz Band, the Morton Red Hot Peppers or any other worthwhile jazz band. For while I do not suggest that Sandy Brown and Al Fairweather belong in that

---

*This was one of the first specialist jazz record shops to emerge after the end of the war and this particular shop provided employment behind the counter at various times, not only to Al Fairweather but Dickie Hawdon, Bill Colyer, James Asman and man-about-jazz, now record distributor, John Jack.

exalted company they do have in common with the finest hot jazz a searching exploratory spirit that keeps them burrowing away into every tune with the concentrated persistence of a couple of terriers.

As recently as December 1988, in a 'Best of Jazz' broadcast on Radio 2, Lyttelton acknowledged his indebtedness to Al Fairweather's trumpet style.

Lyttelton, primarily a musician, could out-write most of the jazz critics of the time, despite the fact that in this critique the acceptable faults in Brown's band were not those he would countenance in the New Orleans pioneers, *vide* his 'Open Up Those Windows' article for *Jazz Journal*. This did not, however, invalidate his percipient assessment of Sandy Brown and his band.

On one of the band's earlier trips from Edinburgh, in September 1953, Lyttelton had himself used Brown and Fairweather on two titles, 'Four's Company' and 'Forty and Tight' (the latter rejected), and continued to laud their recordings so much that he felt compelled, in one review, to write a disclaimer to the effect that he had no ulterior motive in so doing.

The band even registered with Steve Race, not a lover of revivalism, who wrote enthusiastically about their *McJazz* LP in the *Melody Maker*, in his 'Great Records of Our Time' series.

Despite this critical acceptance, the band attracted only moderate crowds, Brown's witty but interminable announcements being above the average fan's head and the shrill edge of his style unacceptable to many. By the time of their reunion the traditional jazz public had become accustomed to, and expected, the familiar repertoire and Brown's 'African' themes, for instance, did not appeal as much as the hackneyed warhorses like 'Muskrat Ramble' and 'Savoy Blues'.

The law of inverse effect certainly applied in this instance: critical praise had little effect on the box office compared with the poor notices but large attendances another Doddsian, Cy Laurie, was getting at his all-night sessions at Mac's Rehearsal Rooms, Great Windmill Street. Laurie, one of the few British Jews to play traditional jazz, was alleged to have thought of himself as the reincarnation of Johnny Dodds. It was unusual for one musician to damn another directly in print but Brown savaged Cy Laurie's attempted emulations of Dodds in his *McJazz Manuscripts*. He wrote:

> The Dodds copyists were Alex Revell, Cy Laurie and Sandy Brown in the UK, Claude Luter in France and Bob Helm and Ellis Horne in San Francisco. Laurie's attempt was inept but desperately sincere. It was also dangerous. As he played his travesty of Dodds's sweeping phrases he described them graphically on his clarinet, and if you played trumpet or trombone on either side of him you stood to get badly cut about unless nimble.

Laurie's Club received considerable press attention, most of it contrived by the nimble mind of publicist Les Perrin. Sensationalist pressmen visited the famed all-night sessions in the hope of seeing use of illicit drugs, but found nothing more than bottles of Merrydown Cider, the traditionalist's favourite tipple, smuggled in to those unlicensed premises.

Laurie disbanded in the mid-sixties and travelled to India to study Oriental mysticism. In 1984 a concert package called 'Mardi Gras' on tour included Cy Laurie and Ken Colyer. Colyer had not seen Laurie for twenty years and ignored him completely. Asked why he had 'cut' Laurie, Colyer muttered, '*He* cleared off to India to stand on his fucking head leaving *me* to hold the fort.'

One of the most musicianly of bands was led by trumpeter Mike Daniels. John Barnes, playing clarinet with the Manchester-based Zenith Jazz Band in 1954, first played with Daniels at the Bodega, Manchester, when Daniels turned up from London without a clarinettist. He joined the band a year later and stayed for six years. He was employed by Daniels in a dual capacity: as clarinettist and as clerk in the firm of Brett Daniels, North London refrigeration specialist, of which Daniels was a director. Like the rest of the staff Barnes addressed his employer as 'Mr Daniels', except when called into the inner sanctum to discuss the previous night's gig. He had no problems in getting off early for out-of-town jobs. If in Manchester, for instance, they would meet outside the Rex Restaurant, Old Compton Street, as early as 10.30 a.m. The Daniels band was much liked, but never made a great impact, probably because of the leader's diffident personality. All the original members are still alive and playing and meet annually for a musical reunion.

George Webb's Dixielanders, Red Barn, Barnehurst, c. 1946: (L to R) Eddie Harvey, Owen Bryce, Reg Rigden, Wally Fawkes (clt), Derek Bailey (at rear), Buddy Vallis, Art Streatfield, Webb

Crane River Jazz Band, Catford Rhythm Club, c. 1949: (L to R) Sonny Morris, Ken Colyer, Ron Bowden, Monty Sunshine, Ben Marshall, John R.T. Davies, Julian Davies

Graeme Bell's Australian Jazz Band: (L to R) Pixie Roberts, Len Carras, Roger Bell, Graeme Bell, Russ Murphy

Mick Mulligan's Magnolia Jazz Band, c. 1953: (*L to R, standing*) George Melly, Pat Malloy, Stan Bellwood, Ian Pierce, Mike Lawrence. (*Seated*): Jimmy Currie, Mulligan, Dave Keir, Jo Lennard, Paul Simpson. Melly, Lawrence and Lennard were dubbed 'the Mulligan choir'

Merseysippi Jazz Band, c. 1952: (*L to R*) John Lawrence, Pete Daniels, Frank Robinson, Dick Goodwin, Trevor Carlisle, Don Lydiatt, Frank Parr, Ken Baldwin

Royal Festival Hall, 14 July 1951. The Marquis of Donegall presents HRH Princess Margaret to (*L to R*) Sid Phillips, Sinclair Traill, James Asman, Ken Lindsey, Pete Payne, Rex Harris, Peter Tanner. Traill's expression, a gem

Leicester Square Jazz Club, 1948: Lyttelton's first band (*L to R*) Wally Fawkes, Lyttelton, Harry Brown, John Robinson, Nevil Skrimshire, Les Rawlings, Pat Hawes

Carlo Krahmer

Ronnie Scott

Club Eleven, Great Windmill Street: (*L to R*) Ronnie Scott, Johnny Dankworth, Denis Rose, Tommy Pollard, Len Bush, Tony Crombie

Club Eleven alumni: (*L to R*) Denis Rose, Johnny Rogers, Harry Morris

Bandleader Ted Heath visits Tito Burns and his band during a BBC 'Accordion Club' broadcast: (*L to R*) announcer/scriptwriter Roy Plomley, Charles Chilton (producer), Denis Rose (*back*), Burns, Alan Dean, Heath, Tony Crombie, Pete Chilver, Bernie Fenton, Jack Fallon, Ronnie Scott (*back*), Joe Muddell

Humphrey Lyttelton (*left*) in Eton garb

London Jazz Club tussle between (*left*) Jimmy McPartland and Humphrey Lyttelton

Humphrey Lyttelton and his band, 1949: (*L to R*) Les Rawlings, Keith Christie (tb), Dave Carey (d), Lyttelton, Nevil Skrimshire, Wally Fawkes, George Webb

Ken Colyer's 'co-operative' band, 1953: (*L to R*) Monty Sunshine, Lonnie Donegan, Ron Bowden (d, *obscured*), Ken Colyer, Chris Barber, Jim Bray

London Jazz Club Riverboat Shuffle, 1951: Keith Christie (tb), Ken Colyer (tpt), Ian Christie (clt)

Bill Cotton, one of Mick Mulligan's two banjoists. He was fired from the band for excessive drinking

Doug Whitton's Jazz Band, one of literally hundreds of traditional bands who appeared in public with the maximum of enthusiasm and the minimum of proficiency

Ken Colyer's skiffle group, with the leader on guitar, unknown bassist and brother Bill on washboard

Two of the skiffle section from Ken Colyer's 'co-operative' band: Colyer (*left*), Lonnie Donegan

George Melly, early 1950s

Poster advertising 'London's Harlem' – Paramount Dance Hall, Tottenham Court Road

Johnny Dankworth Seven, 1951: (*L to R*) Eric Dawson, Dankworth, Eddie Blair, Eddie Harvey, Don Rendell. Pianist Bill Le Sage and drummer Eddie Taylor are out of picture

Band of British musicians who played at the Salle Pleyel, in 1953, on the same bill as Dizzy Gillespie (centre, with hand on Tony Crombie's shoulder). Jimmy Pollard, Ronnie Scott and Dave Usden are on Gillespie's left. Bottom left is Joe Green, bottom right is Tony Kinsey

Ted Heath's band, late 1940s

Ronnie Scott's nine-piece, 1953: (*L to R*) Hank Shaw, Ken Wray, Scott, Phil Seamen, Vic Feldman, Pete King, Len Bush, Derek Humble, Benny Green

Tubby Hayes

Don Rendell Sextet, the Flamingo, 1955: (*L to R*) Pete Elderfield, Rendell, Ronnie Ross, Dickie Hawdon. Missing members: Damian Robinson and Benny Goodman

Kathleen Stobart, the first female jazz musician to break the sex barrier and lead her own band

Alex Welsh, doyen of the 'Condon' bandleaders

The writing on the wall says it all: (*L to R*) unknown banjoist, atypical for Welsh, Archie Semple, Alex Welsh and Merrydown-drinking Roy Crimmins

(*L to R*) Ian Christie, Mick Mulligan, Betty Smith, Alan Duddington, George Melley, Laurie Gold, Denny Wright

Traditionalism Rampant 85

Banjoist Eric Silk and his Southern Jazz Band were one of the early bands that had a continued existence, featuring Alan Littlejohn (trumpet), Ron Weatherburn (piano), Pete Strange (trombone) and Teddy Layton (clarinet). Silk led his band from the front. Other long-standing bands were Steve Lane and his Southern Stompers and Bill Brunskill's band.

Most of the musicians playing traditional jazz were born between 1921 and 1934. One, however, drummer Dave Carey, was born in 1914. He played his first professional engagement in 1929 while still at school, for the sum of eight shillings, became a founder-member of the Croydon Rhythm Club, one of the first of such clubs and, in 1932, was given the honour of welcoming Louis Armstrong on the club's behalf when the great man played the Penge Empire, South London.

An avid collector, Carey was the compiler, with Albert McCarthy and Ralph Goodwin Vaughan Venables, of Britain's first jazz discography, *The Directory of Jazz*, issued in alphabetical instalments, but ceasing at the letter L when the task overwhelmed the collaborators.

Carey also played in Graeme Bell's Australian Jazz Band, recorded with ex-Ellington trumpeter Rex Stewart in London in 1948, joined Humphrey Lyttelton in the same year, then formed his own band in 1952 with Johnny Codd (trumpet), Tony Milliner (trombone), Tony Gibbons (clarinet), Pat Hawes (piano), Bob Mack (banjo and guitar), Eric Starr (bass) and Carey (drums). They recorded thirty-two sides for the Tempo label, Johnny Rowden replacing Codd for the last ten sides.

Several singers emerged at this time and these suffered from comparisons with Americans even more than the instrumentalists, probably because of the historical awareness that jazz on instruments evolved from vocal sources in slavery and while absorption by *musicians* from musicians was acceptable, attempts to sing like the music's black originators were not. Most of this criticism was reserved for those attempting to sing the blues and, plainly, there was in all cases neither the social background nor the vocal equipment even vaguely to approximate to their musical inspirations. But in addition to musicians (trumpeters particularly, for some reason) exercising their vocal cords, there were several women and a few men who essayed the blues.

Of the females, Beryl Bryden, Joan Roberts, Rosina Scudder, Doreen Beatty ('The Angel' with the Saints Jazz Band, later singing under her own name with Mike Daniels's band), Jackie Lynn with Dick Charlesworth's City Gents and Neva Raphaello were the best known. Of the males, George Melly, despite being heavily attacked by the purists, was the most renowned, with a style of his own. John Mortimer described him as 'singing with the raucous charm of an old Negress, so easily attained by those educated at Stowe'. Given that the whole idea of white Europeans singing the blues is something of an anomaly (Leadbelly used to say, 'Never was a white man had the blues, 'cause nothin' to worry about'), many thought others got nearer the essence of the blues: clarinettist Eric Lister, Johnny Silvo and the best of all, Sandy Brown. Melly's triumph was his bravura posturing: he was an extrovert entertainer who, in his stage demeanour, expressed his rejection of social conventions with a defiance that left an imprint on his audiences, if not the critics.

In Greater London dozens of clubs opened to meet the demand for the music that had surprisingly become so popular. Clubs were opened in Wood Green, Edmonton, Croydon, Hampton Court, Putney, Southall, Hitchin, Putney, Luton, Reading, Leytonstone, Woolwich, Maidstone and many other inner and outer suburbs. One of the pioneer club operators was Pete Payne, starting the Catford Rhythm Club in 1948 with Mike Daniels's Delta Jazz Band and, with the same band, the Delta Jazz Club at 6 New Compton Street. Payne also founded the Delta label, recording many early British revivalists, including Mike Daniels and the Yorkshire Jazz Band. He was a founder member of the National Federation of Jazz Organizations and later manager of Dave Carey's Jazz Band. Another durable London club was the Studio 51, Great Newport Street, which eventually went over completely to traditional jazz as the Ken Colyer Club.

The basement of 100 Oxford Street was London's premier

traditional stronghold, becoming the venue of the London Jazz Club, the Humphrey Lyttelton Club, and then Jazzshows Jazz Club, initially managed by Don Kingswell until proprietor Ted Morton installed record-shop assistant Roger Horton as manager, Horton continuing in this role when the premises were renamed the 100 Club.

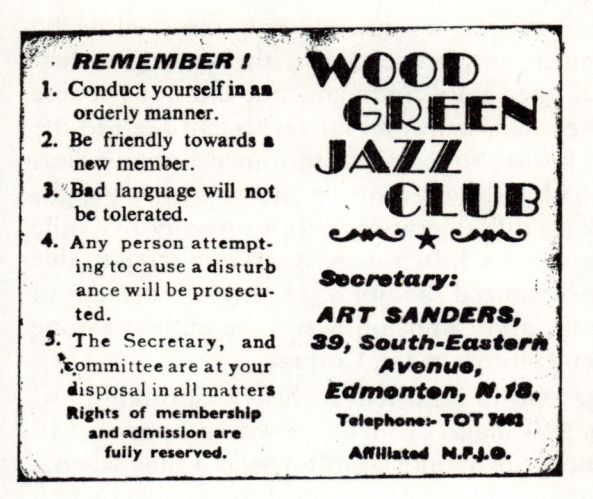

REMEMBER !
1. Conduct yourself in an orderly manner.
2. Be friendly towards a new member.
3. Bad language will not be tolerated.
4. Any person attempting to cause a disturbance will be prosecuted.
5. The Secretary, and committee are at your disposal in all matters
Rights of membership and admission are fully reserved.

WOOD GREEN JAZZ CLUB

Secretary:
ART SANDERS,
39, South-Eastern Avenue,
Edmonton, N.18.
Telephone:- TOT 7662
Affiliated N.F.J.O.

A sternly worded membership card for the Wood Green Jazz Club, run by Art and Viv Sanders

The most favoured restaurant was the Rex, New Compton Street, and over Vienna steak, chips, processed peas, two slices of bread and butter, followed by fruit salad and tinned cream and a cup of tea (2s/6d inclusive), the formation of prototype Hot Fives and Sevens, Red Hot Peppers, Creole Jazz Bands and Black Bottom Stompers was gravely discussed, along with the easing out of stylistically unsuitable or temperamentally difficult sidemen (or sometimes leaders), and the conspiratorially hatched wooing of suitable replacements.

The traditionalists' stamping-ground was in an area circumscribed by 100 Oxford Street to the north (the Blue Posts and Champion public houses being the ancillary watering-holes), the Cottage Club, Lichfield Street and the Faubourg Club, New Compton Street to the east (taking in the Star Tavern, Charing

Cross Road). Only the renamed Blue Posts and the Champion remain.

The Cottage Club, so called because of a rustic facia board, 'cottagey' furniture and an actual thatch over the bar, was opened in 1952 by Al Woodrow and Gerry Cramp, the bar operated by an ex-trapeze artist, Wynne Dinnie. A drinking-club, it opened at 3 p.m. to receive the first influx of hard-drinking members of the fraternity turning out of the pubs, some of whom returned to the pubs at 5.30, or, if musicians, proceeded to their engagements. The Cottage remained open until midnight, but did not become active until eleven, when musicians and fans who had been to the then unlicensed 100 Oxford Street piled in, joined by musicians returning from the bread-and-butter gigs in the ring of jazz clubs (described as the 'milk round') operating within a twenty-five-mile radius of Charing Cross Road. Often there was a jam session, this frequently a highly disorganized shambles. There are hundreds of traditionalists, musicians and camp followers, the author among them, with very fond memories of the Cottage.

The traditional-jazz world boasted a heavy sprinkling of eccentrics, bohemians and 'liggers', many of whom appeared to exist without visible means of support, but this was a time when a room in Soho or its environs could be obtained for as little as two pounds a week, or less. The traditional fraternity were recognizable sartorially: tweed suits, corduroy trousers, Fair Isle sweaters, duffle coats and chukka boots; some affected long hair (before it became a fashion) smoked pipes and were vaguely revolutionary. Many were heavy drinkers of beer and cider. There was also a high degree of sexual promiscuity.

Musically, most were charged with the romance of New Orleans jazz and were anti-bop/swing/progressive music, but as the years passed most came to accept the validity of post-war developments and a few musicians actually leapt the ideological chasm – trombonists Eddie Harvey, 'Rags' Russell, Keith Christie and Ken Wray, trumpeter Dickie Hawdon and clarinettist (switching to tenor saxophone) Dick Morrissey.

A cricket eleven called, appropriately, the Ravers, emerged from the miscellany of characters in this unique milieu. Founded in 1954, its members at various times included Lyn Dutton, his office manager Bert Boud, Mick Mulligan, Frank Parr and Pete Appleby, both from Mulligan's band (Parr ex-wicket-keeper with Lancashire CCC), Monty Sunshine, Micky Ashman, Al Fairweather, Sandy Brown, Wally Fawkes, Jim Bray, and various non-musicians including Max Jones, Don Aldridge and the author.

Occasionally the habitats of these unusual animals were visited by a few from the top of the social scale, mostly when American musicians were in town, Gerald Lascelles one of these. The link man in these sporadic incursions of high-born notables among *hoi polloi* was *Jazz Journal* editor Sinclair Traill. One of the most unlikely of these fringe visitors was Edward Arthur Donal St George Hamilton Chichester, Lord High Admiral of Lough Neagh, Viscount Chichester and the Baron of Belfast, Baron Fishwick, sixth Marquis of Donegall, this last title the one by which he was generally known, although referred to – quite affectionately – as 'The Don'. A bumbling although rather engaging character, he was an aristocrat in the Edwardian mould who, in his fashion, had been a lifelong jazz fan, despite the fact that his knowledge was very limited. He also strained his credibility by possessing every record made by hokum clarinettist Ted Lewis, and considering Sid Phillips the greatest British clarinettist. On hearing a Johnny Dodds record, however, he generously conceded that 'the niggers have got it over our chaps'. Probably because of comments like this, a famous traditional bandleader, who knew a thing or two about the aristocracy, described him as a 'derelict Irish peer', but Donegall had been instrumental in bringing the Original Dixieland Jazz Band to play before King George V and Queen Mary at Buckingham Palace, lending a certain cachet to those young men from New Orleans playing that outlandish music, and he had also helped bring about the appearance of traditional bands before HRH Princess Elizabeth at the Royal Festival Hall in July 1951.

Inevitably, however, the evangelical fervour of traditionalism's salad days slowly diminished. Commercial success and a degree of social respectability were not to the liking of those who once fiercely identified with an impoverished and persecuted minority.

For the record collector, the spate of releases (78s and, later, albums) told almost the entire history of early jazz, and the element of discovery vanished. Collectors who listened to live traditional jazz were able to make unfavourable comparisons between mentors and their emulators. For a host of musicians there was to come a feeling of disillusionment; yet another development, having the opprobrious tag of 'traddy-pop', was to disillusion them, and their followers, even more.

An offshoot of British traditionalism was 'skiffle', a term barely used in the entire history of blues and similar recordings, but used by Ken Colyer in the co-operative to describe the band within a band, with Colyer on guitar, singing US blues and folk songs, the rest of the instrumentation being a bass, washboard and occasionally another guitar. Chris Barber, with his immense knowledge of jazz on record, undoubtedly provided the background information.

Its origins were in the Chicago of the thirties, in the teeming ghettos of the South Side, where immigrants from the South packed the tenements, where poverty was such that conventional instruments could not be afforded and 'rent parties' were held and a collection made to satisfy the landlord.

That the term was used so little on recordings in the US at the time is one thing, but it was no surprise that zealous Britishers should have adopted it; from it sprang a hit record, 'Rock Island Line'. This extraordinary success inspired many essentially amateur groups playing skiffle and a booklet, price 2s/6d, called *Making The Most of Skiffle* was published, giving hints on how to play it, and among the acknowledgements was one to 'Mr Bill Colyer for his tips about the washboard'.

The *Radio Times*, 11–17 February 1984, ran an article by John Collis trailing a programme in the 'Forty Minutes' series in which skiffle was examined. It quoted Chris Barber:

> The term 'skiffle' occurs only twice on old records – a 1929 sampler on the Paramount label, featuring various blues artists and made to sound like a party, called 'Home-town Skiffle', and there's a record made in the 1940s by

Dan Burley's Skiffle Boys. Burley was a journalist who also made piano records – one of which sounded remarkably like 'Bad Penny Blues'!* So we assume from these references that 'skiffle' must have been part of the jazz terminology of the time. We were featuring this music from 1952 onwards – when we'd do part of the set using songs like 'Midnight Special', we called it skiffle.

Until 1952 we were all running amateur bands – people like Monty Sunshine, Lonnie and myself. But we felt that jazz in this country could never get better unless people did it professionally, full time. Then Ken Colyer was deported from New Orleans for overstaying his visa – he got drunk at Christmas and when he woke up it had expired. He was also in trouble for playing with black bands. So he came home, was repatriated first class, and joined the nucleus of the new band; it was called Ken Colyer's Band to begin with. Ken, Lonnie and I were the skiffle line-up *within* the band – we'd do a little skiffle set as part of the show.

I took the band over in 1954, after Ken had tried to sack half of them. We made a skiffle album, with Beryl Bryden on washboard. Then we added drums to the skiffle line-up. At this time, groups who featured the lead singer were the ones who were becoming successful, so Lonnie gradually emerged as the focal point – and the rest, as they say, is history.

Collis takes up the story:

Hand in hand with the nurturing of this music by Barber and Co were their attempts to introduce us to the American blues originals. 'There was a union ban on American musicians playing here, which we felt was wrong – we were being starved of the source of our music, and we believed it would *create* work if they came here. The union wouldn't budge, but then we found a loophole – there was a different rule for *entertainers*, and entertainers included people who sang.

'So we brought over Big Bill Broonzy, Lonnie Johnson (from whom Donegan had taken his stage name); gospel singers such as John Sellers and Rosetta Tharpe; Sonny Terry and Brownie McGhee, Muddy Waters; then the people who settled in Europe, like Champion Jack Dupree and Memphis Slim – the list goes on. But it didn't last.

'We weren't making any money by the time we'd got these people over, but entrepreneurs caught on that there *was* money to be made, by using cheap backing bands, cutting down on rehearsal, and so on. It was a great pity.'

But out of skiffle came the blues boom, which did help to restore the reputation of the great American originals, and keep this essential strand of musical culture alive.

---

*Barber was obviously having a sly dig at Lyttelton's record success.

On both a metropolitan and national scale, traditional jazz was one of the musical wonders of the fifties. So many bands, clubs and fans! Such a financial turnover, such controversy aroused by disputes over the true musical significance of a music that had virtually risen from the dead.

5
Bop on the Road

The boppers' subterranean, semi-private, almost conspiratorial meetings in the Fullado, Metrobopera and Club Eleven were largely born out of their passion to fathom the mysteries posed by the records of Parker and Gillespie trickling into the country. Few of the bop neophytes would have believed that this new form of playing jazz would ever be publicly acceptable. This would have seemed as unlikely to them as the prospect of New Orleans jazz becoming a significant part of British popular music appeared to George Webb's Dixielanders when they were studying the language of Oliver, Morton and Armstrong in the mid-forties.

The young modern musician's livelihood was gained largely in the touring dance bands and it was in this context that the bop figurations and chords were introduced. These bands were to be Trojan horses. This infiltration was not necessarily approved by the bandleaders but, whether they liked it or not, they had to acknowledge the changed situation. In some respects, it was a parallel development to that of the twenties and thirties, when the pre-war jazz musicians, earning their living in 'commercial' bands, prevailed upon their leaders to include the occasional chorus or special 'hot' arrangement.

Some of the leaders, however, realized that there was a public for bop. One of these was Tito Burns and, indeed, his personnel at one time pre-dated the Club Eleven line-ups, with Johnny Dankworth, Ronnie Scott and Co. Burns himself was a young man, but despite his enthusiasm for the new jazz, he was hamstrung by his overriding need to suit the demands of ballroom dancers. It was still too early for a band to play undiluted modern jazz.

Most of the big bandleaders were extremely wary of allowing

anything as 'uncommercial' as bop into their presentations. One of these, Geraldo, frankly announced: 'I'm in the business for money, not for art,' but even he cautiously permitted the occasional solo and in his Sunday concerts (then the fashion) he would feature both a 'modern' and 'dixieland' contingent from the main orchestra. Geraldo was a survivor from pre-war days; as were the far less successful Ambrose and Roy Fox. The latter, an American, had been out of the country during the war and returned blithely assuming he could don his tailcoat, pick up his baton and recommence where he had left off at the outbreak of hostilities.

He engaged a few of the younger musicians: Victor Feldman, who was then mostly playing vibraphone; drummer Martin Aston and tenor saxophonist Benny Green, but his 'society' restaurant associations and the generally sweet-music policy of the band were so much at variance with the splashes of bop that the whole confection proved an unconvincing mixture.

Ambrose, too, employed the young bloods, in post-war situations where he, the most popular and successful of pre-war bandleaders, was finding the going hard. He disliked their music and he disliked them even more. Their waywardness and general demeanour contrasted sharply with that of the respectful and well-turned-out sidemen he had employed before the war. The bloods had been too young for the armed forces, but they had known the irksome restrictions and deprivations of the hostilities and, like so many of their generation, relished new freedoms once the conflict was over.

Changes in public taste compelled him to adapt as best he could. The *Melody Maker*, in July 1949, reported on his appearance at the Royal Star Hotel, Maidstone, Kent – one of the many one-night-stand venues of the time. The report was headed: 'AMBROSE – WITH BOP – ON A ONE-NIGHT STAND'.

> Take a handful of the best boppers in the country; add a few solid section men and a couple of vocalists; and put them all under a maestro with the experience of Ambrose – and something is bound to happen.
> First, any ideas that the young progressive element in the band runs wild throughout can be dismissed at once. The aggregation, consisting of five brass, five saxes and four rhythm, played clean, well-balanced arrangements in an impeccable manner with the rhythm section attaining a good 'loose' beat. The

saxes produced a lovely round tone which, blended with the two trombones, was in several numbers 'out of this world'. It was a pity, therefore, that they were under-amplified and lost in the shuffling of the dancers.

Unlike many bandleaders trying to sound 'modern', Ambrose uses his brass pyrotechnics tastefully and moderately – the moderation making a 'stab' of brass all the more forceful when used. Kenny Baker is definitely the backbone of the band and his playing – particularly in 'Again' – was brilliant, reminiscent of the full-toned, pre-bop Baker. Harry Roche, another of the brass stalwarts, played in his usual sweet-hot manner, in addition to proving his versatility by giving out with some nice Dixieland-styled trombone in 'St Louis Blues'.

The biggest surprise of the evening was the reception accorded to the bop group, who opened the band's second session. They got the biggest applause of the evening – and not merely from a small knot of fans.

Even Ambrose himself seemed surprised at the rising tide of excited approval that greeted Johnny Dankworth and Ronnie Scott taking chorus after chorus on 'Allen's Alley'. The applause was so overwhelming that the maestro was forced to let the boys take a couple of encores, trumpeter Moe Miller joining them for the last. Best solo in the session was by Ronnie Scott in 'Scrapple from the Apple'.

This review encapsulates a few truths of the time. Ambrose, one-time darling of the gentry and on speaking terms with HRH the Prince of Wales (later the Duke of Windsor), could not allow his band to be taken over by the 'progressive element' and, trying to please all sections of the public, he even nodded in the direction of the traditionalist with 'St Louis Blues'. But the applause for the bop group signalled the end of his, and other baton-waving leaders', influence in the business. It can be safely assumed that he did not attempt any 'conducting' during this well-applauded spot. Had he done, it would merely have underlined the fact that his role was purely decorative and soon to be totally redundant.

Ambrose had a few more bands over the next five or six years, employing the young boppers, including tenor saxophonist Tubby Hayes, but he got more and more, publicly, into debt. The hitherto extremely wealthy and revered Bert Ambrose was finding it a hard struggle in conditions totally different from the sumptuous pre-war days.

The 10 December 1954 *Melody Maker* ran an article headed: 'AMBROSE – THE LOST GENERATION – he talks to Maurice Burman':

WHERE are the people of Ambrose's generation today – and why are they still not fans?

WHERE are the present-day equivalent of the whole family who would gather round the radio every Saturday night to listen to Ambrose?

WHERE are the enthusiasts who once hurried home to make sure they did not miss a single number from Roy Fox, Lew Stone and Harry Roy during the week?

WHERE indeed is the enthusiasm which made it necessary for the police to be called out to control crowds *of all ages* whenever these bands made a rare appearance at a dancehall?

What happened, we wondered, to the nationwide popularity and what happened to the West End where it all started? One man, we decided, could answer these questions: Ambrose.

Ambrose harked back to the days when his band broadcast every Saturday night, comparing the current situation of sporadic broadcasts, recalling the days when the bandleader was in complete control of his repertoire, before the publisher's subsidies of the cost of arrangements, but whose price was repetition of numbers the bandleaders didn't necessarily want to play. He blamed the war for a general deterioration in the standards of most bands, the best men going into the Forces and having to take what players they could.

'But the effects of the war on the profession went further even than that. They produced a new generation that had suffered the effects of evacuation and bombing.

'This new generation needed an outlet. It suffered a form of neurosis that found relief in noise and excitement – and there were new bands ready to give it to them. It became a serious thing if more than four bars of melody were heard. In fact melody was now corny and its place was taken by din and discordant arrangements which hid the melody (mainly because, anyway, the melody was so bad that it had to be hidden, usually by loud drum solos and flashy playing).'

While it may have been true that the absence of broadcasts affected the popularity of his band, up-and-coming bands were establishing a following without the help of the BBC. Ambrose (who allowed his pre-war soloists certain headway on a handful of records of his enormous output over twenty years) was the voice of reaction. He used the term 'abominable row' to describe bebop, something a man of his generation could not grasp. In 1958 he gave up bandleading and managed a singer, Kathy Kirby. After a broadcast she made in the early sixties with the Swinging Blue Jeans, Ambrose refused to have her photographed with 'bits of boys'. He died, impoverished, on 12 June 1971 aged seventy-four.

There were few post-war bands where sidemen were given the scope Ambrose alleged, but there was one bandleader with a policy that had strong appeal to the new generation, and to whom it was thought that Ambrose was particularly referring. Ted Heath had been in the business since the end of World War One and had played with Jack Hylton, Geraldo, Sidney Lipton and ... Ambrose. (One of the many stories about the waggish Ambrose was that he persistently and, it was thought, deliberately, referred to his former sideman as 'Fred' Heath.)

Heath astutely gauged contemporary public taste, his highly efficient band playing 'swing' arrangements in the manner of US leaders Charlie Barnet, Tommy Dorsey and Les Brown. He made a feature of cover versions of big hits by American bands, like Tommy Dorsey's 'Sunny Side of the Street', and 'The Champ' by Dizzy Gillespie.

In his 'swing' numbers Heath not only had a powerful nine-strong brass section playing in the triple-forte, 'killer-diller' fashion, trumpeter Kenny Baker accurately hitting high notes and his tenor saxophonists 'honking', but in Jack Parnell he also had a handsome young drummer whose extended solos brought the house down, drum solos having a peculiar fascination for the general public.

But these were the superficial trappings of a jazz orchestra; Ted Heath and His Music was an organization catering primarily for dancers. To handle the pop songs of the day he employed three singers, Denis Lotis, Dickie Valentine and Lita Rosa.

In interviews Heath, too, made no bones about his commercial policy: 'If the dancers wanted me to play the hokey-cokey I'd play it.' He was a dour, colourless personality and had little interest in jazz, but applied a very successful formula.

He employed only the best – trumpeters Kenny Baker, Dave Wilkins, Eddie Blair, Bobby Pratt; trombonists Jack Armstrong, Don Lusher, Keith Christie; saxophonists Ronnie Scott, Johnny Gray, Tommy Whittle, Henry McKenzie; pianists Norman Stenfalt, Frank Horrox, Stan Tracey; bassists Sammy Stokes, Charlie Short; guitarist Dave Goldberg; drummers Parnell and Ronnie Verrell.

There was one particular session, *My Kind of Jazz*, recorded on

Decca, where the jazzmen were allowed considerable improvisational freedom, but such sessions, in a vast output, were few. Indeed Heath once actually recorded an album à la Victor Sylvester's Strict Tempo Ballroom Orchestra. Generally speaking, his jazz talent was wasted.

Other large touring bands were led by Teddy Foster, Ken Mackintosh, Cyril Stapleton, Stanley Black, Eric Winstone, Paul Fenoulhet, Eric Delaney and Basil Kirchin, Frank Weir and the co-operative Squadronaires. Most jazz musicians were constantly in and out of these bands, few remaining for any length of time to become truly associated with them in the way Lew Davis, Max Goldberg, Max Bacon, Sid Phillips and Danny Polo had had long tenures in the pre-war Ambrose Orchestra.

Several small bands jostled with the larger organizations for work in what was then a highly fruitful period for 'members of the profession'. Attracting the most attention by far was the Johnny Dankworth Seven.

Dankworth, born 20 September 1927 in Woodford, Essex, played clarinet (1944) in Freddy Mirfield's Garbage Men, a quasi-dixieland band. He later played with the semi-professional bands of Will de Barr and Les Ayling, then professionally with Paul Fenoulhet and Ambrose.

He was also one of the Club Eleven's founder members, and the Seven sprang from his association with it. The club maintained a fairly strict policy of employing two regular bands which largely excluded other bop aspirants from 'sitting in'. One of these was Ed Harvey who, after a spell in the RAF and then with Freddy Randall, was the first 'renegade traditionalist'. Other sitters-in were tenor saxophonist Don Rendell and trumpeter Jimmy Deuchar from Dundee. Dankworth experimented with the trumpet, tenor, trombone and alto front line at the Club Eleven and in 1950 went on the road with Don Rendell (tenor saxophone), Eddie Harvey (trombone), Joe Muddel (bass), Bill Le Sage (piano), Tony Kinsey (drums) and, pending Deuchar's discharge from the RAF, Terry Brown (trumpet). They signed with the Wilcox Agency, their date sheet at first handled by Les Perrin and later by the author, a novice booker in the organization.

In that year Dankworth swept the board with triple honours in the *Melody Maker* poll as the best alto saxophonist, arranger and Musician of the Year. The Seven topped the small-band section of the poll. It was a considerable feat for a twenty-three-year-old. The band was influenced by the Miles Davis records released on the Capitol label, but the use of a trombone in a bebop band was unusual and Dankworth, in his arrangements, produced a full and distinctive ensemble sound from his unusually constituted front line.

In the May 1950 issue of *Jazz Illustrated*, the first British jazz magazine to give coverage to bop recordings and happenings (Eddie Harvey its modern-jazz critic), Dankworth outlined his aims. The author, then the editor, wrote the introduction:

> Brilliant modern-style altoist Johnny Dankworth has formed a new band of unusual character. Their first performance at a Ted Heath Swing Show puzzled parts of the audience, an omen of the struggle for recognition that every 'uncommercial' band has to face. In many different ways the old rules are being broken by young musicians whose convictions take them outside the slough and limitations of conventional dance music.
>
> This long-overdue breakaway from set practices commenced with the uncompromising George Webb's Dixielanders and although Dankworth's band is entirely different in character the determination to play the music of their own choice shows similar integrity. On 11 May Johnny Dankworth will open his own club, meeting at Mack's Restaurant, 100 Oxford Street, every Wednesday evening. Below, he outlines his policy for *Jazz Illustrated*.

Dankworth wrote:

> My decision to embark upon a project which I knew would be a responsibility and, at times, an anxiety, was brought about by my arrival at two main conclusions.
>
> The first, that modern jazz in England is being represented by two schools, neither of which I could condone. The raucous 'bebop' school with its eye to physical excitement at the expense of musical value, often held my attention, but only in the case of one or two musicians, my respect. The other is the self-styled 'progressives' with their unblushing emulation of the impressionistic composers of the classical world, who may be commended for their gallant attempts to bring better music to the Tin Pan Alley-fed populace, but from a hot-music enthusiast's point of view, their only progression seems to be away from the roots of jazz.

The way seems to me to lie along a different road, probably not a new one, but one which has been overlooked during developments of the past few years. I am attempting, with my new band, to bring back a purely musical sound into British jazz for, after all, melody must surely be the basis of any form of music. The scores which I write for the group will never, I sincerely hope, sound 'smart' for smartness' sake. Similarly, no musical work will find its place in my programmes merely because it is popular (or conversely, because it is *not* popular!) Each number will stand or fall on its intrinsic worth or, at the very least, on the distinction that can be added to in its interpretation.

The second conclusion of mine was this. Jazz, like any other art form, has evolved throughout the years and ceased to be a pure folk music as long ago as 1919 when Bunk Johnson added Irving Berlin's 'Where I Leave the World Behind' to his band's repertoire. This is proved beyond all shadow of doubt when we realize that we find nine out of ten coloured musicians – and, after all, jazz is the American coloured people's music – playing in the evolved style rather than the traditional form. (Even Sidney Bechet confessed to me in Sweden that two of his favourite tunes were 'Laura' and 'How High the Moon', each 'modern' in harmonic structure.)

Thus we find jazz holding an ever smaller following of dancers and an ever-growing entourage of listeners. The obvious step, therefore, is to present jazz in an atmosphere amenable to a listening audience, with a simultaneous increase in dignity of production that this new audience will no doubt demand. The new generation of performers and orchestras can no longer keep a large percentage of intelligent listeners with maudlin sentimentality and music-hall comedy stunts. Thus, from these views, my future musical policy is obvious. It is to present good modern jazz in an atmosphere of musical and social integrity to an audience that has long suffered from the lack of these very qualities.

Dankworth, however, had difficulty gaining bookings, and those he did obtain hardly covered his expenses. Artistic recognition was one thing; economic realities quite another. Allowing for my inexperience as a booker, the stark fact was that the bop associations and unorthodox instrumentation took some time to impress the dancehall public. It was not long, therefore, before Dankworth realized that it would be imperative to compromise; that without dilution of principle there would be no band. Like every other bandleader in that position, he realized that half an artistic cake was better than no cake at all. Bill Le Sage, who also acted as the band's manager, recalls:

As good as the band was – and it certainly should have been, as we used to rehearse practically non-stop – work did not roll in as expected. We were halfway through a week's engagement at the 400 Ballroom Torquay on a small guarantee against a percentage of the takings when John gathered us together in the digs where we were staying and informed us that he had run out of money and we would have to break up. This seemed such a shame after all the hard work we had put into the band that we all decided to go co-operative and take our chances . . .

I found myself managing the band as well as playing piano. It was an art (or, rather, a hell of a job) managing a co-operative band and in the end it was decided that John would have control of the music and I control of the business side. Often counting up didn't take long. I can remember a small school hall where a local jazz-appreciation society ran a dance and where our take was a princely £14/10s. But it was on the way to a tour of the north and it paid the coach bill for the week. In those days a trippers' coach and a driver worked out at 1/6d per hour!

But the band was forced to scuffle for a long time before the offers came automatically (Dankworth even took work playing clarinet in Joe Daniels's 'Drumnastics' recording band). The 'stigma' of their jazz associations worried them to such an extent that they refused a broadcast on the BBC's 'Jazz Club', fearing that this would only serve to establish in the minds of promoters and ballroom proprietors that they were purely a jazz unit.

Some of the more intransigent bebop players levelled the accusation of 'commercialism' against the Seven, but since most of the critics themselves were engaged in various breadwinning activities far removed from jazz, the same charge could have been levelled against them. Within months the Seven returned to play jazz-club engagements.

One of the band's admirers was Edgar Jackson. In the *Melody Maker* of 5 May 1952 he reviewed 'Bopscotch'/'Our Delight' on the Esquire label under the bold heading: 'THE DANKWORTH SEVEN MORE MODERN THAN DIZZY'.

Both these titles have been recorded previously by American groups – Serge Chaloff with his Herdsmen (Esquire 10–074); Tadd Dameron's 'Our Delight' in June 1946, by Dizzy Gillespie (Parlophone R3034).

No one is going to complain about Johnny Dankworth having revived them. For one thing, they are among the most melodically understandable and tuneful of all the compositions from the bop era. One misses in the Dankworth combination the ensemble depth of the Chaloff Herdsmen, resulting mainly from Chaloff's baritone. On 'Bopscotch' one, too, misses the bounce of

Barbara Carroll's grand solo and in 'Delight' the wizardry of Dizzy's trumpet. But the Americans provided nothing to better Johnny's alto and Earl Swope's trombone had little on Eddie Harvey. Also, the Dankworth Seven are more modern than their American counterparts now around; they are neater – and the surfaces of their records are much smoother, giving them a considerably more pleasant overall sound. They take 'Delight' faster than Dizzy. This not only suits the number, but also helps to give everyone longer solos in what is mainly a first-class soloists' showcase.

In 1951 the band's contract with the Wilcox Agency expired and they moved to the Harold Davison Agency and to greater success, continuing to build a reputation until Dankworth announced in the summer of 1953 that he was disbanding to form a big band.

The *Melody Maker*, 5 May 1953, reported:

The Johnny Dankworth Seven, all set to complete its hat trick in next year's polls, is breaking up at the very peak of its career. With the prospect of 365 dates in the next year, Johnny has nevertheless made a revolutionary decision to disband his present combo and form a twenty-piece orchestra with a new sound. The debut of the new Dankworth Orchestra is already set. Its eight brass, five reeds, three rhythm and three vocalists will be heard on 23 October at the Astoria Ballroom, Nottingham.

This gig attracted unanimously favourable notices, with the usual provisos to the effect that time would sort out their few deficiencies. It became one of the most successful touring orchestras although, like Heath, Parnell and Scott, it bowed to the requirements of dancers. Dankworth employed many of the country's most talented musicians, including Eddie Blair (trumpet); Keith Christie, Eddie Harvey, Laurie Monk (trombone); Peter King, Rex Morris, Tommy Whittle, Ronnie Scott, Dougie Robinson, Danny Moss (saxophone); Dave Lee, Dudley Moore, Alan Branscombe (piano); Spike Heatley, Eric Dawson (bass); Kenny Clare, Allan Ganley (drums).

In the *Melody Maker* Big Band Poll for 1955, the Dankworth band, challenging Ted Heath for his crown, were behind by only 123 votes. Dankworth disbanded in 1963, in common with all other touring big bands.

The terms 'modern jazz' and 'progressive jazz' were synonymous from the mid-forties until the early fifties, when the latter designation came to be mostly associated with big orchestras, primarily with Stan Kenton in the United States. The first British band to adopt the style was led by trumpeter Tommy Sampson in the late forties. Sampson disbanded in 1948, and made only test recordings, but Kenton was copied in this country by Vic Lewis.

Lewis was first known for his guitar playing with the Buddy Featherstonehaugh Radio Rhythm Sextet in the mid-forties, then with his Jazzmen (co-led with drummer Jack Parnell). He formed a conventional dance orchestra in 1946, often featuring a dixieland band-within-a-band, and in 1947 made a feature of covering the hits of US bandleader Phil Harris – like 'Darktown Poker Club' and 'Woodman Save that Tree' – he himself imitating Phil Harris's vocal style.

In 1948 he went heavily into emulation of Stan Kenton and in 1950 formed his 'Modern Concert Orchestra', subtitling the package 'Music for Moderns'. It comprised eighteen musicians (the leader himself occasionally playing trombone), a vocalist and a staff arranger, Ken Thorne, and featured compositions associated with Kenton like 'Intermission Riff', 'Design for Brass', 'Theme for Alto' and others, sometimes using arrangements by Kenton arranger Pete Rugolo.

The unit was not without its critics. Ted Heath, in particular, was very sniffy about the Kenton imitations, insisting that Gillespie and Parker were the *real* progressives. The venture, however, was backed by the Wilcox brothers, who promoted a nationwide tour. Jazz critics, though, were generally disdainful of

Typical cartoon from *Jazz Monthly*

so obvious an imitation. Steve Race, writing in *Jazz Illustrated*, February 1950, commented on the concept of 'progressive jazz':

> While I have every respect for Stan Kenton, who maintained his musical standards (whether we may share them or not) in the teeth of financial opposition, and for Vic Lewis, who could have reduced the size of his band months ago and made a small fortune, I'm afraid I don't share his enthusiasm for Progressive Jazz. It has little or no connection with true jazz – Progressive Swing would be a better term – and the contemporary straight music to which it owes its existence is so far in advance that, having learnt to appreciate Kenton, one might as well go the whole hog and learn to appreciate Bartók.
>
> My chief complaint against Kenton and Rugolo is their constant striving for effect, even at the expense of reason. Where Bartók applies an almost mathematical logic to the production of, say, a closing chord, I'm pretty sure the Progressive boys merely find a nice 'juicy' difficult-sounding chord to tack on the end, regardless of context. As a result the music has little head, and less heart.

In the same issue of *Jazz Illustrated*, James Asman, then jazz critic of the *Daily Mirror*, castigated the show – not unexpectedly for someone of his rigidly traditional tastes.

> Good music is the very essence of poetry, and many of the standards are the same. Progressive Jazz, however, merely gabbles gibberish against the wind. The effect is of overwhelming boredom, for the dullness of the pretension is beyond belief. More and more these days we are faced by a determined minority advocating 'modernism' in art and music ... yet most of these esoteric revolutionaries escape from one discipline to one more severe, and of their own making. The narrow laws of bebop, for instance, are now busy laying its ghost ... twenty men labour to produce a bad egg. Surely there are better things to do?

Lewis visited America, was photographed with Stan Kenton and 'conducting' the Kenton Orchestra, but despite considerable publicity and, initially, good attendance at concert halls in major cities, 'Music for Moderns' was a financial disaster, bringing the Wilcoxes near to bankruptcy. Shortly afterwards, Lewis reverted to leading a conventional dance orchestra and, like every other bandleader, drew from the pool of young bebop musicians who bolstered their income with such employment.

The genuine jazz musicians Lewis used during his tenure as a bandleader included Ronnie Chamberlain, Ronnie Scott, Kathy Stobart, Jimmy Skidmore, Tubby Hayes, Roy East, Derek Humble (saxophone); Bert Courtley, Les Condon, Reg Arnold, Hank Shaw (trumpet); Eddie Harvey, Rags Russell (trombone), and Dill Jones (piano).

In the 10 January 1951 issue of the *Melody Maker* Maurice Burman reviewed a broadcast by this conventional orchestra and scathingly referred to Lewis's inclusion of 'The Thing', a novelty tune that had previously been recorded by Phil Harris and comedian Danny Kaye. Lewis was irked by Burman's strictures and, in his reply, reflected the eternal pull between artistic pretensions on the one hand and economic realities on the other. It was headed: 'WHY I BROADCAST "THE THING"'.

> There is a belief among Kenton fans that it is within my power to go along to a BBC studio and broadcast a programme of undiluted progressive jazz. The public cannot be expected to understand the inner workings of the BBC. Mr Burman, however, should know these things and take them into consideration when reviewing a programme. I hope that when he next chooses to review a performance by my orchestra he will do it with a greater degree of responsibility.

Lewis's reply contained many pertinent observations, and Burman, ex-drummer with Roy Fox and Geraldo, must have indeed been aware of the dilemmas facing any bandleader who departs from the accepted norm. But whether ex-musician or not, the temptation to occupy the ivory tower and make solemn pronouncements on the matter of integrity seized Burman (much as it does the rest of us), although a reference to Lewis as 'our pride and joy' was rather overstating his importance to the nation.

Conversely, Lewis can only blame himself for his self-importance and lack of realism concerning the economics of the venture, the same poor judgement as was exhibited by the Wilcox brothers who, to this day, rue their gullibility, especially as it lost them the lucrative services of Humphrey Lyttelton and his band at 100 Oxford Street, and, not much later, their rental of the premises. For they had turned down Lyttelton's demands for a wage increase. Lyttelton and his manager were not slow to note that the revenue from the band's appearances was being squandered on 'Music for Moderns'.

The Burman–Lewis dialogue served (to little purpose) to highlight the BBC's role: to emphasize the corporation's wariness in presenting anything that might offend listeners, even on the Third Programme (then) and Radio Three (now), where jazz of any kind is given short shrift compared with the amount of time devoted to that other minority, the classical-music lover. This coverage includes three- to four-hour operas in foreign languages which, surely, are understood by only a tiny minority of the minority.

The conflict between the desire to play jazz and the imperative need to observe the demands of promoters and public was also one that faced Jack Parnell's Music Makers, formed in 1951. Their first important engagement was to provide the music for *Fancy Free*, a twice-nightly show at the Prince of Wales Theatre starring Tommy Trinder and Pat Kirkwood. Band-member Ronnie Scott, in his *Some of My Best Friends are Blues*, wrote:

> It was a fine band, but after you've played exactly the same music twice nightly, six nights a week, it became increasingly difficult to sustain interest in the musical proceedings. Musicians in those circumstances are constantly seeking distractions and, in that band, most of the distractions were provided by trumpeter Jimmy Watson. There was a pub opposite the stage door and Jimmy had worked out the places in the score to enable him to slip off the stand, hurry to the pub, get his pint and back on the stand in time for the next cue.
>
> The band would take bets on whether or not he'd ever miss that cue, and other distractions were shooting paper pellets at each other, one of which hit Tommy Trinder on his large chin, and creeping up to bite the pianist's ankle. Rather unbecoming antics, but illustrative of the would-be jazzman's sense of frustration at being musically caged.

It was in that band that Ronnie Scott renewed his acquaintance with Pete King, whom he had first met when King was a member of a semi-professional band led by Jack Oliverie at Stoke Newington Town Hall, where Scott had played one-night stands with Tito Burns. King had followed Scott into the Vic Lewis

Orchestra and they now found themselves in the same saxophone section with Parnell. It was to prove a long-lasting and productive liaison.

In November 1951, the show folded – 'We were not inconsolable,' wrote Scott – and Parnell reorganized the band for one-night stands. It comprised Jimmy Deuchar, Albert Hall, Jo Hunter (trumpet); Mac Minshull, Ken Wray (trombone); Derek Humble, Pete King, Ronnie Scott, Harry Klein (saxophone); Max Harris (piano); Sammy Stokes (bass); Phil Seamen (drums – joined by Parnell for two-drum features).

It was a genuinely star-studded ensemble, but Parnell was faced with the inevitable dilemma. In the *Melody Maker*, January 1952, in a feature devoted to his band's debut at Wimbledon Palais that month, Parnell said: 'Compromise? There'll be no compromise. I'm going to be commercial. That means giving people what they want.'

Pete King, a member of the band, recalls:

> With Jack's jazz background, and judging by the guys he booked, it was generally thought that the Music Makers would be a jazz band. Of course, that wasn't possible. Jack just *had* to compromise, whether he liked it or not and being realists, we happily went along with him and were pleased to play whatever jazz we could. That depended much on the venue – some crowds were more receptive than others – and we definitely played more jazz on Sunday concerts.
>
> Overall, I think we probably leaned on Jack to play more jazz than was fair. After all, it was he who had to deal with the managements, and it was he whose bank balance was at stake.
>
> I'd say the jazz content was about thirty per cent, but my main memory is of the privilege of playing with such a talented bunch and, whether jazz or commercial, it was music of a high quality.

The band had powerful solo strength, used extensively when the occasion allowed – particularly on Sunday concerts – and the twenty or so jazz-orientated recordings they made for Parlophone display the band's many qualities. Inevitable personnel changes saw saxophonists Joe Temperley and Tubby Hayes, and trumpeter Hank Shaw, among others, in the band, and it ceased as a touring outfit when Parnell took over leadership of the London Palladium pit orchestra in 1955.

In the *Melody Maker* of 15 November 1952, Edgar Jackson, veteran jazz critic, prefaced his review of Jack Parnell's first record by harking back to his first published review* (from January 1926), of Jack Hylton's Kit-Kat Band, and commenting wryly on its naïveté:

> How much more informed record criticism has been since the *Melody Maker* first started twenty-six years ago, and how much dance music in its more enlightened forms has progressed in the same quarter of a century. For instance, compare those 1926 Kit-Kat Band and Savoy Orpheans with 'The Champ'/'Summertime', by Jack Parnell and his band, Parlophone R3607, 5s/4½d.
>
> Scored by Jimmy Deuchar, 'The Champ', which you may already know from Dizzy Gillespie's record on Vogue V21111, is one of the Parnell band's exhibition arrangements. It could have been a great record, but it just misses it. The supersonic tempo – it goes at nearly eighty bars to the minute – was a bit too much for the band. Or at any rate for a record. Maybe it was because of the sections being too far apart in the studio to hear each other properly, but there are uncomfortable suggestions of grabbing and snatching. Also the balances are not too good. And what happened to the important obbligato by the trumpets behind the trombone passages? It is barely audible.
>
> However, taken by and large the solos by Derek Humble, the trombones and Ronnie Scott are as good as the tempo permits and the band as a whole plays with that enlightened sense of modern jazz phraseology for which it is already noted . . .
>
> 'Summertime' is a totally different proposition. Arranged by Laurie Johnson, whom you may have heard broadcasting with his own light orchestra, it is an effective and delectable slow rhapsodization. Apart from its intro and coda it consists of just one chorus, devised as a showcase for Jimmy Deuchar, and this is played to an accompaniment from one who had considerably more experience in modern band scoring. The Parnell ensemble plays it with a sympathy and finesse that leaves nothing to be desired. This time, too, there are no recording faults. The reproduction is excellent. Jimmy Deuchar caps it with a long, flowing phrase across the twenty-seventh and twenty-eighth bars, which can only be described as inspired, and provides one of those rare moments in it which make jazz the great music it is.
>
> It is a pity that the final touch of perfection was lost by the very last chord being cut short.

The Harmony Inn, like its 'traditional' counterpart, the Rex

---

*See HJB1.

Restaurant, New Compton Street, on the other side of Charing Cross Road, was a hotbed of gossip and intrigues. One bunch of intriguants in January 1953 made a decision that led to the formation of an exciting new band, and to the association between two musicians – Ronnie Scott and Pete King – which culminated in the founding of a club in 1959 that helped to establish London as a major jazz centre.

The Parnell band's mix of 'commercial' dance music and bebop jazz had made them a reasonable box-office draw, but had led to problems in obtaining the broadcasts so necessary to ensure their exposure to a larger public. To achieve this they engaged a female singer, Marion Keene, previously with Ambrose. She made it a stipulation that her husband, tenor saxophonist Ronnie Keene, also joined. Parnell acceded to this and, according to Scott in his book, 'tore the heart out of the band'. When they heard why King had been dismissed, Scott, Deuchar, Humble and Wray gave notice. This incident was to be indirectly responsible for the formation of Scott's first band. Scott wrote:

> We were all sitting in the Harmony Inn one day in January 1953 when we conceived the idea of forming a nine-piece band co-operative – and it turned out to be one of the better ideas we had that year. Derek Humble, Benny Green, Pete King and myself were on saxophones, Jimmy Deuchar on trumpet, Ken Wray on trombone, Norman Stenfalt on piano, Lennie Bush on bass and Tony Crombie drums. And we had a singer called Johnny Grant. We made our public debut in Manchester, in February 1953, followed by a month's bookings in that area, and from the very first night the band took off. In April we played at the London Palladium in one of Ted Heath's Sunday Swing sessions and I remember the headline over the review in the following week's *MM* was: 'Scott punches Heath fans at the Palladium'. It was meant to indicate that the band played with a lot of punch – but then ambiguous headlines were not unknown in the *MM*.
>
> The band went from strength to strength and got good reactions everywhere. It was not only good musically, but we were very commercially minded and concerned with good presentation ...
>
> So we had a good band, great desks and uniforms, a good library, a full engagement book, a fair bus and unfair oil heater. All we needed now was a gimmick. We decided to buy a monkey, dress it in its own made-to-measure band uniform and take it on the stage with us as a sort of mascot. That was one of the worst ideas we had that year. We bought the monkey but as soon as we took it on the bus it went berserk. It was terrified and nobody could get near it

without the risk of having several fingers bitten off. Its behaviour was so erratic that someone observed that it probably had a man on its back . . .

The nine-piece lasted two and a half years and then, inevitably, it broke up. Inevitably, because all bands have an optimum life and it is rarely more than three years. Added to which there were so many stars in the band that clashes of temperament became more and more frequent. But it was tremendous fun – and very satisfying musically. I've never laughed so much in my life as I did with that band.

A novel idea was to have the band rehearse before members of the public and the 27 February 1953 issue of *NME* ran a feature, written by Mike Butcher, that incorporated comments by fans and relatives of the band, including Ken Wray's mother and father, Jimmy Deuchar's wife and Benny Green's father – whose comment was: 'I taught my son, Benny, to play the tenor saxophone, so I'm biased. The band is West End material already.'

But there wasn't a West End berth for a band of this kind; instead, it was an unending succession of one-night stands up and down the country – drill halls, palais, theatres, corn exchanges, miners' institutes, social clubs and jazz clubs, the lucrative weekend dates the pivot of the tours, the midweek dates often merely to pay for the petrol. These usually worked on a guarantee and percentage (whichever was the greater) arrangement. Scott commented:

It was part of the mysterious alchemy of tour organization that if you had a gig at Canterbury one night, the following you would have to be in Perth; then Exeter always precedes Aberdeen. On these all-night bus journeys some of the conversations were hilarious, full of that oblique, sardonic, black humour for which musicians have a unique reputation. For example, we used to make up ideal names for the various categories of people – there was Mustapha Fix, the Turkish tenor player; Pete Bog, the Irish flautist; Mannheimed Stoned, the German trumpet player and the famous Indian jazz critic Pandit Unmer Sifflee – later to figure in one of the club's advertisements.

After the break-up of the nine-piece, Scott formed a big band. He wrote:

If the monkey mascot was the worst idea we had in 1953 the lousiest of 1955 was the one I had to form a big band. To run a big jazz band you have to be obscenely rich or quite insane – so I went into the venture only half qualified. It took me hardly any time to see that the project was a disaster, but it took almost a year to make practical acknowledgement of the fact by folding the band.

There were some fine musicians involved – Dougie Robinson, Joe Harriott, Pete King and myself on saxophones; Stan Palmer, Hank Shaw, Dave Usden and Jimmy Watson (trumpet); Jack Botterill, Robin Kaye, Mac Minshull (trombone); Norman Stenfalt (piano); a Swiss musician called Eric Peter on bass and Phil Seamen (drums). But it was a case of the whole being considerably smaller than the sum of the parts – or maybe some of the parts were full of holes.

The last comment could well be an oblique reference to the difficulties inherent in a band comprised of highly talented and temperamental musicians but, like the nine-piece, the big band received warm critical appraisal. Unfortunately, they made only four records at full strength, but a contingent from the larger band made six sides at the Royal Festival Hall in February 1956.

Some indication of the temperamental side was revealed in an article by Benny Green (who was to have joined the big band) in the *NME*. It was headed: 'FOR PETE'S SAKE' and was a monograph on Pete King, who had managed the ensemble, as well as playing saxophone in the nine-piece, and who was to manage the larger band.

> King's experience as a band manager when first attempting to herd Scott's first band into some sort of coherent formation has been short and perhaps not so sweet. It would seem that there is in the make-up of a jazz musician a strong instinct of defiance of vested authority and contempt of humbug which has always seemed to me one of the most attractive features of life in the jazz world. I have seen so many bubbles of pretension pricked by every grade of humour from epigram to obscenity that I am now convinced that the jazz musician is one of the most beautiful creatures on the planet.
>
> However, defiance has to end somewhere and discipline begin and the trouble is marking the line of demarcation. Pete King used the extraordinary system of chalking his line of demarcation when and where he thought best for the moment. Broadly speaking, his system worked in the Scott Orchestra of 1953–55 for, luckily, there existed a sense of duty to the cause which amazed most onlookers and even some of us inside the organization at times, but King got himself virulently hated and wildly loved in turns. He was popular whenever he considered it prudent to draw upon the band funds to swell the wages, was hated with dangerous hysteria when he suggested that we should settle a bill or save for the proverbial rainy day.

Green could only hint at the manifold problems a road manager has, particularly with a band of stars crammed into a small bus for hours on end. The road network in the fifties contained no motorways. A trip from London to Manchester, for instance, took eight hours or more; the boredom induced by long travelling hours, drink, drugs and temperamental differences became an explosive cocktail. Scott recalls:

> One of my problems was that I (along with other post-war leaders) was not one of the baton-waving brigade. I was a friend of all the guys, I had grown up with some of them, travelled in the same coach: I couldn't possibly be a disciplinarian, like Joe Loss or Ted Heath.
> Considering the idiosyncrasies of the guys, there were differences, of course. Trumpeter Dave Usden and Phil Seamen didn't hit it off and one night at the Winter Gardens, Morecambe, there were ructions on the stand. It was New Year's Eve and we were playing 'Auld Lang Syne'. As midnight struck, I heard a ruckus behind me, looked around, and saw Dave and Phil having a fight. We gamely continued playing.
> Then there were the differences in interpretation of the scores by saxists Dougie Robinson and Joe Harriott. That was a pain, especially as I was a member of the same section. A cameo that sticks in my mind — it was quite a diversion — after a gig was the sight of two women fighting in the street outside a Manchester dancehall. Looking on was a dispassionate Harriott. 'What's going on?' I asked.
> 'Don't worry about it, mun. They're fighting over me.'
> Going back to my first band, I'd like to pay tribute to Derek Humble, a most underrated musician. I think he's the finest jazz alto player we've ever had in this country. As a soloist and a section leader, he was superb; he just didn't seem to attract publicity, and when he went to live and play in Germany, he was sort of forgotten.

One of the most creative and, in economic terms, the least successful musicians was tenor saxophonist Kenny Graham, who led his Afro-Cubists for several years, disbanding and re-forming several times, interspersing his bandleading with spells in the large dance orchestras, one of these being Eric Winstone's, a chore he hated.

The Afro-Cubists' instrumentation was the unusual one of trumpet, tenor saxophone, piano, bass, drums, maraccas, conga drum and bongos, employing the rhythms of the Caribbean along with bebop.

Graham recorded extensively on the Esquire label, his records being highly rated, but the band had little box-office appeal, nor did the gruff demeanour of the leader endear him to ballroom proprietors. The musicians he employed were first class, these including the trumpeters Jo Hunter and Terry Brown; pianists Jack Honeyborne and Ralph Dollimore and the tragic Dickie Devere (drums) who died at the age of twenty-eight.

In the *Melody Maker*, 2 May 1953, Steve Race wrote of Graham:

> For some time now I have been watching a certain British modernist. His name is Kenny Graham . . .
>
> Kenny is the nearest thing we have to a real composer. He has grasped the essentials of thematic development. His band parts, when copied, do not usually consist of twelve bars of notes followed by a sea of chord symbols.
>
> To him, tenor sax and trumpet need not be indissolubly married in unison-at-the-octave. His musical vision is not bounded by a 4/4 time signature. ('Skylon' was written in 12/8: the same thing, perhaps, yet subtly *not* the same thing.) He has that rare gift in jazz, a sense of melodic sequence.
>
> He can create, as in 'Mango Walk', a chord sequence which neither moves chromatically in sevenths, nor treads the well-worn path round the key-cycle. He is not afraid to use two or more themes in one composition, and he can relate them with real ingenuity. His work is interesting melodically, harmonically and rhythmically.
>
> Of course, he has his faults. I don't usually ask people to take themselves more seriously, but at times, I wish Kenny would.
>
> He sometimes shows a touch of musical laziness, for instance. It allowed the ingenious 'Cuban Canon' to degenerate into a mere string of blues choruses just when it should – and in Kenny's hands could – have developed into a real contribution to world jazz. He also showed lack of artistic honesty in claiming 'The Kerry Dance' as his own composition ('Kenny's Jig').
>
> Nevertheless, most of Kenny's work demands real attention, and the news of his 'Afrocadabra', a twelve-minute composition recorded last Wednesday, and slated for issue on an Esquire LP in June, is good news indeed. I haven't heard it yet, but I hope for great things.
>
> For Kenny Graham is a real composer; in embryo perhaps a great one. If only he, too, will remember that fact he may well make an international mark on jazz before very long.

Graham never did make his mark with a wider public, and retired, embittered, in the early 1970s.

Tito Burns's group remained one of the most popular of the small units but this pioneer of bop on the radio on 'Accordion Club' had drastically to alter his policy to fit in with ballroom requirements.

The *Melody Maker*, 25 October 1952, reported on a furore in the ranks by quoting Burns:

> 'There is no room for idealists in a commercial dance band,' said Tito Burns, announcing two changes in a general reshuffle aimed at maintaining his band's policy of providing entertainment as well as jazz. The instrumentalists involved were tenorist Tubby Hayes and drummer Pete Bray. 'Both,' said Tito, 'are first-rate jazzmen but unfortunately they have found their ideals conflicting with my policy of giving the public a show as well as good music for dancing.'

Regarded by many as the finest talent to emerge from the crop of British tenor saxophonists and indeed of all British jazz musicians, was Edward Brian 'Tubby' Hayes, the 'Little Giant', born 30 January 1935. He was playing professionally at the age of fifteen, with the Kenny Baker Sextet in 1951, then with Ambrose, Vic Lewis, Tito Burns and Jack Parnell before forming his own band in 1955.

His playing was characterized by phenomenally fast fingering, a supercharged ferocity of attack, and extensive technical command. He also played flute and vibraphone and was a first-class arranger – a truly remarkable talent.

Despite his abilities and reputation, his band was not a commercial success. A founder member of the band, who stayed with it until its break-up, was tenor saxophonist Jackie Sharpe:

> The first time I can remember hearing Tubby Hayes play was at the 51 Club, Little Newport Street. A cherubic fifteen-year-old youth playing with enthusiasm and authority beyond his years. I was immediately captivated by his playing, little dreaming that he was to become such a catalyst in my life, as, in fact, many other people's lives.
>
> Some time in 1955, I had just acquired my first taxi at the age of twenty-one, only to sell it a few months later without the slightest qualm when offered a place in Tubby's new eight-piece band.
>
> Signed up to agent Tito Burns, we cut our first recordings at the Decca Studios off West End Lane, West Hampstead, for Tempo Records, on 10 March and embarked on our first one-night stands. We couldn't, in fact, have chosen a worse time, although if we had known this it would have not deterred

us in the least. It was the beginning of the end of an era. The touring dance and jazz bands were on the way out. The day of the three-chord guitarists and rock and roll mayhem had begun.

Nevertheless, the eighteen months of Tubby's band was undoubtedly the best time of my life. The band consisted of Dickie Hawdon and Dave Usden (trumpet); Mike Senn (alto); myself on baritone and tenor; Harry South (piano); Pete Blannin (bass); Lennie Breslow or Bill Eyden (drums); and Tubby, with Bobby Breen (vocals). We played some of the most unlikely venues throughout the UK. We often played percentage dates to about twenty paying customers. We were constantly broke, but we had a ball, Tubby proving to be an excellent leader and extremely popular with the minority of dedicated fans who did show up at our gigs.

During that time we passed our BBC audition and appeared on a tea-time broadcast aimed at captive housewives. It was the custom to play very 'commercial' on broadcasts and there were no end of song-pluggers around to press tunes upon us. Our offerings included 'Rock Around the Clock', 'He's a Tramp' and the epic 'Yellow Rose of Texas' introduced by the BBC announcer's Oxford accent with: 'Here's one to set the teacups *rettling*.'

Despite our enthusiasm the rigorous touring had its effect and after a particularly gruelling Scottish trip we were tired, hungry and demoralized. We decided to confront our manager, Tito Burns, and demand more money. As the coach pulled up outside his residence in posh Maida Vale, Tubby and I were elected spokesmen.

The door opened to reveal Tito resplendent in silk dressing-gown. He listened to our tale of woe; our protests that we were totally skint. He beamed a consolatory smile.

'Well, that makes all of us doesn't it?' We terminated the agreement there and then – fairly amicably – and the band broke up.

Of course Tubby progressed from strength to strength. Maturing into a great musician, composer and arranger, accepted worldwide, as we all expected he would. Those early days on the road with the Little Giant were etched into our memories to remain for ever as a tremendous experience – for me, at least, a part of my life that I would not have missed for the world.

His influence remains, and is perpetuated in my own big band, where his compositions and arrangements, together with those of his contemporaries, are played, and which, like all great music, remain undated. The orchestra contains some young musicians who never met him, but all know his music and his genius inspires all of us still. We believe he would be happy with our efforts.

In 1957 Hayes teamed with Ronnie Scott to form the Jazz Couriers, one of the most successful groups, musically and commercially, to emerge from the bop milieu. They made their debut on 7 April 1957 at the New Flamingo Club run by Jeff Kruger. With Scott and Hayes were Terry Shannon (piano); Bill

Eyden – replaced by Phil Seamen (drums); and a succession of bass players including Phil Bates, Jeff Clyne and Kenny Napper.

In *Some of My Best Friends are Blues*, Scott recalled:

> When I got back from that abortive American tour* I teamed up with Tubby Hayes to form what was generally acknowledged to be one of the best modern-jazz groups Britain ever produced – the Jazz Couriers.
>
> Tubby was twenty-two years old and he had already established himself as one of the most gifted, mature and technically accomplished musicians on the British jazz scene. He had been playing tenor saxophone since he was twelve and he invested everything he did with a terrific vitality and enthusiasm. He really made you *want* to play and I learned a tremendous amount from him. I remember our two and a half years together as the most satisfying and musically productive periods of my career.
>
> One of the highlights of the Couriers period was a two-week British tour with Sarah Vaughan. The band also made a few record dates and won a couple of polls. But, once again, the Scott law of optimum durability came into play and by the summer of 1959, though nobody said as much, we all knew the Couriers were running out of steam and getting a little stale. So we decided to fold the band, and on 30 August 1959, we played our last date – at the City Hall, Cork.

Hayes was later to lead specially-formed big bands with the cream of British talent, including Jimmy Deuchar, Eddie Blair, Tommy McQuater, Bobby Pratt, Stan Roderick (trumpet); Keith Christie, Don Lusher, Ray Premru (trombone); Keith Bird, Ronnie Ross, Johnny Scott (reeds); Terry Shannon (piano); Jeff Clyne (bass) and Bill Eyden and Allan Ganley (drums). One of these was the Downbeat Big Band, rehearsing and playing at the Downbeat Club in Old Compton Street.

In the late sixties, Hayes led a regular quartet with Mick Pyne (piano), Ron Mathewson (bass) and Tony Levin (drums), but by now his health was deteriorating. Long-term use of hard drugs was having the inevitable effect. His heart was affected and difficulties with breathing restricted his playing.

He was charged with being in possession of heroin and after being placed on bail, stood in court and received a suspended sentence – and nationwide publicity. In the *Melody Maker*, staffman Bob Dawbarn related an interview with Hayes headed: .

---

*See Chapter 11.

AGONY OF TUBBY HAYES

So what now is Tubby's future? And how did Britain's number-one jazzman come to be standing in a London court last week?

'My problems really began to come to a head when I had jaundice about a year ago. I had dabbled with this and that before then but it never affected my work because I never let it. Up until then I was very busy.

'With the jaundice the doctor advised me to lay off for three months, but for various reasons, I couldn't do it. I decided to do just studio work and cut out the jazz dates and everything that involved travelling.

'Then I got a jazz workshop in Germany. After the first rehearsal I was disgusted with my playing. I hadn't done any jazz for two months and it just wasn't coming. So every night I went to clubs trying to get back into shape for my own peace of mind. Just doing studio work made me so miserable I felt I had to re-form, but found that more and more of a strain.

'The doctor wouldn't allow me to drink and I'm a man who always liked his pint, so that stepped up the drug scene. I felt I just couldn't go on any longer. I was feeling like death and was charging about to get the drugs and keep me going. In the end I just took my phone off the hook, locked the doors and didn't speak to a soul for about ten weeks. After a while I came round and realized I had got to get myself out of this. But that wasn't so easy. You know all those things you read in the papers – well, a friend of mine said, "What carrot can we dangle in front of you to get you straight?" Well, carrots were no good.

'I hope, and believe, that this sentence was the answer. It was the jolt I needed. I've had a pretty horrible three weeks, but it has given me the opportunity to continue my career and at the same time get treatment and get straight. When I went to pieces and took the phone off the hook, I obviously let a lot of people down and got a bad reputation in certain quarters. It's up to me to try and open those doors again. I hope that in time these people will trust me again if I continue to play OK and turn up on time.

'I am sorry I had to pack up the quartet with Mick Pyne, Ron Mathewson and Tony Levin because they were beautiful and we had a lot of good times.

'Recently I have done so little jazz work and I'm really starting from scratch again. I'm doing most of the booking myself, but Pete King has offered to take some of that off my shoulders. There is a possibility of a tour with Peter Burman's Jazz Tête à Tête with Joy Marshall in the New Year. Peter also mentioned that he is hoping to do some concerts with either Carmen McRae or Mel Torme and, if it comes off, he would like to use the big band. One of my ambitions is to do a week or two at Ronnie's with the big band. But the band I have been using is an eighteen-piece, and that makes it impossible. I want to get a thirteen-piece together and that means writing a whole new book. That will take time.

'Studio work? Obviously if sessions come my way, I shall accept some – although I was doing too much of that and it made me very depressed.'

He ended with this message: 'If any of my colleagues – or, come to that, any musicians I don't know – ever get the same sort of problems I have had, for God's sake go to a clinic. Trying to solve it on your own only leads to more problems. And at least in this country, we can do something about these problems.'

Hayes died, after a heart operation, on 8 June 1973, aged thirty-seven.

Another modern band on the road was Ralph Sharon's Sextet, with various personnels. Sharon went to America in the early fifties and recorded with many famous American musicians, including bassists Charles Mingus, Milt Hinton and Oscar Pettiford; drummers Kenny Clarke, Jo Jones and Osie Johnson. He eventually became a very successful musical director with Tony Bennett, Chris Connor, Johnny Hartman, Mel Torme and Rosemary Clooney.

Other modern bands included the Norman Burns Quintet, copying the George Shearing sound; Jimmy Walker's Quintet; the Ken Moule Seven; the Ray Ellington Quartet and Tony Crombie's band.

Crombie, one of the first British bebop drummers, toured with a band that featured singer Annie Ross. She later achieved fame as a member of the Lambert, Hendricks and Ross trio whose forte was vocal interpretation of famous jazz instrumental records. Crombie's bands, at various times, included Dizzy Reece, Les Condon (trumpet); Sammy Walker, Joe Temperley (tenor saxophone); Harry South (piano) and recorded for the Decca, Tempo and Columbia labels from 1954 to 1961, including a big band for Decca in 1960.

Ray Ellington, a drummer with Harry Roy's show band 1937–40, and active throughout the war in many West End drinking clubs, was a frequent visitor to the Caribbean Club, Denman St, Piccadilly. There he heard the resident trio of Dick Katz (piano), Coleridge Goode (bass) and Lauderic Caton (guitar) and employed them to form the Ray Ellington Quartet. This band was instrumental in popularizing bop, recording extensively and touring throughout the UK from 1946 into the mid-1950s.

Another touring band was led by Kathy Stobart, from South

Shields. She arrived in London, aged seventeen, in 1942, and playing with the likes of Jimmy Skidmore and Denis Rose was accepted as the first musician to break the 'sex-barrier' in British jazz. Between two stints with the Vic Lewis big band (1948–9, 1951–2), she led her own regular group, including alto saxophonist Derek Humble, tenor saxophonist Pete King, her trumpeter husband Bert Courtley, and pianist Dill Jones.

Of all the figures in British jazz, pianist Jones was probably the most eclectic, first sitting in with Webb's Dixielanders at the Red Barn in Barnehurst playing in the style of a Joe Sullivan or Jess Stacy, but soon playing in the company of Ronnie Scott, Joe Harriott, Don Rendell and Tommy Whittle. On emigrating to America, he 'returned to type', playing with such dixieland musicians as trumpeters Yank Lawson, Max Kaminsky and Jimmy McPartland. He died, of throat cancer, in 1984.

Tenor saxophonist Don Rendell, who came to prominence as a founder member of the Johnny Dankworth Seven, was another of the most active of modern-jazz musicians, forming his first band in 1953 with ex-traditionalist trumpeter Dickie Hawdon, Ronnie Ross (then primarily featured on tenor saxophone), pianist Damian Robinson, bassist Ashley Kozack and a drummer highly regarded but generally underrated, Benny Goodman, alternating with another fine percussionist, Derek Hogg. Rendell had further significant associations with pianist Michael Garrick, multi-saxophonist Barbara Thompson, and trumpeter Ian Carr, the Rendell–Carr Quintet being probably the most notable of these alliances. The work of Rendell and his associates will be covered in detail in *A History of Jazz in Britain 1970–90*.

During the mid-thirties jazz in Britain was enriched by the presence of West Indian musicians like trumpeters Dave Wilkins and Leslie Hutchinson; saxophonists Bertie King, George Roberts, George Tyndale, Louis Stephenson and Freddy Grant; pianist Erroll Barrow; bassist Coleridge Goode; drummer Clinton Maxwell and guitarist Lauderic Caton. They were often joined, in various combinations, by the Cardiff-born blacks, Joe and Frank Deniz, on guitar.

Only Hutchinson, who later played with Geraldo, and Goode, remained in the business, the latter later being a member of alto saxophonist Joe Harriott's quartet.

The post-war West Indian contribution to the popular-music scene was mainly in the fields of calypso and Latin American music. Expatriate South Africans Louis Moholo, Mongegi Fega and Johnny Dyani aside, the black contribution to jazz was minimal, Harriott, alto saxophonist and flautist Harold McNair, trumpeters Dizzy Reece, Harry Beckett and Shake Keane being the few exceptions that proved the rule.

Harriott was Parker-inspired and, besides playing in conventional bop groups, regularly sat in with traditional bands. He was later to pioneer free jazz in Britain, and on some dates, much to the consternation of both audiences and promoters, alternated, within the same set, between bop and the avant garde.

The *Melody Maker* and the *New Musical Express* ran a weekly listing of the touring bands' calls for the following week, a veritable hodge-podge, comprising literally hundreds of ballrooms, drill halls, corn exchanges, ice rinks, working men's clubs, institutes, colleges and various improvised venues such as aircraft hangars.

The *eminences grises* of this cut-throat business were a handful of agents, mostly London-based, the author one of them. They were wholeheartedly hated by the itinerant troubadours, who saw them as traffickers in human souls, heartless parasites feeding upon creative artists – a myth the troubadours assiduously propagated.

The mix of conventional dance and jazz-oriented bands provided the employment to sustain the young modernist, the opportunity to take to the public that music he had previously played underground and for little financial reward. That such an ostensibly esoteric form of jazz should have reached out further than the grubby dens in which it was nurtured was just one of the revolutions in the British post-war popular-music scene.

6
The Condon Connection, the Three Bs and Traddy-pop

The modernists' relative commercial success was, however, well outstripped by the traditionalists. If the bop musicians were surprised at the degree of their public acceptance, the traditionalists should have been overwhelmed, especially since there were several different categories of their kind participating in this success.

The two main schools could have been described as 'New Orleans Up River' and 'New Orleans Down River' – Humphrey Lyttelton the much-publicized leader of the first and Ken Colyer the less-publicized but no less belligerent protagonist of the second – but there was a further body of musicians, no less sincere in their beliefs, who looked to white music for their inspiration and repertoire, particularly to Eddie Condon and his various bands.

The so-called Condon style was a distillation of the 'Chicago style' of the twenties, when a young group of Chicagoans called the Austin High School Gang avidly listened to jazz records (not unlike many other young men in places thousands of miles from America a generation later) and attempted to copy them. These young Chicagoans, including trumpeter Jimmy McPartland and clarinettist Frank Teschemacher, were also exposed to a cornucopia of great jazz players, the likes of Louis Armstrong, Johnny Dodds and Jimmie Noone, all playing in the 'Windy City' at the time.

More by accident than design, these adolescent tyros employed a slightly different instrumentation from that of the quintessential line-up. They used a tenor saxophone (Bud Freeman) instead of a trombone on their first recording, made in 1927 and issued under the name of the McKenzie/Condon Chicagoans, Condon the banjoist on the sessions, Red McKenzie the 'fixer'.

With this particular instrumentation and, inevitably, putting something of their own into the treatments, they produced a rather staccato, and at times frenzied sound. By the time Condon had switched to the guitar and the Ohian cornettist Wild Bill Davison recorded with him in 1943, the designation had changed from 'Chicago' to 'Condon' style, with its own recognizable characteristics, that had had its genesis in the Austin High coterie so many years earlier.

As mentioned in Chapter 1, the first in this field was Freddy Randall (born in May 1921), his own playing at first much influenced by Muggsy Spanier's and later an amalgam of Spanier's modest range and the explosively volatile Wild Bill Davison, as the latter's records became more readily available. Pee Wee Russell was the inspiration for Randall's clarinettist, Bruce Turner, and George Brunies (a white New Orleanian to be closely associated with the Condon units) the model for trombonist Denis Croker. Randall employed the guitar (with occasional exceptions) instead of the banjo and never the brass bass or tuba; he also used the saxophone in his instrumentation: Pat Rose on baritone and Betty Smith on tenor. His repertoire included many tunes by white composers, particularly those by Nick La Rocca and Larry Shields of the Original Dixieland Jazz Band such as 'Ostrich Walk', 'Original Dixieland One-step' and 'At the Jazz Band Ball'.

Another early British band that emulated the characteristics of the Condon alumni was actually called the Chicagoans, led by pianist Roy Vaughan, but the first band after Randall to become well known for its approximation of the Condon style was that led by trumpeter Mick Mulligan.

Originally titled Mick Mulligan and His Magnolia Jazz Band, they were first inspired by the recordings of Louis Armstrong's Hot Five and Seven. Their early records, for the independent Tempo label, included many Armstrong classics like 'Savoy Blues', 'Struttin' with Some Barbecue', 'Oriental Strut' and 'Skid-dat-de-dat'. In retrospect there can only be wonderment as to why such acknowledged masterpieces of authentic Afro-American jazz should have been covered by a technically limited and out-of-tune band of amateurs, since compared with the originals the Mulligan band versions are crude indeed. To many, it was a waste of time at best and a sacrilege at worst, but direct emulation of the masters was prevalent at the time – 1950 – and the Mulligan band were by no means alone in these seemingly futile endeavours at this stage of their technical development.

The original personnel comprised Mulligan (trumpet), Pete Hull (clarinet), Bob Dawbarn (trombone), Owen Maddock (tuba), Norman Dodsworth (drums) and two banjoists, Johnny Lavender and Jack Richardson (to be replaced by Bill Cotton) and a young art salesman, an expert on surrealism, formerly a Royal Navy rating, George Melly, as vocalist. Melly was a flamboyant personality with an immediately recognizable style derived from assiduous listening to Bessie Smith records.

Their metamorphosis from 'New Orleans' to 'Chicago' was effected by changes in personnel, rather than by any conscious decision by the leader, whose own powerful, sometimes effective, often erratic playing remained in the Armstrong mould. A six- or seven-piece band is, perforce, a democratic unit (unless, of course, led by Ken Colyer) and Mulligan was not unhappy to drop the banjo – or, in his case, two of this instrument.

Roy Crimmins had replaced Dawbarn, Paul Simpson had replaced Hull (to be replaced by Archie Semple, and he in his turn by Ian Christie) and a modern-style guitarist, Jimmy Currie, replaced the banjos, Currie later to be replaced by Bill Bramwell, an ex-Randall player. Bramwell had an exceptional grasp of the blues. Semple was another Pee Wee Russell devotee and Christie's mentor, Albert Nicholas, was a New Orleanian Condonite. By now the influences of the Condon alumni were clearly established.

Scotsman Dave Keir replaced Crimmins, and Kerr was succeeded by an ex-Lancashire CCC wicket-keeper Frank Parr, formerly with the Merseysippi Jazz Band. By the mid-fifties the band had become part of British jazz lore, more for the prodigious drinking and the Rabelaisian behaviour of Mulligan and Melly than for the variable quality of their music, this much affected by the quantity of their alcoholic intake.

In the 12 March 1955 issue of the *Melody Maker*, Max Jones wrote an article headed: 'KING OF THE RAVERS'.

GEORGE MELLY
OWNING-UP

Wally 'Trog' Fawkes's superb drawing of the Mulligan band arriving at a gig.

To understand the colloquial meaning of 'raver' is to be halfway towards an appreciation of the Mick Mulligan character. The expression, oddly enough, is rooted in literature; in Pope's

Fire in both eyes, papers in both hands,
They rave, madden and recite round the land.

Your present-day raver is most often found, glass in hand, somewhere in Soho commenting on the humours of the profession, or on such strident species as the Hooray Henry. He is a jazz-lover, a party-goer, a humbug-hater. He speaks largely in a new vernacular compounded of Cockney, Australian and Runyonese spiced with original invention – and he is no respecter of conventions.

The accepted king of this weird coterie is Mick Mulligan, a traditional trumpet player of essentially amateur outlook who turned professional with immediate and remarkable success. He has a Rabelaisian tongue, the generosity of a public-relations officer, the mimic power of an Al Read and the wit of an Irish playwright. His honesty matches his disrespectfulness and sociability.

Jones's article could only touch upon the character of a wild man who was a law unto himself, but the 'raving' image attracted many to the band's engagements whose lifestyle was exactly the opposite.

The band lasted for twelve years and the ineptitude of their earlier efforts stands in sharp contrast to their later, infinitely superior, recordings in the mid to late fifties.

The band that, more than any other, spread the gospel according to Condon, was trumpeter Alex Welsh's. Welsh, from Edinburgh, played with the Sandy Brown and Archie Semple bands in that city in the early fifties, both bands recording for the S and M label, before he came to London in 1954. He had a good command of his instrument and, like Randall, was influenced by Wild Bill Davison, but his conception and line were steadier than the often wayward Randall's and, unlike Mulligan, was, initially at least, a sober character.

His first band comprised Ian Christie, Roy Crimmins (trombone); Fred Hunt (piano); Nevil Skrimshire (guitar); Frank Thompson (bass) and Pete Appleby (drums). Welsh, only five feet three/four tall, had a pronounced limp, a shy, hesitant manner and seemed an unlikely candidate for the rigours of bandleading. He was not over-conversant with jazz generally, his own record collection being limited and containing a fair proportion of ballads sung by Bing Crosby. But as sentimental pop songs were a known characteristic of the Condon repertoire, this would be consistent with Welsh's approach to jazz. His own playing, like Wild Bill Davison's, was a combination of 'rage and romanticism', as Humphrey Lyttelton put it in a broadcast tribute to the Welsh band after the leader's death on 25 June 1982.

Initially his band was considerably helped by Harold Pendleton of the National Jazz Federation. Pendleton presented the band at the Royal Festival Hall on 30 October 1954, their first major concert, well received. Their next appearance at this prestigious venue, sharing the bill with Ken Colyer's band, was much less of a success. Such were the fervent sectarian divisions of the time that Colyer's followers threw pennies at the Welsh band, this generosity accompanied by cries of 'Play some jazz!'

In a scene where the banjo bands were the most successful, the band had to scuffle, but it became a positive force in British jazz when Semple replaced Christie (Christie taking Semple's place in the Mulligan band) and ex-Randall drummer Lennie Hastings joined. This was a co-operative band and all the members met at the Blue Posts to appoint a nominal leader.

Surprisingly, Semple (who had led a band in Edinburgh with Welsh the trumpeter) and Lennie Hastings (who had co-led a band with trombonist Norman Cave that came out of the Randall band), did not bid for the job and thus the little guy with a diffident manner and a limp became the leader of one of the most exciting and memorable of British traditional-jazz bands.

The Welsh band, in its various manifestations, lasted for an incredible twenty-eight years, and throughout its history maintained an inner strength, a fierce loyalty to the 'family' that transcended the turmoils inherent in any co-operative unit. Like the Mulligan band, they acquired a reputation for 'raving'. Hastings and Semple were ardent tipplers, Hunt and Crimmins fairly moderate drinkers, but Welsh, initially, was strictly teetotal, and somewhat derisively labelled the 'Lemonade King'. The pressures of bandleading, however, soon led him to the bottle and a new soubriquet: the 'Vodka Monarch'.

Welsh, born in Edinburgh on 9 July 1929, started playing in a silver band in his home town. In conversation with Roy Crimmins in *Jazz Journal*, posthumously published in August 1982, he related how he sang harmonies with his father to Bing Crosby records. It was during a tour of Scotland with Mulligan that Crimmins first met Welsh and Semple and recalls how Semple was 'tippling nervously', while Welsh was teetotal and 'shy to a degree of silence'.

'You sound a bit like Wild Bill Davison,' said Crimmins.
'Who?'
'Wild Bill Davison.'
'Never heard of him.'

This disavowal notwithstanding, Wild Bill was to become the major influence on Welsh and in 1953 he came to London to join Dave Keir's short-lived band. On forming his own band in 1954, they trod the well-beaten path to the New Orleans Bier Bar in

The Condon Connection, the Three Bs and Traddy-pop 127

Dusseldorf, playing from 8.30 p.m. to 4.00 a.m. for the German equivalent of £18 per week. Crimmins recalled:

> We were rapturously received, made many friends and were treated like kings by the fans. And here Alex started drinking.
> The next ten years was full of one-night stands, concerts, broadcasts, TV and clubs, booze and arguments. We were a co-operative band; Alex [the pronunciation preferred by the band] took a few pounds more for doing the books and being the leader. Unfortunately he was very secretive by nature and would hold back information until the last second. The other five of us were usually impatient, often drunk and excitable and always very argumentative. Communication was often very strained.
> Our regular London club was at the Fishmongers Arms, Wood Green, run by Art and Viv Saunders. It was a bit like a London version of the Bier Bar in Dusseldorf. We made lifelong friends, particularly Laurie Ridley. In 1960 we started a yearly tour of Switzerland. Arch became ill and was replaced by several clarinettists, mostly Bruce Turner, Al Gay, John Barnes and Alan Cooper.
> Al was asked to join the band. He said, 'I'd love to, I love your music . . . but I don't drink and can't fight', a pointed reference to the boozing and arguments.
> A great moment was being chosen to support the Louis Armstrong All Stars on a tour of Great Britain, and when Jack Teagarden came here with the Earl Hines/Jack Teagarden All Stars in the autumn of 1957 Teagarden invited Alex to return to the States with him. The band accompanied Red Allen, Pee Wee Russell, Bud Freeman, Ruby Braff, Wild Bill Davison and others when the union ban was relaxed. It was a compliment to the band and all praised us warmly.

Crimmins left the band in 1965, to be replaced by Roy Williams, from Terry Lightfoot's band – much to Lightfoot's surprise and chagrin, as he was paying Williams more money than Welsh could afford. Semple left to be replaced by John Barnes, then by Al Gay. Semple died at the age of thirty-seven in August 1965, alcoholism the principal cause of his death.

Of all the characters in the jazz world, the band's drummer, Lennie Hastings, was one of the most amusing. Highly irascible, often drunk, his splenetic outbursts were punctuated with maniacal laughter. He wore a toupee, which he progressively tinted a lighter shade of grey and, eventually, even arranged a 'bald' patch on its crown, to lend verisimilitude to the pretence.

However, in his cups, he would rip it off, hurl it into the air, pretend to use one of his drumsticks as a gun and yell, 'The Glorious Twelfth starts tonight!' On the occasion he 'depped' for the regular drummer in Acker Bilk's band and he and Bilk, both well in their cups, swapped hair-pieces. His famous cry 'Ool-Ya-Koo!', preceding or following a drum break, was echoed throughout the audience and genuinely funny were his imitations of the fruity Austrian tenor, Richard Tauber; trouser-leg rolled up, a coin in his right eye to act as a monocle, his rendering of 'You are My Delight' always brought the house down. Clowning aside, Hastings was an excellent drummer in the mould of Condon regular George Wettling. He had a genuine love of the band's style and was essentially a *band* drummer, intelligently and sympathetically buttressing the soloists. He died of heart failure on 14 July 1973, aged fifty-one.

Other bands with a similar approach to the Welsh bands were led by trombonist Mike Collier and trumpeter Alan Littlejohn, and the many musicians associated with the genre included clarinettist Dave Shepherd (often with Randall), trombonist Jeremy French, trumpeters Bill Thompson, Gerry Salisbury and Alan Wickham, pianist Lennie Felix, guitarist Bill Bramwell and vibraphonist Ronnie Gleaves.

The relative success of the 'Condon' bands presented another side to the face of traditionalism, but their share of the business and acclaim did not match the popularity of the 'New Orleans' groups. These all employed the banjo, an instrument that had been unfashionable since its abandonment by the dance bands in the early thirties in favour of the guitar – its resurgence in the hands of the revivalists proved a boon to its manufacturers. They had never had it so good.

The instrument was the bedrock of these bands and was, as a result, much favoured by promoters. 'Show me a banjo and you show me a profit,' was the plangent and much-quoted cry from the cash register by the 100 Club's Roger Horton, no longer the quiet, self-effacing record-shop assistant he had been when his mother and Ted Morton ran the club.

JAZZ NEWS — Wednesday, April 11th

The Film Treat with the Cool Beat!

"Bursting with youthful vigour, this mixture of music and mirth is a tonic for the blues." — SUNDAY PICTORIAL

YOUR FAVOURITES PRESENT **25 GREAT NUMBERS**

"IT'S TRAD, DAD!"

STARRING

HELEN SHAPIRO

CRAIG DOUGLAS

CHUBBY CHECKER

SPECIAL GUEST STAR **JOHN LEYTON**

GARY (U.S.) BONDS

GENE VINCENT

BROOK BROTHERS

GENE McDANIELS

DEL SHANNON

CHRIS BARBER AND HIS BAND WITH—**OTTILIE PATTERSON**

Mr ACKER BILK AND HIS PARAMOUNT JAZZ BAND

KENNY BALL AND HIS JAZZMEN

TERRY LIGHTFOOT AND HIS NEW ORLEANS JAZZ BAND

TEMPERANCE SEVEN

BOB WALLIS AND HIS STORYVILLE JAZZ MEN

YOUR FAVOURITE DISC JOCKEYS
DAVID JACOBS · **PETE MURRAY** · **ALAN FREEMAN**

Screenplay by MILTON SUBOTSKY   Executive Producer MILTON SUBOTSKY
Directed by DICK LESTER   A COLUMBIA PICTURE
A BLC RELEASE

AND **BATTLE IN OUTER SPACE**

NATIONAL RELEASE STARTS SUNDAY NEXT

NORTH WEST LONDON AT:
† ACTON — Granada
† CALEDONIAN — Essoldo
† CAMDEN TOWN — Plaza
CHELSEA — Essoldo
EALING — Walpole
ENFIELD — Rialto
† FINSBURY PARK — Astoria
○ GOLDERS GREEN — Ionic
HAMMERSMITH — Broadway

HARRINGAY — Essoldo
HARROW ROAD — Prince of Wales
HENDON — Gaumont
ISLINGTON — Gaumont
† KILBURN — Grange
* NEW BARNET — Regal
† NOTTING HILL — Gaumont
QUEENSBURY — Essoldo
SHEPHERDS BUSH — Essoldo

† ST. ALBANS — Gaumont
* WALHAM GREEN — Gaumont
WATFORD — Gaumont (Not showing Wed. 18th)
WALHAM CROSS — Regent
WILLESDEN — Granada

ALSO SHOWING AT:
○ MAIDENHEAD — Plaza
NORWICH — Gaumont

PLYMOUTH — Drake
† SHREWSBURY — Granada
†* SLOUGH — Adelphi (For 5 days only)
†* WINDSOR — Regal

AND STILL AT THE
○ LONDON PAVILION

* 2nd Feature Varies.
† Starts Monday

The progress of British traditionalist jazz in all its aspects, from its beginnings in London suburbs by devotedly enthusiastic and often eccentric amateurs in the mid-forties to the relatively big business of the mid-fifties, was one thing, but for the bands involved in this phenomenon to become prominent in the Hit Parade (once the prerogative of the big dance bands, ballad singers and rock and roll groups), was quite another. It was a dramatic twist in the saga that had many heads shaking in wonderment, especially in Denmark Street, Britain's Tin Pan Alley, and its fellow thoroughfare, Archer Street.

These intrusions into the Hit Parade were indeed a surprising dimension to the popularity of a music once written off as 'archaic'. Such entries were described as 'freakish', but that epithet could apply equally to many other seeming non-starters in the notoriously unpredictable, but extremely lucrative world of the Top Twenty. Two such examples were the 'Third Man Theme' by zitherist Anton Karas and 'Oh Mein Papa' by dance-band trumpeter turned variety solo act, Eddie Calvert. The whims of a capricious public more than the machinations of wily entrepreneurs were the reason for these and other unexpected successes, but none was a jazz or even a jazz-related record.

The tentative entry of Colyer's 'Isle of Capri' into the charts in 1953 and Lyttelton's 'Bad Penny Blues' rising to number nineteen in these listings in 1956 had prepared the ground for this new development, and putting aside 'Rock Island Line' as a non-jazz hit, it was the Barber band, or rather a contingent from it, that was the first to reach the coveted number-one position, not only in Britain, but in America and on the Continent as well.

The record that achieved this stunning success was, like 'Bad Penny Blues', recorded at the end of a session, on 10 October 1956, to use up remaining studio time. The band had not even played this particular tune in public, and as only clarinettist Monty Sunshine knew it well, he recorded it with just Dick Bishop (banjo), Dick Smith (bass) and Ron Bowden (drums). The tune was 'Petite Fleur', a composition by Sidney Bechet. 'Petite Fleur' appeared initially on the LP *Chris Barber Plays – Volume 3* and was first released as a single in Germany and subsequently on the Laurie label in the United States. It had sold a million copies by

1960. Barber, appropriately in the presence of Sunshine, duly received his trade Gold Disc from TV personality Hughie Green.

The traditional-jazz world was amused by the astonished reaction to this success in Denmark and Archer Streets. There followed a stream of recordings of 'Petite Fleur' by orchestras whose leaders had probably never even heard of Sidney Bechet – and if they had, would no doubt have described him as an 'old-time Dixie merchant'. It is also very likely that they had not heard of Monty Sunshine either, although the name of Chris Barber had probably impinged on their consciousness by then.

Those jumping on the bandwagon were Ronnie Aldrich, Stanley Black, Cyril Stapleton, Victor Sylvester's Strict Tempo Ballroom Dancing Orchestra, the Knightsbridge Strings and the song duettists Teddy Johnson and Pearl Carr. In America it was recorded by Jerry Murad and His Harmonica Cats (a mouth-organ group) and by bands with genuine jazz credentials – Edmond Hall, Wilbur de Paris and His New Orleans Band and Gene Krupa. None of these, however, sold anywhere near the approximately two million of that lilting version by Monty Sunshine plus two.

It was yet another of the many ironies peppering jazz history that a master black jazzman, of whom very little was heard for the first twenty-five years of his professional life, who was brought into prominence in the late thirties through the impassioned and persistent advocacy of white critics, who recorded 'Petite Fleur' twice in 1952, both records selling only minimally, was to earn a fortune from royalties on a version of his tune recorded as an afterthought to use up studio time by a young British Jewish clarinettist with the aid of a two-piece rhythm section.

Naturally the effect on business for the Barber band was staggering: full houses for club and concert appearances alike. Large numbers of the general public, not particularly interested in jazz, swelled the crowds, but that these peripheral supporters were not converted into jazz fans proper was proved a few years later, when another kind of popular music, rock and roll in its various noisy manifestations, drew this fringe audience away from jazz.

In 1960 Monty Sunshine left the band and, for a change, there was none of the usual bland protestations that the split was mutual and amicable. In an interview with Max Jones in a *Melody Maker* of December 1960, Sunshine bluntly proclaimed that he had been sacked. Long before the much-publicized dismissal, however, there had been dissension, Sunshine being unhappy with the introduction of an electric guitar and the band's resultant emulation of Muddy Waters's R&B sound, which he likened to a bad imitation of the Shadows, Cliff Richard's accompanying group.

He formed his own band with Rod Mason (trumpet), Geoff Sowden (trombone), Johnny Parker (piano), Dickie Bishop (banjo), Gerry Salisbury (bass) and Nick Nicholls (drums), making his first recordings in March 1961. He has been leading a band ever since, and is particularly successful on the Continent.

The departure of Sunshine did not affect the band's success any more than the farewell of Lonnie Donegan, and its popularity was given a further boost by the addition of a female vocalist, Ottilie Patterson, a schoolteacher from Newtown, Eire. She made her debut with the band at a National Jazz Federation concert at the Royal Festival Hall, on 5 January 1955.

In a monograph on the Barber band discographer Brian Rust wrote:

> The audience was completely bewildered, captivated and amazed by the sight of Miss Patterson, a tiny fairy-like figure in a white frilly dress, looking as if she might manage 'Bless this House' in a quavery soprano, but in fact moaning the blues with a rich sombre majesty that recalled the heyday of Bessie Smith, Sara Martin and Margaret Johnson.

The Barber band was to extend its instrumentation further and embrace in its repertoire material not generally used by traditional-jazz bands. They continued to remain a highly popular band, although later they were forced to play extensive seasons on the Continent, despite attaining some celebrity outside the jazz world by appearing in the screen version of John Osborne's *Look Back in Anger*, the band's trumpeter, Pat Halcox, ghosting for the film's star, Richard Burton.

The inclusion of Bernard Bilk in the Ken Colyer band that

followed the break-up of the Colyer 'co-operative' in 1954 went unheeded, and on the evidence of Bilk's recordings with Colyer, he was just another George Lewis-inspired clarinettist. He had also recorded with banjoist John Bastable's Chosen Six and with trumpeter Bob Wallis.

Bernard Stanley 'Acker' Bilk was born in Pensfold, Somerset, on 28 January 1929, Acker a Somerset nickname for 'mate'. His first job was in a Wills tobacco factory in Bristol. After leaving, he worked for a blacksmith, then in 1945 worked as a builder's labourer for his uncle Arthur. In 1948 Bilk was conscripted in the Royal Engineers and drafted to the Suez Canal Zone where he taught himself how to play clarinet on a borrowed military instrument. He was sent to the glasshouse for sleeping on guard duty, and as a result had many hours to practise in a cell awaiting his court-martial.

Demobbed, he formed his own semi-professional band in Bristol before joining Colyer in 1945. He resumed bandleading in 1958 with West Country musicians, Johnny Stainer (trumpet), Johnny Skuse (trombone), Dave Collett (piano), Jay Hawkins (banjo), Johnny Macey (bass) and Ray Smith (drums), billed as Acker Bilk and His Paramount Jazz Band. After they played a sixteen-day festival in Poland, their return to Britain was headlined in the *Melody Maker*, but referred only to the Paramount Jazz Band, no mention being made of its leader. He, however, in an interview, produced one of the most quoted remarks in jazz. Asked how the band had been received behind the Iron Curtain, Bilk rasped in his strong Somerset, cider-drenched accent, 'Man, they went *beresk*!'

It was the kind of response he was soon to enjoy in his own country with a different band of London-based musicians, but this success was not achieved without a hard struggle. Initially, the band virtually lived in a Plaistow factory owned by a fan, Alan Gatwood, and it was kept together by beating the trail to the Bier Bar, Dusseldorf. This venue, like many other German clubs, was a life-saver for many British traditional bands, the Germans surprisingly conceiving a strong and long-lasting affection for the looseness of New Orleans collective improvisation. On returning to London, Bilk signed to the Lyn Dutton Agency and was helped to become a household name by donning a band uniform, an

NEW ORLEANS JOYS

(FROM THE DIARY OF T. L. GATE, ESQUIRE)

..... BUT lately arrived in London Town, I wandered This Day towards the Eastern Extremities of Oxford Street, there to disport Myself (as I thought) among the Pleasure Booths which surround the Gastronomic Emporium erected by Mr. J. Lyons. It was not to be. More than a Furlong to the West, my Ear was beguiled in so Tempting a Fashion by the Mellifluous Sounds proceeding from a Basement Saloon situate at No. 100 that I could not forbear to allow my Feet to carry me Thither. O Happy Pedal Error! What Transports of Delight derived from so Seemingly Trivial an Incident! For, securely Ensconced on a Dais among the Denizens of this Subterranean Hall, there I descried the Noble Countenance and Dignified Mien of that Pillar of Metropolitan Diurnal Entertainment, Mr. Acker Bilk. Surrounded by his Elegant Ensemble, the Paramount Jazz Men, oblivious of the Clatter of Omnibuses and Hansoms, the Piercing Oaths of their Jehus, and the Mingled Entreaties and Abuse of the Street Hawkers and Peddlers of Drugged Cheroots in the Open Air Far Above, Mr. Bilk bent to his Artistic Will the Intricacies of his Clarionet. Fashioned by the Nimble Fingers of this Paragon and his Myrmidons, the Notes flew out in that Style Much Favoured in the American City of New Orleans : so Spirited in its Execution, so Subtle and Melodious in Conception that I would Fain have thrown Discretion to the Wind and Cast in my Lot with those Disciples of Terpsichore gyrating upon the Floor.

★   ★   ★

In a Trice I had Doffed my Cap, removed my Ulster and handed these, together with my Wallet, Watch and Chain, and a Small Satchel containing Provisions, to a Courteous Usher, and proceeded to avail Myself of the Stimuli Attendant upon the Recital. My Word! These Lads are not Undeserving of their Titular Epithet! Over the Entire Surface of the Globe, can there be another Sextet so Worthy of their Applause ? What a Superlative Crew, indeed!

★   ★   ★

A Civil Enough Fellow clad in a Leathern Jerkin, who chanced to be Seated beside me, favoured me with the Intelligence that it was Mr. Bilk's Wont to Lavish his Art upon the Members of this Establishment at All Times when he was not following the not Ignoble Course of taking his Music to beguile those Citizens residing in Less Fortunate Regions of the Kingdom. Happy indeed, then, said I, are the Members. For, in the Opinion of yr. Scribe, there can be no more Entertaining Pursuit than that of listening to—Ay, and watching as well—its Purveyors, Caparisoned as they are in a Seemly Admixture of Gaily Striped Waistcoats, Pristine Shirting, Sombre Nether Garments and Hard Hats. . . .

★

As, later, I reluctantly mounted the Stairs and emerged into the Ruby, Amber and Green Illuminations which so Characterize Nocturnal London, I could scarce repress a loud Huzzah! —but contented myself by venturing to cast my Cap high into the Air as Some Measure of expressing my Exaltation.

... with Mr. ACKER BILK
AND HIS PARAMOUNT JAZZ BAND

SOLE REPRESENTATION : THE LYN DUTTON AGENCY LTD.
8, GREAT CHAPEL STREET, OXFORD STREET, LONDON, W.I.   GER 7494

Leaflet designed by Peter Leslie.   PUT 0062

inspired publicity gimmick. This apparel consisted of narrow-bottom trousers, pin-striped waistcoats, string ties and curly-brimmed bowler hats. The billing was 'Mr' Acker Bilk and His Paramount Jazz Band and their blurbs were couched in florid Edwardian prose, the names of the leader and the personnel given in full. All this was originally the brainchild of David Backhouse, working for *Jazz News*, but it was later taken up by an astute one-time *Melody Maker* staffman turned publicity officer, Peter Leslie.

The gimmicks aside, the earthy rural personality of the leader was itself an astounding success. George Melly, in *Owning Up*, wrote:

> At first sight he was an unlikely totem for a teenage religion. With his little beard and balding head, and a decided waddle, he looked more like a retired pirate than anything else. He revealed a basic if sympathetic sense of humour based on his West Country burr, the catchphrase 'watch out' and the frequent interjections in his public pronouncements of a noise that can only be described as sounding like a vigorous but watery fart. But none of this can explain his deification in the early months of 1960. As it was, Acker became a password among the young, and the bowler hat, usually daubed round the crown in whitewash, a cult object.
>
> His more extreme followers wore, not only the bowler, but army boots, potato sacks and old fur coats, cut down to look like stone-age waistcoats. This outfit became known as 'Rave Gear', an expression allegedly coined by an eccentric jazz-club promoter called Uncle Bonn (Bonny Manzi) who encouraged the wearing of this gear at his chain of clubs.

The band recorded for Carlo Krahmer's Esquire label, for record-shop proprietor Doug Dobell's '77' label, and Nixa, but their first success was an LP for the Pye label called *Mr Acker Bilk Requests*, which went to the top of the jazz Hit Parade. An LP for Columbia, entitled *The Seven Ages of Acker*, headed the jazz best-sellers for the first four months of 1960, but it was Bilk's first single, 'Summer Set', recorded on 10 March 1959, that became a number-one hit in the UK. Again, this involved only a contingent from the main band, with Bilk, his former West Country colleague (and composer of the piece) Dave Collett (piano), Ernie Price (bass), Roy James (banjo) and Ron McKay (drums).

Colin Smith, formerly with Terry Lightfoot, replaced Ken Sims on trumpet in August 1960, playing with the band that recorded 'White Cliffs of Dover', 'Buona Sera' and 'That's My Home', all hit singles. In July 1961 the band had four records simultaneously in the jazz Top Ten.

It was 'Stranger on the Shore' that established Bilk as an internationally famed star. The idea came from the nimble-brained Denis Preston, who asked Bilk to write a couple of bluesy tunes to be played with the Leon Young String Chorale, assembled for studio work only. Its global sales were staggering – two million, the first million sold by April 1962. It was the first ever record to achieve the number-one position in the UK and US simultaneously. It remained in the charts for a record-breaking fifty-three weeks. The tune was recorded in 1964 by Duke Ellington, featuring baritone saxophonist Harry Carney, but Bilk, while accepting the honour of a Ducal recording of his tune, insists that the middle eight bars are incorrectly played.

'Stranger on the Shore' represented an incredible success for the one-time blacksmith's apprentice who taught himself clarinet in a military gaol and who had come into the Colyer band almost unnoticed. His style of playing has slowly moved away from imitation of George Lewis and he is a much better exponent of the instrument than his critics, contemptuous of his financial success, would allow. He once recorded in the company of Sandy Brown and Terry Lightfoot and, while not matching the flow and inventiveness of Brown, he nevertheless acquitted himself admirably and certainly outplayed Lightfoot.

Ken Colyer's 'Isle of Capri' excepted, the successful British jazz bands in the Hit Parade had been contingents from the bands of Lyttelton, Barber and Bilk (and Bilk with the Leon Young Strings). The first full band success in this elevated area of showbiz fell to Kenny Ball's Jazzmen, with 'Samantha' in 1961, followed by 'Midnight in Moscow', 'March of the Siamese Children', 'Sukiyaki' and 'Hawaiian War Chant'.

Born in Ilford, 22 May 1930, Ball, unlike most trad-jazz musicians, possessed a technique and ability to read. He had played with Sid Phillips's 'Archer Street Dixie' band and with

The Condon Connection, the Three Bs and Traddy-pop

show drummer Eric Delaney's band where he was one of five trumpeters, his previous experience having been with Charlie Galbraith's semi-professional band.

He formed his first band as late as 1957, with Charlie Galbraith (trombone), Dave Jones (clarinet), Pat Mason (piano), John Potter (banjo), Brian Prudence (bass) and Johnny Welling (drums). He also recorded with Terry Lightfoot in January 1958 where on 'Snag It' he displayed the panache of a virtuoso. After the struggles inevitable with a new-formed unit, the success of 'Midnight in Moscow' rocketed the band to the big time.

Shrewdly, Ball continued with the sound that made him so successful and he swiftly became the darling of BBC producers, regularly appearing on 'Easy Beat', on 'Bandbox', 'Saturday Club', 'Parade of the Pops', 'Go, Ma Go' and 'Trad Fad'. On television he appeared on Lonnie Donegan's 'Sunday Break', 'Thank Your Lucky Stars' and 'Showcase'.

It was about this time that the derogatory term 'traddy-pop' was coined and the Ball band became closely associated with this uncomplimentary epithet. The Ball records were pretty, and neatly performed, sanitized revivalism that easily found its way to the drawing-room coffee tables and to the turntables of the disc jockeys, whose own meretricious popularity related solely to the frequency with which they played what the public wanted to hear. The band's formula met with tepid critical response, and not even the leader's own meritorious playing redeemed the general sound in the eyes of these pundits. But then the public generally paid little attention to critics.

The coincidence of the surnames of the three principals in this upsurge of traditional jazz all starting with 'B' led inevitably to the 'Three Bs' tag, promoters falling over themselves to book them, but these represented only the apex of this phenomenon. By the end of the fifties, there were hundreds of similar-styled bands throughout the country; a bubbling nationwide activity.

The trad phenomenon also inspired a book, *Trad Mad* by Brian Matthew, and a film, *It's Trad, Dad*, with Kenny Ball, Terry Lightfoot, Chris Barber, Bob Wallis and their bands, the Temperance Seven and an assortment of rock and roll artistes introduced by DJs Pete Murray, David Jacobs and Alan Freeman, directed by Dick Lester and generally sharing the cinema bill with an epic called *Battle in Outer Space*.

In October 1961, the Bilk and Ball bands and the Temperance Seven were part of the Royal Command Performance at the London Palladium.

The trad boom unfortunately also brought about the only known example of hooliganism at a jazz function. The word 'Raver', hitherto a happy synonyn for harmless hedonism – drinking, dancing, lovemaking – swiftly acquired another and unwelcome connotation. A group of hooligans dressed in 'rave gear' booed the modern band at the Beaulieu Festival in 1959, run by Lord Montagu, and climbed the scaffolding to make their protests. Ken Allsopp, writing in the *Daily Mail*, 1 August 1959, wrote an article attacking the hooligans, and referred to them as being supporters of Acker Bilk's Paramount Jazz Band, a 'brash, noisy, dixieland outfit that is their present darling'.

By 1959 the following traditional bands – in addition to the Three Bs – were 'on the road'. Eric Allandale and His Band, Micky Ashman and His Ragtime Band, Gerry Brown's Jazzmen (from Bournemouth), Ken Barton's Oriole Jazz Band, Ian Bell's Jazzmen, Back o' Town Syncopators, Glasgow's Clyde Valley Stompers and Forrie Cairns (with Fiona Duncan), Ed Corrie Jazzmen, Mike Cotton's Jazzmen, Ken Colyer's Jazzmen, Alan Elsdon's Jazz Band, Trevor Kaye's Trad Kings, Terry Lightfoot's New Orleans Jazzmen, London City Stompers, Mick Mulligan and His Band with George Melly, Dougie Richford Jazzmen, Mike Daniels's Delta Jazz Band, Monty Sunshine and His Band, Sims-Wheeler Vintage Jazz Band, Alex Welsh and His Band, Dick Charlesworth and His City Gents and Bob Wallis and His Storyville Jazz Band. Competing with these were the 'mainstream' bands of Humphrey Lyttelton, the Fairweather–Brown All Stars, Bruce Turner and His Jump Band and, on a semi-professional basis, Wally Fawkes and His Troglodytes.

This listing of bands operating in the trad boom is by no means complete, and the emphasis is on those based in London. Many of these included musicians who had migrated from the provinces and Scotland, some of them, like Alex Welsh, Forrie Cairns, Sandy Brown, Al Fairweather, Acker Bilk, Bob Wallis, Ken Sims and Dick Charlesworth, later to lead bands themselves.

The BBC, not an institution famed for its recognition of jazz, quickly latched on to trad and the bands playing in this style were soon regularly in the studios, Ball in particular.

Agents representing this type of attraction would actually *receive* calls from producers and the contracts department requesting the services of these bands. Prior to traddy-pop a jazz-band agent or manager could make call after call to unsympathetic producers with little or no result. Now the situation was reversed, but nevertheless the booking would invariably be accompanied by the firm instruction that half the numbers out of a total of, say, six, had to be 'bright', meaning up-tempo. Jollity was obligatory.

The publishers in Denmark Street and its environs, long preoccupied with churning out tunes for big bands, and for singers like Alma Cogan and Frankie Vaughan, were suddenly, frantically, searching around for material to offer to the new stars, many apparently unaware that the bands were already playing compositions long in their own catalogues, some from the early and mid-twenties, such as the Jelly Roll Morton compositions in the Darewski catalogue.

Some of the publishers' staffmen attempted to write tunes they thought suitable. 'I've got a really nice Dixie number for you, *bhoy*,' was a phrase that became familiar to bandleaders receiving approaches from A and R men. None of these was of any value compared with the treasury of compositions written and recorded by the New Orleans pioneers in the twenties.

Many Archer Street musicians cast envious eyes on the activity that was affecting their livelihood and one was quoted as saying he would like to know 'how to get in on this trad lark'. Even had he attempted such, it would have been obvious to the trad fans that he was an unwelcome opportunist. Professional dance-band musicians 'doing a Dixie', were met with suspicion by the young people, dressed in their 'rave gear', holding fixed views on the righteousness of trad jazz and imbued, if only vaguely, with an awareness that the music had been born out of struggle.

When the author first came into the business as the manager of George Webb's Dixielanders, there were no jazz-band agents, simply because there were virtually no jazz bands. I was one of the first to form an agency solely to handle jazz bands, starting in 1951 with Mick Mulligan's band, Chris Barber's New Orleans Jazz Band and a newly-constituted Crane River Jazz Band. Others were George Cooper, representing Freddy Randall, and later, James Tate and Ruby Bard representing Bob Wallis and Dick Charlesworth, but we were all small-time operators compared with the success that later attended Lyn Percy Tomlin Dutton.

Dutton was one of the many who took the train from Charing Cross to Barnehurst every Monday to hear George Webb's Dixielanders, travelling and returning with Lyttelton and Fawkes in the mid to late forties. He became Lyttelton's manager when Lyttelton left the Dixielanders, and opened up a small office at 84 Newman Street. This mild-mannered but shrewd man, a one-time member of the Communist Party, later to become an entrepreneurial mogul, was, at the height of the trad boom, representing most of the trad bands, including Acker Bilk and Chris Barber. In one advertisement he listed twenty bands under his direction.

The big dance-band agents, such as Harold Davison, were compelled to recognize the existence of traditional jazz as a money-spinner. Jack Higgins in the Davison office successfully pitched for many of Dutton's bands, including Barber and Lightfoot, Dutton himself eventually joining the Davison organization. This was, however, a short-lived association.

As the smell of blood in the deepest ocean mysteriously attracts sharks apparently from nowhere, so did the trad craze draw all manner of individuals keen to make a killing. Most of them were totally uninterested in jazz. One of them, now promoting music for skinheads and punks, was a veritable Fagin in both reputation and appearance, his name still a byword among musicians of the trad era for his dishonesty.

Commercial success, however, soon brought condemnation from those, many early revivalists, musicians and fans, who despised the emptiness of much traddy-pop. What had once been a genuinely evangelical movement, a stimulating renaissance, had led to dull stereotype with the guilty parties appearing on the stand in all sorts of fancy dress. Not that this bothered what had now become another stereotype: the trad-jazz fan, one who prior to the fad had never collected jazz records and was only dimly aware of the music's history, but who was now very much attracted to the attenuated form that presented itself in a myriad of clubs throughout the country. George Melly, in *Owning Up*, wrote:

> What was infuriating about trad fans *en masse* was their complete intolerance of any form of jazz which fell outside their own narrow predilection. Of course it could be argued that we had been pretty biased in our early days, but in our favour we were fighting for a neglected music in the face of indifference and ridicule and furthermore our idols were the great originals. The trad fans neither knew nor cared about Morton and Oliver, Bessie Smith or Bunk Johnson. It was exclusively British trad they raved about and although it was the better bands that went to the top, any group, however abysmal, was sure of a respectful hearing as long as the overall sound was right. The basis of that sound, the instrument which provided the heartbeat of the trad monster, was the dullest and most constricting of noises, a banjo played chung, chung, chung, smack on the beat.

Even the inventive jitterbugging that had enlivened the clubs in the late forties and early fifties had been replaced by a graceless clodhopping called 'skip jive'.

Jazz Journal editor Sinclair Traill who, in 1950, had initially castigated the tyro revivalists with the admonition: 'Now, kiddies – this won't do', was, in 1952, more kindly disposed towards the obvious improvements that had been made. But in January 1959 he looked back nostalgically to the rough and ready ways of the first traditionalists in his review of an album by Micky Ashman's Ragtime Band.

> During the early revivalist days I reviewed a record by that pioneer 'trad' group, John Haim and His Jelly Roll Kings, playing 'Kansas City Shuffle', and it suffered all, and more, the technical limitations of the other sides under review. But Haim had something – call it heat, intensity, spirit, atmosphere ... whatever ... that is lacking in the Ashman group. The latter has nothing to offset the stereotyped phrases and the general scruffiness. And that banjo! Its grim determination to be heard. Like a malicious zombie it chunters through the ensembles ...

In the issue dated June 1962, Traill was equally caustic about

Sheffield clarinettist Dick Charlesworth and His City Gents' LP injudiciously entitled *Yes, It's the Gents*: 'Everything I don't like about the current trad fad – incompetent musicianship, a thumping rhythm which can't even hold the beat and some of the most awful vocals imaginable. The album's title is perhaps more apt than the organizers of the session believed. Yes, indeed, it's the Gents . . .'

One aspect of the boom which attracted derisory comment was the bands' dress, for the sartorial aspect of Bilk's success was inevitably aped by others. Dick Charlesworth led his City Gents attired in formal City wear – pin-striped trousers, jackets and the 'modern' (as opposed to the curly-brimmed Bilk headwear) bowler hat. They featured a lusty-voiced vocalist from Liverpool, Jackie Lynn.

Trumpeter Bob Wallis, from Bridlington, and his Storyville Jazz Band dressed as Mississippi gamblers, attiring themselves in striped shirts, string ties, box-jackets, high-heeled boots and wide-brimmed hats. Belatedly (and commercially ineffectually), a much older musician, Bobby Mickleburgh, was prevailed upon by his agent, George Cooper, to form a band dressed in the uniforms of Confederate soldiers – called, unsurprisingly, Bobby Mickleburgh and His Confederates, and lasting only a few months.

It was this rash of outlandish apparel that made traddy-pop seem like a comic exercise, but such imitation was to be expected. Just as expected was the attempt by so many bands to produce the traddy-pop hit single that would get them air time and large crowds, but most of them were complete failures. Alex Welsh, with 'Rose Marie' and 'Tansy' (where the ubiquitous banjo was used in a fruitless attempt to cash in), crept into the lower reaches of the charts, but no more.

Some of the bandleaders involved in the trad craze were quoted on the phenomenon in the musical press.

Micky Ashman in *Jazz News*: 'Trad jazz seems to have become a commercial proposition and a good way to earn a living. The real danger to traditional jazz is rhythm and blues!'

Terry Lightfoot in *Jazz News*: 'I will not be forsaking the club circuit.'

Kenny Ball (quoted from an interview with Judith Simons in the

Daily Express): 'Trad was invented by promoters as a stop gap when the pop scene went thankfully flat. The craze is now over.'

But in the general ebullience proclaiming that traditional-jazz musicians had never had it so good, there was one dissenting voice: Ken Colyer's. 'I'll have no truck with trad,' he growled.

It was now a fact, though, that the better-known exponents of what had become nationally and internationally known as trad were in showbiz proper, rubbing shoulders with Frankie Vaughan and the like. Records of the three Bs, particularly Ball's hits and Bilk's with strings, lay alongside albums by Shirley Bassey, Mantovani and Frank Sinatra on the coffee tables. The bandleaders could afford to shrug off the complaints of the righteous. As for the sidemen, even those who shared the disillusionment stuck with it, for the alternative was – to use a cliché of the time – getting a 'proper job'. The philosophy of 'It's better than working' still applied.

If any of the musicians were unhappy about the way traditional jazz had shaped they could always leave. The movement had produced an extraordinarily high number of players capable of playing in the idiom, many working in 'proper jobs' they would gladly have left to play music of any kind full time.

The complaints that the coinage had been debased usually came from those who didn't have to earn their living at music. The commercial success attending this kind of jazz had taken the wind out of the sails of the missionaries, many of whom were miffed that it was no longer a private, esoteric experience but – heaven forbid! – now enjoyed by the masses. And who could really blame the exponents of trad for continuing as they were? In a way their situation was parallel to that of the pre-war dance-band musician who would have preferred to play jazz, but who was compelled to grind out ordinary dance music. The revivalists, with a few exceptions, had to grind out trad.

It was useless to lament the passing of the pristine innocence which had characterized George Webb, Freddy Randall, Humphrey Lyttelton, the Crane River Jazz Band, John Haim, Sandy Brown and the rest of the pioneers. It was not the first time that genuine missionary zeal had been replaced by commercial greed, but there was no doubt that the basic characteristics – the tunes, the phrasing, the collective improvisation – had become impoverished by constant reiteration of their more obvious and publicly acceptable features.

Withal, trad remained, albeit in a somewhat bastardized form, the whites' tribute to the black pioneers from New Orleans, an extraordinary happening that sprang initially from the writings of a few dedicated collectors producing little magazines in their 'dens' in the early to mid-forties. Their espousal of the obscure led to this mammoth interest.

Much as the validity of revivalism and especially its trad manifestation was mocked, it was nevertheless indisputable that many fine musicians emerged in that hyperactive period, Ernest Borneman's avowal that the revival (in Britain and elsewhere) had not produced one player of genius notwithstanding. When, in the sixties, individual US jazz musicians visited Britain to be accompanied by British revivalists they were quite genuine in their praise of the home players and there is convincing evidence of local players' skill on the many gramophone records of the time. Most of these players were not born before 1920, a few had been born after 1930; all were in their adolescence between the beginnings of revivalism and the sixties, and when they retire or die there will be few to take their places: there is virtually no 'Second Line'.

In the late seventies the Tally Ho pub, Kentish Town, north-west London, with a long tradition of jazz under its roof when run by publican Jim Delaney in the sixties, restarted jazz sessions with a young band of musicians barely out of their teens, but they had come to the music too late to absorb its essence, excellent as their musicianship was. Unlike the early revivalists whose record collections were of New Orleans musicians, these young men at the Tally Ho in 1978 had been subject to a massive onslaught of rock and roll. Keen as they were, they hadn't the single-minded dedication of the older men, many of whom had to be called in as 'guests' to bolster this young band: trumpeters like Alan Littlejohn, Colin Smith, Digby Fairweather and Alan Elsdon. The so-called imitators of the fifties were now the accomplished veterans who knew the ropes.

Happily, most of those who commenced playing in the exploratory forties and early fifties are still active, even if, like

Wally Fawkes, Jeremy French, Ian Christie and Alan Littlejohn, they play on a semi-professional basis only. Lyttelton, now in his late sixties, can look back on over forty continuous years of bandleading, an astonishing feat, and not far behind him in longevity is Chris Barber. The culture of another race in another time has been lovingly perpetuated by these British musicians, and the best survived the worst of the trad excesses, but the truth is that by the end of the century those that are still playing will be in their seventies and, feasibly, will be looked upon with the same respectful awe accorded by the zealots to the last of the line in New Orleans in the 1960s. They can look back on great days: the tours, tumbling out of the wagon in the early hours and up a few hours later for another spell on the road, the fans, the girls, the black humour in the bandwagon and, in their early days, the sense of excitement at coming to grips with an alien idiom.

But the trad balloon had to burst. Since the early fifties rock and roll had been slowly gaining ground, coexisting with jazz, with little indication that in the early sixties a manifestation of it was to explode with a fury that would echo round the world, these shock waves emanating principally from two British groups. In *Jazz News* (November 1962) there appeared a small display advertisement, measuring three by two and a half inches and costing approximately ten shillings. It was for a 'rhythm and blues' group called the Rolling Stones. They, and the Beatles, and many more from Liverpool, burst upon the popular-music scene and the impact was to have a shattering effect on jazz. The balloon didn't burst overnight, but Beatlemania and Merseybeat in the early sixties accelerated its end. The forty-odd traditional-style bands on the road were reduced to a mere handful: Barber, Bilk, Ball, Colyer, Welsh. The rest couldn't find the work to keep going. The trad clubs folded. The opportunist promoters quickly latched on to what then was called 'beat' music.

Two of the traditional bands, however, made a fairly successful transition to a combination of jazz and rhythm and blues. Mike Cotton formed his Mike Cotton Sound, backing American soul singers like Doris Troy, Solomon Burke and Sugar Pie DeSanto, running from 1964–71, after which he joined a rock group, the Kinks, before joining Acker Bilk in 1973. Trumpeter Alan Elsdon, after stints with Cy Laurie, Graham Stewart and Terry Lightfoot, formed his own band in 1961, the same time as Cotton, with the end of the trad era in sight. Elsdon then formed his Voodoo Band along the same lines as Cotton, and worked in cabaret with Cilla Black, Dionne Warwick and the Isley Brothers. Reverting to formal jazz, his band temporarily backed George Melly when the latter returned to the road in 1970.

Beatlemania eventually died, but left rock in its wake. Jazz recovered to an extent, and the bands that survived continued to work steadily, albeit not to the enormous crowds they had known in the fifties. Work on the BBC was infrequent, and of all the London clubs that were once home to the ringing banjo, only the 100 Club in its central location still continues its traditionalist policy, although one night is given to contemporary jazz and another two to rock music. It must be an unnerving experience for old habitués of 100 Oxford St, unwittingly walking down those familiar stairs, to hear the screaming of amplified guitars instead of the comforting chug of the banjo.

Even if there are still many who will not accept the British contribution as having any lasting validity, the fact remains that this revivalist activity generally helped to restore to their proper glory many of the pioneers whose fortunes had languished in the thirties, and created a climate in which these pioneers were able to visit us and play to enthusiastic audiences, to our delight and to the edification of local musicians.

During the trad hoo-ha the deaths of two players, utterly different in background and influence, but significant each in his own way, went virtually unnoticed.

In October 1956 clarinettist Harry Parry was found dead in a Mayfair bedsitting room. He was forty-four.

During the thirties he was virtually an unknown musician working in second-division dance bands, before BBC producer Charles Chilton heard him at the St Regis Hotel, Mayfair and booked him to lead the Radio Rhythm Club Sextet playing weekly on the corporation's weekly half-hour jazz allocation.

It was another of the ironies attending the annals of jazz in Britain that this previously unknown figure without a single recording to his name as a sideman or soloist, should have become something of a household name – and on the strength of his BBC shows touring the halls in the late forties. Like his fellow Archer Street jazzmen, however, he was subsequently engulfed by the twin upsurge of revivalism and bebop. He disliked both, but attempted to hop on the traditional bandwagon by making two sides with his 'Ragtimers' that included a banjo and sousaphone. During the fifties he led conventional bands at Butlin's holiday camps. His records, with such excellent musicians as pianist George Shearing, vibraphonist Roy Marsh, trumpeter Dave Wilkins and guitarist Lauderic Caton, stand up well these forty years later. His own playing was neat, the line was somewhat predictable. Purists like James Asman castigated him, but in 1984 BBC Records issued a compilation of his 78s which was favourably reviewed in the specialist press.

In the *Melody Maker* of 26 February 1961 it was announced that Nick La Rocca, trumpeter/leader of the Original Dixieland Jazz Band, had died on 22 February, two months short of his seventy-second birthday. In April 1919, when he and the Dixieland band came to England with their instrumentation of trumpet, clarinet, trombone, piano and drums, and their spirited collective improvisation, it was a culture shock for the natives, and nobody (including the band itself) could have foreseen that the original form of the music they played would be performed by hundreds of bands with similar instrumentation three decades later.

7
Towards the Centre

By the mid-fifties revivalism, in all its manifestations, had become an integral part of the British popular-entertainment scene, but at the same time many musicians passionately committed to the cause were already showing signs of restiveness about the way it was developing, long before the despised traddy-pop became yet another factor to increase their misgivings further.

These musicians became part of a breakaway movement that bore the tag 'mainstream', a term first employed and thereafter assiduously propagated by the English critic Stanley Dance, who went to live and make recordings in America in the late fifties. Dance wrote a regular column for *Jazz Journal* called 'Lightly and Politely' in which he eloquently and dogmatically protested the merits of black musicians, particularly in the bands of Duke Ellington, Count Basie, Fletcher Henderson, Luis Russell, Chick Webb, Claude Hopkins, Don Redman, Lucky Millinder and the like, despite the fact that by the time he was writing his column Duke Ellington and Count Basie were virtually the only survivors of the big black bands that had flourished in the thirties.

Some of these had adapted to the Dixieland style despite never having played in this superannuated way. These players included trumpeters Teddy Buckner (from Lionel Hampton's band), Sidney de Paris (from Don Redman's band), Alvin Alcorn (from Don Albert's band) and trombonists Sandy Williams (from Chick Webb's band) and Jimmy Archey (from Luis Russell's band). Clarinettists Omer Simeon (from Earl Hines's band) and Ed Hall (from Claude Hopkins's band) – both from New Orleans – and Darnell Howard (also from Hines's band) easily fitted into the traditional ensembles. But Dance didn't travel three thousand miles to record 'Dixieland'.

He was extremely critical of revivalism and of modern jazz,

Dizzy Gillespie coming in for his special opprobrium in the latter context. A forthright writer, he made no bones about his likes and dislikes, and he had a particular feeling for the fine soloists from the bands that had broken up, many of whom had been left out in the cold in the fashionable polarization of revivalism and bebop.

Mainstream, in essence, was not new. Small combinations featuring solos in loosely sketched arrangements had been active in the thirties, but many talented players who had become rootless since the big bands broke up were assembled for various sessions to play music that had previously borne no stylistic designation. The first to produce recordings of this kind was veteran critic and record producer (his first supervision going back as far as 1933) John Hammond, these issued on the Vanguard label in 1954. They brought attention to musicians like the white cornettist Ruby Braff and pianist Sir Charles Thompson and revived interest in clarinettist Ed Hall, already known to the British public for his work with Claude Hopkins and on the Brunswick *New Orleans* album.

These records showed the middle way between the extremes of traditionalism and 'modern' bop and certainly the gentle propulsion of pianist Thompson, bassist Walter Page, guitarist Steve Jordan, drummers Les Erskine and Jo Jones (on different sessions) in the rhythm section, particularly caught the ears of those revivalists who were fast becoming disillusioned with the dull metronomic thump of the banjo, so much a characteristic of trad. These recordings were too sophisticated for the dyed-in-the-wool tradder and not harmonically complex enough for the modernist. It was music made for renegade traditionalists!

The Vanguard records, although highly rated, were not given any particular category, but once Dance had his first sessions released on Felsted (a subsidiary of Decca) in 1958, the tag 'mainstream' became another category of jazz, this categorization helping to establish its genre in the buff's vocabulary. There were (and still are) many critics who, nobly professing 'broadmindedness', decried yet another label. 'It's all jazz,' they would declaim – 'away with these divisive pigeonholes!' 'Let's all pull together in splendid amity,' were their pious cries. By now, however, it was a fact that jazz had become an art of many parts, each facet warranting a description in terms of which it was critically appraised and packaged by promoters and record producers. The simple dichotomy of 'traditional' and 'modern' had become subdivided, and by the late fifties yet another development, free-form, had to be added to the list of categories, despite the fact that to many this bore little relationship to jazz as it had been known hitherto.

Of course, there was nothing new in stylistic categorization. Even in the twenties, there had been several classifications. Then there was 'New York' style (Bix Beiderbecke, Red Nichols, Miff Mole, the Dorseys, Joe Venuti, Eddie Lang); 'Chicago Style' (Condon, McPartland, Freeman); white jazz and black jazz; although in those days 'New Orleans', as a style, was barely mentioned – so little was known about the music's origins.

Quite independently of any self-conscious mainstream influences, many British traditionalists had been moving away from what had become a hackneyed stereotype. Lyttelton, for instance – his big-band collaborations with Graeme Bell, using two saxophones, dropping the banjo, his employment of Bruce Turner – these were indications of deviationism. Generally speaking, the renegade traditionalists were happy to identify with Dance's label.

Lyttelton, wearing his critic's cap, warmly espoused these mainstream recordings and, given his earlier departures from the conventional mould, it was no surprise that he rapidly shifted his stylistic ground and was foremost, with his own band, in establishing mainstream jazz in Britain. An international crisis, however, was the catalyst of a crucial personnel change that accelerated his changes in policy. The sixth (including Max Abrams) of his drummers was Stan Greig, the percussionist on 'Bad Penny Blues', but in October 1956, due to the Suez Crisis, Greig, a 'Z' reservist, was called up and sent to Egypt. He was replaced by Eddie Taylor, who had been with the Johnny Dankworth Seven for three years, and then with the Don Rendell Six. It was apparent that his inspiration came from Max Roach rather than Baby Dodds. In his *Second Chorus*, Lyttelton wrote:

> We took Eddie Taylor as a substitute – and quite by accident the metamorphosis took place in the band's style. When Stan returned I had to

make a choice. Both were excellent drummers, both enthusiastic and congenial members of the band. It was a hard judgement to make. But in reality the answer was clear. Musically we had embarked upon a new course and had to stick by it. In a small socially compact unit like a band paying off even a bad and unco-operative musician is distasteful enough. It is doubly so to have to sacrifice a keen and accomplished player through circumstances beyond anyone's control.

While this is true, there is also no doubt that reference to the metamorphosis being an accident is disingenuous. Already the band was vastly different in style from his first in 1948. Already he had been the heretical traditionalist alienating many of his pure-in-heart followers. His next significant step was to replace pianist Johnny Parker with Ian Armit. Again from *Second Chorus*:

> When, in the course of things, it became necessary to alter the composition of our rhythm section, I consulted with Eddie. A rhythm section is a team, and it's always best, whenever possible, to let them choose their partners. Eddie put forward the name of Ian Armit, for years a familiar figure on the traditional-jazz scene, though equipped with rather more finesse and technical prowess than most trad pianists; and Brian Brocklehurst, a name which was at the time unfamiliar to me. Brian was another graduate of the modern clubs, and for this reason I was tentative in approaching him. Despite our abandonment of revivalism, we still maintained a reputation which would scare off the modernist . . .
>
> Ian Armit must have played in almost every jazz band to emerge since the Revival. In the early days, his technically accomplished light-fingered style was unfashionable. Pianists were then expected to pound the piano with both fists in crude imitation of the more primitive New Orleans style. The general attitude can be summed up by the horrified reaction of a pianist[*] in a 'pure' New Orleans-style band on being asked by a recording engineer [Denis Preston was the producer on the date] to play a bit higher up on the keyboard: 'Wot, and sound like fuckin' Teddy Wilson?'

Throughout this book, and its predecessor, the author has repeatedly harped on the many ironies scattered through the history of jazz in Britain, but few were as striking as this case, of a man who chose to lead a scintillating but uneconomic eight-piece band at a time when there was a massive explosion of interest in a

---

[*]His first pianist, Pat Hawes.

style (albeit now with traddy-pop associations) that he had done so much to foster. There are no parallels to such a situation in the whole history of jazz. King Oliver moved from his freewheeling Creole Jazz Band to a larger instrumentation of twelve to fourteen pieces, employing, of necessity, arrangements, and Louis Armstrong from his Five and Seven (recording units only) to a big band, but these transformations happened in totally different circumstances. Their changes in instrumentation were consistent with the trend towards bigger bands demanded by entrepreneurs and public, the belief at the time being that bigger is better, but in his time Lyttelton was pulling against the fashion by forsaking the classic line-up.

Lyttelton threw himself into the new sound with characteristic dedication and energy. The social nonconformist who had become the most publicized of the traditionalist apostles was now the apostate – proclaiming the rightness of musical values he had once condemned and bravely setting the example at considerable financial loss to himself. Of course it was typical of the man to suggest in his attitude and pronouncements that 'what-I-am-doing-is-absolutely-right-and-let-there-be-no-argument-about-it-and-now-fall-in-all-of-you-and-follow-me-into-the-mainstream-quick-march!' This colourful and articulate rebel had not entirely shed his social conditioning!

He was understandably furious with his critics, especially those who alleged that his use of three saxophones was proof that he was going 'commercial'. At the end of Chapter 5 in *Second Chorus* ('Lyttelton's Experiments') he reiterated and answered the question often put to him in those days: 'Why don't you play like you did five years ago?'

> If I tried they would be the first to say, but it's not the same! Of course it's not – and the difference is that five years ago I enjoyed it and believed in it. Today it's just raking over old embers. I must please myself first and if pleasing myself means antagonizing some of the band's followers, then I must take that risk. And, if, in their anger, they tell me I have gone commercial I shall probably let them have it – right between the eyes!

Convinced as he was about the correctness of his changes in policy and supported as he was by most critics, Lyttelton's pursuing that policy imposed a considerable strain on him, mentally and financially. When the young traditionalists and modernists first emerged from underground to play in public, most had no previous reputation by which they would be compared and be judged by, nor, in most cases, did they much care if the public liked them or not. Nor were they overly concerned with financial reward. In the mid- to late fifties Lyttelton was in no such position. He was well aware of his previous standing with the public and defiant as he was in presenting this new image, and defending it in print, he must have been uncomfortably conscious of the fact that a large section of his audience were very critical of the metamorphosis. Furthermore, he now had a large payroll to consider. Ideals are one thing: musicians' fees and the leader's diminishing bank balance quite another.

His dilemmas were sharply illustrated when he toured out of the country, where the audiences were unfamiliar with the changes. An Irish tour uncomfortably crystallized the situation. Audiences were puzzled and cool. The English promoter, a hard-nosed ignoramus (he once described Billie Holiday as a 'Moaning Minnie'), was aghast, and pleaded with Lyttelton to play trad. Relenting, up to a point, Lyttelton said he would play the Louis Armstrong number 'Struttin' with Some Barbecue'. The relieved promoter rushed to the mike and announced that the band was going to play something in the style for which it was famous – 'Struttin' with *Saint* Barbecue'.

He continued to play as he pleased, but the BBC's Jimmy Grant, producer of 'Saturday Club', which started and finished with a Lyttelton composition, 'Saturday Jump' by the eight-piece band, wailed: 'He may play as he pleases, but he doesn't please me.' By now the BBC was trad mad; producers demanded that banjos ring merrily throughout Broadcasting House. It was a hard row, but Lyttelton stuck to his course; he could not turn back, even if he wanted to. The die had been cast. In any case, the public would have been suspicious of a U-turn.

In an interview with the author he spoke about those days.

> The definition of success is doing the right thing in the right place in front of the right people. In fact, we were doing the right thing – producing a good

band, but we were going to the wrong places – traditional clubs, where when we did well, like at St Albans, it was still a problem, because promoters realized that the clientele we attracted would not come back, and that we'd therefore drive away all their regulars (who liked banjos) and leave them in trouble.

You have to grow into a position, to survive all this, where your playing persona is separate from your analysing, academic persona, and that's difficult. I now allow myself the luxury of getting there, doing it, picking up and going home.

It is perplexing why this band, the first of its kind in Britain, was not more successful at the box office. Perhaps because it was neither 'old' nor 'new'; fish nor fowl. Perhaps it was an irrational feeling in many quarters that Lyttelton had become a 'renegade traditionalist' – his own term. He didn't himself attempt to play in the bop idiom either, as – embarrassingly and fruitlessly – had Nat Gonella and Duncan Whyte, but maybe it was because his own style, rooted in an earlier era, seemed anachronistic.

There was, perhaps, a certain amount of identification with an American parallel. Lyttelton's idol remained Louis Armstrong and many of Armstrong's mannerisms (as with hosts of other trumpeters, American and British) were discernible in his playing; understandable in view of the fact that some of the first records Lyttelton heard were those Armstrong made with Luis Russell's band in the thirties. This once particularly virile and electrifying band had become a rather plodding support to Armstrong's bravura trumpet, with only occasional solos from the fine jazzmen still in its ranks, alto saxophonist Charlie Holmes, clarinettist Albert Nicholas and trombonist J.C. Higginbotham.

But here the parallel stops. Lyttelton gave his soloists their head, the arrangements (by Kenny Graham, Eddie Harvey, Harry South and ex-Basie trumpeter Buck Clayton) were often livelier than those employed by Russell, and there was the excitement of 'big-band riffing' behind the soloists, in the best Basie tradition, although Eddie Taylor was not in the class of Russell drummer Sid Catlett. Lyttelton's agent, Lyn Dutton, had unexpected problems. The 'New Orleans' band had sold itself; indeed it was a problem working out whom to refuse. The new band had to be *sold*.

There were soon to be other erstwhile traditionalists joining hands with modernists. For the latter it was an economic expedient. While the mainstreamers were not, by any means, getting as much work as the tradsters, boppers willingly worked with those travelling the middle road. A gig was a gig, ideology notwithstanding.

Bruce Turner, five years with Freddy Randall, mostly on clarinet, and afterwards four years with Lyttelton, primarily on alto saxophone, left (in 1957) to form his own 'jump' band. The verb 'jump' appeared in many tunes played by the pre-war Harlem bands – 'Jumping at the Woodside', 'Jump Steady Blues', 'Second Balcony Jump', 'Do You Wanna Jump, Children?' – and the word connoted the bouncy style of the bands that played these compositions.

Whereas Lyttelton moved slowly towards change, Turner, by virtue of his long-standing taste for thirties black jazz, on becoming a leader, went directly to the formation of the Harlem-style sound that now had the tag of 'mainstream'. But, faced with tepid reactions, he made concessions to audiences at trad clubs by playing trad numbers collectively improvised. Turner, like Lyttelton, composed tunes for his band, but also employed a wide selection of material from a variety of popular-music sources and sketched out the tight arrangements. Initially, however, he had problems in finding suitable players. At that time – to paraphrase Gilbert and Sullivan – a musician was either a 'little traditionalist or a little modernist' and players in the middle ground were few.

'Modern' trumpeter Terry Brown, who had started his professional career in the Johnny Claes band at the age of fifteen (Ronnie Scott, aged sixteen, was another young member) and later played with both the Johnny Dankworth Seven and Ralph Sharon's Sextet, trimmed his bop mannerisms to suit the band. Dixieland trombonist Bobby Mickleburgh also adapted, but it was not until 1959 that a stylistically sympathetic trumpeter, John Chilton (replaced by a Nottingham schoolteacher, Ray Crane) and trombonist John Mumford (replaced by Pete Strange), bassist Jim Bray, drummer John Armatage and pianist Collin Bates from Victoria, New South Wales, were recruited. Turner was then able to consolidate and make some impact on a public that, apart from Lyttelton's 'experiments', had been listening only to trad and bop.

Inevitably, Turner had to scuffle, and while it was a surprise to many that such a seemingly mild and self-effacing individual should ever have considered, much less embraced, the hazards of bandleading, he commanded respect from his musicians, not only for the quality of his playing, but also for his obvious dedication to the music. After a while, the band completely jettisoned the traditional material and, as a result, gained a loyal audience. Their dedication was for a recognizable and praiseworthy virtue and thus deserved support. (Lyttelton, of course, was ploughing a similar furrow but had numerous advantages over his former sideman, not the least of which being the publicity that had surrounded his earlier bands.) This dedication was as much the strength of the mainstreamers as it had been for the revivalists at the Red Barn, Barnehurst, in the mid-forties and for the tyro boppers at Great Windmill Street a few years later. Turner's steadfast integrity attracted further like-minded musicians to his band for very little financial reward and, by the same token, an audience that identified with this personal and artistic struggle. A new band of purists emerged; Ian Christie, writing in the *Sunday Telegraph*, described them as 'mainstream moralists', aficionados as rigid in their views as the followers of trad and bop. They were very welcome to Bruce Turner, and to others who had plunged into the mainstream.

Slowly Turner gained a larger following built up in London at the Six Bells public house, King's Road, Chelsea* and in 1961 the band featured in a forty-seven-minute film directed by Jack Gold and produced by Paddy Whannell and Doug Dobell, shot on 16mm film and a shoestring budget. Called *Living Jazz*, it was embarrassingly low on action, but nevertheless accurately reflected touring musicians' lives and the mechanics of rehearsals. The music and the conviction still come over convincingly nearly thirty years after production.

---

*It was around this time that John Chilton placed a series of somewhat obscurely phrased advertisements in the *New Statesman*, mysteriously including the verb 'jump', this arousing the suspicion of the advertising manager, who smelt connotations far removed from music!

Turner, who in 1984 in his book *Hot Air, Cool Music* berated cults and critics, had, in those halcyon days, no objections to a cultism that supported his endeavours, although he was honest in his perception that many were unimpressed with this so-called mainstream. He mockingly deprecated the genre by quoting those who described it as 'trad without the banjo' and 'modern jazz without the technique'. Turner, a very warm and humorous man, could look dispassionately at the frailties of his ideological stance. Indeed, throughout the mainstream movement there was this awareness of being in a sort of limbo, an unease shared neither by a convinced traditionalist like Colyer, nor by a dedicated modernist like Ronnie Scott. However, they — Turner, Colyer and Scott — all had one thing in common: they were turned down by the BBC as being 'unsuitable'.

It surprised many that Sandy Brown and his partner Al Fairweather became renegade traditionalists for, in many respects, their original band was much earthier than, say, Lyttelton's first band. Like Bruce Turner and, to an extent, Lyttelton with his 'saxophone' band, the Brown band (later the Al Fairweather band without Brown, and this succeeded by the Fairweather–Brown All Stars) had to struggle for engagements and, while this was no great hardship for Brown, who had a healthy income from his architectural business, it was a hard time for those in the band reliant entirely upon music for their living. Critical support, however, was unanimous, and as with Bruce Turner's Jump Band, the Six Bells became their London showcase. Like Lyttelton, both Brown and Fairweather were fully aware that to become a mainstream band was to lose the support of those who had previously championed them.* Like Lyttelton, the personal style of Brown and Fairweather hardly changed, while the overall

---

*The author was the Fairweather–Brown All Stars' agent and was daily concerned with the grim struggle to find work. I once remarked to Brown that he and his partner would have made a lot more money sticking to trad. Brown shuddered, and grunted: 'It wouldn't have been worth it.' I was also representing Wally Fawkes, Bruce Turner and Fat John, struggling in the mainstream.

sound they produced changed drastically. Al Fairweather recalls their reasons for departing from the traditional 'norm':

> We became rather disillusioned with what became known as 'trad'. I'm not completely sure what our reasons for changing were, but we had been playing revivalist music since 1948 and were getting stale. We had introduced the African element quite early on – a departure – and continued to write our own tunes and brought in more 'modern' players – like drummer Benny Goodman, Colin Purbrook, Brian Lemon, Tony Coe and Danny Moss.
>
> We were probably influenced by the written word – as in our fervently revivalist beginnings – and Stanley Dance came into this change of heart. Of course, we had a much broader outlook in London. This wasn't anywhere near as parochial as Edinburgh and there were far more opportunities to hear jazz of all kinds. We came in contact with musicians with tastes different from our own.
>
> Also, hearing the American musicians in person was decisive; people like Hampton and Basie, and like the Teagarden–Earl Hines All Stars, veterans playing mostly the old tunes, but with an approach so different from that of the tradders. We came to doubt the validity of continuing to play in the same old way. In my case I realized there were other trumpet players (Roy Eldridge and Buck Clayton, for instance) who played differently but as well (almost!) as Louis.
>
> This brought about the vague feeling that we should distance ourselves from the then current trad bash-bash sound. This we saw as a caricature of the revivalist jazz we (and so many others) set out to play. Inevitably, I suppose, it had become commercialized and, to an extent, emasculated. My own theory was that trad began with Ken Colyer's visit to New Orleans, was watered down by Chris Barber when he and the rest broke away from Ken, given a bit of a kick and some humour by Acker, and was easy to assimilate and play. I think Kenny Ball played cheery Dixieland – not trad at all. Trad was derived from Bunk Johnson and George Lewis (often very good indeed) and revivalism came from the Hot Five and Seven, and the Oliver and Morton records.

Brown, the acoustic architect, clarinettist, pianist, singer, composer, painter, journalist, author, raconteur and drinker died, burnt out, on 15 March 1975 at the age of forty-six.

Wally Fawkes was another unlikely heretic who abandoned the traditional faith. The first clarinettist in Britain successfully to play the archetypal ensemble role in the fashion of New Orleans, Bechet his primary influence, he (like Lyttelton, Brown and

Fairweather) continued to play in much the same way, but his Troglodytes had, more by accident than design, the sound of the pre-war jam session. This was due to the inclusion, at different times, of players with pre-war experience: trumpeter Dave Wilkins from Barbados, who had played with Ken Johnson's West Indian band at the Cafe de Paris and recorded with Fats Waller during the latter's visit to Britain in 1938 (Len Harrison the bass player and Edmundo Ros the drummer); bassist Russ Allen and pianist Lennie Felix, one of the most eccentric characters in British jazz. He was passionately devoted to the music of Earl Hines, Fats Waller and Art Tatum and occasionally displayed flashes of their keyboard dexterity, being fundamentally a soloist, and not possessing (or desiring, it was thought), the necessary discipline for ensemble playing, or even duets.* This was combined with an equally volatile and inconsistent temperament. He was a person who astutely sized up (with an appropriately narrow-eyed expression and slight twitching of the shoulders) how far he could impose his will or whims. He also possessed an inbred scepticism about people generally and a total mistrust of (and dislike for) agents, managers and bandleaders, but he quickly recognized the counter-menacing deterrent of Fawkes's tilted jaw and tightening lips and – temperamentally – he was no trouble in this band.

For utterly different reasons, the band's problem was the amiable Ian Mackintosh, ex-army captain, timber merchant, fanatically devoted disciple of Louis Armstrong, and father of millionaire impresario Cameron Mackintosh. His claim, often made in his cups (and this was the root of his problem) that he 'played more Negro than any other British trumpeter' was probably true. He had absorbed the essence as well as reproducing the phrases of Armstrong, but lack of practice and his fondness for strong drink marred his talent. As a result the band often sagged, but they made several commendable records for Decca, Mackintosh playing splendidly. Other musicians who played with Fawkes were trombonists Jeremy French and John Mumford, Australian

---

*In 1962 he worked in England with the US cornettist Ruby Braff. They didn't hit it off, Braff exclaiming: 'I asked for a piano player and they gave me a disease.'

pianist Collin Bates, his English near-namesake pianist Colin Bates and drummer Dave Pearson.

Before joining Fawkes, Mackintosh ran sessions under the heading of mainstream at the Humphrey Lyttelton Club, 100 Oxford Street, and in the *Melody Maker*, 21 July 1956, wrote an article germane to the emergence of this new category of jazz, an attempt, he said, to put 'mainstream jazz in perspective'. In this article, Mackintosh expressed his individual preferences: the black big bands of the thirties and their soloists, the names first imparted by John Hammond in his reports to the *Melody Maker* in 1933.*

> None of these men worried as to whether they were traditional or modern, or whether they were playing New Orleans or New York style, but they all played jazz with a maturity of expression. I would say that 1928 was the 'coming-out year' of jazz when the earlier stumblings had been overcome. I think the subsequent six years were by far the most fruitful in jazz history and established a style of playing which has existed until the arrival of Parker, Gillespie, etc. Yet it enjoys no particular name. So we have the strange position whereby the most influential period of jazz is forced to

Wally Fawkes's famous 'Flook', used to advertise his Troglodytes, represented by the author

*See HJB1.

find a name because the pre-1928 copyists and the current modernists have made it appear that no other kind of jazz exists. This is very odd when one remembers that virtually all the great players and bands were playing and recording during this non-defined period.

Tony Coe, born in Canterbury, 29 November 1934, left Lyttelton in 1961 after five years, and formed his own group comprising himself on tenor saxophone and clarinet, with John Picard (trombone), Colin Purbrook (piano), Spike Heatley (bass) and Derek Hogg (drums). As with Lyttelton, Turner, Brown and Fawkes, the band's main avenues of employment were in the trad clubs and they faced similar problems. Jeremy French, an excellent, underrated trombonist and a schoolteacher by profession, who recorded thirteen sides with Fawkes's Troglodytes, wrote a profile on Coe in *Jazz News*:

> Clearly Tony is in the same predicament in which Bruce Turner found himself when he formed his now successful Jump Band. It takes quite a while for a new band to get established, however good it may be, especially if it is a mainstream one. The temptation for the mainstream musician to masquerade as a tradster, to accelerate the process, is therefore a strong one, and I shall long remember the schizophrenic Turner band of three or four years ago. Every swinging Ellington or Hodges number was carefully cancelled out by a tepid trad 'chaser' – to the complete mystification of the paying public.
> 'Got to do it, Dad,' said Bruce at the time. Of course he hadn't, and it wasn't until Turner adopted a consistent and honest mainstream policy that his band started to build up a regular following.

French's observations on the dilemma were apt: the switching from the tightly arranged harmonized passages to stretches of collective improvisation and then back to the arrangements was indeed a case of fish becoming fowl and then changing back to fish again. The same problem applied to drummer John Cox, 'Fat John', whose tastes were for hard bop, but who, strictly for the money, had played with Mick Mulligan before the band split up in 1963. He and Mulligan pianist Ronald 'Bix' Duff formed an excellent band comprising young modernists such as Ray Warleigh (alto), Chris Pyne (trombone) and his brother Mick on piano, but like the Coe–Picard Quintet, it was shortlived.

Although Chris Barber has never abandoned the banjo, his band was to include two saxophones (doubling clarinets), Fender electric bass and electric guitar. It was also to feature material drawn from the wider repertoire of jazz, including John Lewis's 'Golden Striker' and Charles Mingus's 'Better Git It in Your Soul'. Such was the eclectic nature of the band that alto saxophonist Joe Harriott, who had played with Ronnie Scott's Big Band, and who was a key figure in the avant-garde movement of the sixties, often sat in with the band during their appearances at the Marquee Club and recorded with them. In 1964 Ronnie Scott and Jimmy Deuchar also recorded with them on an album called *Good Morning Blues*.

In 1977 the band (by now billed as the Chris Barber Jazz and Blues Band) played at The Hague, Holland, and on the same bill was the multi-instrumentalist, composer, arranger and sporadic bandleader Benny Carter. Chris Barber, white and an atypical product of English public school, then forty-seven and still the starry-eyed enthusiast, approached Carter, then seventy, and said – in genuine modesty in the company of such a revered figure: 'I don't suppose you've ever heard of me, but my name is Chris Barber and I'm a lifelong admirer of yours.'

Carter replied, 'Thanks very much, but I do know you. You're the man who invented trad.'

It was a piquant dialogue, with all sorts of delicate inner nuances. The chances were that more people attended that festival to hear Barber than Carter, but there would be no doubt in the minds of older buffs present that Carter's was the more significant contribution to jazz. Barber's reply is not recorded, but it's likely that he splutteringly denied both responsibility for the Frankenstein's monster trad, and that his band had in any way played in this fashion; indisputably, his later inclusion of material and instrumentation anathema to the purist revealed another nonconformist spirit.

The avowedly mainstream bands were to influence other well-established names in the traditional field, Alex Welsh one of these. Again, however, dilemmas arose. In a conversation the author had with pianist Fred Hunt not long before his death on 21 September 1986, Hunt recalled:

> When we were a straightforward Condon-style band, the fans knew where they stood. When we mixed up the collective improvisation with tight arrangements we were – in the eyes of many one-time staunch fans – neither fish nor fowl. Naturally, they made their complaints known to Alex and the arguments would be rekindled, Alex preferring the band that was, to the band it had become. As for myself, I liked both, but people don't notice the piano so much as the front line and although I had to adopt a different line to the two styles within the band I don't think my solos differed much in either.
>
> In many ways it was both a stimulating and troubled period in Welsh's history and, typically in this tightly-knit family, we were constantly bickering. And yet we had the reputation of being a 'good-time, happy lot'. We must have been good fakers once on the stand!

Roy Crimmins, in the *Jazz Journal* article following Welsh's death, wrote:

> I left England in 1965 and returned in January 1979. Straight back into the band again. Arch and Len were dead. Alex was drinking heavily and it was obvious to me that Alex missed the old family spirit. He told me that the second classic band with John Barnes and Roy Williams had been critically and commercially more successful than the first, but he complained that he ended up just being a lead trumpeter in a swing band, with none of the joyous freedom of leading a free-wheeling ensemble. He admitted that he broke up the band on purpose. I would argue with him that he was foolish, they were great musicians, and that he should have been proud of the band.
>
> 'Oh, I was,' he replied, 'but I was like a fish out of water. I couldn't express myself properly. *They* were expressing themselves and it was *my* band.'
>
> He wanted one more classic band before he retired. The personnel was now Alex, myself, Fred Hunt, Jim Douglas, Pete Skivington and Roger Nobes. The band had its own character, too. In restaurants there were two distinct tables. A with Alex and B with the 'revolutionaries'. It was often more fun at table B.

Whatever the extent and frequency of these disputes within the band, they have left on records and in personal memory a legacy of musicianship and in its various manifestations recognizable identity.

Club and dance promoters fought shy of mainstream. Nearly all were in accord with the sentiment expressed in Roger Horton's aforementioned passionate declamation: 'Show me a banjo and you show me a profit!' Provincial promoters were especially resistant. In his *Hot Air, Cool Music*, Bruce Turner relates his band's embarrassing experience in Bradford. The club manager apologetically presented this mainstream band to his audience of trad-jazz lovers thus: 'All I say, lads, is give 'em a chance.'

The honourable exceptions to provincial lack of interest were the Grimsby Jazz Club, the Manchester Sports Guild, the Mardi Gras, Liverpool and the Redcar Jazz Club.

There were also few mainstream bands in the provinces, the Avon Cities Band in Bristol being the exception. Throughout the country, clubs accepted this doubtful quantity that went by the name of mainstream, and the patrons usually recognized the faces of the bandsmen but realized that their music was different. Slowly, they accepted that it wasn't 'far-out', that good musicianship and genuine conviction were combined to make entertaining and danceable music. What they witnessed was British traditional musicians, more than any throughout the world, expanding their horizons and eschewing the rigidity of the banjo-dominated rhythm section. Most surprising was that a band wholly associated with the trad boom, Acker Bilk's, upset many of their followers and disturbed their agent, Lyn Dutton (in much the same way as Lyttelton had earlier disturbed him), and sent tremors of alarm through the club promoters' circuit, when they adopted mainstream elements.

When the trad bubble burst and clubs closed by the hundreds, most of the traditional bands also collapsed, leaving only Colyer, Welsh, Ball, Barber and Bilk with enough work to keep going. Since the mainstream bands, particularly Fairweather–Brown and Bruce Turner, relied upon sporadic appearances in trad clubs to keep a regular personnel, they too folded. Turner disbanded in 1964, went freelance and joined Acker Bilk in 1966. Al Fairweather joined the same year and, inevitably, the musical thinking of both affected the band's policy, Fairweather writing and arranging several tunes. One of these, 'Big Bill', a tribute to blues singer Big Bill Broonzy, is a gem of a composition and was twice recorded by the band, both recordings a measure of the change the band underwent through the addition of two mainstreamers. They also abandoned their fancy-dress gimmick.

Typically, the trad promoters were displeased by the changes. One of these, Steve Duman, running a club in Catford, south-east London, was overjoyed when Turner left in 1970. He displayed a poster which, for sheer crassness, compared with the notorious 'Go Home Dirty Bopper!' scroll at Birmingham Town Hall in 1953. This read: 'AT LAST! ACKER'S BAND IN ITS ORIGINAL AND UNEXPURGATED FORM. GENUINE TRADITIONAL JAZZ – DEFINITELY NO SAXOPHONE!' Duman's objections to the saxophone were not based on any acute critical assessment of its contribution to a jazz band, they were purely mercenary. 'Saxophone' bands did not draw the same crowds as solid British trad.

Today, Humphrey Lyttelton carries the torch with a highly musical and financially successful seven-piece and both the Chris Barber and Acker Bilk bands are evidence of the sophistication that, as a result of mainstream influences, permeated the ruggedly traditional bands of the fifties.

8
The Ban is Breached

In June 1933, Duke Ellington and His Orchestra played a phenomenally successful week at the London Palladium; a Sunday concert especially for jazz enthusiasts staged by the *Melody Maker* at the Trocadero, Elephant and Castle, South London; and other London venues. Almost coinciding with the news that a return visit was being negotiated, in 1934 a ban on foreign musicians playing in Britain was imposed by the Ministry of Labour.

While this was ostensibly an action by a government department with statutory powers, the real instigators of the embargo were the British Musicians' Union. The ministry's compliance with the union's demands was justified by the practice of ministry officials accepting the recommendations of experts in industry generally, and in respect of foreign musicians and bands the Musicians' Union were seen as those experts.

It was a monumentally stupid prohibition, one that was to deprive jazz lovers of their right to see and hear in the flesh musicians of a kind unique in the whole history of music. Moreover, as later events were to prove, their appearance in Britain could have provided British musicians with work, although the union's rigid enforcement was allegedly to safeguard its members' livelihoods.

It is true that had the ban been restricted to ordinary dance bands – Paul Whiteman's, Jan Garber's, Guy Lombardo's and the like – it would have been valid, and no loss artistically. Those bands played the Tin Pan Alley pops of the day, heavily orchestrated, generally with trite lyrics, the whole usually devoid of jazz content although, in some cases, there would have been the occasional 'hot' chorus from a genuine jazz musician compelled to play in an orchestra of this kind to earn a living. There were sufficient numbers of conventional dance orchestras in Britain without importing them from the United States.

The union refused to accept that *jazz* orchestras were a special case. It was absurd to suggest that, say, Duke Ellington and His Famous Orchestra would put, say, Billy Cotton and his band out of work, or that Louis Armstrong would have Nat Gonella joining the dole queues. The ban was almost total until 1956. Some musicians – like multi-instrumentalist Benny Carter; tenor saxophonist Coleman Hawkins; pianist Art Tatum; trumpeter/singer Valaida Snow; pianist/vocalist Fats Waller; a French group, the Quintet of the Hot Club of France; and one big orchestra, Teddy Hill's, playing only an incidental part in the Cotton Club Show at the Palladium – slipped through this cultural Iron Curtain, in the guise of 'variety' acts.

It was as such that in 1948 Duke Ellington, with trumpeter/dancer/violinist Ray Nance and singer Kay Davis, played the Palladium, with British musicians. In 1949, Benny Goodman and pianist Buddy Greco, again backed by British musicians, played the same venue although not, in the latter case, without spiteful interference from the union, who banned musicians initially booked for the engagement – guitarist Dave Goldberg, drummer Laurie Morgan and trumpeter Leon Calvert – on the grounds that they were in arrears with their dues. By such a pettifogging action they deprived these players of both employment and the prestige such an engagement would have brought them.

A few American musicians made unpublicized appearances. The trumpeters Jimmy McPartland and Rex Stewart sat in with Humphrey Lyttelton and his band at 100 Oxford Street, Stewart actually recording in London, but the official position regarding foreign musicians, with particular regard to Americans, remained unchanged.

The roots of the ban were put down in the early twenties when jazz had become the rage, and since the music originated in America it was American bands (with generally superior technique and showmanship and dominating the gramophone-record catalogues) that the public wanted, albeit under the mistaken belief that these were jazz orchestras. At that time US bands were regularly playing in Britain and many British dance-band musicians argued that if American bands took work here, British bands should play in America, something no British bands did.

The reason for this was brutally simple: there was no demand for them in America. Even had the American Federation of Musicians been interested in 'reciprocity', there would have been no takers among American agents and promoters. This was to be the kernel of the situation in the ensuing years. Certain British musicians could not, then or later, accept this stark economic fact of life, and this blinkered attitude was to form the basis for the union's subsequent intransigence.

In the thirties, there was little outward opposition to the embargo, jazz enthusiasts then being a very small minority. Objections to it in wartime, in the following decade, would have been irrational and futile, but once hostilities ceased constant pressure was mounted on the union to allow American musicians in particular into the country. The diehards at the union's headquarters in Sicilian Avenue, however, were adamant that there were to be no such entries without 'reciprocity'. But the post-war aficionados were more vocal than their predecessors and, to a certain extent, more organized, and with an increasing nationwide interest in jazz, there were more voices to protest against the ban. These entreaties were summarily rejected.

In 1949, desperate measures were taken to defeat the prohibition, and two great American jazzmen, Sidney Bechet and Coleman Hawkins, appeared, illegally, in two separate concerts presented by two promoters. The full story* of these appearances and the machinations behind them and the hilariously comic court case that ensued caused many in the jazz world to wonder about the process and implementation of the law, but are cited here only as two incidents in the chain of events that led to ever-increasing pressure on the union to relent.

In 1951 a Liverpool promoter, Harold Rosen, conceived the apparently bizarre idea of presenting Louis Armstrong and his All Stars on a boat on the Irish Sea. Thus, technically, the performance would not be on British soil and therefore unaffected by the union's prohibition. The author was Rosen's London agent and

---

*See HJB1.

actually went through the motions of enquiring about Armstrong's fee from his British representative Lew (later, Sir Lew) Grade. I had read that Mr Grade started work at 6 a.m. and so I rang him at about eight o'clock one morning. In normal office hours I would never have got past protective receptionists and secretaries. Mr Grade himself answered the phone. It was my intention circumspectly to omit mention of the rather tricky matter of the 'venue' until a price for the All Stars had been established, but I didn't get that far. Grade abruptly enquired if I was an agent, and when I told him who I was, he snarled, 'Then don't waste my time,' and rang off.

Admittedly, Rosen's notion was outlandish, but that it should have been conceived at all revealed how far some promoters would go to meet the demand for American musicians to appear in Britain – or, in this instance, a few miles outside it, on the high seas.

If Grade had regarded my enquiry as a waste of time – the entrenched attitude of the Musicians' Union and their running dogs, the Ministry of Labour, being accepted by this old-school entrepreneur as a fact of life and enquiries for the impossible merely an irritation – there were others with a sharp eye on the profits to be made from the entry of American musicians. One of these was Norman Granz, originator of the 'Jazz at the Philharmonic' (JATP) concerts in the United States; another was the English agent/impresario Harold Davison. The two of them were to join forces in fighting against the ban with the full support of all stylistic denominations – for once united – of the jazz world.

In April of 1952, a year in which determined assaults were made on the union diehards, the *Melody Maker*, 12 April, ran two bold headlines. The main heading read: 'MU REJECTS OFFER OF JATP TO PLAY FREE FOR UNION FUNDS' – with the subheading: ' "No Americans admitted until AFM policy is modified" – Anstey'. (Anstey was then the union's Assistant General Secretary.) The report read:

> Norman Granz, JATP promoter, airmailed MU General Secretary Hardie Ratcliffe from Copenhagen last Thursday offering to bring his unit to London entirely for union funds. Part of his letter read: 'I should like to play London in

whatever is the best and available auditorium with all the proceeds to go to a charity which the union may designate. I would not want one penny of fee or expenses. I would pay all necessary transportation and other expenses for my organization during the day spent in London. I'm extremely proud of my group and the kind of music it plays and want very much for them to play for the British jazz fan.' He added that £2,000 [the approximate equivalent of £40,000 today] or more might be raised by a double concert.

The political affiliations of the MU executive are highly relevant here. They were all members of the Communist Party and their thoughts on receiving what was virtually an offer of charity from this thrusting epitome of *American* free enterprise can only be imagined. It was as though, in politics today, Mrs Thatcher were to offer money from the funds of the Tory Party to Arthur Scargill and the Miners' Union, provided he promised no further industrial action.

Anstey's reply was published in the same issue of the *Melody Maker*:

> Your proposal to donate the proceeds ... to the Benevolent Fund ... is a gesture that is appreciated by us, but is completely unnecessary since any approval that might be given for your concert group to appear in this country would be given in accordance with declared union policy and not upon the disposal of the income from the concert.
>
> The group, all being members of the American Federation of Musicians, must be aware that the policy of the US federation is opposed to the presentation of foreign orchestras and groups of musicians in the US. Therefore the MU states, until the federation policy is modified to provide for a reciprocal exchange of musicians between America and Britain, the union is compelled to oppose the presentation of American musicians here.

On being reminded by the *Melody Maker* that union policy would cause immense disappointment to all the British fans who were eager to hear the JATP presentation, Ted Anstey replied:

> We appreciate that the public – including our own members – would like an opportunity of hearing in person this orchestra and groups of specialists. However, the union has the responsibility of protecting the interests of its members and cannot give *carte blanche* approval to the presentation of foreign musicians in this country without first having the agreement of other countries freely to admit British orchestras and musicians to perform on comparable occasions.

It was unfortunate for the union that the *Melody Maker*'s other front-page story was boldly headed: 'TITO BURNS DUTCH CONCERTS BANNED — SO JATP GOES IN!'

> Tito Burns and his sextet were booked for three big concert dates in Holland over Easter. Now, suddenly, permission has been refused for them to make the trip. It is stated in London that the British Musicians' Union and the NOMA (the Dutch union) will not issue the necessary permits. The concert dates, at Amsterdam, Rotterdam and Scheveningen, will now be played by Norman Granz's Jazz at the Philharmonic group instead.
>
> Tito Burns told the *Melody Maker*: 'This is the most fantastic thing that has ever happened to me. The dates were booked and Dutch agent Lou Van Rees held the necessary permits from the Dutch Government, I can assure you, and I here and now challenge the Musicians' Union to publish the true reason why they have sought to interfere in this unprecedented way.'

So, the front page of the paper that, from 1926, the year of its inception, had spoken for 'members of the profession', carried two stories that hardly put the union, ostensibly acting for the same profession, in a good light, even allowing for the fact that there were some anomalies in the JATP offer report. The headlines referred to 'union funds'; Granz's airmail offer was for the monies to go to 'a charity which the union may designate', but Mr Anstey, one-time theatre pit musician, seemingly interpreted this as meaning the 'Musicians' Benevolent Fund'. Whatever, the *Melody Maker*, rightly, put them on the spot.

In May 1952, the author organized a public meeting at the Caxton Hall, Westminster, to enable well-known and respected figures in the business to speak against the ban. They were Pat Brand (editor of the *Melody Maker*), Ray Sonin (editor of the *New Musical Express*), Ernest Borneman (anthropologist, author and critic), Humphrey Lyttelton (musician and critic), Bob Farnon (composer and orchestra leader) and Steve Race (pianist, critic and composer). Clearly, with such speakers as these it was not a frivolous exercise, and it was an achievement for me to get the respective editors of the *Melody Maker* and *New Musical Express* even to mention each other's names and papers — something, in their fierce rivalry, they had not done before. (It turned out to be my only accomplishment in this exercise.)

I issued a statement published in both papers:

JAZZ, SWING, DANCE FANS!!

... DO YOU WANT ...
AMERICAN MUSICIANS TO PLAY
.. IN THIS COUNTRY? ..

Would you like to hear ARMSTRONG, BECHET, DAVIS, ELLINGTON, GILLESPIE, HERMAN, J.A.T.P., KENTON, PARKER, TEAGARDEN, and other Great Musicians

IF SO — Attend a Protest Meeting against the British Musician's Union policy of refusing admission to these U.S. Instrumentalists

— AT THE —

CAXTON HALL 10, 11, 24, 29, 39, 46, 134 Buses — and Westminster Tube —

CAXTON STREET, WESTMINSTER, S.W.1

at 8 p.m. (Doors open 7.30)—*Please Come Early*

MONDAY 12th MAY, 1952
(NO ADMISSION CHARGE)

Speakers include: **PAT BRAND** (Editor Melody Maker)
ERNEST BOURNEMAN, BOB FARNON, STEVE RACE, HUMPHREY LYTTELTON, RAY SONIN (Editor Musical Express)

ORGANISER: JIM GODBOLT, 85 NEWMAN ST., W.1   MUS. 5260

This is no anti-union meeting, but strictly a demonstration against the MU's short-sighted and destructive policy with regard to the importation of foreign musicians. The speakers have all agreed that the meeting be held at the earliest opportunity to make clear to the union and interested sections of the public that responsible figures in the entertainment business are determined to fight for what they believe to be in the best interests of the profession.

All the speakers have fully supported the MU in its endeavours to raise standards and working conditions. However, the speakers are strongly opposed to the MU's complete unwillingness to acknowledge reasonable requests.

The union lost no time in stepping in, forbidding the MU members – Race, Lyttelton and Farnon – to speak, under the threat of expulsion. This doomed the meeting. It was essential that the platform be as broad-based as possible, and without the musicians it might appear that the two editors were concerned only with publicizing their papers – with the help of an 'intellectual' writer (Borneman) and a 'parasitic' agent (Godbolt) – and were heartlessly unconcerned with the best interests of musicians.

As for the 'parasitic' agent myth, there appeared in the 10 May 1952 issue of the *Melody Maker* a letter from a Charles Pude of Orpington:*

> Why doesn't Big Business, as represented by Messrs Godbolt and Co, come right out in the open and admit that it is not really interested in the advancement of English jazz ideas by allowing American jazzmen into this country, but rather more in lining its own pocket as exploiters of public entertainment?
>
> Certainly the MU is right in refusing to sanction an American invasion. Let these agents and bookers encourage the British bands who have most of everything the Americans have and are fast becoming creators, as opposed to imitators, in style.
>
> Let Godbolt and Co lay off the MU, too. It is only the presence of the union that keeps the exploiters of musicians where they can do least harm.

---

*Mr Pude played novacord with Arthur Young's Sextet at the swank Hatchett's Restaurant, Piccadilly in 1942. Violinist Stephane Grappelli was a featured member of the band. The notion that I was associated with 'Big Business' in any way was laughable. I only wish that it had been true!

The *Melody Maker* replied:

> No one has proposed an 'American' invasion. What has been suggested is that the MU consider the controlled entry into Britain of one or two foreign star musicians, not only to inspire local musicians (see letters above) by first-hand and up-to-the-minute example, and feasibly to be the means of creating extra employment for them, but also to re-create among the general public the national enthusiasm for dance music that has been lost by our 'isolated' musicians during the past few years.

In June 1952 the National Federation of Jazz Organizations of Great Britain and Northern Ireland booked two American and two European musicians for concerts to take place at the Royal Festival Hall and British musicians were engaged in support. The NFJO actually obtained permits from the Ministry of Labour and proceeded with their press announcements and advertising. They sub-contracted one of the artists, New Orleans blues singer/guitarist Lonnie Johnson, to Lyn Dutton for a nationwide tour, to be supported by British musicians. The *New Musical Express*, 9 May 1952, reported:

> The Ministry of Labour has issued work permits to guitarist/blues singer Lonnie Johnson and white barrelhouse pianist Ralph Sutton. This gratifying news suggests a change of heart on the part of the authorities which may lead to the free entry of selected American jazzmen. In addition to Sutton and Johnson, the traditional concert on the 28th will feature Humphrey Lyttelton and his band, the Christie Brothers Stompers and Ambrose Campbell's West African Rhythm Band.
>
> The concert on the 30th is for modern jazz fans and will have as guest stars Dutch trumpet man Rob Pronk accompanied by Brits Chuck Gates (piano), Dickie Devere (drums) and Bruce Wayne (bass), and Swedish alto saxophonist Arne Domnerus accompanied by Tommy Pollard (piano), Lennie Bush (bass) and Tony Crombie (drums).

Also booked for the programme was Dizzy Reece and his band and Cab Kaye and his band. The *Melody Maker*, 4 June 1952 headline was: 'BRITISH JAZZMEN TO TOUR WITH LONNIE JOHNSON'.

Just why the Ministry of Labour saw fit to issue permits in this instance will now never be known. Perhaps it was the decision of a solitary official, a new man perhaps, someone unaware that his ministry had long bowed to the union or maybe, naïvely, he thought it was the department's right to issue permits if they so wished and it was no business of a non-statutory body like the Musicians' Union. Perhaps the usual man was on holiday; whatever, it was a seeming change of heart, a sentiment not echoed, though, in Sicilian Avenue. They promptly banned their members from appearing in either concert. Despite this, certain bands and musicians defied the ban to enable the concert to take place. These were Ron Simpson's Commodores, pianist Gerry Moore, drummer Dickie Devere and alto saxophonist Joe Harriott.

There were strange repercussions from these jazzmen's defiance. There were resignations from the National Federation of Jazz Organizations by some musicians, many of them publicly opposed to the union's embargo, but of the opinion that strike-breaking was unacceptable in any circumstances. These musicians were Humphrey Lyttelton and Steve Race, joined by Peter Leslie, Ernest Borneman and Mike Butcher, all of them expressing anti-'blackleg' views. The Humphrey Lyttelton Club and the New Jazz Society withdrew from the organization.

These were indeed puzzling times. All these individuals strongly opposed the ban, but all were members of the union. Nevertheless, Humphrey Lyttelton declared in his first book that he would have been prepared to suffer imprisonment to play with Bechet at the Winter Garden in November 1949. It may not be an unfair view of their resignations, these many years later, that these individuals, while genuinely pro-unionist in the general sense – as indeed was the author – were cloaking their dissatisfaction with the administration of the federation with these fraternal sentiments.

The shows were a shambles, although not because of the Musicians' Union action. This could have been the opportunity to give even greater prominence to the visitors but, in the case of the traditional concert, this was not to be. Max Jones, in the *Melody Maker*, 5 July 1952, wrote:

> Forgetting for a moment the bans and last-minute panic, here we had two solo artists that the bulk of the jazz public wanted to see. It would have been sufficient, in my estimation, to provide a curtain-raiser in each half and leave the rest to the USA ...

It's an ill wind, we thought (even from Sicilian Avenue) that blows nobody good. The federation, we hoped, would make a virtue of necessity and present the two Americans in a bold and satisfying way. Instead . . .

The burden of Jones's criticism was that the Americans were under-used and that the bands booked at the last minute – Lonnie Donegan's band and a reconstituted George Webb's Dixielanders – did not compare with the established names like Lyttelton and the Christie Brothers who had obeyed the union's edict.

The publicity surrounding the ban on union members, imposed after a government department had given its blessing to the visitors, at least served to highlight just what an obdurate bunch the MU executive were, particularly with regard to Lonnie Johnson, bluesman from New Orleans. Since this country had no blues singers, who were the artists deprived of employment by his appearance? And what of the employment and prestige lost by the Lyttelton, Crane River and Merseysippi bands and the Ray Foxley Trio who had been booked to appear with Johnson at various stages of his tour?

The union was totally unrepentant and issued a statement after the concerts, their phraseology indicating both their annoyance at the Ministry of Labour's effrontery in issuing permits to foreign musicians, and their own highly authoritarian attitude towards the matter of entry.

> The union objects to the appearance of foreign musicians unless under arrangements approved by the union. Arrangements were made for these two concerts without consultation with the union by the NFJO, who first wrote to the union asking for consideration of the 'ban' [MU's quote marks] only on 25 June, received on the 26th. The first concert was on the 28th.
>
> The Ministry of Labour decided in April that foreign musicians could perform, but merely informed the union without any prior consultation, despite the fact that such consultation is the usual procedure. We are not willing to be told by the ministry; we should have been consulted by them before the NFJO bookings were made. The NFJO admitted that this should have been done by expressing 'deepest regret' on 25 June, but it was too late then. Relations with other countries are not involved in this case. We will discuss any scheme to regulate foreign bookings but will not be ignored by the NFJO until a few days before the concerts.

That mysterious reference to 'other countries' probably relates to a criticism regarding the executive's attitude to America generally. Communists, they would have an automatic anti-American bias.

Had there been any well-known Russian jazz musicians at the time, it could be safely assumed that they would have been welcomed to Britain by the MU with open arms, such visits accompanied by fervent proclamations of everlasting fraternity between the Russian and British proletariat and the assurance that relations between these two entities would be forever cemented as a result. Actually there were very few Russian jazz musicians then, and on the evidence of those who made gramophone records* it was a merciful blessing that they did not appear here, not that musical considerations would have bothered the ex-theatre-pit-musician comrades on the union's executive, to whom only the political colour of the performers would have been of relevance.

By now the British jazz movement had become an extremely painful thorn in the MU's side; a bunch of vociferous fans, banding themselves together under long-winded names or simply individuals, journalists and letter-writers, were hammering them in the musical press with enthusiastic editorial support. And there was more discomfort for these backwoodsmen in the offing.

In January 1953, 150,000 acres of East Anglia were flooded with the loss of 370 human lives, some thousand head of livestock and with considerable damage to property. A Flood and Tempest Fund was launched by the Lord Mayor of London to aid the stricken area and British bands combined in concerts to make their contribution to the fund. It was yet another opportunity for Norman Granz to make a gesture. He offered the entire JATP package to appear at two concerts in London, the entire proceeds to be donated to the Lord Mayor's fund. Permission was granted by the Ministry of Labour.

It was a grim irony attending the history of jazz in Britain that a regional disaster of some magnitude was the catalyst for the change allowing American musicians to appear on a British concert stage with official blessing. Whatever the union executive

---

**Jazz and Hot Dance in Russia* – Harlequin HQ7012. An extremely interesting album, but more notable for its historic than musical value.

may have privately thought about Granz's opportunism, they could not be seen to be standing in the way, or even forbidding the British bands that volunteered, free of charge, to appear on the same concerts. In fact, in all the enormous publicity that surrounded the Ministry of Labour's permission for these concerts the union's executive was unusually, and significantly, quiet. Not a peep out of them!

Of course, Granz's gesture was not altruistic: a rich man, he would not notice the loss of profits on one concert and, as everyone knew, his move was to put the already beleaguered MU executive in a spot. This time even they could not finagle their way out of a tight corner.

The *Melody Maker*, 18 February 1953, reported: 'JAZZ AT THE PHIL TO PLAY LONDON'.

> Jazz at the Philharmonic will play two concerts in London on Sunday week (March 8th). For the first time in eighteen years, an American unit will be playing for the British public. Relaxation of the Ministry of Labour ban on US bands is due to the fact that all proceeds from the concerts will go to the Lord Mayor's National Flood and Tempest Distress Fund.
>
> Jazz at the Phil will appear at the Gaumont State, Kilburn, in a duo-concert presentation organized by impresario Harold Fielding, in conjunction with the *Melody Maker*. Fielding was discussing flood concerts with the *MM* when JATP boss Norman Granz phoned from Stockholm. His all-star unit is now touring the Continent, and as soon as he heard of the *MM*'s concert plans he offered to fly JATP across to London and give two entirely free shows for the fund. He could do it on March 8th.
>
> Immediately application was made to the Ministry of Labour for the necessary permits. By Wednesday night the ministry announced they would relax the ban. The ruling would remain, however, in principle, and instead of receiving working permits the Granz men would be given a special entry note from the Home Office.
>
> Jazz at the Philharmonic will appear in two concerts – 3 p.m. and at 7.30 p.m. Seats are bookable at 7/6d, 10/6d and 15s.

In the same issue Max Jones reported on the formation of the Visiting Orchestras Appreciation Society, their aim to bring pressure on the Musicians' Union to allow foreign, particularly American, musicians to play here.

The *Melody Maker*, 7 March, carried the banner headline: 'GRANZ 'PLANES INTO LONDON AS FANS AND MUSICIANS BLITZ

"STATE"', and reported that 'after an unprecedented night-and-day demand for seats the concerts were a sell-out'. The names of the JATP package were given: Charlie Shavers (trumpet), Lester Young, Flip Phillips and Willie Smith (saxophone), Barney Kessel (guitar), Oscar Peterson (piano), Ray Brown (bass), Gene Krupa and J.C. Heard (drums) and Ella Fitzgerald, supported by British bands – Ronnie Scott's, Harry Hayes and his band, the Eddie Thompson Trio, the Tito Burns Sextet and the Norman Burns Quintet.

The report quoted an intriguing comment from the theatre manager, Mr G. Conway. 'You're mad,' he said.

But both concerts were sell-outs, irrefutable proof that there was an overwhelming desire on the part of the British public to see American jazz musicians and, as the *Melody Maker* reported, despite the group's 'modern' propensities, traditionalists comprised a large proportion of the numerous fans who phoned the paper to congratulate them on getting the JATP to appear in this country. In fact, the *Melody Maker*'s role was to publicize the event, and therefore themselves, but it deserved to congratulate itself after years of opposing the ban, and giving this event major publicity.

The *Melody Maker*'s 14 March issue carried the headline: 'SENSATIONAL JATP SHOWS RAISE £4,000 FOR FLOOD FUND'.

> The fog that shrouded London lifted on Sunday morning and Jazz at the Philharmonic flew into town in brilliant sunshine. Twenty-one hours later, as the fog was closing in on London Airport, the unit flew out again to the Continent. In between, Norman Granz's jazz stars played two concerts and added over £4,000 to the Lord Mayor's flood fund.
>
> The miracle had happened. After eighteen years, the *MM*, aided by impresario Harold Fielding, had brought an American jazz group into Britain. The fact in itself was so unreal that many of the 8,239 people who packed the Gaumont State, Kilburn, found it difficult to believe their eyes and ears . . . The Gaumont manager, Mr Conway confessed: 'I take back what I said. In twenty-six years in show business I've never seen anything like it.'

Melody Maker staffman Tony Brown wrote a full-page report of the concerts, headed: 'ONE DAY THE IMPOSSIBLE HAPPENED'.

> They came from all over the country. Some got up in the morning darkness to buy their tickets. First was a youthful enthusiast from Willesden. 'I want to see

American jazzmen. I'm mad at the Musicians' Union for banning them . . .'

The *Melody Maker* had sacrificed a valuable Sunday-morning sleep to watch the JATP musicians fly in. It had picked out Ella Fitzgerald and the others easily. Its fascinated eyes followed Lester Young of the fabulous hat and creeping gait. He looked like some high priest of some dark devilry. We had driven back with them in the coach, had shown them Buckingham Palace and a trooper of the Household Guard. Lester squirmed with merriment when a guardsman stamped out his about turn. 'Man, dig that crazy routine!' . . .

The English bands accepted the situation good-humouredly and played well. Ronnie Scott was brilliant and, even better, was able to convince the crowd of it. Eddie Thompson amused with some clever keyboard doodling.

Now the great moment had arrived: Norman Granz strode on from the wings and called on the almost legendary figures one by one. The broadly grinning J.C. Heard; a youthful-looking and glossy Ray Brown; Barney Kessel, tall and with a professorial stoop; the monolith of a man that was Oscar Peterson; Charlie Shavers, small and aggressively confident; a poker-faced Flip Phillips; Lester Young, who glided in to the biggest applause of all . . .

Before playing, Lester Young, his face a benign mask, struck his pose and sagged there, seeming by some strange illusion to be supported by his saxophone. He looked wonderful and we applauded him mostly for it.

Ella Fitzgerald did much to prove she is one of the greatest-ever jazz singers. Her pitching was a joy to hear. She, too, did her share of crowd-fetching. The biggest roar of the day greeted Gene Krupa. He played with Peterson and Phillips in the afternoon. In the evening Willie Smith replaced Flip. Krupa did his stage performance, complete with personal spotlights and personal shadows. When he went into his long drum solo, his companions wandered off the stage and left him to hammer it out alone. For the climax J.C. Heard joined him.

Undeniably, the star of the show was Oscar Peterson. This enormously talented pianist played jazz of several styles with virtuosity. He has marvellous harmonic inventiveness and very fast and accurate fingering . . .

The great afternoon show became wonderful entertainment in the evening. Somehow the atmosphere came to life then, with the audience reacting to artists with wild enthusiasm. The Ronnie Scott band drew a tremendous ovation. Tito Burns, the Norman Burns group and Harry Hayes registered well. Said one British musician before the event: 'We'll play the music; they'll get the crowd.' Another solemnly declared that the JATP unit didn't play jazz. On challenge, he substituted the word bop for jazz.

This kind of confused thinking may explain the deficiencies that are certainly to be found in home-produced jazz. One musician only in the English contingent was fit to take a place in the JATP unit. But, individually and collectively, we don't swing like the Americans. Too many of our jazz players are worrying about the notes played, when the essence is *how* they are played. But there were many musicians who came to learn and admire. Like Don Carlos, who thought Peterson the greatest pianist ever. Like Harry Hayes who was left limp by the dynamic playing of Willie Smith. Like the professional drummers who, in unashamed hero worship, had come to exchange words with Krupa, to shake hands with him if possible. And what is wrong with healthy hero worship anyway? Krupa met one of the heroes of his youth in the course of the evening. He was our own Max Bacon.

Maybe it takes hero worship to produce heroes.

It was instructive to read the comments of certain musicians.

Bandleader Ted Heath: 'It's hardly fair for me to comment as I was backstage most of the time, but what I heard of the afternoon show was great musical salesmanship!'

Guitarist Frank Deniz: 'Well, Peterson was *the* thing, so far as I'm concerned, but the rest came up to expectations.'

Trombonist Harry Roche: 'I thought it was GREAT! Like a shot of adrenalin in the arm. I'd like to see it happen every couple of months. Peterson was fantastic, and Ella . . . well, of course, she goes without saying. Also, my favourite altoist has always been Willie Smith. He didn't disappoint me.'

Tenor saxophonist Rex Morris: 'They're all phenomenal musicians but, to me, the highlight was the Peterson Trio. Their music was pleasing to the ear, tasteful *and* commercial.'

Baritone saxophonist Harry Klein: 'Some of it I liked, some of it I didn't. But the showmanship was wonderful and the whole thing proved the adage – it's not what you do, but the way you do it.'

But bandleader Vic Lewis wasn't that impressed: 'Oscar Peterson? Wonderful! But as for the rest . . . I think there was nothing the best of our musicians couldn't have done.'

In the same issue Steve Race commented on the musicians' reactions, the composition of the audience and Oscar Peterson:

> Despite the fact that the stage at last Sunday's JATP contained such a thrilling cross-section of the world's leading jazzmen, I did find time to glance around the auditorium in search of familiar London faces. There were plenty; in fact, it is safe to say that everyone who wasn't doing a Sunday concert elsewhere was there that day.
>
> Conspicuous by their presence were many of the old-timers who have been clicking their tongues at the 'Let-them-play-here' drive, together with some strong MUnionists whose battle-cry has always been: 'Britain's jazzmen are second to none.' I also saw one of Britain's top swing bandleaders who is privately opposed to the entry of foreign musicians.

Presumably the 'British leads' brigade went to the Gaumont State to have their point proved. I hope they were satisfied. But since my particular interest is the piano, perhaps one of them will tell me which British pianist is a superior jazzman to Oscar Peterson. Jazz aside, perhaps one of them will write and tell me who has a superior technique, a finer touch, or a more advanced harmonic sense. For good measure they might like to add the name of one British dance-band pianist who is fit to dust the piano lid for him. I'll print the names of all nominations, and we'll let the nominees decide. Let's hear from you, gentlemen!

Race did not receive any letters, or any other kind of communication, in response.

Self-confessed 'mouldy fygge' James Asman, reviewing the concert from a traditionalist's perspective in the *New Musical Express*, gave some of the JATP musicians qualified praise, and added that on leaving the theatre and crossing the road to catch a bus, he caught sight of the fascia of a gents' outfitters bearing the name 'George Lewis'. 'Ah,' said Asman, 'if only that name had been on the billboards of the Gaumont State that night.' He was to have his day.

These many years later, it is still a matter of wonderment that a disastrous flood should have been the reason for American musicians to be allowed to play in Britain with *official* sanction and – albeit tacit – acceptance from the body that had so resolutely made a blanket refusal to allow American musicians to play here without so-called reciprocity from the American Federation of Musicians.

The JATP's visit largely occupied the correspondence columns of the *Melody Maker* and *New Musical Express* for the following weeks, but although the headlines concerning projected visits of US musicians were depressing many of the stories offered hope that some would materialize. The *Melody Maker*, 16 May 1953, carried news which was promising:

HEATH FOR NEW YORK: MU AGREES PHILLIPS–BONANO EXCHANGE
The *MM*'s JATP concerts have proved the 'Open Sesame' for the first Anglo–US exchange in eighteen years. Mellowed by the MU's 'gracious attitude' towards Jazz at the Phil, James C. Petrillo, president of the American Federation of Musicians, has relaxed his hitherto unrelenting embargo on British bands.

The Ted Heath-for-Carnegie project now has AFM approval. In addition, Petrillo has announced an exchange deal between Britain's Sid Phillips and America's Sharkey Bonano. Bonano, famed New Orleans trumpeter, will lead a sextet for a Coronation concert at the Royal Festival Hall. Phillips is expected to lead a British six-piece at a club in the Crescent City's Bourbon Street. Both the Heath and Phillips deals are being negotiated by British jazz celebrities.

The Heath project is being carried through by Syd Gross, former London 'Swing Shop' promoter and now a US disc jockey. The Phillips–Bonano switch is in the hands of the Marchioness of Donegall.

The project almost inevitably ran into difficulties. A tangle of moves and communications to break the deadlock followed and it was piquant that two scions of the aristocracy, the Marquis and Marchioness of Donegall, were treating with the Communist-dominated executive of the MU, but what the American public would have made of Phillips's polite Archer Street Dixieland will never be known. Conversely, what the patrons of the Astor Club, Mayfair (where it was mentioned in another report Bonano would be playing) would have made of Bonano and his pungently direct style, will also remain a matter for conjecture. This was one more project that foundered.

Jazz musicians, however, still filtered through to the UK despite the ban. On the grounds of his being a 'variety' artist, permission was gained for the US pianist Teddy Wilson to appear at the Royal Festival Hall, on Sunday 20 September 1953, promoted on behalf of the *New Musical Express* by its new proprietor, Maurice Kinn. With Wilson were the bands of Harry Gold, Freddy Randall, Kenny Baker and Basil Kirchin. According to the *NME*, seven thousand attended this concert.

On the same date, another concert took place, at the Theatre Royal, Dublin, promoted by veteran British bandleader Joe Loss and Irish promoter Bill Fuller in association with Harold Davison, and, in its way, it proved that Harold Rosen's idea of presenting the Armstrong All Stars on a boat was not, perhaps, so bizarre after all. True, the Theatre Royal was on dry ground, but of the seven thousand who attended the two concerts, by Stan Kenton and His Orchestra, the majority of these were British and most had travelled by boat across the Irish Sea to hear a band they were denied hearing in their own country. Reporters from both the

NME and the *MM* covered the shows and returned with rave notices. Both those concerts again demonstrated that there was a colossal demand for American bands of this calibre from British fans, many prepared to brave a sea passage to hear them.

Another loophole was provided by the presence of USAF bases in the UK. On what was virtually American soil, American bands were able to play at will, a fact that must have enraged the Musicians' Union executive. One of these was at Sculthorpe, Lincolnshire, and prior to that historic Dublin concert, the Kenton band played there for American servicemen.

The *New Musical Express* carried a lengthy report by Tony Hall and a photograph of the Ronnie Scott band, who also played that engagement, looking on in wonderment at the assembly of stars in their presence. Hall's report also quoted Kenton's highly favourable comment on the Scott band: 'I'm proud to have heard Ronnie's band. It's certainly the greatest we've heard since leaving the States.' This was a sentiment that was echoed by Kenton's trumpeter Conte Candoli, and saxophonists Zoot Sims and Al Cohn. Kenton continued:

> It proves that your musicians are fighting a myth and a jinx. This whole thing reminds me of the US jazz scene back in 1935. At that time the general opinion was that jazz was the Negroes' music and only Negroes could play it. White musicians were put down on all sides. That has been proved a fallacy and now we have white musicians and Negroes sharing the bandstands together and, in a lot of cases, the Negroes base their styles on some of the white boys.
>
> It's the same with your British musicians, compared with the Americans, if what I have heard tonight is anything to judge by. If, as we all sincerely hope, this union trouble is overcome, and our musicians are allowed to play in each other's countries, the American jazz public will be really astonished by bands like Scott's.
>
> But I foresee one real danger of a band exchange. Some American musicians who happen to have big 'names' in Europe because of records, yet are not playing well any more, could come to London and share the bill with a band like Scott's. The British boys might well be the better band, but the others would get more applause because they're Americans. And that's got to be all wrong.

There were many truths in Kenton's comments, although his allegedly anti-black bias later earned him a reputation as a racist.

Certainly, British musicians were suffering a marked inferiority complex; on the other hand, few could claim to be on a par with the vast number of superior American musicians. Whatever the improvements made by the local musicians, jazz, in all its manifestations, was still better, infinitely better, as played by most Americans. And, in respect of the union issue, the fact remained that Americans could draw the crowds; far more than the British playing at home or abroad.

Where 1953 had proved to be an eventful year with the JATP concerts, Teddy Wilson in London and the Kenton concerts in Dublin, 1954 saw many now familiar announcements in the musical press of this and that exchange project being mooted and abandoned. Despite the banner headline in the *Melody Maker* that Heath was to play the Carnegie Hall, New York, for charity to reciprocate Granz's generosity, there was no sign that it – and other projects – would actually take place. All the attendant publicity served only to draw attention to the fact that the ban still existed.

The *Melody Maker*, 10 February 1954, reported that promoter Harold Fielding, hitherto concerned mostly with classical music, was 'battling' with the Musicians' Union to let him present the Oscar Peterson Trio and Ella Fitzgerald, with no success.

In April 1954, Norman Granz offered London Palladium boss Val Parnell the services of the Oscar Peterson Trio and Ella Fitzgerald free. To an outsider, unaware of the background to this crazy patchwork of attitudes and events, this apparent generosity would have made Norman Granz the biggest American philanthropist since Rockefeller, but this time such munificence was to no avail: no flood or other disaster to warrant acceptance, to justify official permits, to ensure MU acquiescence.

In May, Woody Herman and His Orchestra played the USAF camp at Sculthorpe, and at the Royal Theatre, Dublin, again to packed houses, again mostly of British enthusiasts who had braved the crossing – a particularly rough one on this occasion, so much so that Herman's flight was delayed and British musicians who had travelled to hear the band kept the show going until the Herman band eventually arrived, resulting in laurels for British musicians: Woody Herman commissioned Scott drummer Tony

Crombie to write arrangements and invited Ronnie Scott to join his band.

In August 1954, it was reported in the *Melody Maker* that Caesar Petrillo had turned down an application for Ken Colyer to play in New Orleans and that the British Musicians' Union had refused an application for veteran trumpeter Jimmy McPartland, the man who had taken Bix Beiderbecke's place in the Wolverines, to play in Britain.

It was one of the many ironies attending this charade that, at a time when so many New Orleans musicians had died and, of the remaining practitioners, the brassmen, particularly, were past their peak, Colyer, soaked in the nuances of New Orleans ensemble style, would have been an extremely welcome addition to the bands of that famous Louisiana city. Later Colyer played a tour of New England colleges with George Lewis and his band, significantly not in the South, where such multi-racialism would have been hostilely, perhaps violently, opposed.

In November, Petrillo rejected an end-the-ban plea from Ted Heath. Again, that outsider who saw Granz as an extremely generous philanthropist might be excused for thinking that in this impasse the American union were just as intransigent as their British counterparts. They were; but the fundamental economics of the situation were still that American bands were in demand in Britain and British bands in America were not. The demand for reciprocity, however admirable morally it may have appeared, did not square with market realities.

In January 1955, permission was granted for a concert tour of the Oscar Peterson Trio and Ella Fitzgerald to commence in February, two English musicians, drummer Tony Kinsey and bassist Sammy Stokes, in the package. There were reports of incompatibility in the *Melody Maker*. In the same month, Johnny Dankworth turned down an offer to play in a country that pleaded for British musicians: South Africa, Dankworth objecting to segregation. In June it was reported – *ad nauseam* – that the AFM saw little hope of a proposed Stan Kenton/Ted Heath exchange, but the *Melody Maker*, 15 October 1955, carried a banner headline: 'KENTON FOR BRITAIN! TED HEATH FOR US CONCERT TOUR'.

This epoch-making news broke this week when it was revealed that James C. Petrillo, boss of the American Federation of Musicians, had lifted his twenty-year-old ban on British dance-band musicians to permit Ted Heath to make a concert tour of America. Only the actual dates remain to be fixed.

Harry Francis, Assistant Secretary of the MU, told the *Melody Maker*: 'This is the sort of exchange we approve of in principle. We have no objections to a tour here, subject to Ministry of Labour approval, and provided Ted Heath plays a similar date-for-date tour of the States.'

Asked whether the MU would object if the Kenton personnel proved to be slightly larger than Heath's, Francis added: 'I don't think this would be a stumbling block,' this seen by the *MM* as 'an important concession', for in the past the union had stipulated that exchanges should be on a man-for-man, hour-for-hour basis.

The immediate reaction to this was scepticism. Tell us the old, old story . . . as the song ran . . . and, indeed, on the opposite page another headline and report told us that the Musicians' Union were truly the masters and could override the Ministry of Labour. The headline read: 'UNION EXPLAIN BAN ON HORNE BASSIST'. It was reported that the union had objected to singer Lena Horne bringing over her bass player, George Duvivier. Ted Anstey, the union's Assistant General Secretary, was quoted: 'When the Ministry of Labour, despite our known objections, has *thought fit* [my italics] to issue work permits, we have reserved the right to take what action (the banning of Duvivier) we consider appropriate.' This was a clear example of a body without statutory powers overriding the decision of one that had them.

No wonder there was scepticism! But the 5 November issue gave further details, and there were more in the 24 December issue, giving Kenton's first date – at the Royal Albert Hall on 11 March. On 31 December the first provincial dates were announced. It really looked as if, after a gap of twenty-three years, at least one American band would play in Britain and conversely (although frankly, this was of lesser interest to the British jazz enthusiast) a British band, Ted Heath's, would play in America, the first band to achieve this feat.

Not since it was announced that the ban would be relaxed to allow the JATP to play those two memorable concerts in London was there so much pleasurable anticipation among jazz aficionados, even though the traditionalists were not over-enthusiastic.

But, as events were to prove, they also were to experience the joy of seeing in the flesh musicians they had for so long revered on records.

9
First of the Giants

Throughout January and February 1956 the *Melody Maker* and the *New Musical Express* continued to give readers details of a projected Stan Kenton tour of the UK. It now seemed a certainty, the American Federation of Musicians having agreed to 'exchange' them for Ted Heath.

At last! A real breakthrough, one that would never have happened without the years of constant pressure from the strident jazz minority, a battle cry taken up by astute entrepreneurs who saw the possibilities of financial gain. It was significant that the bands germane to this operation were, exclusively, those with strong jazz associations. There was no suggestion whatever that ordinary dance bands were considered. This was, of course, consistent with the claim that had long been made by aficionados that it was only jazz musicians they wanted, thus presenting no threat to those employed in the bands of Geraldo, Joe Loss, Cyril Stapleton, Stanley Black and the like. But what an inordinate length of time it had taken and how many great jazzmen had died during this absurd and self-defeating embargo!

Interest in the Kenton tour was overwhelming. Promoter Harold Davison had to book an extra appearance in London and extend the provincial tour before the orchestra even arrived. It was proof positive that a large section of the British public was desperately keen to see as well as hear American bands.

The *Melody Maker*, due to a printers' strike which eventually spread to daily newspapers, was not able to cover Kenton's opening concert, nor the best part of a tour that involved a massive sixty-two concerts in thirty-three days. It must have chagrined the doughty *Melody Maker*, for so long the champions of the entry of US jazz musicians, to see their rival, the *New Musical Express*, not only covering the Kenton tour in depth but publishing a photograph of *MM*'s ex-editor Ray Sonin (lured from them by proprietor Maurice Kinn on his taking over the paper) with Kinn and Harold Davison, the caption reading that Kinn and Davison were responsible for the Kenton tour. Moreover, Ray Sonin was the announcer for that historic opening concert. More chagrin for the *Melody Maker* was heaped on them by the astute Kinn who, realizing that a public deprived of their accustomed newsprint supply would buy *anything* for a read on the train or bus home, ordered his non-union printers to print large numbers. These were eagerly bought by commuters to Shenfield, Hitchin, Haslemere and Tunbridge Wells who, perforce, became acquainted with, if bewildered by, such divers names as Norrie Paramour, the Beverley Sisters, Winifred Attwell, Edna Savage, Denis Lotis, Jimmy 'Organola' Leach, Denny Boyce, Joan Regan, Teresa Brewer, Slim Whitman, Nat Hentoff, Humphrey Lyttelton, David Whitfield and . . . Stan Kenton. These no-choice-but-new readers were to learn much about Kenton, his orchestra and his involvement in a historic event.

It must have been a puzzling kaleidoscope of names and reportage, and it must remain a matter for conjecture how many converts, if any, were made to the various kinds of popular music encompassed in the pages of the *New Musical Express* in this virtually newspaperless country.

Kenton's orchestra comprised: Ed Leddy, Vinnie Tano, Phil Gilbert, Lee Katzman, Sam Noto (trumpet); Bob Fitzpatrick, Kent Larsen, Don Kelly, Carl Fontana (trombone); Fred Fox, Irving Rosenthal (french horn); Jay McAllister (tuba); Spencer Sinatra, Bill Perkins, Lennie Niehaus, Jack Nimitz (saxophone); Stan Kenton (piano); Ralph Blaze (guitar); Mel Lewis (drums); Curtis Counce (bass).

Mike Butcher, in the paper whose circulation had rocketed so unexpectedly, wrote in the 16 March 1956 issue an ecstatic 1,500-word critique of the opening concert at the Albert Hall on Sunday 10 March 1956.

> Royal Albert Hall, Sunday afternoon – by 1.55 the atmosphere is supercharged with the barely containable force of a physicist's atom. You're scared to strike

a match in case the place explodes. Within five minutes it *does* explode.

Lighting the fuse, editor Ray Sonin's brief, still-hard-to-believe announcement . . . but to see is to be convinced. It's true. The Kenton boys are here.

They file casually on, soberly suited in grey with plain black ties, the Herculean giant called Stan Kenton – introduced by his number-one champion Vic Lewis – follows in line behind the rest after a few agonizing moments of suspense.

He sits at the Steinway, towering over it like a blond Gulliver in Lilliput. The trumpet team picks up claves, a cowbell, maraccas, a gourd. The french horns merge with the reeds, the tuba with the trombones, Curtis Counce tightens his G-string a little . . .

Then, like an almighty roar, the most blazing band event in the memory of post-war Britons catches fire to blow the Albert Hall's dome heaven-high. 'Artistry in Rhythm' hurls upwards to the roof and down again in an unforgettable riot of brilliance. We're on the scene while history is being made, at the start of an era . . .

After twenty-two[*] years, one of America's 'Big Four' bands – by far the biggest of them all in the eyes and ears of Kenton fans – had jumped the barriers, made friends all round within seconds as soon as it breezed into town, and was now right in front of us. A civilian crowd in the heart of London.

Butcher acknowledged the impossibility, in the height of such an emotive occasion, that he could be objective with the admission:

> To attempt an ordered summary of such a show would be virtually impossible. It would also be as dead as a blueprint of a flashingly active, galvanic machine, so I'll try to set down an unmeasured, unsequential, overall word picture of the kicks, the surprises, the possible disappointments, the familiar things and the fresh – in short the impression made on me by the Stan Kenton band in Britain, 1956.

His wholly eulogistic review ended: 'There's so much to revel in.'

As Kinn was owner of the *New Musical Express* and co-promoter of the concert, it was unlikely that a house journalist would have been critical of any aspect of the proceedings. But it's also certain that Butcher was genuinely enthusiastic. It was a time of charged emotions: here was the first major jazz orchestra to visit Britain since 1933, when Duke Ellington had startled

---

[*]Butcher was dating the length of the ban from Cab Calloway's 1934 visit, and overlooked the appearance of Teddy Hill and His Orchestra at the Palladium in an accompanying role in 1937.

audiences at the London Palladium and other selected venues. The orchestras of Cab Calloway (in 1934) and Teddy Hill (in 1937) had both contained several notable soloists, mostly under-employed, but these orchestras were not of the high technical standard of the Kenton aggregation, and it had been all those long years (excepting the 'variety' performances of Duke Ellington and Benny Goodman in 1948 and 1949 respectively, and the visit of JATP in 1953) since American musicians had been *allowed* to play in Britain – the performances of Bechet and Hawkins (1949) both having been unofficial.

In the same issue of the *New Musical Express* there was fulsome praise from bandleaders Cyril Stapleton, Ted Heath and Vic Lewis, and a photograph of the usually beaming but here grim-visaged Lewis, a smiling Kenton and a characteristically dour Heath. (Lewis was miffed that it was not his band going to America in exchange for Kenton. He claimed to have instituted the idea of exchanges, whereas it has been the idea and efforts of many.) Kenton's visit was also reported and commented on in the post-strike *Daily Mirror, Daily Express, Daily Sketch, Daily Herald* and *Evening Star*.

However, opinions on the Kenton band were not unanimous. In the *Melody Maker*'s first issue (2 April) after the industrial dispute was over, Tony Brown quoted various British musicians who reflected some of the heretic rumblings in the profession, many of its members no longer prepared to accept American superiority as gospel. Bandleader Basil Kirchin, who heard the Kenton orchestra at Luton:

> I was brought up on that legend, British musicians hadn't a chance. These men were our gods. The curtains weren't even drawn when the Kenton men ambled on then Stan loped to the piano and started playing. Wonderful psychology, I thought, because we were all waiting for that fabulous Kenton brass.
>
> After I heard the trumpets I felt sorry for Kenton. They had no range. I only heard a few Fs and a couple of Gs and from one of the section we saw a childish display of irritation over a fluff. It must have been a bad night. Was this the legendary musicianship? Thank goodness for that drummer. Great. But my band agrees with me that if Ted Heath used those arrangements he'd show up the Kenton band on that standard. Only a couple of numbers swung.

Vic Lewis (who by then had introduced the band eight times):

> As a unit it's as good as anything Kenton has ever had and swings more than most. The programme, I'd say, retrogresses from the music played by the Innovations Orchestra of 1950. But I'd say that the Americans lead us in two respects. Their drummers are relaxed and they swing; the arrangers know how to write and are *free* to write well. Our picked soloists are as good.

Drummer Allan Ganley was another British musician Brown interviewed: 'I admired Mel Lewis, but noted the absence of really original soloists such as Zoot Sims and Conte Candoli.'

Leader/drummer Eric Delaney found Lewis 'disappointing' and Keith Christie thought the arrangements 'doomy' – 'boring him to tears'. He also opined: 'There's not much scope for soloists. Fontana and Fitzpatrick are brilliant and Perkins fine on tenor. Whittle or Scott, though, could be as good or better.' Delaney introduced a defiant note: 'Let them all come. They don't frighten us. However much jazz they may play our bands can still hold their public and they can entertain it.'

These opinions were undoubtedly sincerely expressed (and, true, there was no major soloist with Kenton on that historic visit), but the larger indications were that British jazzmen were feeling more sure of themselves. It is possible that, as a reaction to long-standing feelings of inferiority they indulged in overly enthusiastic references to the quality of their British contemporaries – and by inference, to themselves. There was, however, to be a development during the tour that effectively substantiated these beliefs.

Critics and musicians gave vent to their opinions on the historic Kenton appearance; thirty-three years later critic Brian Davis recalls:

> On that never-to-be-forgotten Sunday, 11 March, fifteen of us went up in three cars to London in a state of heady delirium. Having first heard Kenton on AFN in 1946, we had waited ten years for this. We would have been just as euphoric about seeing *any* American band. After all, didn't the whole population converge on the Kilburn State three years earlier, almost to the day, to take in the JATP Flood Relief Fund concerts? It was just that to us Kenton was something else; a different, albeit highly controversial leader who at times had strayed into some pretty rough musical terrain, some of it distinctly dubious in

jazz terms. Still, since the 'Prologue band' of 1953 with Kamuca, Sims, Rosolino etc, the whole concept seemed to concentrate on much more swing.

After we had arrived and installed ourselves eleven rows back, Ray Sonin introduced the band. Then he did a very strange thing! Bassist Curtis Counce was the only black in the band and in front of the assembled multitude, Sonin stepped back and deliberately shook Counce's hand. This action was of kindly intent but unspeakably wrong-headed, let along patronizing, but in those days the British man in the street was relatively innocent about any act which would today be unthinkable in racial terms – or was it unwitting arrogance? In the event the house emotionally cheered to the echo, and in the Albert Hall that was some echo! We can only hope that Counce had his appalling embarrassment, astonishment, disbelief, justifiably rising anger or whatever, somewhat alleviated by sensing the collective heart-in-the-right-place if monstrously gauche reaction of his public.

Bandleader Vic Lewis was now on stage. Who better with his unabashed admiration for all things Kenton, to introduce his idol – and there he was, this great tall figure striding to the piano. More cheering; he was playing unaccompanied – listen! Yes – before our very eyes he was unfolding that glorious 'Artistry' theme. Suddenly the others came to life, with much Latin rhythm effects from the remaining brass as the reeds took up the theme in half-tempo while those fantastic trombones (plus the depth of the tuba) countered with a variation on the 'Artistry Jumps' figure. Kenton was now out front; a dinning crescendo on the cymbals and in came those beautiful 'impossible' trumpets for the first time – a wall of sound, hitting the dome and coming back down again, resembling the visual effect of photographs slightly out-of-focus.

God! Those Albert Hall acoustics, but who cared? This was the *real* thing. During those forte final measures of 'Artistry in Rhythm' I turned to a friend with whom I had shared these ten years of growing up in jazz, but neither of us could speak. Our combined mutual experience of the first shockwaves of Kenton's 1940s records over AFN, the British band 'substitute' discs, then the originals coming along – and here and now the live Kenton sound washing over us, was all too much! This was one of the few times in my life I shed tears of joy.

Before the ovation had subsided, the band had kicked off its first number. What else but 'Stompin' at the Savoy'. Guitarist Ralph Blaze was first up (just like the record, we mouthed happily) – then the band – a boppish trumpet solo, identified as Sam Noto (who, unfortunately, was given far fewer opportunities later than the rather flashy Vinnie Tano) – more band, and now here was Bill Perkins up on his feet, tenor tone soft-edged but sinewy – again that great sonorous band sound but now we could *see* Mel Lewis do that incredible bit, as on the record, where he phrases with and between the ensemble, creating an impetus with such admirable control and colossal swing.

Thus it went on, a memorable mixture of Kenton standards: 'Intermission Riff' (marvellously inventive Carl Fontana), 'Painted Rhythm', 'Peanut

Vendor', 'Concerto to End All Concertos', '23° North 82° West'. Ordinary standards – 'Polka Dots' (more riveting Fontana), 'I've Got You under My Skin', 'Yesterdays' (cool swinging and rhapsodically mellow Perkins, respectively); and the new things, especially 'Royal Blue' in honour of Princess Margaret. And so on – the band could do no wrong; the audience was ecstatic and hanging on to every bar.

In the *Melody Maker*, 7 April 1956, it was reported that two of the Kenton personnel, baritone saxophonist Jack Nimitz and tenor saxophonist Spencer Sinatra, had suddenly returned home. The reasons given were that they were exhausted by this arduous tour, that they found their expenses exorbitant, but – it was whispered – they had been caught smoking marijuana. Whatever the reason behind their abrupt departure, British musicians had to be quickly co-opted. Harry Klein came in for Nimitz, and Tommy Whittle (to be replaced because of Whittle's later commitments by Don Rendell) for Sinatra. Klein and Rendell also continued with Kenton on the Continental leg of the tour.

Whittle's recollections, published in the *Melody Maker*, 21 April 1956, were illuminating and while, naturally, he made no comment about the validity of his own contribution or the reactions of his fellow musicians and leader, he illustrated the divisions that still existed between the technique and approach of American and British musicians.

Whittle had to travel to Taunton, 240 miles, and join the band without rehearsal. His reaction was overwhelmingly positive:

> The timing and sound of the band blasted me and I sizzled and went with it. I found a confidence and reserve of concentration I didn't know I had. The music is extremely difficult to play . . . the musicianship in the band is of the highest standard and the timing and swing of each individual musician is a thrill to sense and work with.
>
> The performance that these musicians put on during the strain of an extremely strenuous tour is nothing short of incredible. The stamina which is required to do this never seems to be lacking and there is always a zest and enthusiasm on or off the stand, particularly in the playing.
>
> Having worked in many name bands in this country, it is possible for me to make comparisons. In a British band there seem to be so many different viewpoints on how to play, and so many conflicting ways of feeling the beat. This internal difference of opinion is, I believe, the big reason for this second-rate feeling that we seem to be stuck with. It creates lack of spirit,

inferiority complexes and worst of all, cynicism. To be less abstract: in the Kenton band each individual musician seems to have the correct method of production and, even more important, a good sense of rhythm and timing or beat or swing – or whatever else you like to call it. In a British band only the highest-paid has anything like uniform production and the sense of time is almost completely ignored; certainly it is given no importance.

There are a great many musicians in this country who are capable of playing rhythmically. But how often do they have to suffer the excruciating agonies of a dragging rhythm section? And how touchy musicians are when it is suggested they are dragging.

Of Kenton himself, I can only say he put me right at ease with his natural manner. He is obviously a man of great sincerity; his music is a reflection of his ideals.

Of Whittle, Kenton (same issue) was quoted as saying: 'He is one of the greatest ever.' Unfortunately, Klein's contribution received no such accolades, maybe because his was a 'section' role, whereas Whittle had solo spaces.

But in the *Melody Maker*, 14 April, Kenton was quoted as saying: 'I would like to take Don and Harry back with me. Of course there are union difficulties to be overcome and I cannot say whether I shall be taking these musicians or not. I think they are fine players and I am happy to be taking them on my Continental tour.'

Despite these grandiose happenings, the *Melody Maker* and *New Musical Express* continued to feature news items that reflected the humdrum level of activity in 'the profession', but were redolent of an era coming to its close. One of these concerned saxist Brian Soothill, who had ended a long association with Les Garrat's teatime hall band at Bradford and had been replaced by former Cameo Club altoist Joe Markey. On the jazz scene, the *Melody Maker*, in February 1956, recorded that trumpeter Johnny Claes had died at the age of thirty-nine. Claes, a Belgian, came to England and established a reputation as a trumpeter who made a passable living as a jazz musician. Ronnie Scott and Max Jones (tenor saxophone) were two of his alumni.

It was next the turn of the traditionalists to hear someone in the flesh who had long been their foremost idol on record: Louis Armstrong, whose last visit to the UK had been in 1934. In April 1956, it was announced that in the following month Louis Armstrong and his All Stars would be playing a ten-day (two concerts a day) season at the Empress Hall, but as late as 28 April the *Melody Maker* struck a note of uncertainty, reporting that at the time of going to press no permits had been issued for Armstrong and company by the Ministry of Labour. The buffs were not surprised. The union-ban wrangle had been played out for so long that they would believe the appearance of their beloved Louis only when they actually saw him.

And most of the thousands that did see him (some every day, twice a day) had never been to, or knew anything about the Empress Hall, Earls Court, and would have no advance idea of the dire circumstances in which the world's greatest jazz trumpeter ever would play on the occasion of his first visit for twenty-two years. But the *Melody Maker*, 5 May, ran a banner headline: 'YES! LOUIS IS REALLY HERE!'

> Tonight's the night! After weeks of rumours, Louis Armstrong and his All Stars are scheduled to kick off their British tour at the Empress Hall tonight (Friday) at 6.15 p.m. The opening strains of Louis's signature tune, 'When It's Sleepy Time Down South' will mean that a British audience is hearing the great Satchmo in person for the first time in a generation.
>
> Louis and his party will arrive at London Airport on Thursday morning. With Louis are the All Stars: Trummy Young (trombone), Billy Kyle (piano), Edmond Hall (clarinet), Barrett Deems (drums), Jack Lesberg (bass) and singer Velma Middleton. From tonight for ten days the All Stars are to play twice nightly at the Empress Hall for about one hour and forty minutes. Supporting the All Stars will be singer Ella Logan and dancer Peg Leg Bates, with Britain's Vic Lewis Orchestra . . . Freddy Randall and his band are going to America in exchange, touring in a rock and roll package with Bill Haley's Comets, the Platters, the Colts, the Flamingos, La Vern Baker and the Red Prysock band . . .

The following week's issue carried a lengthy report of the Earls Court performance by editor Pat Brand, who would normally have given such a 'traditional' assignment to staffman Max Jones. Brand had obviously claimed the honour himself. He wrote:

SAN FRANCISCO CHRONICLE 1/23/62

Lively Arts

Satchmo---A Giant Upon This Earth

— **Ralph J. Gleason**

LOUIS ARMSTRONG, who is appearing now at the Venetian Room of the Fairmont Hotel in what can only be described as an exquisitely enjoyable show, represents something unique in our culture. We shall not see his like again, more's the pity.

While he is here with us at the Fairmont, you should see him and you should bring the youngsters to see him because he is, like Stravinsky and Casals and Picasso, a giant upon this earth: an original, the only one of his kind and there will be no more when he is gone.

It is fitting Louis Daniel Armstrong should be appearing in the top supper club on the West Coast on the hill that is a symbol of San Francisco's own stature. It is only sad that it took him so long to get there, climbing slowly from one grim joint to another over the years.

Now that he's there, it seems like he was always there and should always have been there. His personality, never mind the points to which the militants object, is a breath of fresh air because he is human in a way that most performers on that circuit never are. Even his contrivance is without pretense; at the least it is contrivance within the human scope.

That his show has genuine roots in the real folk history of this country may be overlooked by those to whom names like Joe Oliver and places like Storyville are unknown.

But Louis is real and he is America and to a great part of the world he represents the best of America. To the extent that we deny him that acceptance here, we do ourselves, more than him, an injustice.

As show business, Louis puts on a great performance, as music it runs from echoes of New Orleans street parades to bebop syllables straight out of a Juilliard School of Music stream-of-consciousness nightmare. Louis sings the corny ballads and they come to life, have meaning and move. When he plays, just like when the other real ones play, you know that this was it the first time it happened and it has never been equalled in his lifetime nor ever will be. Louis is more than a musician, more than an entertainer. Wrapped up in his music and in his sandpaper voice, is a way of life, a point of view and an attitude that this world will be much the poorer without. Don't miss him.

Thank you MR. GLEASON, Thank you very much.

Satchmo

● *Currently touring*
GREAT BRITAIN
for
HAROLD DAVISON

● *Extended European Tour*
Commencing APRIL 5 thru JUNE 10
Embracing
GREAT BRITAIN — FRANCE
GERMANY — SWITZERLAND
NORWAY — DENMARK
ITALY — HOLLAND
SPAIN — PORTUGAL

Booked Exclusively by
ASSOCIATED BOOKING CORPORATION
JOE GLASER, *President*
50 WEST 57 STREET, NEW YORK 19   JUdson 2-7700

CHICAGO ● MIAMI ● HOLLYWOOD ● LAS VEGAS ● DALLAS ● LONDON

'Yes! – Louis is really here!' So ran the headlines on the front page of last week's *Melody Maker*, ending the uncertainty that had existed for days before this announcement as to whether the fabulous Armstrong actually would be allowed to play his trumpet in the British Isles. He was really coming! Seven days later he would be fronting his All Stars in London's Empress Hall.

Doubts were stilled.

But the growing anger of the fans was not.

What was promoter Harold Davison doing, booking him into this vast arena whose acoustics were, to say the least, extremely suspect. And on a revolving stage! What was this – a circus? With 'supporting' acts! Why couldn't Louis fill the whole bill himself, as Kenton had done?

And the prices! More for an hour show by this sextet than for a two-hour show by the sixteen-piece Kenton Orchestra – which had itself upped the prices of seats far beyond that for any previous bandshow.

Angry letters poured into the *Melody Maker* offices.

At 6.15 on the night of Friday 4 May, the lights dimmed in the Empress Hall and the first of the twenty concerts was on. When it ended two hours later there was only one answer to the question of whether or not the protests were justified.

And the answer was yes.

The Vic Lewis Orchestra had opened the programme with a selection of 'oldies' that were, from my seat, practically inaudible. Then, on to the central stage, stumped Peg Leg Bates; an artist whose dexterity is unquestionable, but whose frequent references to his disability were the very reverse. For twenty minutes we watched him dance himself into a lather of sweat, then were introduced to Ella Logan.

Nobody could fault Miss Logan's ability as a performer. One could certainly fault the promoters for expecting a singer of ballads to hold a jazz-hungry audience for twenty minutes. The slow handclap she was given could more properly have been directed at them.

And then, at 7.30 p.m. came the All Stars. Now, every ear attuned to the centre-stage – and let's face it – within a few bars of 'Sleepy Time Down South' we knew our fears were coming true. The echoing of Barrett Deems's drums; the almost complete absence of sound from Billy Kyle's piano and Jack Lesberg's bass; the fluctuating volume as the front line swung slowly round – towards us, at us and past us. Those who paid twenty-five shillings a seat had every reason to complain.

Brand continued his report by noting improvements in the sound balance on the following Tuesday and he pronounced himself pleased with the fact that Peg Leg Bates's and Ella Logan's spots had been cut to ten minutes each. But after an absence of twenty-two years, he complained, the fact that the world's greatest trumpeter had to play on a revolving stage was an artistic disgrace and he opined that the profit motive, however inescapable and understandable, should not have been allowed to ruin a performance for which this country had waited so long. He also hinted at financial wheeler-dealing behind this outrage.

> There remains the question of the prices, and some startling facts emerge from the enquiries I have made, which can best be summarized as follows. First, why were prices higher than for Kenton? Because, I am assured, the payroll for the sextet is higher than that for the entire Kenton Orchestra; it is probably the highest-paid combination in the world. To this outlay must be added the cost of halls, cost of billing, cost of transporting the All Stars from America and back, and during their tour of Britain.
>
> Further, *there is the cost of the Randall tour in America* [Brand's italics]. Before Louis was permitted to arrive here by the Musicians' Union I am told that the promoters had to put down the entire amount that the Randall band was to get in the States. To this is added the cost of 'bolstering' [Brand's quote marks] the Randall package with Bill Haley and the Comets and supporting attractions, and although Freddy's success in America is assured, he is at present an unknown drawing power.
>
> To cover this fantastic outlay the promoters of the Armstrong tour were forced to hire halls with the biggest capacity, to spend money on the best possible amplification equipment – and to charge higher prices.
>
> Is it worth paying to see and hear Louis, Velma Middleton and the All Stars? Unhesitatingly, I say yes!

An unusually interesting critique, if only because it touches upon the economics of the exchange, something Max Jones, in his preoccupation with the music, would probably not have mentioned. Undoubtedly the financial considerations were exceedingly convoluted and the details of them will, most likely, never be known. Perhaps Brand, aware both of the long, long years without American musicians in this country and of the tortuous negotiations that preceded the appearances of Kenton and Armstrong, did not wish to upset the apple cart by divulging more. On the other hand, Brand, not very conversant with jazz, was seeing events from an ordinary reporter's viewpoint and, as a result, his observations are highly relevant.

The payment to artists to 'bolster' Randall's American trip was obviously the nub of the impossibility of a *genuinely* reciprocal arrangement. Randall was virtually unknown in the States and it was necessary to surround him with – or rather that he be a part of – a rock and roll package in which his contributions would have been out of place, to make it appear that the exchange was legitimately conducted. Armstrong, on the other hand, was a famous, revered figure in England and, irrespective of the nature of his presentation, was assured of massive support.

But that presentation! Harold Rosen's apparently hare-brained notion of Louis and his All Stars playing on a boat offshore from the UK to escape the palsied hand of the MU now seemed, in the light of that appalling revolving stage at Earls Court, to be a *good* idea, given a reasonably large boat and a fairly calm sea. Modern-jazz fans had already proved that they could brave the Irish Sea in all its capricious moods to hear Kenton and Herman, and it would be inconceivable that the duffel-coated, chukka-booted and sandalled traditionalists in the Blue Posts or Cottage Club would not have risked seasickness and missed hearing the great Armstrong.

Naturally, there was an overwhelming desire on the part of the trumpeter's admirers to meet their idol, and his dressing room was besieged to such an extent that Humphrey Lyttelton took it upon himself to place his sixteen stone and six foot three inches at the entrance, like a centurion guarding Caesar. One of those who did gain admittance was alto saxophonist Harry Hayes – rightfully so, since he was a member of Armstrong's only white band, on the great man's 1932 visit. To Hayes's delight, Armstrong, looking up, immediately recognized him. Another welcome visitor was Nat Gonella, whose own playing was fashioned in the Armstrong mould and projected on the variety halls and on hundreds of recordings during the 1930s.

While the JATP Flood Relief concert had breached the ban, it was the appearances of Kenton and Armstrong, representing opposite extremes of jazz, that prepared the ground for a steadily increasing number of subsequent jazz visitors. For 1956 was an epochal year for the UK jazz enthusiast. The historic visits of Kenton and Armstrong were to be followed by more giants: Sidney Bechet, virbraphonist Lionel Hampton and an unexpected early return of

Louis Armstrong in somewhat bizarre circumstances.

Bechet arrived in Britain in September. (His first visit to Britain had been with Will Marion Cook's Southern Syncopated Orchestra in 1919 and the second had led to his playing with Humphrey Lyttelton's band in November 1949 and to promoter Bert Wilcox being put on trial at the Old Bailey for contravening articles and sections of the Aliens Order Act 1920.) His 1956 visit, however, had the stamp of official approval. Promoter Harold Davison did not have to fear prosecution in arranging a tour for Bechet, accompanied by a French traditional-style band led by clarinettist André Reweliotty.

Humphrey Lyttelton's band played the support set. By now Lyttelton had a different band from that of November 1949, an infinitely more rounded and generally more accomplished unit. They would, in fact, have given Bechet much better support than that provided by Reweliotty, but again the politics of 'exchange' determined the situation.

Jack Hutton, reviewing the concert for the *Melody Maker*, remarked: 'Bechet's effect on the Reweliotty band (who played the opening numbers on their own) was amazing – he made them riff and generate a little swing, but when they opened up with "Down in Honky Tonk Town" it sounded like the "Charge of the Chasseurs Afriques".' Hutton also made reference to the effect Armstrong's All Stars had had on the Lyttelton band, and expressed the view that their solos and riffing were infinitely superior to the French band. It was a pity, in the light of this improvement, that Lyttelton was not given the chance to redeem the faltering support his band had given Bechet in November 1949.

The audiences for the importations so far – Kenton, Armstrong and Bechet – were almost reverent in their attention, their physical reactions no more than head-nodding and applause and some cheering, but a 'happening' at the Empress Hall, Earls Court in October 1956 saw frenetic response to a visiting orchestra. The 20 October 1956 issue of the *Melody Maker* reported that Lionel Hampton and His Orchestra would be appearing in the country the following month and that a special midnight matinee for 'serious jazz enthusiasts' would be held at the Royal Festival Hall on 13 November, arranged by the Visiting Orchestras Appreciation Society, in association with the National Federation of Jazz Organizations. This announcement echoed a similar one in the same paper in 1933, when great emphasis was laid on a 'special' concert by Duke Ellington's Orchestra to

> feature some of these quieter and more individual compositions of his which have not hitherto been played in London. We have promised him a quiet and attentive audience which will know what to expect and how to listen. The applause should come at the end of each number and not in the middle in the distressing and irritating way which has marred the work of the band elsewhere. Let us show that ours is the real public.

Hampton, who had played on so many classic jazz recordings with the Benny Goodman Quartet and Quintet, and made recordings under his own name with the cream of US jazz musicians, black and white, in the late thirties, played in this country with a fifteen-piece band seemingly hell-bent on whipping up hysteria. The audience jived and jitterbugged, stamped, applauded and cheered in a most un-British fashion. Bob Dawbarn reported:

> It was amazing, extraordinary, fantastic and any other adjectives you like to add. Britain has never seen anything like the show put on by vibraphonist-drummer-pianist-juggler-bandleader-showman Lionel Hampton.
> Along with 6,800 others I attended the Empress Hall on Sunday afternoon for Hamp's British debut. I don't think any of us will ever forget it. Trying to review the occasion and analyse one's feelings about this unique circus is not that easy. I wonder what the people who complained about Armstrong's excessive showmanship will make of Hampton? He makes the Danny Kayes and the Johnny Rays seem the rawest amateurs at crowd-raising. It was like taking part in a super colossal revivalist meeting.
> The extraordinary part of the show was the way Hampton built up to a climax in the second half. His gyrations and incitement of the crowd became wilder until he reached his *tour de force* – 'Flying Home' . . .
> As Eddie Chamblee honked and squealed into the mike for chorus after chorus, Hamp led Elsie Smith and four or five more of the group out into the audience and round the arena. The audience stood to see what was going on and, like the Pied Piper of Hamelin, he led them back with him. Young men and girls poured down the aisles to pack the gangways and area in front of the stage. One young hopeful climbed on to the back of the stage – but fled at the sight of a burly commissionaire. A few wooden seats fell over, but there was

never any sign of trouble or 'rioting', although the national press naturally made the most of it next day. One young man, who had behaved throughout the faster numbers as if testing a new jet pilot's ejector seat (much to the discomfort of Maurice Burman who was sitting in front of, and at times underneath, him), was now undoubtedly 'gone', standing on his seat with arms outstretched in supplication to Hampton, who looked as though he was being worked by strings.

Eventually Hampton, reluctantly acting on instructions, went into 'God Save the Queen', some twenty minutes before the scheduled end of the concert. When I left ten minutes later, the arena was still dotted with groups shouting for 'Hamp'.

The *Melody Maker*, 17 November, reported on the special concert, the notice unsigned:

> Lionel Hampton was the star of the midnight concert at the Royal Festival Hall on Tuesday, but Britain's Johnny Dankworth became the focal point when he shouted: 'What about playing some jazz!' The Hampton band has been the centre of controversy throughout its tour and Tuesday was no exception. The show was advertised as being an all-jazz concert for musicians and real jazz fans. On the Wednesday the *MM* was inundated with telephone calls from dissatisfied customers who protested that the concert was no different from those seen at other venues.
>
> In a conversation with the *MM*, Johnny said he made his vocal protest after watching Hampton throw his drumsticks in the air and pretending to catch them. 'There were murmurs of agreement around me, so others in the audience felt the same. In the interval two members of the audience approached me and asked why I didn't leave if I objected to what was being played. In fact, I decided to do so. I have asked for my money back and shall continue to ask for it. After all, it was specifically advertised as a jazz concert. And I understand that Hampton was very carefully briefed. It was not my intention to create any sort of disturbance, merely to offer a suggestion. I shall, in fact, write to Hampton explaining this.'
>
> Johnny added that in all fairness he should say that opinions on the matter were evenly divided and Hampton may have felt that he had to please all sections of the audience . . .

The report by Burman read: 'I blame the VOAS and the NJF and Hampton – for hogging the show. There were some marvellous talents in the band – largely wasted, and Hampton's antics deserved the booing. The action of Johnny Dankworth vocally demanding more jazz was unconventional, but I wish I had had the courage to join him.'

Dankworth, the jazz enthusiast, was forgetting that he, too, had had difficulty in getting over a purely jazz policy and had been forced to compromise. Not a strict parallel; but his outburst did at least illustrate the eternal conflict between artistic beliefs and economic realities, although it is unlikely that Hampton was unduly bothered by such ideological considerations.

Humphrey Lyttelton, in his *Second Chorus*, wrote:

> Two organizations, the Visiting Orchestras Appreciation Society and the National Jazz Federation, arranged to present a midnight concert especially for musicians and 'serious' jazz lovers. It was promised that Lionel Hampton would drop his usual presentation and put on a concert of highbrow jazz for the cognoscenti. When he turned up and presented his normal stage show with all the trimmings, there was a furious outcry. Nobody quite knew what they had expected, but it wasn't this. Hampton had insulted the 'jazz-lovers'.
>
> But it was really the other way round – the jazz-lovers had insulted Hampton by trying to impose their wishes and demands without bothering to find out how he felt about it. They had asumed that he would leap at the chance to turn his back on the public and play something special *for the élite*. It was quite clear that he had no wish to do anything of the sort. He was bewildered by the whole proceedings and looked thoroughly unhappy and ill at ease until some members of *hoi polloi* who had impudently gained admission began to clap and whistle and stamp their feet.
>
> The moral to all this is that if you want music for eggheads, you must find eggheads to play it. If you start to apply the same treatment, the same critical approach to jazz as that which is traditionally applied to serious music, sooner or later you will run into absurdity.

The Dankworth outburst also prompted a tart observation from Stanley Dance in *Jazz Journal*, January 1957.

> Hampton's midnight matinee poses some interesting new questions. 'What about playing some jazz?' bawled by one musician to another suggests the bandleader is able to recognize jazz when he hears it. What we would like to know is whether Dankworth attended the Kenton concert. If he did, was he heard to bawl the same question? If not, why not?
>
> We sat through the Kenton concert indignant and incredulous without bawling once, because we knew that in the audience there were several hundred jackasses who had come long distances to hear the noise.
>
> But suppose we go to a modern-jazz concert and find the musicians not playing jazz, are we not, with this precedent, more than entitled to bawl?

The flooding of an area of East Anglia had led to an officially recognized performance of American jazz musicians in England in 1953, but the brutal invasion of Hungary by Russia in October 1956 brought the UK the bonus of Louis Armstrong, appearing in the country for the second time in the same year. The occasion was a concert at the Royal Festival Hall in December 1956, in aid of the Lord Mayor of London's Hungarian Relief Fund, Armstrong playing with the Royal Philharmonic Orchestra under Norman Del Mar and a quintet of British musicians: George Chisholm (trombone), Sid Phillips (clarinet), Dill Jones (piano), Lennie Bush (bass) and Jack Parnell (drums).

More irony: no objections, no demands for reciprocity, from the comrades at Sicilian Avenue, although what their private feelings were that such a concert was arranged because of naked aggression by the country they revered most can only be imagined. Although they gave BBC TV permission to film the event they forbade any recordings being made. They had to make some petty gesture to save face. In the event, no television cameras were present and perhaps it was fortunate that neither these, nor recording engineers were present. On the other hand, had the shambles the concert turned out to be been filmed or recorded it would have illustrated just what a totally misguided concept was this alliance of a classical orchestra with a jazz musician. It was yet another pathetic example of those seeking to give jazz 'respectability', by having, in this instance, a distinguished jazzman combine with an orchestra in this prestigious venue in aid of a good cause; but to precious little musical effect.

If Armstrong had just played with the British musicians booked to accompany him – who, incidentally, were not mentioned in the programme – it could, musically, have been a much better presentation than at the Empress Hall on that revolving stage, and with no Peg Leg Bates or Ella Logan to hold up the proceedings. But the occasion was to have the hocus-pocus of formal trappings – the stuffed shirts, the baton-waving for a 'special' orchestration of 'St Louis Blues' – a totally pretentious gallimaufry.

Insufficient rehearsal was one reason for the concert's failure, but the misalliance of jazz musicians with symphonists was a fundamental cause of the breakdown in communication between two entirely different musical cultures. Humphrey Lyttelton's comments on the concert in his *Second Chorus* were sharply apposite:

> Now, in Britain we are at a disadvantage. We have few, if any, conductors who are familiar with the jazz idiom. Leonard Bernstein, who conducted the orchestra for the New York concert, was able to converse with Louis in the technical jargon of jazz. When a passage turned up for the small jazz band to play on their own, he had only to ask Louis, 'How many choruses, Pops?' for the whole thing to be settled. In this respect, poor Norman Del Mar was at sea.
>
> At the first rehearsal he bounced about the piano stool like an agitated teddy bear. 'Stop, stop, stop! I realize that you fellows are flexible, but I must know where I am to bring in my chaps!' It was impossible to leave a gap in the score for the little group to fill in. Every bar that was to be played had to be marked on the score. Where a jazz player would recognize, by ear, the exact point he should come in, the conductor had to have it down in black and white or he was lost.
>
> Louis himself was all calm and reassurance at the rehearsal. He addressed Mr Del Mar indulgently as 'professor', 'daddy' and, on one occasion, 'Fats'. (This is a lovely story. One wonders how Del Mar reacted to being described as 'Fats'!) When Mr Del Mar, pounding out the orchestral part on the piano, roared out a desperate enquiry about the tempo, Louis put a hand on his shoulder. 'Hold that one, Daddy . . . you got a good tempo there, boy!'
>
> When the concert time came round next day, the Royal Festival Hall was filled to capacity with the most heterogeneous audience it has ever seen. Dinner jackets, fur stoles, white-tie-and-tails, rubbed shoulders with duffel coats, sweaters and jeans. The occasion was charged with the sort of bogus dignity at which the British excel.

On reflection the concert and its rehearsal should have been filmed and/or recorded, if only to have enshrined on celluloid or shellac Louis Armstrong referring to Mr Del Mar as 'Professor', 'Daddy' and 'Fats'. The film would also have caught the sorry spectacle of Del Mar sitting on the dais with his head buried despairingly in his hands. It would not have occurred to him that on that very day it was likely that there were literally hundreds of orchestras plodding through, as he had done, Liszt's 'Hungarian Rhapsody'; the audience could well have done without another rendering, especially if the alternative was the magic of Louis Armstrong on a bonus visit.

Like the crowd that attended the two JATP concerts at the

Gaumont State, Kilburn, three years earlier, the *raison d'être* for the occasion was not uppermost in this audience's minds, but generally the feeling was that Hungary had been savagely overrun. There was one dissenting voice in the bar after the show – Denis Preston's, his left-wing past re-emerging as he bitterly denounced the deposed Hungarian regime as 'fascists'.

What a year 1956 was for the jazz community. The high-powered bombast of Kenton's men impressing with their colossal musicianship; the Armstrong All Stars with Louis still in command, and Ed Hall's clarinet a joy; Bechet's third and this time official visit, but with an inferior foreign band, an infinitely superior British band playing only a supporting role; a riotous (though riot-free) Hampton extravaganza; and the fiasco of pairing Louis Armstrong with a 'long-hair' orchestra at the Royal Festival Hall in the name of charity. There were, however, more delights – and more controversy – to come.

Jazz had become a highly varied music, eliciting highly varied reactions. Overall, though, the British jazz public remained divided into traditionalists and modernists, these respective factions supporting only the music of their choice.

10

The Invasion Mounts

The traumatic events of 1956 led to constant visits to these shores by the bands and musicians who had fashioned the language of jazz in the land of its birth.

In January 1957 Eddie Condon and his band 'hit town' – an Americanism that had almost literal application to these wild and not so young, men. Condon, guitar (fifty-two); Wild Bill Davison, trumpet (fifty-one); George Wettling, drummer (fifty); Gene Schroeder, piano (forty-two) and Cutty Cutshall, trombone (forty-six) were high-livers. The rest of the unit soberly comprised Leonard Gaskin, bass (thirty-seven) – the one black player in the band – and Bob Wilber, clarinet (twenty-seven), a revivalist in the company of seasoned veterans with a 'history'.

It is no reflection on Wilber's skills that the Condon enthusiasts would have much preferred to see veteran Pee Wee Russell, so long a member of the Condon alumni, instead; or Tony Parenti, Volly de Faut, Ernie Caceres, Sal Franzella, Joe Dixon, or Creole Condonite Albert Nicholas from New Orleans, all of whom had a history. But Wilber, although he was American and had played and recorded with Sidney Bechet, trumpeters Henry Goodwin, Buck Clayton and Clark Terry, trombonists Jimmy Archey, Lou McGarity and Vic Dickenson, bassists Pop Foster and many other veterans, was, in the eyes of a great number of aficionados, virtually in the same mould as, say, Wally Fawkes, Sandy Brown, Ian Christie, or Monty Sunshine. He did not have a *history*.

But to the Condon admirers, the very presence of the legendary leader and the equally legendary Wild Bill Davison and George Wettling was excitement enough. Surprisingly, Bechet had been met by only four people on his arrival at London Airport in September the previous year. On the day of Condon's arrival, however, there was a posse of musicians and fans to greet what George Melly described in *Owning Up* as 'ageing delinquents'. *That* comment, coming as it did from a declared libertine, revealed that the excitement attending their visit was as much social as musical, and it was not long before the welcoming aspect of this visit was in full swing.

Bottles of whisky were produced by the well-wishers at Heathrow, and the visitors, already intoxicated, were naturally delighted with the reception. Eddie Condon accepted a swig from Max Jones's bottle, looked at Max's totally hairless head, and said, 'Don't bother with the name of your barber, just give me the address of your distillery.'

Jones toured with the band and recalled this experience in his book *Talking Jazz* in a chapter called 'Eddie Condon'.

> On the morning of their arrival the band booked in at a hotel in Piccadilly. Condon tentatively asked if he could have a whisky for breakfast. The waiter replied: 'In an English hotel, sir, a guest can get alcoholic refreshment at any hour of the day or night.' Condon turned a bleary eye to Dick Gehman (Condon's publicist) and announced, 'Dick, I'm taking out papers.'

Jones, in the 26 January *Melody Maker*, reviewed the band's Glasgow concert.

> Davison dominated the band, and the qualities we expect – humour, wildness, assertive attack and drive, and tremendous dynamic contrast – are all present in his style, and he combines them with considerable artistry, keeping everything healthily alive by the fullness and feeling in his tone.
>
> The band sports a sound rhythm section and a fine degree of in-tuneness: there are less extended ensemble 'ride-outs' than I had hoped for. As for Condon, he seemed the most dispensable member of the group after the first or second number. His guitar was not heard nor, unfortunately, were many of his casual announcements. The excessive informality of the presentation was not to the liking of the audience.
>
> The band met with a very mixed reception at St Andrew's Hall, Glasgow. A member of the audience yelled: 'You're drunk, why don't you go home.' Condon retorted: 'OK, let's have your keys.'

In his write-ups on touring with Condon ('No Rest Cure'), Max Jones commented on the quiet and serious Bob Wilber, and it was ironic that it was this sober young man who was the only one to arrive late for a concert. He overslept in a Leicester hotel and Bruce Turner, who was with the Humphrey Lyttelton band on the show, took over.

Pat Brand in *Melody Maker* wrote: 'One aspect of the Anglo-US band exchange ... Bruce Turner's remarkable *tour de force* at Leicester last Friday when he took over Bob Wilber's spot in the Condon band at literally a minute's notice and brilliantly busked an hour's concert, was a revelation to the Americans, and an eye-opener to most of the audience.'

Wilber relates the experience in his autobiography *Music was not Enough*. Like many Americans, he has a strange notion of British dialect and accents.

When I woke up and looked at my watch it was already past seven. The first performance of the double concert started at six! In a total panic, I jumped out of bed, pulled on my clothes, grabbed my horn and ran downstairs to call a taxi. It should have been no surprise to me that taxi drivers are the same the world over.

'Take me to the concert.'
'Which concert, mate?'
'The Eddie Condon concert.'
'The Eddie who concert?'
'The Eddie Condon band, from New York.'
'Where is this 'ere Condon bloke playing?'
'I don't know, but surely you must know.'

By trial and error, we eventually arrived at the concert hall just as the band was about to go into 'That's a Plenty', our big finale. Now that band contained some of the fastest-living and hardest-drinking legends of jazz, such as George Wettling, Wild Bill Davison, Cutty Cutshall and Gene Schroeder, not to mention Eddie himself. It appealed to Eddie's sense of humour to recall in later years that the only member of the group who ever missed a concert was the young, serious and sober Bob Wilber. Bruce Turner, however, was a capable [sic] deputy. In fact he was the main topic of interest in the newspaper reviews the next day. I got to know Bruce quite well on the tour. He had been playing dance music on the boats in order to come to New York to study with Lee Konitz. When he was warming up his alto in the dressing-room, he sounded just like Konitz, but on the stage his clarinet sounded like Edmond Hall, and his alto like Johnny Hodges. Finally I said to him, 'Bruce, I don't understand. You sound just like Lee Konitz backstage but on stage it's all Hall and Rabbit. You're a great musician but I haven't heard Bruce Turner yet.'

'Dad,' he said, 'you wouldn't want to hear that!'

Allowing that in the jazz world there are an enormous number of us who are pots calling kettles black, this question, coming from the eclectic Wilber (who has been 'Bechet', 'Bigard' and 'Goodman', to mention only three in his career) smacked of true gall.

Humphrey Lyttelton wrote the tour up in the *Melody Maker*, a report Wilber himself reproduced in full:

> Needless to say, [Eddie Condon's] now legendary Silent Guitar caused a certain amount of comment. Some writers seem to have acquired the notion – from what source I cannot think – that Eddie Condon came here as the world's greatest guitarist. No one who has read Eddie's own autobiography, *We Called It Music*, will imagine that this description found any favour with him. Nothing could be more devastating than his own self-definition when referring to a famous Louis Armstrong session – 'They let me sit in a corner and hold my banjo.' . . .
>
> Opinions about his role as compere and organizer are mixed. In many places, where he inadvisedly spurned the microphone, his wisecracks fell on the stoniest ground. A pity, because when he was on form and when he found a good-humoured member of the audience who could act as a stooge, he was very funny . . .
>
> Summing up, one could fairly say that those writers who knew their jazz accepted and appreciated Eddie's role as master of ceremonies.
>
> The most receptive and appreciative places were London and Edinburgh, from which you may draw your own conclusions. Comments about the rest of the band varied. Once again, total ignorance begat a certain amount of disappointment. The West Country critic who asserted that Condon has 'long preached purity in traditional jazz' (did you ever hear such rubbish!) naturally went away disgruntled. 'All we got was a "pop" concert,' he grumbled. On the other hand, the music appears to have had the most curious effect on one listener north of the border. He said in relation to Cutty, ' "Sentimental Journey" featured ex-Goodman bandsman Cutty Cutshall. The smooth, liquid flow fom his tenderly handled trombone crystallized in the Cutshall-created cathedral chill to form the bluest of blue stalactites above a hushed audience's head.' I must say I liked Kingsley Amis in the *Observer* about Wild Bill, whose cornet 'constantly seemed about to produce not just notes but a wisp of black smoke or a shower of gravel'. I am less enthusiastic about his schoolboy assessment of Bob Wilber – 'whom any half-dozen British practitioners might have replaced with advantage'. The spoilsport curtails our merriment by withholding their names. I know at least two eminent British practitioners who agree with me that Wilber was the most exciting and impressive musician in the group.

Lyttelton curtailed *our* merriment by not naming those two eminent British practitioners.

Alan Elsdon

Freddy Randall

Kenny Ball

Terry Lightfoot's New Orleans Jazzmen, with trumpeter Dickie Hawdon reverting to a traditional role

Chris Barber

Acker Bilk

Bob Wallis and his Storyville Jazzmen are fanatic Traditional Jazz Musicians who sought their inspiration direct from the great masters like Louis Armstrong, Kid Ory and George Lewis, who promulgated this American Negro music of New Orleans at the turn of the century.

Bookings were plentiful in the Honky-Tonks and Gambling Dens of the notorious suburb Storyville - where tunes were frequently requested at gun point.

Passing Storyville is the famous Mississippi River which during the Season abounded with pleasure boats. Traditional Jazz and gambling were features of the trips and many of todays most famous Trad men played aboard them in their youth. The Storyville Jazzmen are attired as Mississippi Gamblers of that period.

Bob Wallis in a typical traddy-pop handout

Paddy Lightfoot

Monty Sunshine, star of Chris Barber's best-selling 'Petite Fleur'

Humphrey Lyttelton's band, 1954: (*L to R*) Micky Ashman (b), John Picard, Lyttelton, George Hopkinson, Bruce Turner, Freddie Legon, Johnny Parker, Wally Fawkes

Humphrey Lyttelton's 'saxophone' band on 'This is Your Life', 1958: (*L to R*) Lyttelton, Eddie Taylor, Eamonn Andrews, John Picard, Brian Brocklehurst (b), Tony Coe, Ian Armit, Jimmy Skidmore, Joe Temperley

Sandy Brown, a 'renegade traditionalist'

Bruce Turner's Jump Band: (*L to R*) John Picard, John Armatage, Turner, John Chilton, Jim Bray, Collin Bates

MELODY MAKER March 14, 1953

For one day, the impossible had happened

TILL THE END OF THE WORLD
Recorded by BING CROSBY, LES BAXTER and JIMMY WAKELY
By VAUGHN HORTON, writer of "Mockin' Bird Hill"
SMALL ORCHESTRATIONS 3/-
SOUTHERN MUSIC PUB. CO.
8 Denmark Street, London

A gathering of UK jazzmen pays homage to the Master with unknown interviewer: (*L to R*) Mike Collier, Ian MacIntosh, Humphrey Lyttelton, Freddy Randall, Al Woodrow, Ian Christie, Diz Disley, Alan Leet

Stan Kenton (*left*) discusses a score with Pete Rugolo

George Lewis and Ken Colyer bands combined: (*L to R*) Mac Duncan, Johnny Bastable, Joe Watkins, Jim Robinson, Kid Howard, Colyer, Lewis, Colin Bowden, Ian Wheeler

Condon disciple Mick Mulligan (*left*) with his mentor and Al Woodrow (*right*) at the Cottage Club

Jack Teagarden (*left*) and Earl Hines are greeted by a host of musicians including Chris Barber at London Airport

Al Woodrow with Billie Holiday at the Cottage Club

Eddie Condon introduces (*L to R*): Archie Semple, Bruce Turner, Bob Wilber, Cutty Cutshall

Zoot Sims with Jackie Dougan

Bruce Turner with Ben Webster

New Orleans All Stars Glasgow, 1966

The jazz scene abounded in memorable characters: (*top left*) Eddie Harvey, first 'renegade traditionalist'; (*top right*) Wally Fawkes, Britain's first 'New Orleans' clarinettist; (*bottom left*) Lennie 'Herr' Hastings; (*bottom right*) Gypsy Larry, skiffle broom stylist

Norman Granz

Denis Preston, Britain's answer to Granz

Doug Dobell

Glasgow promoter Bob Gardiner with George Lewis and his manager Dorothy Tait

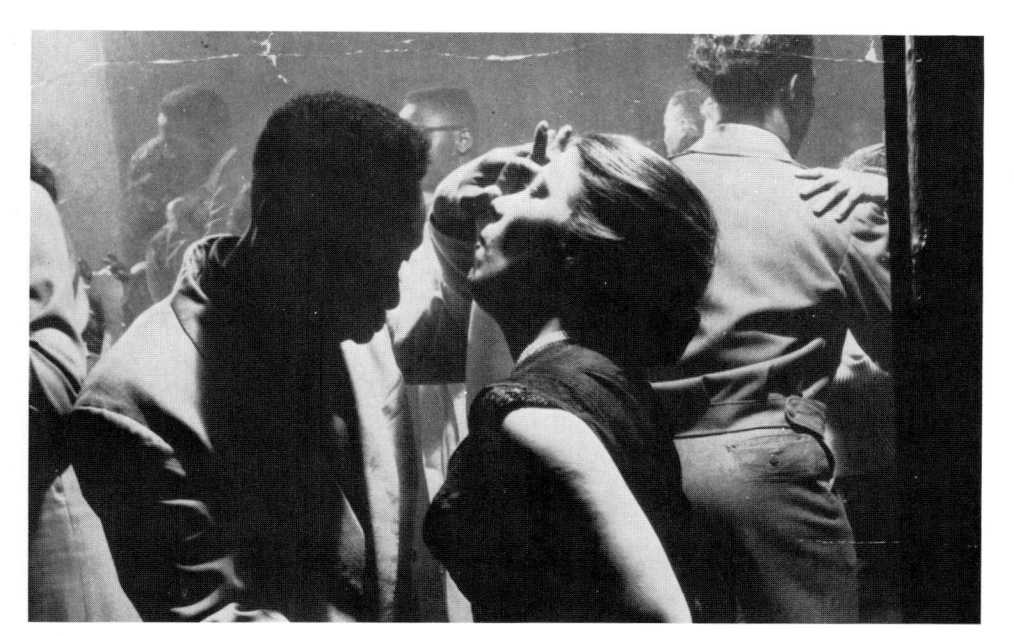

Sunset Club, 1953

Avant-garde pioneer Joe Harriott blowing with traditionalist Chris Barber

Rex Harris

Max Jones

Returning to London, the Condon high-livers met up again with their British counterparts, particularly in the Cottage Club in Litchfield St, and spent a great deal of time drinking with the likes of Mick Mulligan, Ian Christie and Frank Parr.

The tour, however, was not a financial success, and Condon never returned to Britain. In his survey on jazz in London in Leonard Feather's *Encyclopedia of Jazz*, Benny Green referred to the band as 'a circus'.

The next arrival, in April 1957, was Count Basie and His Orchestra. Their initial concert took place at the Royal Festival Hall in the presence of HRH Princess Margaret. Regarded as one of the four top great black orchestras in the thirties, Basie had managed, unlike most of his contemporaries, to maintain a large unit. It was his first visit to England and, inevitably, the 1957 personnel was unfavourably compared by older collectors with the thirties band that had trumpeter Buck Clayton, trombonists Dicky Wells and Benny Morton, baritone saxophonist Jack Washington, alto saxophonist Earle Warren, tenor saxophonists Herschel Evans and Lester Young and what many regarded as the greatest rhythm section of all: drummer Jo Jones, guitarist Freddie Green, bassist Walter Page and the Count himself at the piano.

Only Basie and Green remained. The band was totally different in character; now more polished, the arrangements more sophisticated, but with a still impressive array of soloists. Its personnel was Reunald Jones, Thad Jones, Wendell Culley, Joe Newman (trumpet); Henry Coker, Benny Powell, Bill Hughes (trombone); Marshall Royal, Billy Graham, Frank Foster, Frank Wess (saxophones); Freddie Green (guitar); Sam Jones (bass); Sonny Payne (drums), Count Basie (piano) and Joe Williams (vocalist).

The reports were mostly enthusiastic, despite the older hands vainly pining for the pre-war band. These were referred to by Humphrey Lyttelton as 'neurotic'. Max Jones in the *Melody Maker*, 6 April 1957, said: 'This is a beautiful band. It swings irresistibly: partly because the arrangements encourage it, partly because the rhythm team provides a perfect foundation, also because every man is a swinger and every section is a knockout.' It was left to the *News Chronicle* to provide the most eccentric account: 'Princess Margaret tapped her feet to negro rhythms . . . the Count later said: "I'm gonna call my baby (his wife) and tell her of this honour." '

In the same issue, certain bandleaders and musicians offered their opinions.

Bandleader Johnny Dankworth: 'I haven't got over it yet; an object lesson.'

Bandleader Eric Delaney: 'Honestly, it makes you feel like chucking everything in.' (Cf Delaney's comment on Kenton drummer, Mel Lewis, on p. 193.)

BBC Show Band leader Cyril Stapleton: 'One of the most exciting bands ever – we must have the wrong sort of blood in our veins.'

But the most illuminating and refreshingly honest comment was from Ted Heath: 'At last we have been able to hear the real spirit and feeling of jazz. It proves it is useless sending jazz to America. You have to send them something different.'

Heath had expressed an incontrovertible truth concerning the innately superior jazz sense of the Americans, and however unpalatable it may have been (especially to the Musicians' Union executive) he hit the nail on the head regarding a specific market reality.

The next American visitor was in total contrast to the Armstrong package with its elements of vaudeville, the high-powered bombast of the Kenton Orchestra, the swooping majesty of Bechet overriding an inferior accompanying unit, the alcoholic quipster in Condon, and the sophisticated and powerful Basie band, but in many respects his was the outstanding success story.

In Chapter 4, 'Traditionalism Rampant', I referred to the extraordinary impact made on young British musicians by the recordings of the New Orleans musicians who had not joined the trek to Chicago and New York in the twenties, and who were largely unrecorded, in print or shellac, until historically-conscious researchers publicized and recorded them.

In April 1957 came the first visit of an almost mythical figure who had been virtually deified by the fundamentalists, clarinettist George Lewis. Truly, there was something saintlike about this frail black man with the unique style and a poverty-stricken background, an irresistible combination for zealous traditionalists, their heads as full of ideologies as of musical values.

The tour was organized by young Northern entrepreneur Paddy McKiernan, who had his university-degree initials on his notepaper, in collaboration with the National Federation of Jazz Organizations. According to Jay Allison Stewart, Lewis's biographer[*] (and manager under her real name, Dorothy Tait), Lewis accepted the English offer provided that Ken Colyer's band accompanied him in the UK and then the leader played with Lewis's band in the United States in exchange.

The State Department had obviously been apprised of Colyer's defiance of the immigration laws during his much-heralded pilgrimage to New Orleans and they delayed their decision, but once the dreary politics were eventually sorted out, Lewis, on 10 April 1957, boarded a BOAC plane as a first-class passenger bound for Manchester. On arrival he was greeted by a brass band composed of Colyer's band and like-minded musicians, Colyer's band then comprising Ian Wheeler (clarinet), Mac Duncan (trombone), Johnny Bastable (banjo), Colin Bowden (drums), Ron Ward (bass), Bob Kelly (piano) and Colyer himself.

Weighing barely ninety pounds, stricken with a variety of illnesses and semi-illiterate, Lewis had had fame thrust upon him in a manner he could never possibly have visualized in the twenties and thirties when he had played occasional gigs in and near his home town after performing humble tasks by day.

In a tough, hard-working life, Lewis had been a stevedore, and many collectors treasure a copy of a superb photo-book, *Jazzways*, published in 1946 and edited by George S. Rosenthal and Frank Zachary, in collaboration with two scholars of New Orleans music, Frederic Ramsey Jnr. and Rudi Blesh. It includes a stark photograph of Lewis in singlet and dockworker's cap working as a longshoreman, shifting sacks of coffee heavier than himself, his face registering weariness and resignation, its lines

---

[*]*Call Him George*, Jazz Book Club, 1963.

deep, while the muscles of his shoulders and arms stand out in stark contrast to his emaciated frame.*

Leonard Feather's entry on Lewis in his *Encyclopedia* was not the damning monograph he penned on Bunk Johnson, although he managed to be allusively critical. 'Though some critics, both in the US and abroad, have belittled Lewis as superannuated and mediocre, he was described by Rudi Blesh in *Shining Trumpets* as "perhaps the greatest clarinettist since Johnny Dodds".' Feather would, no doubt, have been dumbfounded by the clamorous reception given to this slight and ailing folk hero at the Manchester Free Trades Hall by over three thousand people on the night of 10 April 1957. They rose to their feet in a spontaneous gesture of welcome, Lewis unable to hold back his tears.

October 1957 saw the appearance of the Earl Hines/Jack Teagarden All Stars. Both commenced recording in the twenties, both had led big bands, Hines from 1929 to 1947, Teagarden (after long stints with Ben Pollack and Paul Whiteman) from 1939 to 1946 but, perforce, both had subsequently earned a living in post-war Dixieland groups. Hines had done this very unwillingly; understandably for a black musician who had been leader of a large unit for so many years and had been compelled to play in bands redolent of social and racial attitudes he, a very outspoken man, obviously detested. When he left the Louis Armstrong All Stars, which Hines often alleged should have been billed simply as the 'All Stars', Armstrong was asked how he felt about the departure. 'I miss his playing, but sure don't miss his ego,' was the reply.

Teagarden was a player equally at ease in both large and small bands, but he and Hines were obviously at odds during this tour. At the opening concert, at the Royal Festival Hall, and the Coliseum Theatre, Kingsway, Hines's exhibitionistic posturing often threw Teagarden. (At the Coliseum the author can recall

---

*This, in fact, was a little journalistic sharp practice to emphasize Lewis's proletarian and deprived background. That photo was taken once Lewis had established a name as a musician. No one was likely to take such a professional-looking shot of an unknown black stevedore.

him, in solo flight, stopping to look behind him to see what grimace or gesture of Hines had caused the audience to laugh.)

The much-esteemed trumpeter Max Kaminsky, then fifty-one, had lip problems, and clarinettist Peanuts Hucko – like Wilber before him with Condon – was neat, but lacked identity. The clarinettist originally mooted for this tour was New Orleanian Pete Fountain; he would have been a better choice.

But to old aficionados, actually to *see* as well as hear Hines and Teagarden, and Max Kaminsky, all making their first visits to the country (the only trips for Teagarden and Kaminsky) was a joy that transcended the musical problems caused by the lack of group unity.

At the St Andrew's Hall, Glasgow, they packed both houses, and were mobbed, in contrast to the meagre 200 that comprised the first house and the half-full second house of Gerry Mulligan's visit in May of that year – the provinces being well behind the metropolis in supporting modern jazz.

During his visit, Teagarden was a guest of Roy Plomley on the BBC's 'Desert Island Discs'. It was a rather sad interview. He rationalized his commercial failure as leader of a big band, commenting that his former Ben Pollack sidemen, Benny Goodman and Glenn Miller, were in strong opposition, but as the recordings of 'Big T's' big band reveal, he had an infinitely better sound than Miller's, in many respects (in the author's opinion) superior to Goodman's. All the records he chose for 'Desert Island Discs' featured himself.

On 19 October 1957, Lionel Hampton, without his orchestra, played at the Royal Festival Hall with Humphrey Lyttelton and his band and Johnny Dankworth and his orchestra, the proceeds going to Christian Action for the South African Treason Trial. Max Jones was impressed: 'Hamp could not possibly have been carried away more completely if he had been promised the takings for himself.'

In December 1957, the Modern Jazz Quartet made their first visit.

Their reputation for 'chamber' jazz had been established, but these four musicians, in black jackets and pin-striped trousers, swept on to the stage of the Royal Festival Hall on 1 December 'like a diplomatic delegation', according to *Melody Maker* staff writer Tony Brown's description in an article entitled 'Jazz in a Bowler Hat' in the 7 December 1957 issue. He continued:

> The first few bars of music killed any notion that a sombre formality in presentation derives from something fundamentally phony. The musicianship is first-rate and I don't expect to hear more beautiful bass playing than that of Mr Percy Heath. Drummer Connie Kay plays with skill, sensitivity and intelligence. Milt Jackson must be credited with improvisational gifts of an unusually high order ... it would be easy to underrate the work of John Lewis at the piano, so circumscribed is his solo function, but if the strength of the man lies in founding an attractive group style based on sound musical instincts and good taste, then this may be forgiven. More, he has brought off the minor miracle of bringing his music to a large and enthusiastic audience both in America and Europe – eschewing tricks of salesmanship and grotesque posturing on-stage. Of course, the attitudinizing of Lewis is bound to bring charges of gimmickry down on his head, and unjustly, I fancy. I regard his approach as a misguided attempt to bring dignity to jazz. He has obviously set his face too sternly against Uncle Tom antics. The pity is that he apes the ridiculous formality of concert practices instead of relying on the natural dignity of the music.

In the same issue, Humphrey Lyttelton wrote:

> So many people have come up, eyes sparkling with anticipation, to ask me what I thought of the MJQ that, at the risk of being mistaken for a critic, I feel called upon to mention here the two concerts I attended. Freddy Mills has a word for it – 'Phenomenous'.
>
> Most 'phenomenous' of all and evidence of the almost hypnotic power of the group – it must be something to do with that tinkling triangle – was the audience reaction. During the opening spot by the Rendell band (something to be proud of, with Bert Courtley's 'Packet of Blues' a high spot on each occasion) the packed house showed itself, by sundry vocal interruptions and by the clapping of soloists, to be a normal representative jazz audience. Yet it sat, in awed cathedral silence, through announcements by John Lewis which, on the last concert especially, were only rescued from the depths of tedium by their unconscious hilariousness. It says much for the compelling power of the music and the magnitude of the quartet's reputation that the hall didn't ring with earthy cries of 'Git on wiv it' and 'Call 'im orft'.
>
> As for the music itself, it was for the main part so excellent as jazz – solid,

swinging, with deep roots in tradition – that I resented the too-frequent intrusion of twee out-of-tempo, mock-classical trimmings which, let's face it, could for the most part have been supplied off-the-peg by any moderately gifted music-school graduate. The jazz was of exceptional quality, which brought delighted grins to the faces of almost everyone except the four studiously dead-pan performers. There were moments which I shall cherish. These were the passages which achieved genuine dignity because they spoke in honest, forthright terms and in a manner which, in its own right, is unsurpassed. We all know what John Lewis is trying to prove. The trouble is that for many of us, it was proven long ago in the music of jazzmen through the ages. John Lewis and Milt Jackson prove it again when they swing the blues so lovingly. After all, the morning suits, the classical trimmings and the solemn posings add nothing to what we already know. There is a hint of concealing prudery about them which I find alarming and distasteful.

Lyttelton ended this typically percipient critique on a characteristically pugilistic note: 'And the first person who says, "Would you sooner see them running about in grass skirts and rings in their noses?" can punch himself in the eye and save me the bother.'

In February 1958, the controversial Dave Brubeck Quartet toured Britain. With pianist Brubeck were alto saxophonist Paul Desmond, bassist Eugene Wright and drummer Joe Morello.

Steve Race, in the *Melody Maker* of 15 February, reviewed the group's concert at the Royal Festival Hall. Race had long been a champion of Brubeck and his eulogy of the concert was no surprise.

> Patrons of the first of the two Festival Hall shows may like to know that, with the exception of one brilliant flash of inspired playing from Dave they had the better of the two – Morello unquestionably the most musical drummer I have heard, a man whose primary interest is tone, even though his business is rhythm. His solos are in their way as tuneful as those of the front-line men.

In Race's eulogistic appraisal of Brubeck's complex performance of a waltz, he allowed that he 'may not have been playing jazz according to strict definitions' but he ended his critique:

> And so the first European concert by the Dave Brubeck Quartet came to an end. This is an example, if ever there was one, of a group which must be heard

more than once. And not only *heard* but *listened* to, with every ounce of attention one can command. The reward for such attention is tremendous, and it is offered only by this one group in the whole wide world of rhythmic music. One regrets it was wasted on so many.

Other *Melody Maker* contributors were less ecstatic, undoubtedly coming into Race's category of the many on whom Brubeck was 'wasted'. Tony Brown:

A man is measured, inevitably, against his pretensions. Dave Brubeck has claimed to be an innovator, a man seeking to extend the frontiers of jazz ('... even Kenton thought I was too far out ...') and his work must be examined with this in mind.

At the Festival Hall last Saturday night he didn't persuade me that his is one of the really creative brains on the jazz scene. I carried away the impression of rather grandiose expositions of simple ideas of nineteenth-century variations on twentieth-century themes. He is prone to express himself emphatically – but none the less rhythmically, with great double-handed chords ... it was as a jazz *soloist* that I felt Brubeck was the least convincing.

Bob Dawbarn, one-time trombonist with Mick Mulligan's Magnolia Jazz Band:

From what I heard at the first of the Royal Festival Hall concerts on Sunday, I should say there is only one thing wrong with the Dave Brubeck Quartet – the pianist. If this is the stuff that wins polls I shall expect the *MM* readers to vote Liberace top jazz pianist of 1958.

What offended me most about Brubeck was the glutinous sentimentality of his piano solos – not romanticism, but sheer sickly sentimentality. He seemed to alternate florid ramblings containing little logic and less inspiration with monotonous chord thumping presumably to inject some excitement into the proceedings. The music bore little resemblance to either jazz or classical music, being close in spirit to the froth of 'Cornish Rhapsody' and 'Warsaw Concerto'.

The pity of it all was that on the same stage Joe Morello was superb, to put it mildly, and altoist Paul Desmond and bassist Gene Wright were fine.

May 1958 saw the first fully authorized appearance of Norman Granz's Jazz at the Philharmonic since 1953, when it had made the initial dent in the cultural Iron Curtain erected by the Musicians'

Union. The personnel this time comprised Dizzy Gillespie (his first visit to England since coming as a sideman with Teddy Hill's band at the London Palladium in 1937), Oscar Peterson, Stan Getz and Coleman Hawkins. This was Hawkins's third appearance in England – the first time was back in 1934, where he found himself touring with Mrs Jack Hylton's band (and recording with Jack Hylton); the second, illegally, was in 1949. Appearing here for the first time were drummer Gus Johnson and bassist Max Bennett. The British support was the Dill Jones Trio, with clarinettist Dave Shepherd.

By this time a virtual cross-section of bands from the home of jazz had played in a country that for over twenty years had been arbitrarily denied their presence and the tastes of all the denominations had been largely met, but announcements in the musical press in August 1958 advised of a proposed visit that had the community of all ideological hues agog with anticipation.

Duke Ellington and His Orchestra were to tour Britain in October, the orchestra's first visit since that sensational appearance in 1933. It was well known from the hundreds of records released in the UK since that epochal visit that the orchestra had changed in personnel and character, and for many old buffs who a quarter of a century earlier had sat listening wondrously and been stunned by that extraordinary constellation on a vaudeville stage, following 'blue' comedian Max Miller at the London Palladium, it was an anxious time. On the opening night at the Royal Festival Hall, however, they were there to a man!

Several had set opinions: one of these was that clarinettist Jimmy Hamilton was, for many Ellington buffs, merely keeping Barney Bigard's seat warm, and the latter had been out of the Ellington orchestra for over fifteen years! The revered 'Tricky Sam' Nanton had died, but veteran Quentin 'Butter' Jackson adroitly essayed the manipulation of mutes that was Nanton's supreme ability. Apart from the urbane Duke, however, only alto saxophonist Johnny Hodges and baritone saxophonist Harry Carney remained. Old buffs were reassured, though, by the presence of trumpeter Shorty Baker and saxophonist/clarinettist Russell Procope, both of whom had played in pre-war bands, Baker with Don Redman, Andy Kirk and Teddy Wilson, and

Procope with Jelly Roll Morton, Fletcher Henderson and Teddy Hill. Such a tally of associations was very much an old jazz buff's yardstick of quality.

But these old hands looked with baleful eyes at the information that Ellington was bringing with him three vocalists.* Each was seen as supernumary, and brought back unpleasant memories of their 'time-wasting' predecessors in 1933: dancers Bessie Dudley, Bailey and Derby and singer Ivie Anderson, the latter just acceptable. (Almost all the Ellington aficionados attending these 1933 shows had regarded each vocal refrain as taking up valuable solo space which would have been much better used by any of this extraordinary company of improvisers. It also stirred up unhappy recollections of Peg Leg Bates and Ella Logan appearing with Louis Armstrong as recently as 1956.)

In the event, it proved to be a highly controversial visit. The more devout the Ellingtonian, the more intense the disappointment at this second coming. It wasn't only the vocals that jarred, however, it was Duke's programme planning as a whole. Of course (as in 1933, when he had met with similar criticism) it was Ellington's very fecundity as composer and orchestrator, exemplified on hundreds of records, that militated against him – he could not possibly please everyone in one two-hour concert – but there was no question that the faith of many of the devout had been severely shaken. And – no doubt due to the frustrations of being denied by the embargo on American musicians for so long – the reactions to their actual presence at long last aroused fierce passions, to the extent of a musician/critic threatening physical violence should he hear criticisms of Ellington in his presence.

In the October *Melody Maker* two utterly reverential Ellington worshippers expressed their disappointment. One was Max Jones:

> So far as I am able to interpret the event, the story of Duke Ellington's opening concert at the Royal Festival Hall was the story of a superlative orchestra playing a programme not quite worthy of this historic occasion.
>
> In view of the array of talent mustered last Sunday, I know it seems ungrateful to find any fault, but it must be done. This is the world's foremost

---

*In the event, only Ozzie Nelson appeared, but to the old hands, it was one Ozzie too many.

jazz orchestra – the instrument of the most imaginative and completely original jazz composer in the jazz field; from it, quite naturally, we expect a preponderance of Ellington creations played in full for all their worth. In fact, we got very few – and very imposing they were. We also got several shortened versions, a song from 'Drum is a Woman', some 'Showcase' numbers (including a long-drawn-out solo), a French ballad and a pot-pourri of Ellington hits.

Let me make two things clear at once. The band was marvellous and I thoroughly enjoyed the concert.

The contentious tone of Jones's opening paragraph had been tempered by his overwhelming desire to be pleased, and after a breakdown of the show, he concluded:

There is no question of the orchestra's ability. Ellington still leads the world's richest, most rewarding jazz band. But this is no reason for glossing over what I believe were shortcomings if this is viewed as a jazz concert.

As a musician, whose faith in jazz was restored by the occasion, said: 'You've heard Ellington '58. What do you expect? Utopia?'

From Duke, I suppose I do.

Another Ellington worshipper, Vic Bellerby, in the same issue wrote:

After the second Ellington concert I heard a teenager ask: 'Why didn't the band play?' It was an innocent remark which at once exposes the weakness of the two Festival Hall concerts.

For, from the opening 'A Train' to the final 'Diminuendo and Crescendo in Blue', not one single band number was played. Forgetting the boring monotonous drum solo and the commercial vocals – though I still refuse to accept their necessity – the main trouble was that Duke, with typical modesty, wrongly demonstrated his unrivalled solo strength by asking nearly every member of the band to take a solo routine. And all the time we felt conscious of the hundreds of Ellington compositions waiting to be played.

The true secret of Ellington's genius is his uncanny ability to weave his soloists into an original composition, continually absorbing our interest by the ever-changing pattern and colour. We were not given one number in which this happened. It was like a series of great actors delivering their favourite soliloquies rather than contributing to a great Shakespeare play.

Basie was quite confident to let his band sit back, find the beat and play number after number, improving all the time; Duke, the showman, played safely – far too safely – thus giving jazz lovers a sad disappointment.

That storm petrel from Eton and the Brigade of Guards, Humphrey Lyttelton, pronounced in the same issue:

IF THEY CRITICIZE DUKE I MAY GET VIOLENT

The visit of Duke Ellington brings another living legend into our midst. The semi-myth becomes fact, and many preconceived ideas will be shattered to be replaced by a rather more concrete impression.

Some will be shocked – indeed, the old familiar cries were to be heard during the two opening concerts: 'Too much comedy! . . . Not enough jazz! . . . Why didn't he do this . . . Or that?'

Those who went to hear the first serious jazz composer were no doubt startled to be confronted with a sophisticated entertainer who treated his audience and himself with an air of urbane frivolity.

One of the most salutary effects of these visits is the drastic spring cleaning of legendary cobwebs. Jazz mythology is fine in its way; it does us no harm to believe that on a clear night, Buddy Bolden could be heard three, five, ten miles away across Lake Pontchartrain (though in irreverent moments we may well ask what the people standing ten feet away felt about it). I often wonder how the process of historical selection which goes to make up a legend begins. Who told whom that when the newly joined Lil Armstrong asked King Oliver about the key of a number he replied: 'You're a musician ain't you? Hit it, gal!' And why do they not go on to say, as is probable, that Lil played a four-bar intro in A flat, and the band came in on C. Legend records how King Oliver, hearing his musicians praising rival cornettists, ordered pianist Richard M. Jones to 'beat it out in B flat', and then walked out into the street to seduce the customers from clubs several blocks away with a (presumably) ear-splitting blues. It does not record what Jones said when he found himself left in the basement beating out in B flat on his tod.

But, hush! These legends are inviolable. The heroes are dead and it is an altogether hamless and endearing tendency to picture them slightly larger than life.

Legend about living artists is a different matter. It has grown up in the unnatural climate brought about by distance and the MU ban, when our knowledge and judgement of musicians was based almost exclusively on gramophone records. And we have seen over and over again how discrepancy between the legend and reality has led to impaired judgement and bewilderment.

Louis Armstrong, Lionel Hampton, Earl Hines, Eddie Condon – all have met with criticism for being themselves and failing to conform to mythical roles. You may be sure it will happen with Duke, too. If so, I hope in the interest of public order that I am out of earshot. For, after the two opening concerts by one of the most perfect musical combinations in the world, I remain in a state of enjoyment, into which cutting criticism enters only at the risk of violence.

In the following *MM*, the author wrote: 'Ellington, like Lyttelton, even, is a fallible mortal who can make mistakes in programme planning. In underestimating the occasion and, conceivably, listening to highly suspect advice. All this is rather sad, but sadder still that the articulate and influential Lyttelton should demand uncomplaining acceptance, or he'll thump you one.'

A waggish sub-editor added a footnote: 'Perhaps Jack Solomons would like to stage the Lyttelton–Godbolt fight.'

Brian Blain (later Music Promotions and Public Promotions Officer of the Musicians' Union) wrote:

> Humphrey Lyttelton is right when he says that the shattering of the romantic myths of the jazz world is a good thing. But he, and others, are guilty by their sycophantic attitudes of an even worse myth-building – the refusal to admit in the face of aural evidence, that a great jazz artist has given much less than he is capable of giving. This is the real reason for the controversy around his list of jazz greats.

In the *Melody Maker*, 25 October 1958, Lyttelton wrote: 'If Vic Bellerby was disappointed, I was not. If Max Jones was not left limp, I was. If Jim Godbolt and the gentleman who writes off my enthusiasm as "sycophancy" found themselves assailed by dissatisfaction I can only commiserate with them.'

In the same issue, Bellerby protested that the Ellington concerts were a sad disappointment and, surprisingly for a buff, quoted adverse comments in the national press, an entity not normally considered to have much validity in jazz matters by the aficionado!

> Humphrey Lyttelton's sudden uncritical adulation of Ellington follows his usual near-hysterical praise of all visiting musicians. Like the fanatical convert, he threatens physical violence to people having a little sagacity and sense of Ellington perspective. He really thinks that Hodges's 'All of Me', 'Terry', 'Perdido', and Carney's 'Sophisticated Lady' are Ellington *band numbers*. How silly can you get?

Bellerby, however, allowed that there were two magnificent concerts at the Davis Theatre, Croydon, and the Empire State, Kilburn, adding, 'If more critics had possessed the guts to criticize the opening concerts, things might have been very different.'

It is by no means certain that Ellington read a single notice of his concerts and, if he did, that it affected his programme planning one iota, but the fact remained that many were grievously disappointed.

Ellington brought his orchestra to Britain again in 1963 and *Jazz News and Review*, 16 January, carried a front-page photograph of a titled trio: Lord Montagu, Duke Ellington and the Honourable Gerald Lascelles. It also ran a searing attack on the band by Daniel Halperin.

> Who would dare tilt at the master? . . . Who has the nerve to say that something of Ellington is less than good? . . . he has coasted along relatively free of criticism and that, I admit, has not done him any good at all. As far as this critic is concerned the time is long overdue for taking an acid-etched look at Duke Ellington.
>
> The glibness has set in . . . the smooth nothingness for which, in some respects, I blame Billy Strayhorn whose fey romanticism was OK in small doses and fatal in extended forms . . . the glories of the early 1940s orchestra were attacked by an almost fatal disease: bureaucracy. In this case, the listless centralization of authority in the hands of two rather weary super sophisticates, Duke and Strayhorn.
>
> Between them, through the years, they have slowly allowed a once-great orchestra to fall into a state of inanimate suspension, dangling from the girders of what was once a great musical strength. In the great days, Duke's soloists, Duke's phrasing, Duke's voicing, not to mention his undeniably superb compositions, were the wonder and mystery of jazz. They baffled as they entertained. They were objects of reverence and pleasure. In the fifteen years of great decline, Duke has solidified, like some jewel-encrusted mummy of fabulous age. Now the band just goes through the ancient paces. Gone is the verve, the drive, the passion, the total engagement in the production of wonderful music, in the expression of moods and colours heretofore unexpressed in jazz.
>
> Throughout the years Ellington has relied increasingly upon his charm in wooing the natives with tinsel trickeries, where he once showed a capacity to astonish and excite. The blandness of security has set in. Why upset people? That seems to be Ellington's slogan. It's so much more pleasant to kid them along cynically, to throw them the crap about being a great audience, to tell them 'he loved you maaaaaadly' than to send them home disturbed and, possibly, profoundly moved.
>
> Ellington, Strayhorn and Co has become a thing in itself, a crumbling thing. Honour the man by all means. His past contributions efface any present lack. Hear this orchestra; its professional competence is unbeatable. It is the most superior relic in jazz.

There were no reports of Mr Lyttelton doing Mr Halperin a serious injury.

For two happy years, buffs of all shades of opinion had been offered a choice of bands right across the stylistic board and, despite the reservations by critics and enthusiasts about Ellington's showing, this was regarded by many as a highlight. The next band from America, however, was the very antithesis of Ducal sophistication.

This startling contrast was provided by the full George Lewis band arriving in January 1959. With Lewis (fifty-seven), were trumpeter Kid Howard (forty-nine), trombonist Jim Robinson (sixty-seven), drummer Joe Watkins (fifty-seven), banjoist Lawrence Marrero (fifty-seven), pianist Joseph Robichaux (fifty-seven) and bassist Alcide 'Slow Drag' Pavageau (sixty-nine). Apart from Robinson, they were not 'old' by present standards of longevity, but their hard lives had prematurely aged them, Lewis particularly. He, Marrero and Watkins were in poor health. Despite this, their performance was spirited, the regenerating spirit of jazz pulsing through their aged and ailing bodies. They possessed an aura of intriguing antiquity, and it was a priceless opportunity to see and hear their historically significant camaraderie, representing direct the music's turn-of-the-century originators: trumpeters Buddy Bolden, Buddy Petit and Manuel Perez, and clarinettist Alphonse Picou.

To the rigid purist their supreme virtue was that only they and musicians of their ilk played the 'Real Jazz'. Feelings were fiercely strong about music of this kind played by people of this background. Their segregated second-class citizenship and the poverty of their circumstances in the US undoubtedly – illogically, but understandably – enhanced their musical appeal. (Conversely, the supporters of 'modern' jazz equated 'newness' with intrinsic quality.)

Jay Allison Stewart, in her book on Lewis, wrote of his tour:

> The reviews were, in large part, excellent; some, written by Britain's counterparts of America's 'musicologists' were snobbish displays of intellectual

exhibitionism; a few, obviously written by those sincerely devoted to 'mainstream' jazz, were written without any comprehension of the music on which they were commenting; and the general, non-musical press commented at some length on the great age of the band: 'Jazz granddads' was a favourite phrase. One of these was in such bad taste that I doubt if any American editor would have passed it. The lead, referring to George Lewis, started: 'The mouldiest fig this side of decomposition . . .' continuing with a description of George's extreme thinness and general appearance, before discussing the band – which the writer had apparently just heard of.

In many cases the appearances of these veteran musicians, black or white, were the last chance to see as well as hear (and to meet) a minstrelsy the like of which will never be seen again. Some, particularly the brass players, were past their best; the relaxation of the ban had come too late for home audiences to hear them in their prime. Nevertheless, even players below their peak were a pleasure to hear and, for journalists and fans alike, the privilege of speaking with those who had fashioned the course of jazz history from the early twenties helped compensate for their failing powers.

April 1959 saw a visit by an American bandleader that had special significance. Woody Herman toured with seven Britishers and two Canadians resident in Britain. This was not a publicity stunt; not, even, another stratagem to comply with exchange requirements. It was a genuine musical association, a mark of respect to those local musicians who had made such progress, mostly by listening to records, that they could take their places in a crack American orchestra. They were trumpeters Bert Courtley, Les Condon and Kenny Wheeler (a Canadian resident in Britain); trombonists Eddie Harvey and Ken Wray; saxophonists Don Rendell, Johnny Scott and Art Ellefson (another Canadian resident in Britain). The Americans were trumpeter Nat Adderley and Reunald Jones, trombonist Bill Harris, guitarist Charlie Byrd, pianist Vince Guaraldi, bassist Skeeter Best and drummer Jimmy Campbell.

In October 1959, trombonist Kid Ory, famous for his association with Louis Armstrong on the historic Hot Five and Seven recordings of the late twenties, came with Red Allen (trumpet), Bob McCracken (clarinet), Cedric Haywood (piano), Alton Redd (drums) and Squire Girsbach (bass), all making their debut in the UK.

Ory, whose associations with New Orleans jazz went back further than Jim Robinson with the George Lewis band, was seventy-three when he made the trip. His lip was in good shape, and the band, although comprised of veterans, played in a light and agile manner and employed such tunes as 'Sentimental Journey' not usually associated with a New Orleans band.

Obviously the US traditional-style bands who visited this country had trouble in finding clarinettists to fit the bill (Edmond Hall in Armstrong's first visit and Lewis excepted). Even Louis Armstrong in 1964/5 had an erstwhile bopper, Eddie Shu, who was less than inspiring, and many a British clarinettist – Sandy Brown and Wally Fawkes particularly – would have filled the role more effectively. The Teagarden–Hines show had the characterless Hucko, Condon had Wilber, but Ory, the father of jazz trombone, introduced to British audiences a virtually unknown but excellent white clarinettist in McCracken.

The band was surreptitiously, illegally, recorded. The excellent results were later issued, as a memento of this visit, by a member of the first black* jazz band, Spike's Seven Pods of Pepper, to make gramophone records in Los Angeles in June 1922. Ory, of course, was bombarded with questions about his history, but was asked by the British trombonist Graham Stewart if he had any advice to budding trombonists. He replied, 'Yeah, don't ever play for nuthin'.'

---

*Throughout this book I have used both 'coloured' and 'black' to describe members of the Negro race, although aware that even 'Negro' is no longer acceptable to many members of the ethnic group to which it once applied without question, nor to many whites. Ory died in January 1973 and Charles Fox, in a radio programme, referred to him as 'black'. This drew a protesting telephone call from Ory's widow in Britain at the time: 'My husband was *not* black. I wouldn't have married him if he was!' Ory was a pale-skinned Creole, and for what may have been the general attitude of Creoles to pure blacks see *Mister Jellyroll*, Alan Lomax's biography of Jelly Roll Morton. In this, Lomax reproduces letters from Morton to his sister, berating Negroes, and twice referring to them as 'niggers'.

After the long, barren years in which an insensate ban on the entry of American musicians had been ruthlessly applied, these had been fruitful times, and not a few illusions had been shattered. There were more delights to come, in the shape of visiting soloists backed by British bands.

11
Entry of the Soloists and Coals to Alabama

Throughout 1960/1961 Pete King, the manager of Ronnie Scott's club, engaged in long and tedious negotiations with both the American Federation of Musicians and the British Musicians' Union in an attempt to arrange for the appearance of solo jazz musicians from the US, to be backed by *British* musicians on a regular basis. This was in accordance with a precedent established by George Lewis with Ken Colyer in 1959. The outcome of this time-consuming, frustrating (and financially exhausting) effort involving numerous flights to America, was the appearance of tenor saxophonist Zoot Sims with Stan Tracey (piano), Kenny Napper (bass) and Jackie Dougan (drums) at Scott's club for a four-week season in November 1961. Tubby Hayes played the Half Note club in New York in September that year as the exchange musician, and recorded with James Moody, Roland Kirk, Walter Bishop Jr, Sam Jones and Louis Hayes.

This booking of soloists provided many British musicians not only with remunerative and prestigious employment, but the pleasure of actually playing with musicians they had long admired, and from whom they had learned so much. Thereafter at the Scott club the Tracey Trio coped regularly with a myriad of problems, musical and temperamental, offered by a succession of visitors that included tenor saxophonists Benny Golson, Lucky Thompson, Roland Kirk, Stan Getz, Dexter Gordon, Bobby Jaspar, Johnny Griffin and Yusef Lateef and trumpeters Art Farmer, Freddie Hubbard, Dizzy Gillespie and many, many more.

The appearance of the temperamental Stan Getz prompted one of Scott's most famous *bons mots*: 'I got a slipped disc bending over backwards to please Stan Getz.'

The traditional/mainstream bands who played with the visitors included those of Humphrey Lyttelton, Alex Welsh, Alan Elsdon, Bruce Turner and John Chilton, all acquitting themselves with ease and proficiency behind guests including saxophonists Bud Freeman, Don Byas, Ben Webster, Benny Waters; clarinettists Pee Wee Russell, Albert Nicholas; trumpeters Ray Nance, Rex Stewart, Buck Clayton, Red Allen, Ruby Braff, Wingy Manone, Bill Coleman; trombonists Vic Dickenson and Dicky Wells; pianists Teddy Wilson, Ralph Sutton, Earl Hines and many more.

Chris Barber, who had become a director of the National Jazz Federation Ltd, brought over and played with musicians as widely differing in style as clarinettists Ed Hall and George Lewis, pianist John Lewis (from the MJQ), alto saxophonist Louis Jordan, trumpeter Alvin Alcorn, organist Wild Bill Davis and trombonist Trummy Young, as well as many blues and gospel singers. His band adapted themselves admirably to guests with whom, at one stage of their careers, they could not possibly have envisaged themselves playing.

The facility of British bands in the sixties was fortunately a far cry from the technical standards obtaining in the late forties and early fifties. An unpremeditated event was a bolster for pride in British musicianship. Tubby Hayes (as trumpeter Jimmy Deuchar had done eight years previously for Jimmy Williams in Lionel Hampton's band) deputized for Paul Gonsalves in a Duke Ellington concert at the Royal Festival Hall in February 1964. The background to this was that Gonsalves's well-documented drug abuse was a constant source of irritation to his leader, who knew well, however, the saxophonist's worth and suffered his foibles accordingly. On the day of the concert, Gonsalves had over-indulged, and with the connivance of Douggie Tobbutt, the tour manager, Tubby Hayes was booked as a deputy. In the event, Gonsalves recovered, but Hayes still took his place – the only British player ever to perform with the great Ellington orchestra.

While most of the visitors and their accompanying bands were compatible enough, there were, however, the occasional upsets and there was one imbroglio that resulted in a veritable furore. In May 1964, Red Allen guested with Humphrey Lyttelton's band at the Manchester Sports Guild. The row that blew up reflected a tangle of stylistic differences and attitudes, and indicated that the hard-line approach applied as much to certain modernists as it did to diehard traditionalist. In this instance an entrenched attitude had unhappy results.

To fill in the background: bop, like revivalism, was successful only because of the protagonists' intense belief in what they were doing, and in the heat of their passion, some modernists vehemently deprecated previous styles. The clarinettist Pip Gaskell, who played and recorded with Lyttelton in the band's early stages, went to Paris in 1948 where a famous stylistically mixed bill at the Salle Pleyel comprised Hot Lips Page, Sidney Bechet, Dizzy Gillespie, Miles Davis and Charlie Parker. Gaskell, backstage listening entranced to Bechet, praised him to James Moody, playing with Dizzy Gillespie's band. Moody replied: 'Man, we don't listen to that old shit.' His leader, Dizzy Gillespie, also viewed traditional music with a certain wry amusement. Bob Wilber, in his *Music was not Enough*, tells the following story:

> ... we were very much into the sound and repertoire of the King Oliver Creole Jazz Band. We rehearsed in a studio on Broadway called Nola's, where all the big bands rehearsed. One afternoon we were wailing away on 'Snake Rag' when the door opened and Dizzy Gillespie, who was rehearsing his new band down the hall, looked in. Eyeing us quizzically, he asked: 'What kinda stuff you guys playin'? Man, that's some crazy shit! You cats are so far in, you're far out!'

Bop was not an overnight invention by the Minton alumni. It came of an evolutionary process, but reached fruition in the mid-forties, and one suspects that now, acknowledging this, neither Moody nor Gillespie would make such comments and would, conceivably, be apologetic about the things they said so many years back. (Conversely, many traditionalists wish they had not been so damning of bebop.)

With Lyttelton in Manchester were Tony Coe, Joe Temperley (saxophone), Eddie Harvey (piano, doubling on trombone), Pete Blannin (bass) and Eddie Taylor (drums), sidemen with 'modern' beliefs. Many of them almost certainly held attitudes similar to those of Gillespie and Moody, and the story goes that as Allen stepped on to the stand he overheard a remark that, in effect, was a scornful reference suggesting that a 'period' situation was confronting these 'up-to-date' musicians. Allen, a mild-mannered and extremely co-operative man (as the author can testify from numerous business and personal dealings with him), took umbrage at this remark, but his presence with that particular Lyttelton band in the light of his own history, and theirs, threw up a host of ironies and contradictions. Allen, although from New Orleans, had not, even in the early days of his professional career, been a 'New Orleans' player. He had been more a solo stylist in the big bands of Luis Russell, Fletcher Henderson, Charlie Johnson, the Louis Armstrong band (Russell's) and Lucky Millinder, and in these bands (Johnson's apart) he had made many records demonstrating his skills as a powerful, arresting, if at times erratic, soloist.

Although he played on many small-band sides in what would now be called mainstream, it was not until the Brunswick *New Orleans* album, made in 1940 (companion sides to those made by Armstrong and Bechet), that he made records in the New Orleans style and was much criticized by the purists for his wayward line. After the break-up of the big bands he was compelled, like so many of his contemporaries, to fall in with the current fashions for employment, and much of this was in the so-called traditional bands in which he did not excel as much as he had with the orchestras of Russell, Henderson and Milliner, his solos leaping from the ensembles with remarkable vigour and passion.

This was a novel situation: he was now a featured soloist in a band whose leader had dramatically moved away from the music that Allen, in recent years, had been compelled to play to earn his living, and yet the style of Lyttelton's band itself had its genesis in those bands in which Allen had proved to be a master soloist.

G.E. 'Eddie' Lambert, reporting on Red Allen's appearance in Manchester in *Jazz Journal* May 1964, praised the various bands that accompanied him, the Alex Welsh, Sandy Brown and Bruce Turner bands, but was highly critical of the backing by Humphrey Lyttelton's band:

> There was nothing wrong with the instrumentation – so often a sore point among Lyttelton listeners although one fails to see why – or with the standard

of musicianship. Basically the trouble resolves into a question of style, for the modified Basie small-group manner of the Lyttelton band, which suits a man like Buck Clayton so well, is quite the wrong backing for a player of Henry Allen's environment and methods. The modern style of the band's soloists other than the leader sounded mechanical when placed against the more personal methods of their guest. The Lyttelton sidemen produced a well engineered, rather brash sound and seemed to regard this as enough in itself; there was more formality in the music and less smiling on the bandstand on this evening, and the players showed little disposition to adapt their music to the needs of their eminent guest.

Indeed Eddie Harvey persistently refused to follow Red's directions regarding the chords and seemed quite indifferent to the whole affair. All this obviously affected Red . . . One wonders if the band is running into the same sort of impasse which they faced in more traditional fields prior to Bruce Turner joining the group in the early fifties. At that time Humph's taste, intelligence and musical courage prevented the band from foundering in the morass of mechanical 'trad'. Let us hope that he sees any dangers in his present situation with the same clarity.

In the July issue of the same journal, even Steve Voce, a fervent admirer of Lyttelton, made references to the Lyttelton rhythm section sounding 'uncomfortable' with Allen. In the same issue, Lyttelton replied to his critics in typically crisp and acerbic style:

I have thought twice before commenting on G.E. Lambert's review of my band with Red Allen. Red's visit generated such high-voltage emotion that to barge in with mundane observations is rather like crashing into a cathedral on roller skates. Furthermore, the name 'G.E. Lambert' – like H.G. Wells, G.K. Chesterton or H.M. Customs – exudes an authority which one hesitates to challenge. I am grateful to Steve Voce for telling me that 'G.E. Lambert' really answers to the name of Eddie and that he is 'a magnificent fall-about specialist who goes off like a cuckoo-clock after a fixed number of pints'. Reassured that he is really just like you and me (well you, anyway), I charge fall-about Eddie with gross unfairness to Henry Allen. To suggest that a man who was born just one year before fellow-New Orleanian Lester Young is unable to settle into 'modified Basie small-group' surroundings, whatever they may be, is surely a gross libel on his musicianship. We heard him five years ago in New York sitting in with 'Sir Charles' Thompson's Trio – and we didn't notice that 'Sir Charles' insulted his guest by switching on a special style for him.

Worse still is the suggestion that Henry Allen is some worthy but unfortunate old character from the past who has 'known so much neglect in recent years'. Throughout the fifties Red fronted the house band at the Metropole – second only to Birdland as a New York jazz Mecca. Since then he has fulfilled regular engagements at the Embers, the much-sought-after venue from which Jonah Jones was launched to his pop success. Only the grossest kind of sentimentalizing can equate the Embers with the ricefields of New Iberia or Red Allen with a sort of latterday Bunk Johnson. Looking round at the fate of some of his contemporaries, Red may well count himself a persistent success, and expressions of saccharine sympathy about his 'neglect' are hardly flattering, if well-meant.

Having said this, let me agree with G.E. Lambert that our session with Henry Allen was not a happy one. Indeed, it was probably my least enjoyable experience in fifteen years of bandleading. The reason for this may well make fall-about Eddie go off like Big Ben, but it must be stated. The afternoon rehearsal went off smoothly, and our offers to adapt our instrumentation to suit Henry were emphatically turned down. 'Just you play your way, and I'll be with you.' It was all the more surprising, therefore, when shortly after the start of his first set, Red took violent exception to the expression on the back of Eddie Harvey's head – an area which I have hitherto regarded as just about as scrutable as a coconut.

It became obvious that something was wrong when Red began interrupting all the piano solos by calling in another soloist and shouting for chords which Eddie was actually playing at the time. It's ironical that this fate should have befallen Eddie Harvey, who was drummed out* of George Webb's Dixielanders seventeen years ago for copying J.C. Higginbotham and who knew the chords of 'Patrol Wagon Blues' when G.E. Lambert was falling about on ginger pop at Chadderton Grammar School.†

It was an odd accident that brought things to a head. All bands have standing jokes, and one of ours is that record by Willie 'The Lion' Smith in which he purports to give a history of piano styles – '1926 – we're movin' up!' Red referred in an announcement to a recording session 'in 1929', and Joe Temperley, partly by reflex action and partly to relieve the tension on the stand, murmured, 'We're movin' up!' Overhearing this, Red misinterpreted it as a dig at himself and, momentarily losing his temper, started to harangue the band over the microphone, stating, 'I can move up on you guys any time!' . . .

Fortunately, Red recovered before the end of the night and most of the audience, barring one man who informed me at every opportunity that 'he comes from New Orleans' and offered to teach me 'Muskrat Ramble', seemed to be quite happy about it all. At the end of the session, a man who might well

---

*An exaggeration: true, an inquisitorial meeting, the author present, was held with Harvey in the hot seat, and explanations demanded of him why he was playing with a local *dance* band and caustic references were made to him deserting 'tailgate' principles, but he left the Dixielanders because he was called to do his National Service in the RAF.

†One wonders how Old Etonian Lyttelton knew that Lambert had attended a provincial *grammar* school. Was his informant the body who apprised him of G.E.L.'s alcoholic intake? Eddie Lambert died in 1987.

have been G.E. Lambert himself, except that he was vertical and seemed quite steady on his feet, asked me why 'it hadn't happened tonight'. Well, now he knows . . .

The moral of this story is that critics who succumb to emotion and who make deductions from musicians' comments, are forsaking the fact-finding which good journalism demands and invariably end up on their backsides, with or without the aid of a fixed number of pints.

Despite Lyttelton's assurance that all ended well, Red Allen's rejoinder, in a letter to *Jazz Journal* in September 1964, suggested that he was still very sore about the affair.

I heard Humphrey Lyttelton in London five years ago using Luis Russell's arrangement of 'Swing Out' and my solo as recorded. I suggest Humphrey stop gorilla-ing jobs and let his superiors Bob Wallis and Ken Colyer have a chance. Old Humph should spend some time with such great musicians as Sandy Brown and Bruce Turner or at least spend a week with Alex Welsh's full band (contact manager Phil Robertson). If Humph should reorganize, get ideas from my man Diz (Guitar) Disley, John (Dobell) Kendall, Jack (MSG) Swinnerton or Alan (Coloroll) Gatward. We movin' up my man Humph. I may move to England.

That letter, unique in its way, was the unfortunate end product of a veritable merry-go-round of differences, misconceptions and misunderstandings, and perhaps considering Red's highly individual style it was not the best of ideas to put him with a band that, in some respects, did not have the unanimity of purpose that would have been found in a wholly traditional or wholly bop band.

There were no such artistic or personal problems in the Lyttelton tours with singers Jimmy Rushing and Joe Turner and trumpeter Buck Clayton, whose arrangements were used in all three tours. Here, the problems were economic. In a taped conversation at the author's flat, Lyttelton recalled: 'When we toured with Jimmy Rushing, we drew only 350 in 1,000-seat venues. What kept me going was the internal excitement in the band. Now, of course, the venue problem wouldn't arise – Jimmy Rushing, were he still alive, would be a large enough draw wherever you decided to book him.'

One of the most compatible of pairings, despite the visitor apparently playing in a constant alcoholic trance, as if only by instinct, was clarinettist Pee Wee Russell with Alex Welsh and his band – a union of Condonites. It was an opportunity, following an appearance at the Manchester Sports Guild in July 1964, for Eddie Lambert, in a favourable review, to deliver a side-swipe at another Northern critic. In *Jazz Journal* he commented: 'a fine session . . . but they had to contend with Steve Voce bawling encouragement in true Merseyside fashion'.

Another compatible tour was that of Ed Hall with Alan Elsdon and his band. For a man who was used to playing for audiences sometimes numbering in their thousands with Louis Armstrong's All Stars, it was a contrast for him to play before barely a hundred people. One evening in the summer of 1963, he played with Elsdon's band at the Fox and Hounds, Haywards Heath, to an audience of this size. Returning to London in Alan Elsdon's car (the author and Lennie Felix fellow passengers) this normally benign man – a non-drinker, and certainly not a drug taker – gave vent to his spleen: about George Gershwin for stealing 'Summertime' on a visit to Georgia to research material for *Porgy and Bess*; about Pee Wee Russell: 'He plays *nothing*!'; about New Orleans which had awarded him an honour (I can't recall under what auspices) which Hall, mindful of the colour bar still operating in his home town, swore he'd burn before acknowledging. Following this unexpectedly savage outburst he was particularly scathing about the Elsdon clarinettist – 'He plays *shit*!' It was an extraordinarily atypical outburst from an otherwise gentle soul. The understandable resentment of the New Orleans musicians about status under the laws of their home town contrasted strongly with their worldwide acceptance as masters of their art.

The author once entertained Albert Nicholas, in the company of Max and Betty Jones. (A genial evening, with conversation, food and drink, with Nicholas chuckling in recollection at 'cutting' Sidney Bechet on Jell Roll Morton's 1941 'High Society'. 'Yeah, I think I gave him a bit of trouble there.' He suddenly erupted, however, when, in some context, the name of the white Original Dixieland Jazz Band came up.

'*Bastards!* White shit stealin' our toons!' Suddenly remembering the pigmentation of his companions, he broke off. The subject was quickly changed.

There were curious twists in the tales of racial discrimination in the States by visiting musicians, black and white. Trumpeter Ray Nance, touring Britain with Bruce Turner and his band, told of an occasion, with Earl Hines and His Orchestra, when they stopped at a roadside diner. Hines was addressed by the white counterhand as 'Boy!', a derogatory term from a white to a black man in the US. Nevertheless, Nance, clearly having no pleasurable recollection of Hines, told the story with relish and, chuckling, repeated it.

One of the categories of person to emerge from this influx of American jazz musicians became known derogatorily as 'JMFs', meaning 'Jazz Musicians' Friends': these were individuals who fastened like limpets on to the visitors, basking in their reflected glory. A classic case was collector/amateur trumpeter Doug Whitton who, though having contrived to act as Judas by getting Sidney Bechet surreptitiously to record for Melodisc on the morning of the historic Bechet/Lyttelton concert on 14 November 1948, managed to seat himself (and get photographed) in the Royal Box with Bechet and the Wilcox brothers before Bechet was 'called' to the stage by Rex Harris. Some, like Max Jones, were legitimately attached to their 'heads'; others, like Lyttelton's archetypal 'men-about-jazz', were there for the glory by association; others compulsively moved towards the famous.

The author was once talking to Mick Mulligan trombonist Frank Parr in the Blue Posts, when Max Jones entered with cornettist Muggsy Spanier. Jones looked warily around as he came in with his 'head', and Parr leapt away from me in the direction of Spanier and Jones with the agility he displayed behind the stumps keeping wicket for Lancashire CCC and the Ravers CC, leaving me for dead.

In varying degrees, most British jazz musicians were aware of American musicians; indeed they would not have been jazz players otherwise, but almost without exception American jazzmen were totally ignorant of the abilities of their British counterparts, if only because most didn't collect records (least of all the few British ones issued in the States) or read British jazz magazines. It was therefore a surprise to them that some of the natives had been so successful in absorbing the jazz language. Wild Bill Davison, for instance, warmly and sincerely praised Archie Semple as 'the greatest since Ed Hall'.

Overall, it was a happy experience for visitors and the musicians who accompanied or supported them. Long-lasting friendships were struck and aficionados were able to attend performances by those they had heard on record. There were some surprises, however. A few incidents shattered myths. John Barnes recalls:

> After a gig at the Manchester Sports Guild with Earl Hines, he requested that the band assemble in the secretary 'Jenks' Jenkins' office. Just the band. No one else. We had no idea what to expect. Were we that inadequate to the job of accompanying the world's greatest pianist? We were totally mystified. The reason we had been called soon became clear. Nothing to do with our music. In fact, Earl went to great pains to say how much he enjoyed working with us, but objected strongly to us drinking and smoking on the stand. 'It's so unprofessional,' he said.
>
> We were flabbergasted. It's something we had always done at clubs; in a way it was part of our style. But bowing to the master's admonitions, we didn't drink or smoke on the stand for the rest of the tour. Once the tour with Hines finished, we of course reverted to type.

That the British jazz scene was enhanced by this stream of distinguished visitors is to the credit of the many who persistently campaigned for their entry.

The fate of British musicians involved in the exchange deal was less than ideal. A major problem was the enormous number of miles British bands had to travel in the States in order that the charade of reciprocity could be seen to be implemented. In his despatches to the British musical press, this was the main complaint by Ted Heath, whose orchestra was the first British attraction involved, indeed the first British band ever to tour in the United States. In a mixed bill, which included the Nat King Cole Trio and June Christy, and which witnessed an unpleasant racial incident in Alabama, the reactions to the Heath orchestra were variable, but at the end of the tour it enjoyed a tremendous success at New York's Carnegie Hall, an historic event that was recorded.

Entry of the Soloists and Coals to Alabama   241

In such a vast population, the number of people interested in jazz was proportionately lower than in the British Isles and so the Britishers, with few exceptions, played in rock and roll packages, before audiences who generally had previously never even heard their names, let alone being aware of what sort of music they played. Of all the visitors to the US, only Ted Heath, by virtue of his records, was known there, and the extent of his popularity was limited.

The economics were geared to this simple fact: it was profitable for American entrepreneurs to have their bands play in Britain, not only for the tour revenue but from increase in record sales. It was not a viable proposition for American businessmen to promote British acts, but in the devious and intricate machinery of entrepreneurism various stratagems had to be devised to lend some credence to the concept of fair exchange.

As Ronnie Scott (who played the US in exchange for Eddie Condon's All Stars) succinctly put it in his *Some of My Best Friends are Blues*:

> We had been, quite incongruously, booked into a tour with an all-black rock'n'roll package that included Fats Domino, Chuck Berry, La Vern Baker and Bill Doggett. In some places our names weren't even on the billing, but when they did appear, they just about outranked the printer in type size. We played our one number on each date to enormous and totally indifferent audiences and then got the hell off. They needed a British bebop band like they need a synagogue in Damascus.

Freddy Randall and his band, in exchange for Louis Armstrong, had frightening experiences playing venues in the Deep South. The 21 May 1956 issue of *Melody Maker* carried the headline: 'JUNGLE MUSIC CRY AT RANDALL US SHOW'. The report, by Leonard Feather, read:

> The white citizens of Birmingham, Alabama – who were responsible for the attack on Nat King Cole during Ted Heath's concerts – again caused trouble when Freddy Randall appeared at the Civic Auditorium. The Randall band, in a package including rock'n'roll king Bill Haley and his Comets, played before a segregated audience at the Auditorium on Sunday. Council pickets paraded outside the hall carrying signs reading: 'Down with rebop. Christians will not attend this show. Ask your preacher about jungle music.'

Whatever doubts that could be entertained about the kind of Christians these citizens believed themselves to be, clearly they were not conversant with popular-music terminology. Randall playing *jungle* music? And where was the 'rebop' in this show? Birmingham, Alabama, in May 1956 had echoes of Birmingham, Warwickshire, in 1953, when Bruce Turner was hooted because he appeared playing the alto saxophone. It was the supreme irony that white men from east London who, in essence, played white men's jazz, suffered abuse by Southern rednecks for playing 'nigra' music. There was even a bomb-scare.

The report added that since Randall had been booked in Alabama, Tennessee, South Carolina, Georgia, Florida, and at the National Grand Armoury, Washington, 'this means that Randall, like Heath, will get a very untypical view of America, playing the same Jim Crow theatres and auditoria', but ended by quoting Randall bassist Jack Pebberdy as saying that the band's appearance in New Orleans was a great success, and that people were surprised at such fine 'British Dixieland'.

The next British band to play in the United States was Vic Lewis's. He left England on 8 October 1956, the tour lasting until Sunday 4 November. The *Melody Maker*, 20 October, splashed a banner headline: 'EIGHTEEN MEN FLY TO THE STATES TO PLAY — FOR SIX MINUTES! THIS IS AN INSULT TO BRITISH BANDS.' Leonard Feather reported scathingly on the working conditions, the extensive travelling and the amount of time allocated to British bands in the packages in which they were compelled to appear. There could be no question of them objecting; they were totally in the hands of the tour promoters. In a foreign country, they would be utterly stranded if they kicked up a fuss. Feather continued:

> British bands are being insulted. And it's not a question of the money they're being paid in comparison with what American bands are getting in Britain. Nor is it a question of whether the best bands are being sent. What's wrong is the farcical way they're being used.
>
> Ted Heath was lucky. True, he played only a dozen numbers in a variety show that was top-heavy with acts, at least two of which added nothing to the entertainment value or the box-office draw, and merely subtracted from Heath's playing time. Moreover, apart from New York, the band was not able to appear in such American key cities as Boston, Philadelphia, Chicago, Kansas

City, Los Angeles, etc. But Ted's was red-carpet treatment compared with what followed. Freddy Randall, in an exchange for Armstrong, was shipped over here and dumped into a rock'n'roll show so obscure, and so far south, that when I happened to mention it to George Shearing's wife, Trixie, she said: 'What? Was Freddy Randall's band in America? When?' Trixie and I were in the Armoury in Newark, because this was the nearest 'The Biggest In-person Show of '56' would ever get to New York. That's the name of the rock'n'roll vaudeville show in which Vic Lewis is almost heard.

Vic has one advantage over his predecessors: only five southern dates; less Jim Crow, even a couple of nights in Canada. But man, that show! Bill Haley and his Comets are the only white act aside from Vic's band, but rock'n'roll is ghastly, regardless of race, creed or colour. There are umpteen acts in the show with names like the Platters, the Clovers, the Teenagers, the Flairs, etc. In Newark it didn't matter how out of tune they sang or how bad the diction because the acoustics of the hall were so shocking and the amplification so poor that nothing anybody said, sang or played all evening could be discerned, anyway. The audience seemed to be about sixty per cent coloured. Because the show had been switched from another venue at the last minute to the vast, gloomy dark barn of a place called the Armoury, the attendance was disappointing. Customers paid one dollar for a big, twenty-eight-page souvenir programme. Photos on the cover of everyone but Vic.* Biographies of everyone but Vic. Not even a mention of Tommy Whittle anywhere in the book. No listing of Vic or Tommy in the order of acts. Vic's band got on the bandstand at 10.18 and was off at 10.24.

In those six minutes they played 'Intermission Rock', 'In the Mood' and Tommy Whittle's solo 'Just One of Those Things'. The band, though Vic told me he was sinking to the level of his audience, as far as possible, sounded good: Tommy sounded in good form.

It was the only music I heard played all evening. And for these six minutes on the stand somebody paid return fare across the Atlantic for eighteen people (including Vic's manager). For these six minutes Vic and his men are traipsing all over the country in a show that needs the band about as much as the North Pole needs more ice.

On his return from the US Ted Heath maintained a stout patriotic stance, claiming in the *New Musical Express* that certain British bands were as good as anything in the States. In Heath's despatches, he reported June Christy complaining to the tour promoter, Carlos Gistal, that it was a crying shame to bring these

---

*This must be the only occasion in his career on which Vic Lewis was not photographed. In his *Music and Maiden Overs*, there are over 100 pictures of Lewis with everyone from Viv Richards and Louis Mountbatten to Jayne Mansfield and Stan Kenton.

nice English boys all this way and make them play in some of the bad parts of the huge USA. Gistal curtly replied: 'I haven't brought the Heath band to America to admire the scenic beauty, but to make some money. But I suggest at the end of the tour, June, that you hire a bus, and drive the band to all the nice places for a couple of weeks.'

Johnny Dankworth's trenchant comments on the situation were headlined in the *Melody Maker* of 4 January 1958:

'IT'S A FARCE,' says Johnny Dankworth.
  Johnny Dankworth has rejected an offer for his orchestra to tour America in exchange for the Glenn Miller Orchestra's visit to Britain. He has done so 'in disgust' at the schedule offered him. [Dankworth was then quoted]:
  For the best part of two years now I have been continually asked: 'When is your band going to the States?' And I have consistently given the same answer. First: when we are well-known enough to mean something out there. Second: when we are guaranteed a fair showing – to a jazz audience; and regrettably, I was forced to add a third condition: when we are assured of a tour that will cause no embarrassment to negro musicians or enthusiasts [i.e. by playing to non-segregated audiences].

In August 1959, Dankworth played a successful season at Birdland, New York, but one wonders what consternation his headlined strictures caused in Sicilian Avenue.

In October 1959, the *Melody Maker* reported that Ted Heath had turned down a tour of the 'Frozen North'. In the same month Humphrey Lyttelton and his band toured America, but at least he was included in a package totally devoted to jazz that included singer Anita O'Day, the Lennie Tristano Quartet, Thelonious Monk Quartet, George Shearing's Big Band, Julian and Nat Adderley. In his *Take It from the Top** he wrote of the mishaps on the tour, and referred to one show in particular, at the New York Hall, as a shambles.

Lyttelton had one moment of joy in a prickly interview with Henry Morgan, a TV anchorman whose stock in trade was a studied, smirking offensiveness to everybody in range. Trying to needle Lyttelton he enquired, in a tone of amused surprise, what

---

*This chapter was titled 'Coals to Newcastle'.

an Englishman was doing playing jazz in America.

'Just the same,' retorted Lyttelton, 'as the Americans are doing speaking English in England.' That smart-arse American commentator quickly learned that he shouldn't have tangled with an Old Etonian who was a master of the put-down.

In terms of financial success and audience acceptance – it was the first British band to appear on the 'Ed Sullivan Show' – the band that probably had the most success in America was Chris Barber's, due to their having had a hit-parade success with 'Petite Fleur' and, before that, 'Rock Island Line'. In an interview with Bob Dawbarn, however, in the *Melody Maker* (18 August 1959), on his return from eight and a half thousand miles and forty days in the US, Barber was, according to Dawbarn, 'prepared to talk enthusiastically of the rare King Oliver recordings he discovered and bought at the Chicago home of blues singer St Louis Jimmy, [but] he remains vague about the success of his tour'.

Dawbarn enquired: 'How much did "Petite Fleur" contribute to the ready acceptance of the Americans?' Barber replied:

> 'So far as the audiences were concerned, not at all. It did help us to get recognition in the music business itself – from bookers and agents. The audiences at our shows couldn't really associate "Petite Fleur" with the rest of our music. In any case the jazz fans liked the backing of "Wild Cat Blues" better. One thing that amused me was when George Brunies told me he had lost twenty dollars on a bet that Sidney Bechet was on our record.'
>
> I asked Chris if it was true – as a member of the band had told me – that audiences were surprised to find that he wasn't a clarinettist.
>
> 'I didn't give them a chance to be surprised,' said Chris, 'I let them know straight away which was Chris Barber.'
>
> I found Monty Sunshine under a new Sing-Sing haircut and asked him about *that* tune.
>
> 'We hadn't played "Petite Fleur" for ages and on the first shows I was terrified in case I forgot it,' confided the clarinettist. 'We have played it so often now I wouldn't mind forgetting it again.'

Dawbarn asked Barber to assess the standard of the average American trad musician. 'Cy Laurie and Mick Mulligan,' Barber tersely replied. Dawbarn concluded: 'The fantastic Barber success story seems to go on and on and on.'

There was more to this dialogue than immediately hit the eye.

Barber, an immensely self-assured young man, would not wish to have it thought that he required the artificial stimulus of a hit-parade success to impress audiences, nor that the band's success was attributable to one member of the band – the clarinettist on the trio recording of 'Petite Fleur' – and as it was soon to transpire in the dismissal of Sunshine from the band, all was not well between him and the leader. Barber obviously didn't think much of the Laurie and Mulligan bands.

The Barber band was highly praised by John S. Wilson of the *New York Times*, who commented on the irony of British bands being so good at performing what he termed 'home-grown traditional jazz', a form originally not indigenous to their island. Another British success was Alex Welsh's 1958 performance at the Newport Jazz Festival, but these isolated triumphs by Heath, Barber, Welsh and Lyttelton were the only bright spots in this doomed attempt at reciprocity. It has to be repeated: the British public wanted the American bands; the American public didn't want British bands.

How the entrepreneurs in America and Britain contrived to give the exchange system any semblance of what the British union demanded we will never know. Suffice it to say that within the terms set by the unions, it was totally inoperable and all attempts to make it appear viable reflected very badly on British bands playing in America. It was not long before another irony attended this charade. British rock and roll groups *were* much in demand by American audiences and, for the first time, a natural market force applied. The Americans wanted British rock and roll; the British jazz enthusiast wanted US jazz musicians. A genuine quid pro quo was therefore established.

Before that, the so-called reciprocity was indeed a farce, but its one advantageous outcome was the presence in Britain of those who were responsible for America's single great contribution to music: its jazz musicians.

12
Jazz City

The regular appearances of US musicians significantly heightened London's throb of activity to make it, in the fifties and sixties, a jazz city. Benny Green's 1961 report on London in Leonard Feather's *Encyclopedia of Jazz* noted:

> In the past few years, with interest stimulated by American visitors and the subsequent belated acknowledgement of the existence of jazz as something more than a source of delinquency and viciousness, the little clubs went from strength to strength until soon they were not so little. Crowds of a thousand were not unheard of during the brief but glorious life of Jazz City; nor are club programmes of three nights a week of music at the Flamingo. It is calculated that on a normal Saturday night in London, about five thousand people pay for admission into the little clubs, with an equal division between traditional and modern.

Such activity was in sharp contrast to the picture in 1933, when a handful of head-nodding jazz enthusiasts, rarely exceeding a hundred or so, attended the No. 1 Rhythm Club to sit and listen to a recitalist 'spinning discs' on a portable gramophone. The No. 1 was essentially a record recital club for dedicated collectors, and it was not until 1941, when Joseph Feldman opened his Swing Club at 100 Oxford Street on Sunday evenings, that there was any dancing to jazz music, and with it the introduction of jiving and jitterbugging to Britain.* Feldman's closed its doors in December 1954, after nearly thirteen years of continuous operation. Starting as a jam-session haven during the war for Archer Street jazz musicians, to be joined by neophyte boppers trying out the figurations they had picked up from those rare 78s coming over on

---

*Particular only to the Feldman club, thanks to the GI presence; the Bell band truly introduced the fashion.

the boats, it eventually became a totally 'modern' club, the old Archer Street hands beating a retreat. Their regular Sunday night was taken over by the Humphrey Lyttelton Club, taking their total to seven nights a week.

Feldman's holds a very special place in the hearts of older buffs, and this writer, for one, would have loved to have been present to observe the expressions of Coleman Hawkins and Kenny 'Klook' Clarke after the 'forbidden' concert at the Princess Theatre on the afternoon of 4 December 1949. On the stand, blowing lustily, was the Crane River Jazz Band! It could be safely assumed that these highly sophisticated musicians would have been stunned at what they heard.

During 1950, drummer Leon Roy, an extrovert showman, formed a mixed band of West Indian and English musicians to play on Monday evenings at the Paramount Dance Hall, Tottenham Court Rd, in London's West End. His West Indian players included Pete Pitterson (trumpet); George Roberts and George Tyndale (saxophones). The local players included trumpeter Denis Rose and Dave Usden; trombonist Mac Minshull; saxophonists Harry Klein, Pete King and Derek Neville – the latter a pre-war veteran of the West End's bottle-party sessions – and bassist Lennie Bush. An occasional vocalist was Roy's sister, Shani Wallis, later to be star of the show *Paint Your Waggon*.

The band's style was an imitation of the Dizzy Gillespie Big Band, and Roy had obtained printed Gillespie scores. Like the Gillespie band, it was a high-powered, uncompromising bop band, but considerably rougher, even, than the Gillespie aggregation. It was basically a rehearsal band.

The male clientele was predominantly West Indian, their clothes, demeanour, speech, deportment and loose, expressive style of dancing, and the wildness of the band combining to transform the interior of an average palais into a highly charged approximation of a Harlem ballroom in the thirties, the proceedings justifying the billing, 'London's Harlem'.

Harry Klein recalls:

> The guys were paid something like twenty-five shillings a gig, and, naturally, if anything better turned up, you took that, but I loved the excitement of Leon's

band, even if it was for a peanut. The atmosphere was great, the girls terrific and the dancing marvellous to watch. I, for one, got a charge from that. I can't be sure, but I think the management got a bit worried about certain substances being handed around and put a block on it. Leon Roy went to America and he's become devoutly religious, preaching for one of the sects they have over there. In my time he was a wild, likable, and very entertaining character, not that good a drummer, but he had the feel and that's what counted in that band.

The author recalls going over the top in a report on one Monday-evening session in *Jazz Illustrated* but in those days black activity in London, especially jazz activity, was a novelty and, perhaps, there was the naïve wish that the likes of a Harlem ballroom would be a permanent feature of London's entertainment scene.

The traditional clubs continued to flourish and multiply. Particularly successful in London were 100 Oxford Street, the Wood Green Jazz Club and Cy Laurie's 41 Great Windmill Street; their all-night sessions were invariably packed. Although the traditional clubs continued to show a superiority in numbers and attendances, a number of clubs were devoted to modern jazz, following the Fullado, Metrobopera and Club Eleven. Many of these clubs were short-lived, among them the Zan Zeba, 39 Gerrard Street. Open from midnight to 4 a.m., the club employed a house band led by West Indian trumpeter Dizzy Reece, often with another West Indian tenor saxophonist, Sammy Walker, drummer Dickie Devere, with occasional visits by Laurie Morgan and Denis Rose. The band (when in sufficient numbers) played, like Leon Roy, the arrangements of Dizzy Gillespie's Big Band. The personnel and instrumentation varied from night to night. This was bop underground; the musicians were transitory, their cash rewards minimal.

These haphazardly run places were, inevitably, replaced by clubs with normal facilities run on business lines. One of the first of these was the Studio 51, Great Newport Street, off Charing Cross Road, run by Vi Hyland. It opened in 1951. The smallness of the room predisposed it to a small-group policy: the Ronnie Ball Trio, Tony Kinsey Trio, and the Tommy Whittle Quartet. Bix Curtis was the compère. The 51 was hired on special nights each week by various bandleaders, including Kenny Graham and

Johnny Dankworth. In April 1956, however, modern jazz was supplanted when it became the Ken Colyer Club, running four nights a week.

A short-lived experiment, the Bandbox, run in a large hall in Leicester Square, was opened by bandleader Denny Boyce in 1954, and needed a crowd of about five hundred to make it a going proposition. Ted Heath's band made several appearances there, but the enthusiasts preferred more intimate settings, and it soon closed.

Jeff Kruger and his father Sam had been running Jewish dances in a luxurious room under the Mapleton Restaurant, Coventry Street, Piccadilly, and saw the possibilities for jazz promotion. On Sunday 31 August 1952, they opened their 'Jazz at the Mapleton' with the Johnny Dankworth Seven and a re-formed Kenny Graham's Afro-Cubists. Thanks to some astute publicizing of the event, police had to be called out to control the crowds. Laurie Henshaw reported in the *Melody Maker*, 6 September:

> Inside, the atmosphere was as torrid as a stoke-hole of a ship ... Compère Tony Hall pleaded in vain for the pressing throng to give the band boys breathing space, but, like King Canute, they wouldn't budge the tide an inch. A few hep cats tried to dance; most preferred to perspire standing still.
>
> USAF serviceman Richard De Gray (ex-bassist with Tommy Dorsey and Jimmy Zito) summed up the scene when he said he never expected to see anything like this outside New York. The musicians caught the swing fever and sweated out some first-rate jazz. For me the Dankworth Seven proved the high spot (how I wish they played like this on records!) but the Afro-Cubists were swamped with applause as they announced their 'come back' with the strains of 'Flamingo'.
>
> Actress Joan Dowling, accompanied by husband Harry Fowler, cut a rug – a real one – in the novel opening ceremony. Both promised to be regular visitors. Next time some of their admirers may be able to see them.

Later, it was running twice, then three nights weekly, and called 'Jazz at the Flamingo'.

The Kruger family ran the business in a respectable fashion; somewhat in contrast to another entrepreneur who operated from the same premises at different hours. From the early fifties, one of the most colourful of club promoters was Rik Gunnell, a one-time Smithfield Meat Market porter who knew little about jazz but was attracted to its ambience. If there was one aspect of the London jazz-club picture that could be described as shady it would be the clubs that Gunnell ran. He had a fondness for the company of villains at a time when gang warfare in Soho was rife. One of his clubs, the Star Club, Wardour Street, was dubbed the 'Scar Club' on account of its razor-wielding clientele.

One of Gunnell's early ventures was the Two-Way Club, running on Thursday nights at 100 Oxford Street in the autumn of 1952. Its title related to his vain attempt to introduce a policy of traditional and modern jazz on the same night. The *New Musical Express* ran a story about the venture under the heading 'FIGS AND FUTURISTS UNDER ONE ROOF'. It opened with Mick Mulligan and his band with George Melly and the Johnny Dankworth Seven, to a sparse audience and, to add a ecumenical touch to the proceedings, Dankworth, on clarinet, joined with the Mulligan band on the final number, a tear-away version of 'When the Saints Go Marching in', the traditionalists' anthem.

The Two-Way Club lasted for four Thursdays. It was going to take more than an opportunistic promoter (for Gunnell's motives were hardly ideological) to entice the opposites to share an evening together and rarely did this policy work elsewhere, in clubs or on the concert platform.

Gunnell opened the Club Basie, in the Tavistock Restaurant, Charing Cross Road, in 1955, which he described as the 'most luxurious jazz joint in town' and another, the Blue Room, but neither lasted long. Even modern-jazz followers, who regarded themselves as more sophisticated than the traditionalists, seemed wary of plush surroundings.

At that time none of the jazz clubs was licensed, patrons making use of local pubs for alcoholic refreshment and so Gunnell entered into an arrangement with the proprietors of premises in Denman Street, off Piccadilly, to run their former billiard hall as a club with a full menu and licensed bar. Gunnell called it the Piccadilly Club, but sensing failure after the opening night, opted out after two nights, leaving the author naïvely to continue with the club.*

Gunnell's most successful operations were his All-Night Ses-

---

*See *All This and Many a Dog*, by the author.

sions, first in the basement under the Mapleton, and thereafter at 33/37 Wardour Street, under the name of the Flamingo Club.

These commenced at midnight and ran through to 6 a.m. and attracted a highly cosmopolitan audience of ordinary jazz fans; US servicemen – mostly black – from the US Army camps then dotted around London; film stars like Peter Finch; two of the most celebrated *demi-mondaines* in the history of British politics, Christine Keeler and Mandy Rice-Davies; and lesser-known ladies of the night.

The premises were unlicensed, but Gunnell overcame this tiresome difficulty by selling bottles of Coca-Cola spiked with whisky at what then seemed the exorbitant price of 10/- a bottle. The US servicemen, armed with duty-free liquor, traded with the resident West Indian blacks for various drugs. This illegal sale of alcohol was never discovered – or, at least, Gunnell was never charged with such – but the raffishness of the proceedings and certainly the activities of some of the clientele attracted police attention.

The music was provided by the best of Britain's modern jazzmen, but in some glaring cases, their contempt for the public, and the condition in which some of them appeared, alienated them from the crowd and Gunnell turned to the emerging R&B musicians to please his clientele, the main attraction being Georgie Fame and the Blue Flames.

One of the inner suburban clubs was Klook's Kleek, at the Railway Hotel, West Hampstead, run by Dick Jordan. It opened in January 1961 with a modern-jazz policy, but within two years the enthusiast Jordan also became disillusioned with the attitude of the musicians: turning up late, extending their numbers up to forty minutes and taking breaks of up to ten minutes between them. Jordan had a dancing policy, but the forty-minute marathons placed a considerable strain on the stamina of his patrons and, changing to a R&B policy with Manfred Mann and Georgie Fame, he did good business with musicians who considered the requirements of the dancers rather than their own inward-looking self-indulgence. The club closed in January 1970.

The author was another who ran more jazz clubs than were good for his pocket, although the Six Bells flourished for ten years

the GAFF

Monthly Club Puffo

The above are caricatures of Stars regularly appearing at the GAFF. They are drawn by WALLY FAWKES known to "Daily Mail" readers as 'Trog', whose comic strip 'Flook' from time to time features many well-known figures in the Jazz World. The story line of this strip is written by GEORGE MELLY, who in addition to singing the blues also comperes B.B.C. "Jazz Club". SANDY BROWN, in addition to playing clarinet, singing, composing and arranging, is an Artist of distinction as a hobby and an acoustical architect by profession. AL FAIRWEATHER also is a gifted Artist and some of his satirical drawings will be appear-

SIX BELLS
KING'S ROAD, CHELSEA
Saturday, May 6th, 8 p.m.
JOHN CHILTON'S SWING KINGS
JITTERBUGS WELCOME

387
Dopey Dick's jazzhouse
railway hotel
west hampstead
SIGNATURE:

Dopey Dick's was the other name for Klook's Kleek, the Railway Hotel, West Hamsptead, run by Dick Jordan

from 1959. His other, less successful, ventures were the Gaff, at the Green Man in Blackheath, and the Hideaway, Hampstead, the last aptly titled, since so few people appeared to discover its presence.

One of London's most jazz-active streets was seedy Gerrard Street, now Chinatown. Many small clubs operated there so it was nothing unusual when yet another opened, at number 39, on Friday 30 October 1959. The *Melody Maker*, 25 October 1959, ran an advertisement:

RONNIE SCOTT'S CLUB, 39 Gerrard Street, W1. Fri. 7.30 p.m. Tubby Hayes Quartet; Eddie Thompson Trio and the first appearance of Jack Parnell in a jazz club since the relief of Mafeking. Membership 10/- until January 1961. Admission 1/6d (members).

This jocular advertisement was the forerunner of many another similarly humorous notice, one of which, on 14 November 1959, read: 'At tremendous expense and great loss of life – now open seven nights a week. Come along and see the fun next week – we're holding a musician's ball.'

This elicited a prim letter from the *Melody Maker*'s advertising manager, informing the club that the paper could not accept any more advertisements containing that kind of *double entendre*. Ironically, not many years later the same paper's lovelorn advertisers frequently used four-letter words and made sexually explicit offers in an extensive agony column.

These advertisements, composed by the waggish Scott, established the spirit and atmosphere of the club, sustained by his impishly witty announcements.

> 28 November 1959: Saturday, midnight to 6 a.m. – the late, late, late, late show. Now featuring a tremendous step towards inter-racial relations – ham bagels.
> 5 December 1959: Free admission! – for Somerset Maugham, Sir Thomas Beecham and Little Richard.
> 12 December 1959: Ronnie Scott's Club – sponsored by the Shoreditch Tsetse Fly Protection Society.
> 2 January 1960: Special offer to our 1,000th client – a pair of exquisitely matched giant bird-eating spiders, or a week in Manchester. Personal appearance of Alfred Hinds. The food must be good – 3,000 flies can't be wrong.

Musicians were paid approximately three pounds a session and a resident player like Stan Tracey about thirty-five pounds a week. Staff received between ten and twelve pounds a week, and as with so many other little clubs that had been opened, particularly in Gerrard Street, some even at No. 39, the life expectancy of the Ronnie Scott Club, managed by Scott's partner, Pete King, was held to be short. No one, certainly not the principals, could have visualized its running nearly thirty years later, and in premises infinitely plusher than the one-time taximan's haunt furnished with second-hand chairs, sporting an ancient upright piano, albeit made to look a little cheerier for the opening night by the application of a few pots of paint.

The Scott club's opening at rather dingy premises set them in opposition to the infinitely more luxurious Flamingo, where the resident compère was Tony Hall. Hall, a bland character, made certain comments in December 1959's *Jazz News*, replied to by Scott in the same paper. Somewhat acrimonious correspondence raged in the paper for some weeks afterwards, and led to the following piece, written by Daniel Halperin and entitled 'Storm Over Soho'.

'This damp, depressing evening we have with us, strictly for financial peanuts, and because they have nowhere else to go, the most maudlin group on the modern-jazz scene.

'The alto saxophonist who is its leader is young enough to know better but he persists in playing his Bird-burdened solos which are received by those who have heard worse with widespread nausea ... The pianist was bitten by a bunch of Monk records nine years ago and has been biting them back ever since. The trumpet player lives rent-free in another world and every other member of this group agrees that is a good thing. For your delectation and dubious delight they will play a number of moth-eaten arrangements in a manner much modified by the creeping mental *rigor mortis* which afflicts them all.'

A cozy little introduction along the above lines would, I submit, make a mite more honest jazz-club listening in view of the tempestuous Scott–Hall controversy. I refer to Ronnie Scott's piece in the 3 December issue of *Jazz News* and the piece, on another page in this issue, by Mr Tony Hall.

Mr Scott weighed in first with a strong slap at the 'cheapskate huckstering' and 'merciless haranguing' of jazz-club compères. Mr Hall shoots back, believing that Mr Scott's bludgeon was aimed at him ...

On today's high-pressure scene, music is being peddled to the masses with every cunning commercial connivance and contrivance. The kids are bombarded with messages from every angle. They have been talked into listening to and paying for pops, rocks, beat, trad – you name it, they've bought it.

Meanwhile modern jazz languishes low. Surely, whatever the involved reasons for this sad situation, and one of them is undoubtedly the fact that for a long time many modern jazzmen spurned audiences quite obviously, this kind of music has urgent need now in Britain of all the help it can get in putting itself across to the public.

I'm not suggesting that the day of the determined huckster is at hand.

What I am saying is: EVERYONE ON THE MODERN-JAZZ SCENE MUST DECIDE NOW HOW MUCH PROPULSION TOWARD THE PUBLIC THEY ARE WILLING TO ACCEPT, WHAT EFFECT IT MIGHT HAVE ON THE MUSIC AND WHAT FORM THE PAYLOAD ROCKET SHOULD TAKE.

That is, really, what Mr Scott and Mr Hall are arguing about.

Having extracted my little column from this storm in an eggcup, I flee to that mythical jazz club where the reluctant compère tells the truth (how refreshing that would be, my friends, and how impossible): 'For the last number, ladies and gentlemen, our second-rate talents will mangle a little tune entitled "How Come You Don't Do Me Like I Do You?" which is based, awkwardly, on a misunderstanding of the chords in "If I Had the Wings of an Angel, I Wouldn't Lend 'em to You, Baby." '

Scott's club featured the cream of British musicians, but these players didn't draw the crowds. In Scott's words: 'The problem was that we suddenly came to discover what a legion of friends we had among musicians – and, naturally, we couldn't ask our friends to pay admission charges when they dropped into the club. Sometimes we had more sitters-in in the audience than payers.'

The club obtained a supper and liquor licence in 1960, opening till 1 a.m. It was a start towards the informal sophistication that characterized the later club, but even with these increased facilities business was indifferent, and Scott and King were constantly beset with financial difficulties. The only solution was to engage the more famous Americans, and although an exchange system for bands was in operation, no such scheme existed for solo acts until Pete King successfully negotiated with both British and American musicians, resulting in the appearance of Zoot Sims playing a four-week season at the Scott club in November 1961.

Sims's appearance was the turning point in the club's history, providing a memorable season that was to be followed by a stream of US jazzmen. They not only drew the crowds, but also gave work to British musicians, brought in to accompany the visitors. This arrangement provided proof that British musicians had developed the considerable prowess needed to support their better acclaimed contemporaries from across the Atlantic. Their grasp of the idiom was, unquestionably, vastly superior to that shown when they first followed the innovative records played 'up at Carlo's'.

In *Some of My Best Friends are Blues*, Ronnie Scott reflected on this period:

> It was no secret that European players in those days had an inferiority complex with regard to American musicians and this, when combined with what in some cases was genuine inferiority, often created disastrous tension and atmosphere in pick-up Euro-American groups. Generally speaking, the Americans were entitled to act in a superior way because many of them *were* musically superior to their European colleagues; but there were certain

American jazzmen who clearly took a delight in humiliating European rhythm-section players and in emphasizing the discrepancy between their playing and that of their accompanists rather than trying to achieve a musical compromise so that the audience at least got acceptable music.

Zoot Sims was beautifully easy-going and adaptable. He clearly demonstrated right from the start that his primary concern was to find common ground with his rhythm section. It was a good team by any standards: Stan Tracey (piano), Kenny Napper (bass) and Jackie Dougan (drums) – it would certainly hold its own with any of the top American horn players.

Although Tracey was an outstanding example of how British musicianship in the field of modern jazz had developed in such a relatively short space of time, there were one or two drummers who cracked under the strain of accompanying temperamental guests.

The appearance of famed American soloists gave the club stability and a growing reputation, but the premises' capacity was uneconomic. Scott and King got to the stage where every Sunday night they pondered as to whether they could open the following week.

In the summer of 1965, Scott and King found premises in 47 Frith Street that would enable them to expand, to have proper kitchens, a lengthy bar and more band space. They had to borrow something like £35,000 to achieve this, and their saviour was Harold Davison. 'We made him an offer he could refuse,' wrote Scott.

They opened on 17 December 1965 with tenor saxophonist/flautist Yusef Lateef and singer Ernestine Anderson. The premises were in a state of complete chaos: no front doors, electrical installations incomplete, wires trailing on the floor; it was also a few days before there were separate ladies' and gents' lavatories. Out of the chaos, however, arose an institution, though one not without further crises.

The success of the club, the continuously high standard of the music aside, lay in the disparate characters of Scott and King, each complementing the other. Scott's humour, manifested in the repetition of the same jokes for over a quarter of a century – protesting that 'what was good enough for my dear old Dad is good enough for me' – is as much a part of the club's lore as the quality of the music, while the chore of club administration fell to Pete King.

Scott and King continued the lease on 39 Gerrard Street, calling it the 'Old Place' and using it for both old hands and new bands, such as that of Chris McGregor.

A club of an entirely different character was the Studio Club, Swallow Street, founded in 1919 by artists for artists (the painter Augustus John was a founder member). It continued its artistic associations over the years, but during the fifties it saw an influx of musicians, managers, agents and record producers from the jazz world. The resident pianist was Alan Clare, a consummate musician with a vast repertoire of tunes, supported by a variety of willing volunteer (unpaid) bass players and drummers, and often joined by the musician members.

It was a feature of the club that the music was casually accepted. Perhaps surprisingly, this apparent indifference on the part of the members was actually appreciated by the musicians, many even declaring it was a pleasure to play without being gaped at.

Famous visitors included Cab Calloway, Sarah Vaughan, Mezz Mezzrow and Mary Lou Williams, the inviter invariably Max Jones. In an article for the *Melody Maker*, Jones described the Studio Club as the nearest thing to a pre-war jam-session club.

Although much fewer in number than the clubs catering for the traditional enthusiast, a sprinkling of clubs devoted to modern jazz operated in the suburbs. One of the most successful, and certainly the longest running, was at the Bull's Head in Barnes, south-west London, overlooking the Thames. Run by publican Albert Tolley, seven nights a week, it featured all the foremost modern-jazz musicians, its resident trio initially led by pianist Roy Budd, and from 1966 one of its resident bands was the Be-bop Preservation Society, conceived by Bill Le Sage, with Hank Shaw (trumpet), Peter King (alto saxophone), Spike Heatley (bass), Bryan Spring (drums) and Le Sage (piano).

While it was a fact that traditional and bop musicians were rarely seen together socially, meeting up mainly on stylistically mixed Sunday concerts or in transport cafes while on tour, there was one club in London, the Downbeat, Old Compton Street, run by saxophonists Mike Senn and Jackie Sharpe, where they met fraternally. There was a resident trio, usually led by pianists Alan Clare and Pat Smythe, and 'modern' musicians would sit in. (The Downbeat was also the home of a big band led by Tubby Hayes.) Although the clientele was a mix from both camps, an incident one evening reflected the yawning chasm between the two stylistic opposites.

Pat Smythe was leading the resident trio when a young traditionalist trumpeter, thinking to essay a little bebop, got up on the stand uninvited. Smythe, a highly respected musician but a rather Calvinistic, unsmiling character, immediately stopped playing and the drummer and bass player, rather embarrassed, followed suit. The neo-bopper slunk away. Intermixing of the clientele was one thing; Smythe was not going to countenance it on the bandstand.

One memorable afternoon Billie Holiday was brought into the club and sang to a mere handful of people. During her performance, someone with absolutely no sense of occasion decided to use the payphone near the bandstand, resulting in Kenny Graham having to be physically restrained from attacking him.

In April 1958 the National Jazz Federation opened the Marquee in Oxford Street – not many yards from 100 Oxford Street – with a mixed policy, that included regular appearances of Humphrey Lyttelton's 'saxophone' band, this making fewer and fewer appearances at the club that bore the leader's name (the Humphrey Lyttelton Club closed on Sunday 15 September 1959 and was taken over by accountant Ted Morton and Mrs Molly Horton, pursuing an almost wholly traditional policy).

In 1959 Johnny Dankworth opened his own Sunday Club at the London Dancing Institute, 29 Oxford Street, and that well-known shopping centre became a club battleground. The Marquee was to become known as the foremost R&B venue, one of the first bands to be booked being the Rolling Stones. The author recalls a traditional night when he spotted a young man seated at the end of the bandstand scowling at whatever traditional band was playing that night – Dick Charlesworth's, I believe. There was something about his cast of features that enabled me later to connect him with the name of Mick Jagger, once he became a world-famous figure.

But it wasn't the Rolling Stones that made an impact as the Marquee's first big attraction. That fell to the unlikely figure of a former traditional-band banjoist, Alexis Korner, and it was his efforts that fostered the entire R&B movement in Britain. For it was from the Marquee that a movement sprang, an amalgam of blues and jazz, that generally went under the title of rhythm and blues. In the early sixties, the Marquee booked Alexis Korner and his Blues Incorporated with little expectation that such a mixture would attract much attention, but Blues Incorporated turned out to be a riotous success, drawing crowds as large as a thousand.

Korner was born in Paris in April 1928, the son of a Greek mother and an Austrian cavalry officer. By the late 1940s his blues quartet was part of Chris Barber's band, playing a thirty-minute set on Barber's concerts. Unlike most traditionalists, he accepted bebop, a fact that he assuredly would have kept to himself when he recorded (on mandolin and guitar) with Colyer's Skiffle Group: Colyer (vocal, guitar), Micky Ashman (bass) and Bill Colyer (washboard).

In the mid-1950s Barber was bringing over American blues artists such as Big Bill Broonzy and Muddy Waters. Both of them played electric guitar, an instrument that was anathema to the jazz purist. Korner, however, was booked for a spot on these concerts and decided that the power of the electric instrument was for him. His band also featured Cyril Davis on amplified harmonica.

Rejected by the fundamentalists, Korner was soon moving in the company of modernists such as saxophonists John Surman, Art Themen, Alan Skidmore, Dick Heckstall-Smith and Ray Warleigh; trumpeter Kenny Wheeler; drummers Phil Seamen, Ginger Baker, John Marshall and Charlie Watts; bassist Jack Bruce; organist/saxophonist Graham Bond and singers Long John Baldry, Paul Jones, Mick Jagger, Eric Burdon and Robert Plant.

Tenor saxophonist, now the *Evening Standard*'s jazz critic, Jack Massarik, was once a member of Ronnie Jones's Blue Jays. He recalls some of the prominent names involved in Britain's R&B boom.

Alexis Korner's Blues Incorporated was to inspire a rash of similarly blues-oriented groups and thus give yet another dimension to British jazz. One of the foremost of these groups was fronted by John Mayall. Mayall, discovered by the Gillespie-influenced Mancunian trumpeter John Rowland playing barrelhouse piano in a Salford pub, the Black Lion, quickly followed Korner's lead, turning professional within months of singing with the first band to include him, Blues Syndicate. Eric Clapton joined him the following year.

The influence of modern jazz was a significant ingredient in the R&B boom. Whereas the lead singers in R&B bands were influenced by black US R&B artists, the backing musicians had a healthy respect for the work of such giants as Sonny Rollins and John Coltrane on tenor, Wes Montgomery on guitar, Lee Morgan on trumpet, Art Blakey on drums, Jimmy Smith on Hammond organ – and for such skilful 'crossover' figures in the US like King Curtis and Junior Walker on sax, Billy Preston and Donny Hathaway on keyboards, Stix Hooper and Bernard 'Pretty' Purdie on drums.

Some of the singers were also instrumentalists: Georgie Fame, having broken free of the glamour-boy mould created for him by the Svengalian Larry Parnes, formed his Blue Flames, singing in a style closer to Louisiana than his native Lancashire and playing Hammond organ. Tony Knight, singer and drummer, led the Chessmen, who included a youthful Lol Coxhill playing growling tenor sax and doing the two-step shuffle that was an obligatory part of any R&B stage act in those days.

Many of the bands were thus fascinating hybrids of blues and sixties modern jazz. Cliff Barton, Fame's Fender bassist, was punching the strings with his thumb instead of a plectrum years ahead of his time, while the drummer Red Reece was a protegé of the ubiquitous Phil Seamen, and Glen Hughes took fine solos on baritone sax, an instrument played by very few modern jazzmen in Britain (Ronnie Ross and Harry Klein had the field largely to themselves) at that time.

Brian Auger, an excellent jazz pianist originally motivated by Horace Silver's work with the Jazz Messengers, took the Jimmy Smith route to the Hammond organ and founded the Steam Packet, which originally featured Long John Baldry and Julie Driscoll on vocals, helped out by an anorexic-looking adolescent called Rod 'The Mod' Stewart, later destined to leave transport cafes far behind.

Auger's guitarists, Vic Briggs – now living in California – and the brilliant Gary Boyle, were both influenced by Wes Montgomery. Ronnie Jones's band, in which he played alto sax and Hammond (but not simultaneously, as the amazing and sadly missed Graham Bond used to do) also featured the Coltrane-influenced New Zealand tenorist Brian Smith (later with Ian Carr's Nucleus) and drummer Clive Thacker (later to tour the US with Auger and appear at Ronnie Scott's with Ernestine Anderson and several other jazz artists).

The R&B phenomenon was thus a striking example of a nationwide movement springing from the activities of a single club.

Another feature of the London scene was the regularity of jazz concerts, one series of which were those described as 'Jazz Jamborees'. These had been running since 1938 and were generally notable for having only a minimum of jazz content. The use of the word 'jazz' was a hangover from days in 'the profession' when it was applied to non-improvisational and unswinging dance music, but by the late fifties the Musicians' Benevolent Fund who ran these events had, belatedly, realized that the musical content of these shows should be consistent with their title. In 1958, the bill thus comprised Johnny Dankworth and his Orchestra, Ted Heath and his Music, Humphrey Lyttelton and his Band, the Jazz Couriers, Tony Kinsey Trio, Ray Ellington Quartet, Chris Barber, but – as if in a sort of rearguard action from the old hands – also present were the bands of Oscar Rabin, Edmundo Ros and ... the Big Ben Banjo Band led by Norrie Paramour.

The 1959 jamboree was a genuine jazz occasion, presenting Tubby Hayes and his Band, Ronnie Scott and his Orchestra, the Tommy Whittle Quartet, Jack Parnell and his Orchestra, Annie Ross, the New Jazz Group – Derek Smith, Allan Ganley, Sammy Stokes and Harry Klein – and Tony Crombie and his Band. They were intoduced by the long-standing compère of these shows, Tommy Trinder, as 'Tone Cumberland and his Boys'.

Trinder was ignorant about jazz, and was not a particularly sensitive compère, either on this occasion or on his regular BBC programme, 'Sunday Break' featuring jazz bands. On one occasion, he announced that the following week's attractions would include the black bass baritone Paul Robeson, ending the announcement with a whooped '*Yowsah!!*' The following week, actually introducing Robeson, he was unctuousness personified. 'It gives me *very* great pleasure ... ladies and gennelmen ... it is a *very* great *honour* indeed to present to yew – a *very* fine singer and a *gennelman*: Paul Robeson!'

Before the war shops specializing in jazz were virtually unknown.

Levy's in Aldgate, Morris's in Tottenham Court Road and the City Sale and Exchange, Fleet Street, had made a feature of stocking jazz records in the thirties and Dave Carey had opened his Swing Shop in 1938, but shops devoted entirely to jazz and blues were mainly a post-war phenomenon.

The first was Dobell's, 77 Charing Cross Road. Doug Dobell, demobilized from the army in 1946, was managing his father's antiquarian bookshop at this address and initially set aside a small area for the sale and exchange of 78-rpm records. The takings were put in a tin, there being no proper till for the small cash turnover. In 1950 the shop went over completely to jazz and blues, its knowledgeable salesmen over the years including George Ellis, Bill Colyer, Alf Lumby, John Kendall, Don Sollash, Brian Peerless and Tony Middleton.

It became both a collector's Mecca and a dropping-in point for visiting musicians. Dobell's (whose slogan was 'Every true jazz fan is born within the sound of Dobell's') continued at 77 Charing Cross Road until approximately six o'clock on 31 December 1980, when representatives of Westminster City Council came to put padlocks on the door. The sounds of jazz still defiantly issuing from inside marked the end of an era. No. 77, with the entire parade of Victorian shops and dwellings, was then demolished by the City Council and a characteristically charmless construction erected in its place.

In November 1981, Dobell reopened at 21 Tower Street, WC1. He died in 1987 – on his annual pilgrimage to the Nice Jazz Festival.

Other specialist shops were the International Bookshop, Charing Cross Road; John Rowe's Attic, 84 Newman Street (next to the Blue Posts); Dave Carey's reopened Swing Shop in Streatham, south-west London; and Jim Asman's at 23a New Row, St Martin's Lane (opening in 1953 and specializing mostly in pre-bop issues). Colletts opened a shop for jazz and blues, at 1 New Oxford Street in 1953, managed by Ray Smith, who continued in this capacity when the shop moved to 180 Shaftesbury Avenue in 1982, and taken over by him in 1985.

In 1960, pioneer jazz-record-shop proprietor Doug Dobell founded his '77' label (after his address in Charing Cross Road), recording both British musicians and American visitors. For the vintage-jazz enthusiast (and the lover of twenties dance-band music) there were various compilations, notably *Jazz in Britain – The Twenties*, *Jazz in Britain – The Thirties*, *Home Made Jam, Volumes 1 and 2*, and *My Baby Loves to Charleston*, an album of British bands with tracks by various Bert Firman Orchestras including the Rhythmic Eight, the latter with a sleevenote by the indefatigable discographer Brian Rust, who wrote of clarinettist/saxophonist Perley Breed, an American resident in London in the late twenties, that 'he needed no introduction' . . .

Other small specialist record companies helped to meet the growing demand for jazz records: Tempo, Vogue, Melodisc, Nixa and others. Many were subsequently to be absorbed into the larger companies, who themselves were catering with increased issues for the jazz enthusiast. Decca, for instance, had four staffmen committed to jazz: Peter Clayton, Peter Gammond, Keith Howell and Geoff Milne.

There were also a few independent producers, foremost among them Denis Preston who, at one stage, described himself as St Denis Preston. He was alleged to have been a child prodigy on the violin and he had been in the Royal Army Pay Corps during the war stationed in Sidcup; otherwise, little was known about this enigmatic operator. One thing, however, was certain: he was always astute enough to avoid the bondage of a nine-to-five job. He had a lordly arrogance that would have precluded such a mundane way of earning of living.

Max Jones knew him well, and in his obituary of Preston in the *Melody Maker*, after his death on 28 October 1979, wrote: 'I found Preston erudite, unpredictable, Rabelaisian, mentally alert, opinionated, often outrageous, warm-hearted, flamboyant in dress, manner and motor cars, dedicated to cricket, food, drink, discussion and the music of Duke Ellington (these often overlapped), enthusiasm about motor racing and gangster and boxing books. He was eloquent in tongue and pen.'

Preston was genuinely in love with jazz and although patently no philanthropist, often recorded bands for his own pleasure, or even for sentimental reasons. One such recording featured veteran trumpeter Nat Gonella in 1959, playing on different sessions with a mixture of traditional and modern musicians at a time when the major companies were totally uninterested in a man whose recordings (on the pre-war Parlophone label) sold steadily. On these recordings Gonella played in a looser, more relaxed style than he had with his Georgians in the thirties.

Preston opened Lansdowne Studios, in Notting Hill Gate, in 1955 on borrowed money, opening it up for the business in general but also starting the label, Lansdowne, for which he personally recorded hundreds of sessions, most of them in the mainstream mould. He saw himself as the British Norman Granz, and on several sessions followed the 'Jazz at the Philharmonic' pattern. One such session was with British alto saxophonists Joe Harriott, Bruce Turner and Bertie King, *à la* Charlie Parker, Benny Carter and Johnny Hodges.

Never one to hide his light under a bushel, he told Max Jones he thought he was a better producer than Granz, but that he was hampered by lack of home-grown talent. The new trends he took in his stride, recording Joe Harriott's avant-garde 'free-form' group, the Harriott–John Mayer 'Indo-Jazz' fusions, and Stan Tracey's famed *Under Milkwood* suite.

He also recorded the spoken word, from calypso singer Lord Buckley to philosopher Bertrand Russell, and recorded an interview with Frank Richards, creator and writer of the Greyfriars and St Jim's schoolboy stories.

His other issues included albums by Kenny Baker's Half Dozen, memorable albums by Humphrey Lyttelton's band and various sessions by Sandy Brown and Al Fairweather, all recordings that have stood the test of time. He also recorded veteran Buddy Featherstonehaugh, featured on baritone saxophone. He was a convert to modern jazz, and recorded with young players like Leon Calvert and Kenny Wheeler (trumpet), Roy Sidwell and Bobby Wellins (tenor saxophone) and Jackie Dougan (drums).

Although Preston showed an amused contempt for trad, he quickly saw the commercial possibilities of the genre and made several highly profitable recordings, apart from those of Chris Barber. He even claimed that he invented the word 'trad' for a

1958 album *It's Trad* by Terry Lightfoot, but he was undoubtedly being characteristically flippant since the term was in use and in print as early as 1956.

Despite this intense activity in the clubs, on the concert platform and in recording studios, plus the increase in specialist shops and a spate of books relating to jazz, the BBC characteristically showed little interest. Allocation of air-time to the music that had taken such a hold on the nation was grudging and parsimonious. While it would clearly be invidious to try to apportion blame for this state of affairs in such an amorphous organization, it is nevertheless the case that many producers were laws unto themselves and revealed precious little interest in jazz, while other minority musical forms, and subjects – literary, historical, whatever – *were* acknowledged, often at length. Even in the BBC's Third Programme, set up in 1949 to serve minority interests, it was not thought that jazz deserved much air-time.

Uncharacteristically, however, BBC TV ran a memorable series produced by Terry Henebery called 'Jazz 625', from 1964–6. Among the American and British artists enshrined on film for future generations to see were: Duke Ellington, Woody Herman and his Orchestra, Ben Webster, Buck Clayton, Wes Montgomery, Thelonious Monk, George Lewis, Oscar Peterson, Dizzy Gillespie, the Modern Jazz Quartet, Willie 'the Lion' Smith, the Alex Welsh Band with Dicky Wells and the Bruce Turner Jump Band with Don Byas.

In 1961 a film, *All Night Long*, described by David Meeker, author of *Jazz in the Movies*, as a 'ludicrous combination of *Othello* and jazz jamboree that falls flat on both counts', was made in Britain. The music direction was by Philip Green (leader of several near-'Dixieland' recordings with Archer Street musicians in the thirties under the name of the Ballyhooligans), and it featured the US pianist Dave Brubeck, composer/bassist Charles Mingus and many British musicians, including Johnny Dankworth, Tubby Hayes, Keith Christie, Allan Ganley, Kenny Napper, Bert Courtley, Colin Purbrook, Harry Beckett, Harold McNair, Jackie Dougan and, on the soundtrack only, Cleo Laine.

If for nothing else the occasion was notable for the belligerent observations of Mingus, who took a poor view of British musicians, and at one point sarcastically enquired, 'Who invented jazz? Tubby Hayes and Kenny Napper?' But he had complimentary things to say, not only about saxophonists Joe Harriott and Harold McNair and trumpeter Harry Beckett (all three West Indians) but also about Ronnie Scott: 'Of the white boys, Ronnie Scott gets closer to the Negro blues feeling, the way Zoot Sims does.'

Not that eccentricity was restricted to visiting Americans; London, Jazz City, had its fair share of the home-grown article. One such was Gypsy Larry, who played a home-made single-string bass in the Cottage Club skiffle sessions and who was later a cleaner-*cum*-general factotum at Ronnie Scott's. He was no respecter of persons and once hurried Miles Davis and friends out of the club when they had felt disposed to sit around. Another was ex-publican Don Kingswell with his wide range of rich malapropisms who, when road manager with Teddy Foster's band, helped Foster to meet the contractual number of musicians in some halls by 'playing' the trombone before checking the takings, and who later managed Cy Laurie's atmospheric club in Great Windmill Street.* There were also dedicated promoters, fired by a genuine love of jazz, who were sporadically successful in their endeavours: triers like one-time drummer Peter Burman, cousin of Maurice Burman. A Jew, but virulently anti-Semitic, he championed and supported Tubby Hayes during the musician's last, sad days; he promoted the best of modern musicians in his Jazz-Tête-à-Tête and eventually became road manager for Humphrey Lyttelton's eight-piece band. Others included Bix Curtis, who lost more money than he ever made promoting; and Harry Morris, the sundries salesman and Club Eleven manager, the supreme Sohoite who felt he was 'out in the sticks' in Marble Arch.

There were, of course, some nasty people – like the agent whose business tactics and neighing laugh earned him the soubriquet of

---

*See the author's *All This and Many a Dog* for more anecdotes about Kingswell.

the 'Braying Mantis' – but generally the warmth and flow of the idiom attracted similarly mercurial characters. Many are dead – Gypsy Larry, Don Kingswell, Harry Morris, Bix Curtis, Peter Burman among these – and others, inevitably, have drifted into suburbia and respectability.

Archer Street had been an integral part of the dance-band industry in which so many jazz players made a living, some fulfilling their roles as improvisers, others, in the more commercial bands – like Kenny Graham with Eric Winstone – merely reading the dots.

'The Street' was both social club and labour exchange and the latter function was exploited by the 'fixers' for bands ranging from trios to thirty-strong orchestras for TV extravaganzas. They knew that they would find in the denizens of this tiny thoroughfare musicians who could sight read a score as easily as they read the sports results in their daily newspapers.

For the dance/jazz musicians Archer Street's Harmony Inn was practically a second home, denizens of the Street inhabiting it all day for the price of a cup of tea or coffee. The leaseholder of the premises was a bald-headed Czech emigré called George Siptak who opened up business in 1950. Recognizing where most of his trade was likely to come from, he christened his cafe with an apposite name and had badly drawn murals, saxophones the predominant motif, all over the interior. Benny Green, in an article on Archer Street in *Topic*, August 1962, wrote of Siptak: 'He had never seen the inside of a jazz club and yet he knew better than any critic about the relative abilities of his customers, perhaps from digesting the small talk, perhaps from an instinct for human nature.'

In the same article, Green correctly stresses that the traditional jazzman was not present:

> He is a specialist, usually with no ability outside the narrow confines of his own style, and could be disastrous at a conventional hotel dance. The modernist, being far better equipped technically, does frequent the Street and often augments his income from playing a few dance engagements, although fixers were chary of giving work to jazzmen, who they feared might turn out to

be 'characters', which might mean anything from eccentricity of dress to the failure to turn up at all.

Green skirts the true reason why so many bandleaders were reluctant to give employment to 'characters'. This was the usual description for drug addicts and they could, at the least, be disruptive or, at worst, attract the attention of the police and the undesirable publicity that would go with such investigations.

Towards the end of the fifties the numbers to be seen in the Street declined week by week and while it seemed inconceivable to most of its denizens that such a solidly entrenched form of entertainment as the dance band (and the variety theatre) should expire, expire they did. Musicians continued to say 'see you in the Street', but as the weekly listing of band calls in the musical papers shrunk, so did the once teeming throng. In Green's piece on Archer Street in *Topic* he told the stock 'Street' story concerning a disturbed musician who had the recurring dream that he went to Archer Street one Monday and found that nobody had turned up.

For a musician who, say, had been abroad since 1950 and had been totally out of touch before returning in the early 1960s, that nightmarish dream would have materialized. He would have found that the Street had become a ghost street. A colourful part of London's street lore had disappeared never to return.

Thanks to Denis Rose, however, there exist on film, shot on Rose's cinecamera, many characters who haunted this little street, and who were so much a part of the burgeoning modern-jazz scene in the fifties. The faces that flit silently across the grainy, flickering pictures are marvellously evocative of the time and its ethos. They included Ronnie Scott, Pete King, Joe Temperley, Harry Morris, Ronnie Ross, Tony Kinsey, Reggie Dare, Joe Harriott, David Smallman, Ken Wray, Jimmy Deuchar, Derek Neville, Norman Stenfalt, Dickie Devere, Tony Crombie, Laurie Morgan, Jeff Ellison, Dizzy Reece, and two African characters, one 'Jazz', the other dancer Teddy Hale, whose name was later linked with the drug-related death of tenor saxophonist Wardell Gray in a Las Vegas hotel in 1956. Two from the traditional scene are also briefly seen: guitarist Diz Disley and singer Beryl Bryden.

Also in the films were some of the lovely Windmill girls, much admired by the musicians, and various equally lovely young ladies, groupies of their time. There were also some Soho villains, like gangster Jack Spot, uneasily peering into Rose's lens. The adjacent Windmill Theatre, which despite its proud boast 'We Never Closed' (relating to the war), eventually closed its doors in 1963. Its demise more or less coincided with the 'death' of the Street.

Ronnie Scott recalls:

> I didn't realize it at the time – one never does – but I now appreciate how lucky I was to have been a part – an almost daily part – of that wonderful camaraderie. It was a ritual to go to the Street when in town. Even if you didn't pick up any work, it was the social atmosphere that was so wonderful. There was nothing like it anywhere in the world. It was great. The guys, the girls, the Soho characters: everything about it was marvellous. My bands were formed in the Harmony Inn there; I met some loves there. Often, when I'm sitting in the club's office, I dearly wish I could pop down to the Street, have a chat, or joke. Of course there's nothing to stop me going to the Street. It's still there. But there's *nobody* there.

13
A Flood of Literature

During the twenties, the so-called Jazz Age, there was virtually no writing on jazz (the real thing, that is), and what comment there was came from the pen of Edgar Jackson, in the *Melody Maker*, from its inception in January 1926. This writing was ill-informed – hardly surprising, since Jackson had no discographies, histories or biographies to consult, and the musicians concerned were 3,000 miles away.

Nevertheless, Jackson was indisputably well-intentioned and the claim, in the preamble to his review of Jack Parnell's 'Summertime'/'The Champ' in the *Melody Maker*, November 1952, that he was the first writer in the world *seriously* to approach jazz records, was perfectly justified.

The *Gramophone* (largely devoted to classical music) ran some jazz reviews in the twenties but it was not until the arrival of *Rhythm* in 1929 that the emerging cognoscenti were able to read notices other than Jackson's. Spike Hughes was one of *Rhythm*'s contributors and it is indicative of racial attitudes of the time that he could blithely refer to records by 'nigger' bands (*Rhythm*, June 1929) he had bought from Levy's shop in Aldgate, East London.

The mid-thirties saw the arrival of two shortlived, home-produced, specialist magazines, *Hot News* and *Swing Music*, though the *Melody Maker* continued, throughout the decade, to give jazz its support. During the war, albeit much reduced in size, and its print minuscule, *MM* continued to acknowledge the jazz enthusiast.

After hostilities ceased, the *Melody Maker* continued its championship of this generally beleaguered music and future jazz historians (if any) might well ponder on why a trade paper relying for its sales and advertising on its coverage of dance bands should have given continuous support to a minority interest, and these years later many veteran buffs look back with nostalgic affection to the old *MM* appearing every Friday. It was a special event in their calendar.

Despite this, the paper continued to be vilified by the pure in heart. In the *PL Yearbook of Jazz 1946*, edited by Albert McCarthy and published by Editions Poetry, McCarthy, quite unfairly, described *MM* as:

> a newspaper of wretched aspect designed for the British dance-band musicians and those who make their living out of dance music in this country. The reviews of Edgar Jackson are of no interest whatsoever to the genuine jazz enthusiast. The writing is often a poor imitation of the worst sort of American journalese and the only thing of interest is a collector's column run by Max Jones and Rex Harris.

Describing his own magazine, *Jazz Forum*, published from rural Fordinbridge, Hants, with painter Augustus John among the artistic community as his neighbours, he claimed, rightly, that it specialized in serious analytical criticism, collectors' features, and poems by William Everson, Kenneth Patchen, Nicholas Moore, Louis Adeane and Howard Sergeant, all pretty weighty stuff if often precious and turgid. McCarthy, a working-class boy, was enraptured by literati.

None of these esoteric features could possibly be considered by a trade weekly and had it indulged in such it would have been hooted out of Archer Street. The main body of the *Melody Maker*'s readership, and the few who bought *Jazz Forum*, lived in different worlds, although McCarthy and his contributors often found their way into the *Melody Maker*, mostly as querulous correspondents.

The purist's main *bête noire* was Edgar Jackson and in the same *PL Yearbook*, Charles Wilford, in a chapter entitled 'Jazz Over England', while bowing to the fact that Jackson was Britain's first ever jazz critic, wrote:

> There are, at this moment in England, only two periodicals which regularly review new records, the *Gramophone* and the *Melody Maker*. In each, the reviewer is Mr Edgar Jackson and indeed he furnishes the two magazines with

almost identical reviews, distinguishable only by the canny usage of what Fowler would call elegant variation. Now it is understandably fair that Mr Jackson should have his word, particularly as his experience of jazz goes back further than any other journalist in the country. It is, however, undesirable that any one man should have what is virtually a complete monopoly of comment on jazz. It is particularly undesirable since Mr Jackson's peculiar prose style, crammed with inversions and double negatives, is intelligible only with difficulty; it must have repulsed many readers who have approached it genuinely in search of knowledge. Here is a random sentence, as a specimen: 'In fact, if only for the elasticity of its highly improvisational style Sleepy John Estes's singing can be no more described as idiomatically dull than it can be said not to present the blues in one of their at once earliest and so more authentic forms.'

The *Melody Maker*'s monopoly on dance- and jazz-music journalism was challenged in 1948 with the launch of *Musical Express* by the founder and editor of *Rhythm*, Julian Vedey. (*Rhythm* was acquired by Odhams Press, publishers of the *Melody Maker*, and later incorporated into the sister paper. Vedey became a small-part film actor before returning to journalism.)

Vedey ran the *Musical Express* on a limited budget with the aid of his daughter, Georgette, and the lack of capital and staff showed, but it was read by members of the profession and jazz enthusiasts, its jazz writers including Tony Hall, Mike Butcher and James Asman. It represented little threat to the *Melody Maker*, then edited by Zahl Ray Sonin (the paper's third editor, Jackson being the first, Percy Mathison-Brooks the second), but in 1950 the *Musical Express* was floundering. Les Perrin, working on the paper for a nominal salary, approached wealthy entrepreneur Maurice Kinn to take it over. Allegedly the figure than Kinn paid for the title was £2,000. Kinn's first act was to entice Sonin from the *Melody Maker* in 1952 to become its editor; the format was improved, *New* added to its title and its circulation rocketed. It became another force in popular-music journalism, and still continued to give jazz coverage. Ironically, the paper was eventually bought out by IPC, Odhams' successors.

Pat Brand, a journalist on the *Melody Maker* from just before the war, a naval rating during hostilities, became its fourth editor, still allowing the jazz writers their head. He died in 1955 and was succeeded by Jack Hutton, from Dundee.

It was under Hutton's editorship that the *Melody Maker*, reflecting the rising popularity of jazz, reached its peak from the jazz perspective. Hutton, a traditional-jazz trumpeter, in addition to having old hands Max Jones, Laurie Henshaw, Chris Hayes and Bob Dawbarn in his team, recruited another Scot, Bob Houston, a 'modernist' in his tastes, to effect changes in the format; and traditionalist banjoist/guitarist, Diz Disley, to contribute finely drawn cartoons. He also solicited contributions from the cream of jazz writers, including Steve Race, Humphrey Lyttelton, Charles Wilford, Ernest Borneman and ... Edgar Jackson, the old retainer. The paper, while of necessity appealing largely to fans of pop and dance music, had a strong, influential and highly readable jazz character. Even the censorious Albert McCarthy could not have reasonably complained about this fertile period in the *Melody Maker*'s history – but he probably did.

In the paper's thousandth issue, 15 November 1952, the editors of 'Collectors' Corner' looked back on the Corner's eleventh year. The article was headed: 'A Feature was Born in a Jam Session' and carried a photograph, taken in 1941, of Corner founders Bill Elliott and Sinclair Traill peering intently at a 78-rpm record.

> In the old days the Corner was solely a 'feature for Discophiles'. But the jazz scene here has utterly changed since then. There are more discographical works available now, and nearly all the 'standard' listings have been published somewhere or other. We try to include up-to-date discographies from time to time, but there is naturally not the demand for them there once was.
>
> The British record business has altered completely, with enthusiasts now having the output of more than a dozen independent companies to chose from. Almost certainly, the jazz policies of the 'small' labels have forced the two major concerns to drop their rather snooty attitude towards jazz ... The biggest change of all has occurred among amateur and semi-pro jazzmen. The bursting out of scores of local jazz bands has resulted in (whatever else it may have done) an enormously increased number of jazz fans – in the widest possible sense.
>
> We think the Corner has mirrored this wider interest within the limits laid down by its title and function in the paper.

The paper's long-standing tradition of supporting jazz was continued by Hutton's successors Ray Coleman and Richard

"Thus we conclude a round-table discussion on the subject, 'Early New Orleans Jazz Compared to Modern Hot Music'."

One of the many cartoons in *Record Changer* affectionately mocking the factions in the traditional v bop war

Williams, with able young writers like Chris Welch and Steve Lake joining the team, but editors thereafter, younger, more attuned to the rock and roll mania and bowing to managerial pressure, slanted the content for adolescent consumption until in the early 1980s, jazz virtually disappeared from the paper that had championed it since 1926.

Edgar Jackson died on 15 September 1967, aged seventy-two.

During the war, a new wave of home-produced specialist music magazines appeared. The little magazines, a cottage industry, were constantly on the brink of expiry, their income forever lagging behind their expenditure but, in the naïvely self-deceiving belief that a right-thinking community would rally to ensure the continuance of these so righteous and informative papers (as their creators saw their products), these losses were rationalized.

Those so committed never begrudged the time they obsessively spent on their broadsheets but, in the event, enthusiasm for the project was one matter, continued financial losses quite another. Inevitably, many of these little magazines were shortlived, heartfelt pleas for support in their editorial columns going unheeded. But in view of the economic cards constantly dealt against them, some had a surprisingly long life.

Jazz Music was edited by Max Jones and Albert McCarthy from 1942 until 1945. Jones continued alone until 1950, when the title was taken over by Tony Starke, operating from Southampton, with Jones and Reg Cooper as associates.

Max Jones recalls:

> I contributed a few pieces, but did nothing editorially. I'd had enough of all that editing, and sending out invoices and statements, the addressing and posting of envelopes. Doing all this had been interfering with my wage-earning duties at the *Melody Maker*. At one stage, Steve Lane took over the title and ran it with various helpers until 1960.

In January 1950, the Wilcox brothers launched *Jazz Illustrated*, the first two of its eight issues edited by Stan Wilcox and Kenyon Jesse, the remaining six by the present author. Its contributors, modestly paid, included Humphrey Lyttelton as cartoonist along with Smilby, Charles Wilford, Steve Race and Ernest Borneman.

The cost of producing a photo magazine was prohibitive and when the Wilcox capital was poured into Vic Lewis's ill-fated 'Music for Moderns' *Jazz Illustrated* was one of the first resulting casualties.

Albert McCarthy launched *Jazz Monthly* in February 1955. It continued until April 1971, reappeared as *Jazz and Blues* (incorporating *Jazz Monthly*) but finally folded in December 1973. Leonard Hibbs became an associate, though not a contributor. This was a link with the beginnings of the home-produced magazine history in Britain, Hibbs having founded and edited *Swing Music* in 1936, which soon folded. *Jazz Monthly*'s title page solemnly read: 'the magazine of intelligent jazz appreciation', the editor and contributors considering themselves a cut above their principal rival *Jazz Journal*.

John Postgate, a respected critic, recalls *Jazz Monthly*, its particular ethos and the idiosyncrasies of its contributors:

> I first encountered the *Jazz Monthly* crowd early in 1958. I had been writing for the magazine for less than a year but was by then sufficiently established for its editor, Albert McCarthy (Mac) to invite me to its occasional gatherings of contributors. At a typical gathering there would be at least two sub-groups: Mac at one table with his group of acolytes and Alun Morgan, with a distinct group, at another. Among those present might be Charles Fox, who would leave early, Paul Oliver, Max Harrison (whom Mac knew well enough to call 'Peter'), Michael James, Ronald Atkins, Jack and sometimes Ann Cooke, Raymond Horricks and Tony Russell. Stanley Dance came at least once, before emigrating, so did Max Jones; Charles Fox dropped out fairly soon, Brian Priestley was around in later years. We all believed that we, through *JM*, were doing something to upgrade jazz criticism and the appreciation of our beloved music: to heave it out of the 'Bird swings like the clappers' kind of writing. We needed such dedication because the odd gathering, and our names in print, were almost our sole rewards. *Jazz Monthly* and its coterie of contributors (several of whom re-emerged in print in the 1980s writing for *Jazz Express*) were already an anomaly, even in the 1950s. It was a left-over from the 'little' cultural magazines of the 1920s and earlier. The collective dedication of its contributors to a cause; its tolerance of affectation and pretentiousness in the quest for critical standards; the individualism; the fury with which we attacked each other in print; the willingness of the anarchic editor to publish almost anything unedited; these attitudes were relics of an earlier expansive era: the

low-circulation, highbrow magazines dedicated to poetry, art, literature and so on, most of which died in the Second World War. Commercialism never entered our (or Mac's) head: the idea of rejecting a poor record review so as not to offend the advertiser, now commonplace, was unthinkable. And the idea of pulling one's punches because someone was a fellow contributor was also unthinkable: the reverse was true.

Perhaps that is why *JM* lost advertisers – and readership (for slanging matches in print are only fun for others in small doses). Anyway, it began to fold in the early 1970s, briefly becoming *Jazz and Blues* (under Max Harrison's editorship) before being engulfed by *Jazz Journal* about 1972. For all its reputation for pretentiousness, it did a lot to pull jazz writing and criticism up by its bootstrings and the element of turbulent outspokenness is sadly missing from today's jazz magazines.

The record reviewers in *Jazz Monthly* were particularly hard on trad. Charles Fox on the Merseysippi Jazz Band, June 1952:

> Only a month or two ago Mr Malcolm Menzies, that inveterate grasper after truth/life, suggested that critics try to reconstruct the events in musicians' hearts. Baffled for a moment to sum up the Merseysippi Jazz Band, I'm inclined to plump for the Menzies line. As lads on the Liverpool wharves, what would these jazzmen have been? A rusty old dredger, perhaps, scraping off the bottom of the Mersey? Or the last tram grinding slowly past the Royal Liver building? Yes, Mr Menzies, it all seems to be here. Seriously though, this is sprawling mixed-up music, out of King Oliver by Lu Watters. The two trumpets battle bravely, Don Lyddiat nips about lissomely, Frank Parr on trombone snarls like a chummy grampus. But however enthusiastic the musicians their jazz never comes alive.

Burnett James on Micky Ashman's Ragtime Band, December 1961: 'Someone said that you should try anything once in this life except incest and folk-dancing – with a strong hint than an exception be made of the former. For myself I have been tempted to put trad jazz into the latter category.'

The contributors' continual attacks on trad were, of course, preaching to the converted, for it is certain that any of the paper's classic-jazz collectors would have turned ashen at the very thought of Micky Ashman or Terry Lightfoot nestling against King Oliver or Jelly Roll Morton on their shelves and, conversely, most of the fans who stomped to the strains of trad with the mandatory banjo predominating would never have heard of *Jazz Monthly*.

Ironically, had even a small proportion of these tradders taken out a subscription, the paper would have been put on a sound commercial footing.

One of the raciest, most informative and stimulating of magazines was undoubtedly *Jazz News*. It ran from 1951 to 1962, by turns monthly, bi-monthly and weekly. It had a succession of dedicated editors – John Martin, Ian Maclean, Peter Clayton, Brian Nicholls among them – who handled a melange of news, features, humour, discographies and club listings. Contributors included Charles Fox, blues specialist Paul Oliver, Kitty Grime, Brian Rust, Daniel Halperin, the author and a pseudonymous John Merrydown, who energetically stirred up controversies – and there were plenty of these!

The jazz world of today is altogether more ordered than it was then. The magazine was packed with literals – hardly surprising, since the typesetters were Polish. The quality of the newsprint was suggestive of low-grade lavatory paper, but the magazine took jazz seriously, not solemnly. It had originated with NJF boss Harold Pendleton finding himself, as the result of some business deal, the owner of a printing press, and of a pub conversation concerning how he could make use of it. The outcome was this worthy addition to jazz literature in Britain, a genuine reflection of the ethos of the jazz community in the fifties and sixties.

One aspect of that ethos was the continuing internecine warfare between the various jazz factions. *Jazz Journal*, first published by co-editors Sinclair Traill and Tom Cundall in May 1948, provoked many disparaging references in *Jazz Monthly*, including lampoons of the *Journal*'s December covers, adorned with holly, mistletoe, robins and Father Christmas. None of this festive flim-flammery for atheist (as well as anarchist) McCarthy.

There was no love lost between Traill and McCarthy. Traill, with his middle-class upbringing, his banking career, five years in the officers' mess, and many assiduously cultivated hours in the company of the Marquis of Donegall, the Honourable Gerald Lascelles, Sir Edward Lewis and Lord Montagu, was hardly a person who would have time for a working-class anarchist who adopted literary airs and graces, continually thrusting barbs at his *Jazz Journal*.

But Traill (Cundall soon dropped out) had the last laugh. The *Journal* easily outlived *Jazz Monthly* and is now (1989) forty-two years old, a world record for an English-language jazz magazine.

Traill was one of the more picturesque characters then populating the jazz scene. Born in December 1904 in Leamington Spa, educated at Blandford, a collector in his thirties, he founded the Birmingham Rhythm Club in 1935, came to London, co-founded *Melody Maker*'s 'Collectors' Corner' and went straight into a commission in the RAF. (It was said that he had 'specialist' knowledge gained while working for Decca. What this was few knew, but one could never visualize a man with such a grand manner ever being a mere ranker.) He returned to 'The Corner' on demobilization, founded *Pick-Up* in 1946, then *Jazz Journal* in 1947, in whose columns he stoutly denied any financial responsibility to creditors in connection with the former paper.

There are literally hundreds of stories about Traill. Most of them concern his deceits, conceits, snobbery, affectations and meanness yet, in retrospect, this outrageous wheeler-dealer is spoken of with affection, if only by virtue of his extraordinary feat of keeping *Jazz Journal* going for so long. It was the only magazine of its kind to survive its founder.

He died on 10 January 1981 of a heart attack, but memories of him are strong, people still giving imitations of him flicking his carefully trimmed moustache with the forefinger of his right hand as he expressed pained surprise at having forgotten his wallet when it came to his round (it was always the case with him that others 'stood' first), claiming to have received a letter from Louis Armstrong or Duke Ellington that very morning or recalling a dinner party at Buckingham Palace with the Honourable Gerald Lascelles just the night before.

He got to know Armstrong well in the fifties, but first met him when the great trumpeter was touring Britain in 1934. When Louis Armstrong arrived at Nice in 1948, there was a large crowd of well-wishers to greet him with cries of 'Hello Louis'. Armstrong, his own PR man, randomly waved, addressing the crowd with 'Hello Pops'. Traill turned to Humphrey Lyttelton standing alongside and murmured (with a characteristic brush of his moustache), '*Heavens*, I didn't think he'd recognize me after all these years.'

The many obituaries in *Jazz Journal* following his death were understandably laudatory, but two who paid tribute lightly touched upon aspects of his character widely known in the jazz world. Peter Clayton in the *Sunday Telegraph*:

> Precisely how the occasionally exasperating but always entertaining Traill kept *Jazz Journal* going for some parts of the thirty years he was the editor I suspect only he knew. But he managed it. Having been briefly, hilariously and – on a minor scale – disastrously involved in the production of a jazz magazine myself I have a dim notion of the mixture of cunning, dedication and ruthlessness it must occasionally have required.

Mike Hennessey, who edited the magazine for eighteen months when *Billboard* owned the title, wrote: 'Sinclair was a very special person. The jazz world will be a much more drab and cheerless one without him. On the other hand the angels will now have the benefits of his wit and wisdom – though they'll have to jog his arm when it's his turn to pay for the ambrosia.'

The durable *Journal*'s present editor and owner is Eddie Cook and among his team of contributors are one of the original writers, Stanley Dance, still using the royal we under the heading of 'Lightly and Politely', and the maverick Steve Voce, whose column 'It Don't Mean a Thing' has been in the thick of controversy for over twenty-five years.

By the 1950s, jazz was also increasingly featured·in the mainstream press. Of all the writers in the lay press, poet/man of letters/librarian Philip Larkin was surely the most literate and readable if – in a particular sense – he was 'dishonest'. For Larkin, generally, hated 'modern' jazz, yet his brief in the *Daily Telegraph*, for which he wrote a weekly record review from 1961 to 1971, was to include a cross-section of the review copies sent him.

In his lengthy and absorbing introduction to these pieces published in book form by Faber in 1970 and 1985, Larkin admitted to adroitly using words that would not give offence to 'demonstrative devotees of modern jazz', but which cloaked his true feelings, and those who read jazz literature would have been deprived of a rare facility of expression had he been genuinely true to himself. After all, what does a little dissembling matter if the upshot was prose of such excellence for so long a period in the jazz column of a quality daily? As Larkin put it:

> I tried in writing my criticisms to be fair and conscientious, but there were many times when I substituted 'challenging' for 'insolent', 'adventurous' for 'excruciating' and 'colourful' for 'viciously absurd' in a thoroughly professional manner. Although my critical principle has been Eddie Condon's – 'as it enters the ear, does it come in like broken glass or does it come in like honey?' – I've generally remembered that mine is not the only ear in the world. Above all, I hope my pieces suggest I love jazz.
>
> I began by saying how much pleasure it has given me, and when I imagine how much I would have missed if, instead of being born on 9 August 1922 I had died then, I realize how great my debt is. How dreadful to have lived in the twentieth century, but died before King Oliver led his men into the Gennett Studios, Richmond, Indiana, or before Frank Walker auditioned Bessie Smith ('fat and scared to death') or Bubber Miley joined Duke Ellington's Washingtonians! If I have any message for my readers, it's that.

Larkin's position-cum-dilemma was no different from that of the few jazz-record presenters in the BBC clinging to their miserly allocation to jazz. If any of these presenters were overtly to show individual preferences, a liking for one epoch more than another, assuredly there would be many bitter complaints from partisan listeners. Larkin continued:

> To say I don't like modern jazz because it's modernist art simply raises the question of why I don't like modernist art: I have a suspicion that many of my readers will welcome my grouping of Parker with Picasso and Pound as one of the nicest things I could say about him. Well, to do so settles at least one question: as long as it was only Parker I didn't like, I might believe that my ears had shut up about the age of twenty-five and that jazz had left me behind. My dislike of Pound and Picasso, both of whom pre-date me by a considerable margin, can't be explained in this way. The same can be said of Henry Moore and James Joyce (a textbook case of declension from talent to absurdity). No, I dislike such things not because they are new, but because they are irresponsible exploitations of technique in contradiction of human life as we know it. This is my essential criticism of modernism, whether perpetrated by Parker, Pound or Picasso: it helps us neither to enjoy nor endure. It will divert us as long as we are prepared to be mystified or outraged, but maintains its hold only by being more mystifying and more outrageous: it has no lasting power. Hence the

compulsion on every modernist to wade deeper and deeper into violence and obscenity: hence the succession of Parker by Rollins and Coltrane, and of Rollins and Coltrane by Coleman, Ayler and Shepp.

In a footnote to the second edition, Larkin wrote:

> I went on writing these articles for three more years, and the additional pieces are printed here for the sake of completeness. While I enjoyed doing them (listening to new jazz records for an hour with a pint of gin and tonic is the best remedy for a day's work I know) they seem on rereading to carry a deepening sense of depression.
>
> The kind of jazz I liked was dying with its masters: George Lewis, Pee Wee Russell, Johnny Hodges, finally Armstrong himself, the great oak uprooted at last; what claimed to be succeeding it grew more and more astringently chaotic...
>
> What was actually succeeding it – the inescapable whanging world of teenage pop – had dominated the music industry to such an extent that the 'hot record' was becoming as hard to get as when my story started. Review copies were supplied less willingly...
>
> Consequently in July 1971 I wrote suggesting that the late Alasdair Clayre should review pop records every other month in place of me... but all that happened was that my pieces were not printed. In December that year I brought my contributions to an end.
>
> I am sure I was right. I had said what I thought about jazz and there was no point in repeating myself.

In his crusade against what he regarded as the pretentiousness of many modernist critics, Larkin referred, though not by name, to one of his severest castigators, Richard Williams. Reviewing a John Lennon album in the *Melody Maker*, 15 November 1969, Williams wrote: 'Sides Two and Four consist entirely of single tones maintained throughout ... constant listening reveals a curious point: the pitch of the tone alters frequently, but only by microtones ... this oscillation produces an almost subliminal beat which maintains interest.' Williams had been sent a review copy in which two sides were merely engineers' test records. But Williams, one of Larkin's principal critics and a writer apparently totally uninterested in pre-bop jazz, fell heavily here and made a fool of himself. Larkin (in this footnote) wrote: 'I wish I had got that into my original introduction.' He died in December 1984 at the age of sixty-three.

The October 1957 issue of *Jazz News* reported that a Father Beaumont had completed a twentieth-century folk mass, a work he undertook 'believing that popular rhythms and modern musical styles might help to lure young people back into the churches'. The mass was recorded by Paxton Records and sympathetically reviewed in the *Church Times*. It also brought that paper a letter from a certain Charles Cleall:

> I am mildly surprised to find the matter of Father Beaumont's mass flowering into a discussion. I believe it is an important spiritual issue to stop as soon as possible notions that 'jazz is as much the outcome of a mighty earnestness as is music', and that church music should be entertaining the masses. Jazz is certainly entertaining to the masses: not because it is an art, but because it is an aphrodisiac.
>
> Far from spurious compositions having been spurred on by its rhythms, jazz imitates (clumsily and unsuccessfully) the intricate rhythms of sixteenth-century polyphony. How can one discuss an interest that boasts only three books published in the United Kingdom? It has no literature because its devotees can hardly read a book from cover to cover.
>
> There is an unpleasant correlation between jazz and drug-taking: between swing fanatics and juvenile delinquency. Let jazz inside our church and our music will rot.

Mr Cleall revealed monumental ignorance in asserting that only three books about jazz had been published in Britain. By 1957 there were scores of volumes on the subject, indicating that devotees, far from being unable to read, had an omnivorous appetite for literature on the subject. For a music appealing to a minority, jazz was documented by a disproportionately large volume of literature.

All About Jazz by Stanley Nelson, published by Heath Cranton in 1934, was the first attempt by a British author to write a history of jazz. Nelson, of course, was limited by lack of genuine information, his book coming alive only, at a late stage in its preparation, after he had listened, in astonishment, to Duke Ellington and His Orchestra at the London Palladium in June 1933. Overall, however, it was a hodge-podge of scanty historical detail with too much emphasis on what was thought to be jazz, the ephemera played by Paul Whiteman in America and Jack Hylton in Britain, and their like.

An infinitely superior work was *A Critic Looks at Jazz* by Ernest Borneman, published in 1946 by Jazz Music Books, one of the book-publishing ventures of the magazine *Jazz Music*. Borneman, Vienna-born, a refugee from Nazism resident in Britain from the early thirties, was at once an anthropologist, film-maker, journalist and novelist with an exceptional command of a language he had adopted. He originally published the book serially in the US magazine *Record Changer*, under the title *An Anthropologist Looks at Jazz*, bringing to his work the scientific approach of the anthropologist and sociologist, utilizing his specialized knowledge of Africans and their cultural traditions. It was a short book, only fifty-one pages, but evidence of a keen intellect was manifest in every line.

The next Englishman to attempt 'an account of jazz's origin and growth from the early drum rhythms of Africa to the highly developed Western music of the day' was Rex Harris in his book *Jazz*, published by Pelican in 1952, at two shillings (10p).

Harris, born 1904, full name Aubrey Rex Vivian St Leger-Harris FBOA, HD, FSMC, was an ophthalmic optician and Freeman of the City of London who came to jazz at a relatively late age – in his thirties – well beyond the usual time, adolescence, at which most aficionados come to the music. A much younger Max Jones introduced him to its joys.

During the war, Harris managed Cyril Blake and his Jig's Club Band, became a co-editor of 'Collectors' Corner', a regular broadcaster and, with Dr Ralph Hill presenting the 'classical' viewpoint, he gave lectures to the armed forces, various educational bodies and music classes.

Harris had a much greater fund of information to draw upon than Nelson, but by the time Harris began to prepare his lengthy work – it was some two hundred and fifty pages long – revivalism was in full flood. He had assiduously read what many purists considered to be their bible, *Shining Trumpets*, by Rudi Blesh, in which he dogmatically alleged that Ellington never played jazz. Harris quoted lengthily from Blesh, and his volume turned out to be more of a panegyric for the old, 'real' jazz, than an examination of the music's larger history. Its foreword read:

> After the long and wearisome years of 'swing' which has overlaid the traditions of jazz there has arisen a new generation which is anxious to learn of the roots and growth of this fascinating music. So much confusion exists in the public mind regarding the word 'jazz' that it was felt necessary to present a genealogical table which would make the subject clearer.
>
> This book is an attempt to vindicate the integrity of those who have kept jazz alive during the long years of its eclipse behind the meretricious blaze of artificially exploited swing music.

Harris's book was severely censured even by revivalists and from its publication and reprints, and from further books by him published by the same company, arose the rather contemptuous term 'Pelican Jazz'.

Harris slavishly followed the fundamentalists' party line, was critical of the bands, white and black, who used arrangements and riffs and berated many creative musicians he, in his 'Corner' days, had praised; among them multi-instrumentalist Benny Carter.

> Benny Carter (born 1907), one of the leading musicians of the McKinney Cotton Pickers, was responsible for organizing the well-known recording group, the Chocolate Dandies. Carter is an astonishingly versatile instrumentalist, playing clarinet, trumpet, and saxophone, excelling as an alto saxophonist. Most of his solo and arranged work warrants the same comment as that of Redman – that as a musician he possesses tremendous talent. His powers of invention, technique, tone, all are of the highest order, yet lacking the essential warmth and drive of the true jazzman, he never entirely satisfies. Listening to Benny Carter is listening to a *demonstration* of beauty; it is self-conscious, never completely relaxed; and it never imparts that sense of urgency which is an essential to jazz performance. The records by the Chocolate Dandies and later orchestras, including some composed by British musicians, have an atmosphere about them which is coldly beautiful, refined, delicate, and *studied*. Jazz is none of these things.
>
> It is not without interest to imagine what would have been the position if, when with Billy Fowler's band in the rough and ready days of the early twenties in Chicago, Carter had not had the advantage of an university education. Possessing an inherent musical instinct as he did he might well have joined forces with Ladnier and sought self-expression in the same way as did that fine trumpet man – from the heart rather than from the mind, the orthodox musical word of crotchets and quavers . . .

Ernest Borneman, *Melody Maker*, 26 April 1952, questioned Harris's account of jazz's African origins, derived largely from Borneman's own writing. Like Humphrey Lyttelton, also critical, he did not allow Harris's praise of his (Borneman's) erudition to deter him from challenging his admirer's received wisdom:

> Rex Harris's new book, *Jazz*, reminds me in every respect of that phenomenally successful American compendium, *Reader's Digest*. It is reasonably priced, printed in vast quantities, popular, easy to read – and digested from all the best magazines . . .
>
> There is, for instance, a lengthy passage in Chapter One in which Rex propounds a hypothesis on African music which I first advanced in the late thirties and which Max Jones later reprinted in *A Critic Looks at Jazz*.
>
> Only two kinds of books can really help us to bridge the gaps in our knowledge of jazz and its history:
> 1. Straight field work of the kind at which William Russell has always excelled – and which has made books like *Jazzmen* and *Mr Jelly Roll* so disproportionately important in jazz research.
> 2. Independent analysis which challenges the traditionalist commonplaces as much as those of the modernists. For to quote and paraphrase either of them at this late stage means little more than to perpetuate errors and compound fallacies.

Borneman did not quote the gaffe that made Harris a laughing stock. In his denigration of big bands generally, he put down the famous bands of Duke Ellington, Count Basie and Fletcher Henderson and addressed himself to the matter of their soloists, and in a footnote to a dissertation on their unjazzlike qualities he wrote: 'The tenor saxophonist Coleman Hawkins possessed great powers of improvisation which, had they been canalized into a different medium of expression, e.g. the clarinet, might well have secured him a permanent place in jazz.'

There cannot be many comments in the whole history of jazz journalism that have aroused greater fury (even from traditionalists) than Harris's asinine footnote. He never lived it down. However, as there was a strong purist antipathy to the saxophone family at the time, Harris's extraordinary hypothesis was acceptable to many. Indeed, not long before, Humphrey Lyttelton, himself totally converted to the same fundamentalists' convictions, had expressed views antipathetic to the saxophone and Harris himself quoted Lyttelton who, being questioned on a broadcast, stated, 'If being broad-minded means saying I like something when inwardly I know I detest it, then I'm narrow-minded and proud of it.' (See Chapter 3 for Lyttelton's dismissal of Benny Carter in the same vein.)

Harris echoed those sentiments:

> This book takes a similar attitude. If being catholic in its outlook on jazz means accepting as jazz forms of music which are utterly divorced from the real thing then this is a purist book and proud of it.
>
> Nevertheless, the outlook is not the extreme one of condemning all forms of 'hot' music as being completely worthless; much of Henderson, Redman and Lunceford is good music of its kind; most of Ellington is unique as an original musical form; but it is not jazz in the strict sense.

Harris commenced writing his book in 1950, or thereabouts, and, absorbed with the task, was not aware that the man he was quoting (and fulsomely praising) had undergone a radical change of heart. In fact, Lyttelton's startling heresy in *Jazz Journal* appeared the same year, 1952, as the first edition of Harris's book.

In 1962, Harris published another book, *Enjoying Jazz* (Jazz Book Club), to a similarly hostile reception. John Postgate, in *Jazz Monthly*, January 1962, wrote:

> It has given me no pleasure to review this silly book. Rex Harris, with Leslie Perowne, was instrumental in introducing me to jazz by way of their broadcasts in 1940–41.
>
> It is a rehash of his notorious Pelican *Jazz*. Much shortened, converted into nursery language with a six-page chapter entitled 'Bop, Progressive, Cool and Mainstream' in which Harris makes a pathetic attempt to deal 'impartially and truthfully' with what he regards as modern jazz.
>
> I saw only a few factual errors. But it is the sense of values and taste that are distorted on a grand scale. The time has passed when 'I-know-what-I-like-and-what-I-don't-like-isn't-jazz' formed even a humorous basis for writing about jazz. For adults this is a sorry piece from one who might well have deserved our respect. For children, who will know no better, it is lamentable.

The Jazz Book Club published David Boulton's *Jazz in Britain* (1958), with a foreword by Chris Barber, the first attempt to delineate the music's introduction to and progress in the UK, commencing with an outline of the music's Afro-American origins and covering early misconceptions and misapplied uses of the generic term – like the Murray Club Jazz Band, Alfred Delmonte's

Jazz Band, the Boston Jazz Band, Billy Tell's Jazz Band and the Indeanola Jazz Band, all British, before the arrival of the Original Dixieland Jazz Band from New Orleans in 1919.

Humphrey Lyttelton's *I Play as I Please* and *Second Chorus* were reprinted in the series, as was Dorothy Baker's fictional account of the life of Bix Beiderbecke, *Young Man with a Horn*. Membership of the club cost, initially, 45/-, that being the total arrived at by ordering six books, the minimum number allowed.

An interesting view of the jazz scene in Britain in 1957 was provided by one such Jazz Book Club publication, *My Life in Jazz* by Max Kaminsky. This book said as much about American misconceptions concerning the UK as about its ostensible subject but Kaminsky did acknowledge the fact that European audiences were well informed:

> In 1957 they were still, except for the hard core of avant-gardists, madly appreciative of hot jazz and of the chance to see us, and I'll never forget the warmth and enthusiasm they accorded us ... They are touchingly appreciative, and jazz to them is a much more serious business than it is to Americans,

Jazz Book Club

builds—builds—builds

'cats' to be proud of . . .

'CATS' who dig the whole jazz scene, who are knowledgeable, informed, discriminating.

JBC covers every aspect of that fascinating and endlessly interesting literature of jazz.

In JBC's lists you will find history, theory, practice, biography, classic volumes and new, enriching ones.

In fact the more one explores this literature of jazz the more one is surprised and delighted by its range.

Is it reasonable to suggest that if you like jazz music you will also like to read some of the many books about that music ? We believe it is and that is why the Jazz Book Club was started.

Whether you are a concert goer, gramophile, amateur jazzman or just a happy listener, the Jazz Book Club offers you an opportunity to add to your pleasure—inexpensively !

p.t.o.

who naturally think of it as a more everyday thing than a rare art form. The European fan is highly intellectual and analytical, partly because with their main source of hearing jazz limited to recordings, they can't possibly get the whole picture ... The English have always loved jazz and have formed many, many bands faithfully modelled after everyone from Kid Ory to Count Basie to Stan Kenton to Gil Evans. The 'traditional' jazz band has long been their favourite, however, as it has been here, too, where every college has its stereotyped Dixieland band. In one city in England, I forget where, Peanuts, Lesberg, and I were invited by the jazz club of the local college to give a lecture on jazz. We were led into a large auditorium and as soon as we were seated on the platform one of the boys unrolled a huge map on the wall which looked like a family tree and bristled with names like traditional, neo-primitive, mainstream, urban jazz, modern, etc. After we were presented to the assembly, Peanuts stood up and said, 'The first thing to do is to throw away that chart,' and he went on to talk about how that sort of thing was the cause of the whole trouble in jazz, the attempt to pigeonhole every style and even every lick a musician might feel like playing and trying to rule on whether it was right or wrong. 'It's not right or wrong,' Peanuts ended up grandly, 'it's just either good or bad!' and he sat down to thunderous applause and cries of 'smashing' and 'wizard'.

The first autobiography from a British writer/musician was Spike Hughes's *Opening Bars*. He followed this with *Second Movement* in 1951, each book more about Hughes's showbiz life than his involvement with jazz.

The first autobiography to be written by a wholly committed post-war British jazz musician was *I Play as I Please* by Humphrey Lyttelton, published in 1953 when he was thirty-two. Highly readable, it described a period when young men were passionately following in the footsteps of their New Orleans mentors, an epoch of high idealism. It was twelve years before another autobiographical book dealt with the traditional *mores* combined with personal recollection: *Owning Up* by former Mick Mulligan vocalist – turned writer – George Melly.

Melly, whose first articles were for *Jazz Illustrated*, had become the scriptwriter for clarinettist/cartoonist Wally Fawkes (Flook), drawing a strip cartoon in the *Daily Mail* under the pseudonym of Trog. Melly also wrote TV and film criticism for the *Observer*. The one-time blues shouter had become a pundit and tele-person, knowledgeably expounding his views on modern art. The book, bawdy, funny, honest and the first to paint impressions of a musician's life on the road, was generally well received, but Philip Larkin, writing in the *Observer*, took exception to Melly's bad language and moral attitude.

> I could never watch (the verb is chosen advisedly) George Melly singing without feeling embarrassed, and the same goes for reading his book. He is so anxious to tell you which birds he had it off with, what character's armpits smelled like the hallway of a cat-infested slum, and who peed in a washbowl where someone else had left a lettuce to soak that, free speech or not, one soon wishes he would belt up. It's not so much an adolescent desire to shock (though that element is there) as an adolescent sense of humour . . . For students of the jazz scene in this country, however, there is much to be learned from it. Melly, as most of his readers will know, sang with the Mick Mulligan band throughout the fifties, and the value of his account lies in the picture he gives of how jazzmen actually earned a living at that time rather than in any perception of trends . . .
>
> Perhaps it is as a portrait of a band that the book is most successful: Melly is very good at describing the genesis and development of the kind of asinine group-joke that becomes a routine or cliché in the fatigued early hours – for instance, the 'points' game, or the teasing of personalities. The Mulligan team was noted for this kind of lark, and to some extent resemble the Condon crew described some ten years earlier in *We Called It Music*. The difference is that whereas Condon made you want to be one of his crowd, Melly makes you profoundly grateful you're not.

Steve Voce, in *Jazz Journal*, December 1965, commented, 'It would be a shame if the book becomes known for its bad language, rather than acclaimed for the brilliant use of the rest of the language.'

It is a testimony to its validity as an evocation of a period as well as a personal memoir that it is still in print. He captures the ethos of a touring musician beautifully. One of the book's highlights is his graphic account of the notorious (but of sweet memory) 15s-a-night boarding house in Brunswick Road, Manchester, run by a slatternly Mrs Mac (although not named as such by Melly as she was still alive when the book was first published).

This establishment was renowned for the cat that roamed at will over the dining table and the 'velvet' covering the lampshade that turned out to be layer upon layer of dust. Mrs Mac's walls were adorned with photographs of the bands that she 'accommodated', and among these was a postcard of the Queen on which was written 'Lovely digs, Mrs Mac' and which was signed 'Liz and Phil'.

In 1961 the UK saw the publication of jazz's first comprehensive reference work, *The Encyclopedia of Jazz*, by British emigré – now a US citizen – Leonard Feather. He had contributed to the *Melody Maker* as far back as 1933 and was responsible for Benny Carter's surprising appointment as staff arranger to Henry Hall's BBC Dance Orchestra. He was also the organizer of many seminal British recording sessions, including those by the Danny Polo Swing Stars and George Chisholm's Jive Five. Feather did British musicians proud by listing over fifty of them, including Keith Christie, Ken Colyer, Tubby Hayes, Humphrey Lyttelton and Bruce Turner, and provided a balanced representation of traditionalists, mainstreamers and modernists, each receiving a full, informative entry, but his prejudices against traditionalist musicians were displayed in his note on Chris Barber (possibly influenced by Benny Green's contribution on British jazz): 'Barber's position in England is comparable with Turk Murphy's in US: though attacked by many critics as musically worthless, his band has enjoyed phenomenal success in the past couple of years and has played to packed houses in concert halls all over Europe.'

Apart from autobiographies, books about British jazzmen were non-existent, the scribes generally uninterested in the home product, but in *Concerning Jazz* by Sinclair Traill, published in 1958, the editor wrote on traditional bands (and included praise for entrepreneur Lyn Dutton) and Brian Nicholls, in a better-written article, traced the history of British bop. Similar chapters were also included in David Boulton's *Jazz in Britain* and in *The Decca Book of Jazz*, edited by Peter Gammond, with contributions from many British writers, including the Honourable Gerald Lascelles.

Naturally the main subject matter of British writers was the American music, but the first thorough examination of 'modern' jazz by British authors was *Modern Jazz – A Survey of Developments Since 1939* by Alun Morgan and Raymond Horricks, published by Victor Gollancz in 1956.

A feature unique to the British jazz scene was the number of musicians who, unlike their American counterparts, whose books were invariably ghosted, were also writers: Humphrey Lyttelton, George Melly, Sandy Brown, Digby Fairweather, Ian Carr, Brian Priestley, Benny Green, Dave Gelly and John Chilton.

Chilton, trumpeter with Bruce Turner's Jump Band from 1959 until 1962, collaborated with Max Jones in 1970 to produce *Salute to Satchmo*, a definitive volume on Louis Armstrong, and a more detailed and factual book than the autobiography *Satchmo – My Life in New Orleans* (no 'ghost' writer credited) published by Jazz Book Club in 1957. Jones and Chilton updated and enlarged their book in 1971 with *Louis*.

In 1972 Chilton, through his own company, Bloomsbury Books, published his *Who's Who of Jazz*, a book that has become a standard reference work. It was an incredible achievement for a Britisher who had never been to America, to elicit, by dint of intensive correspondence and diligent research, a mass of information on over a thousand American jazz musicians, the data including their geographical movements, various employers and associates. Subtitled 'Storyville to Swing Street', the book limited its entries to those musicians and vocalists born before 1920 but – and this is consistent with his own tastes in jazz – omitted Dizzy Gillespie (born 1917), Charlie Parker (born 1920, a borderline case perhaps, but he had played with Jay McShann's pre-bop swing band), Stan Kenton (born 1912) and Kenny Clarke (born 1914), all associated with 'modern' jazz. In subsequent editions all the above, excepting Parker and Clarke, were included. In a conversation with the author, Leonard Feather himself expressed a tremendous admiration for such an exhaustive work.

Fictional books with a jazz background were few. Sinclair Traill wrote *Way Down Yonder in New Orleans*, Ernest Borneman wrote a thriller with references to jazzmen, and Peter Clayton with Peter Gammond wrote their *Fourteen Miles on a Clear Night*, a series of satirical pieces lampooning certain attitudes and practices.

An unintentionally hilarious novel was *The Gabriel* (1951) by William Morum, which encapsulated practically every Fleet Street misrepresentation about jazz and dance musicians. One suspects the author, casting around for a subject, read some nonsensical report concerning jazz musicians in a newspaper and – eureka! – decided his book would be about a young brass-band trumpeter who is seduced to 'red-hot music' by reading the *Rhythm Weaver* – a laboriously contrived synonym for the *Melody Maker*. In the *Rhythm Weaver* the surprised youth, Jimmy Ware, reads that Monty Midas and his Seven Scroungers take the floor at the fashionable Robert Hotel. England's Hot Momma goes to town on three new discs! Hot Lips Hartman's three-hour jam session! Squeeze Box Wizard in new line-up with Scats Scanlon! Dizzy 'Fingers' Burton* tapping the ivories for new rhythm trio!

Turning over a page, the hero read, 'How to Whip and Smear' by Terry Tanner, England's hottest trumpet ace, with the following from Mr Tanner:

> It's no good listening to the discs of our old friend Satchmo (trumpet) Armstrong, and trying to copy his tricks if you have an idea how he does them. Now, you've all heard the master whipping and smearing in his latest version of the 'Tiger' and no doubt you've had a bash at it with your local gig outfit. It didn't come off, did it? And was your face red? Save yourself the embarrassment by studying my instructions carefully. The smear is quite simple really. All you do is . . .

An understandably bemused Jimmy asks a fellow member of the dance band he has joined, 'What does all this mean?'

The answer: 'Look here, Sonny. That's a crazy paper. A jazz wallah's Gazette. I only bought it for a good laugh.'

Eventually the hero finds himself at Murton-on-Sea with the Merry Mexicans, playing such items as 'Meeting My Cutie on the QT' and the leader of this band, one El Bandelero, patently Jewish, announces Jimmy's solo feature thus: 'Ladies and shentleman, tonight I hat a beeg surprise for you. Tonight it is my pleasure to present to you the boy wizard of the trumpet!' With a dramatic gesture he turns to Jimmy: 'Ladies and shentleman, I give you – El *Chicko*!'

Back in London, he studies at the 'Philharmonic', alights from a

---

*It was pure coincidence that, later, a real Dizzy Burton (who played trumpet), operating in Manchester, recorded in London for the Esquire label in 1959.

tram to see a poster outside a dancehall announcing Buddy Bonnington and his Red Hot Rhythm Aces, and he thanks his lucky stars he is finished with all *that* but, events lead him to a certain street in London's West End. Someone asks him: 'Where you heading? The Street?' 'Which Street?' Jimmy enquires. 'Who's fooling now, pal? Archer Street — where else, you mutt?' And so on . . .

An advertisement for the book appeared in the *Melody Maker* with an endorsement from author J.B. Priestley: 'The author has dealt in an unpretentious, convincing and spirited fashion with a kind of life that has rarely found its way into fiction — the life of the instrumentalist and orchestral player.'

Jack Hylton, pre-war bandleader turned impresario, contributed a blurb in the same advertisement: 'William Morum's book has the rare virtues of simplicity and authenticity. His people are real, his descriptions of the life of musicians true and his writing simple and clear.' Hylton had previously written a muddled foreword to Stanley Nelson's *All About Jazz*.

Novelists continued to entertain bizarre notions about jazz and jazz musicians, but thanks to the weight of jazz literature generally, the literati and the public at large were better informed than Mr Morum.

This partial examination of the books on jazz published between 1950 and 1970 gives the lie to that Christian bigot Mr Cleall's allegation that jazz was without any weight of literature and that jazz enthusiasts were illiterate. Indeed, the spate of literature continues unabated to this day.

14
Twenty Extraordinary Years

In the closing chapter of my *A History of Jazz in Britain 1919–50* I wrote: 'By 1950 Britain stood on the brink of its first real jazz era, and very different it was from the "Jazz Age" (so-called) of the twenties.' I trust that this book, with all its acknowledged omissions, confirms the truth of that statement.

Certainly, the proliferation of British jazz bands, the entry of American musicians, the mass of recordings released, the spate of literature and informed media coverage would have been beyond the wildest expectations of late-twenties collectors eager to spend their half-crowns on the next Parlophone 'Rhythm-Style' release of Louis Armstrong, Duke Ellington, Bix Beiderbecke or Joe Venuti 78s, and their sixpences on the then monthly *Melody Maker*, the bible of jazz and dance-band enthusiasts in those palmy days.

Of course, much of what has happened in the twenty years covered in this book owes a great deal to prior events, not only to those first exciting releases of records by American jazz giants and the championship of jazz by the *Melody Maker*, but to the first 'rhythm clubs', gatherings rarely numbering more than thirty or so people solemnly nodding their heads to the beat and joining in the intense discussions that followed, earning their devotees the appellation that still sticks: 'jazz fiends'.

The 1939–45 conflict that brought about the beginning of so many social changes also opened up opportunities for jazz-minded musicians, professionals in the dance bands and emergent amateurs dedicated to a totally different approach: emulation of the music of the New Orleans pioneers. During this period, when shellac was scarce, the record companies, albeit sparingly, continued to issue jazz records. The break-up of the big dance bands due to call-up resulted in the formation of jazz units such as Harry Parry's Radio Rhythm Club Sextet, to be replaced by Buddy Featherstonehaugh's Sextet formed in the RAF. Changing social conditions also resulted in the emergence of a myriad of drinking clubs in London's West End which featured jazz rather than polite dance music. The stage was being set for a minor revolution in public taste.

It was during the war, too, that the music of the black New Orleanians began to receive belated attention. Home-produced magazines like *Jazz Music*, edited by Max Jones and Albert McCarthy, and *Jazz Record*, edited by James Asman and Bill Kinnell, were to be the forerunners of many enthusiast magazines that helped spread the gospel according to New Orleans. In addition, the release of significant records, many of them reissues, inspired George Webb's Dixielanders to adopt a strict 'New Orleans' policy. This band, with all its limitations, conveyed a rough honesty that challenged the indisputable technical superiority of the jazz by Harry Parry, Buddy Featherstonehaugh and the Vic Lewis/Jack Parnell Jazzmen which appeared on major labels.

The almost coincident arrival of bebop brought a further startling new dimension to a scene which had not previously known such a variety of endeavours, such multi-faceted activity leading to a situation unthinkable before the war: British musicians actually earning a living playing jazz.

After the end of the war the jazz enthusiast who wanted to hear music 'live' was able to choose from a great variety of jazz styles: from the small-ensemble simplicities of George Webb, Freddy Randall and the Crane River Bands to the orchestral bombast of Ted Heath and Vic Lewis's Kenton-type orchestra; from the much-publicized Humphrey Lyttelton band to the controversial Club Eleven boppers and the smoother Dankworth Seven and many more. For the record collector there was a sudden plethora of releases and the introduction of the LP in the early fifties resulted in modern jazz musicians extending themselves more fully. In addition, compilations of classic and obscure recordings from collections all over the world became available, along with a stream of books on the subject.

Perhaps the most significant development in the period 1950 to

1970, however, was the immense improvement in the standard of British jazz. There were, of course, a great number of pre-war British musicians, all of them in dance-band employment, but when the quality of their performances is compared with those of the post-war years, the difference is astonishing. It should be remembered that pre-war jazz musicians indulged their personal tastes only occasionally and that their emulation of the art was rooted solely in their listening to gramophone records. This was equally true of the first revivalists and most of the beboppers, but they were both eventually able to hear at first hand, and play with, the greatest of American jazz musicians. This connection demonstrated the local musicians' thorough absorption of the idiom, proved by their success in accompanying and complementing the Americans, notable examples being Stan Tracey's various trios, backing a formidable array of star soloists accustomed to only the best of collaborative musicianship; Alex Welsh's bands, successfully riding the stylistic problems of performing with players as diverse in their approach as Bud Freeman, Red Allen, Pee Wee Russell, Earl Hines, Ruby Braff and Dicky Wells; and Humphrey Lyttelton's bands backing Buck Clayton, and singers like Joe Turner and Jimmy Rushing. By the 1960s, there existed a category of roving musicians who could play in almost any stylistic setting: for instance, trombonist Roy Williams with the US alto saxophonist Spike Robinson, and the supremely adaptable pianist Brian Lemon, who accompanied alto-saxophonist Art Pepper during the latter's stint at Ronnie Scott's in 1980.

The invitations by US bandleaders – Woody Herman to Ronnie Scott, Jack Teagarden to Alex Welsh, Count Basie to Tony Coe and George Lewis to Ken Colyer – to play in their bands were no mere publicity stunts; they were genuine offers, a sincere acknowledgement of British prowess.

Victor Feldman had unqualified success in America playing with Woody Herman, Cannonball Adderley, Peggy Lee and many others, and it was a testimony to Tubby Hayes that he was fully able to take Paul Gonsalves's place in the Duke Ellington Orchestra at the Royal Festival Hall in February 1964, and to Jimmy Deuchar that he was able to play with Lionel Hampton in 1956. This resulted in a somewhat back-handed compliment frequently being paid: British musicians could copy the US idiom better than many. In recent years there has been less emphasis on comparisons with Americans. As the language of jazz is now spoken internationally, non-American contributions can be seen in a wider perspective, and the number of young and talented British musicians occupying the stage in the late 1980s augurs well for the future.

A healthy situation which owes much to the musicians and writers who, from the late 1920s onwards, realized that such a potent method of musical expression deserved their zealotry. The penultimate paragraph of my first volume read:

> That jazz should have emerged in its own breeding ground is one phenomenon. That it should permeate the musical activity and public consciousness of so many other countries and Britain in particular is another, and is quite incredible in its extent and ramifications. The history of jazz in Britain is a remarkable story of missionary zeal, of the propagation of its values right from the early gramophone records, and of the determined assimilation of its essence by successive generations of British musicians.

I echo those sentiments to conclude this book.

Discography and Bibliography

This listing is intended as a guide to musical examples pertinent to the various chapters. It is not a discography in the academic sense nor does it pretend to be either complete or up-to-date. With so much material appearing on permutations of discs, cassettes and CDs it is impossible for even quarterly-produced record catalogues, such as those published by the *Gramophone* magazine, to maintain a position of near-currency. I have restricted the listing to partial details of titles and personnels for brevity, believing that the facts as noted here should be sufficient to give the flavour of the music contained on the records. Unless otherwise listed, all the recording sessions which went into the production of these examples took place in London. A listing of abbreviations used for instruments etc will be found at the end.

Alun Morgan

Discography

1 New Orleans to Barnehurst to Royal Festival Hall

George Webb's Dixielanders:
Owen Bryce, Reg Rigden (cor); Eddie Harvey (tbn); Wally Fawkes (clt); George Webb (p) etc.   Derby – 1945
New Orleans Hop Scop Blues, Come Back Sweet Papa, Dippermouth Blues, Riverside Blues   Melodisc EPM7-70

Humphrey Lyttelton – George Webb:
Collective personnel: Humphrey Lyttelton, Reg Rigden, Owen

Bryce (cor); Harry Brown, Eddie Harvey (tbn); Wally Fawkes (clt); George Webb (p); Art Streatfield (b); Derek Bailey, Roy Wykes (d). 1946–7
Smokey Mokes, The Saints, Come Back, Sweet Papa, Dippermouth Blues, Black Bottom Stomp, London Blues etc.
Jazzology J22

Humphrey Lyttelton – *Delving Back with Humph*:
Collective personnel includes Humphrey Lyttelton (cor); Harry Brown, Keith Christie (tbn); Wally Fawkes, Ian Christie (clt); George Webb (p); Nevil Skrimshire (g). 1948 & 1949
Ole Miss Rag, Panama, Cake Walkin' Babies, The Thin Red Line, High Society etc Esquire ESQ310

King Oliver and His Creole Jazz Band:
King Oliver, Louis Armstrong (cor); Johnny Dodds (clt); Lil Hardin (p); Baby Dodds (d) etc Richmond, Indiana – 1923
Canal Street Blues, Weather Bird Rag, Dippermouth Blues, Snake Rag, Alligator Hop, Working Man's Blues etc
Rhapsody RHA8023

Bunk Johnson's Jazz Band:
Bunk Johnson (cor); Albert Warner (tbn); George Lewis (clt); Lawrence Marrero (bjo) etc. New Orleans – 1942
Big Chief Battleaxe, Franklin Street Blues, Sobbin' Blues, Weary Blues etc Teldec AG6.24547

Ken Colyer and the Crane River Jazz Band:
Ken Colyer, Sonny Morris (cor); Monty Sunshine (clt); John R.T. Davies (tbn); Pat Hawes (p); Bill Colyer (vcl) etc. 1950 to 1953
Down by the Riverside, Milenberg Joys, A Miner's Dream of Home, Deep Bayou, If I Ever Cease to Love etc Dormouse DM18

Chris Barber's New Orleans Band and Washboard Wonders:
Keith Jary, Ben Cohen (tpt); Chris Barber (tbn); Alec Revell (clt) etc. 1951
Snake Rag, Oh Didn't He Ramble, Everybody Loves My Baby, Whoop It Up Esquire (S)333

2 On the Boats and Up at Carlo's

Johnny Dankworth – Ronnie Scott – *Bop at Club Eleven*:
Dennis Rose (tpt); Johnny Dankworth, Johnny Rogers (alt); Ronnie Scott (ten); Tommy Pollard, Norman Stenfalt (p); Tony Crombie, Laurie Morgan (d) etc.   1949
Wee Dot, Coquette, 52nd Street Theme, Bremavin, Loverman, Second Eleven, Scrapple from the Apple, Night in Tunisia etc
Esquire ESQ315

Victor Feldman – *The Young Vic*:
Johnny Dankworth (clt); Eddie Thompson, Tony Crombie (p); Vic Feldman (p, vib, d); Lennie Bush (bs) etc.   1948, 1951 & 1954
Mop Mop, Moonlight in Vermont, Jolly Rogers, Evening in Paris, Pakistan, Serenade in Blue, Body and Soul, Monkey Business etc
Esquire (S)327

Jack Parnell and His Quartet:
Bobby Pratt (tpt); Reg Owen (clt); Tommy Whittle, Ronnie Scott (ten); Ralph Sharon, Norman Stenfalt, Frank Horrox (p); Dave Goldberg (g); Charlie Short, Jack Fallon, Sammy Stokes (bs); Jack Parnell (d, vib, vcl).   1946, 1947 & 1950
On the Alamo, I'll Never be the Same, On the Sunny Side of the Street, Scrubber Time, Sweet Lorraine, Old Man Rebop, Jukebox Jumba, Quickie   Decca LF 1065

Melody Maker Columbia Jazz Rally:
Collective personnel: Dave Wilkins, Reg Arnold (tpt); Woolf Phillips, George Chisholm (tbn); Frank Weir, Carl Barriteau (clt); Bertie King, Harry Hayes (alt); Ronnie Scott, Tommy Whittle (ten); George Shearing, Ralph Sharon (p); Dave Goldberg, Pete Chilver, Frank Deniz (g); Jack Fallon (bs); Jock Cummings, Norman Burns (d).   1947
Who's Sorry Now, Blue Moon, I've Found a New Baby, Confessin', C Jam Blues, Thrivin' on a Riff
(Note – these titles have only ever appeared as 78-rpm issues.)

Harry Hayes and His Band:
Collective personnel: Kenny Baker, Jimmy Watson, Leo Wright, Alan Franks (tpt); Jock Bain, Lad Busby, Nobby Clark (tbn);

Harry Hayes (alt); Tommy Whittle, Aubrey Frank (ten); Norman Stenfalt, George Shearing, Pat Dodd (p); Jack Fallon, Charlie Short (bs); Norman Burns (d). 1944 to 1947
Titles include: First Edition, Drop Me Off in Harlem, No Script, Midnight Prowl, Swingin' on Lennox Avenue, I'll Close My Eyes, High as a Kite, From A Flat to C, Scuttlebut, Ol' Man Rebop, Dinner Jacket, The Bebop
(Note – these titles were recorded for HMV and, with the exception of one which appeared briefly as part of a British jazz compilation, none has been issued on microgroove in Britain.)

3 He Played as He Pleased

Humphrey Lyttelton and His Band – *A Tribute to Humph* – Volume 1:
Humphrey Lyttelton (cor); Keith Christie (tbn); Wally Fawkes, Ian Christie (clt); George Webb (p); Mickey Ashman (bs); George Hopkinson (d) etc. 1949 & 1950
Memphis Blues, Maple Leaf Rag, Careless Love Blues, Snake Rag, Hop Frog, Snag It, I Like to Go Back in the Evening etc
                Dormouse DM1

A Tribute to Humph – Volume 2:
Same personnel as before. 1950 & 1951
Dallas Blues, Cakewalkin' Babies Back Home, 1919 March, Panama Rag, Buddy's Habits, On Treasure Island, Trog's Blues, Wolverine Blues etc   Dormouse DM2

A Tribute to Humph – Volume 3:
Personnel as before but Ian Christie omitted and Johnny Parker (p) replaces Webb on last session on LP. 1951
Kater Street Rag, Mezz's Blues, Suffolk Air, Yes Suh!, The Old Grey Mare, Tia Juana, Chicago Buzz, One Man Went to Blow etc
                Dormouse DM3

A Tribute to Humph – Volume 4:
Collective personnel includes Humphrey Lyttelton (tpt, clt); Wally Fawkes, Freddie Grant (clt); Bertie King (alt); Johnny Parker, Mike McKenzie (p); Fitzroy Coleman, Freddy Legon (g); George

Hopkinson (d); George Browne (conga). 1952
Fidgety Feet, Friendless Blues, Original Jelly Roll Blues, King Porter Stomp, London Blues, Mike's Tangana, Ain't Misbehavin', The Onions etc Dormouse DM4

A Tribute to Humph – Volume 5:
Collective personnel includes Humphrey Lyttelton, Al Fairweather (tpt); Wally Fawkes, Sandy Brown (clt); Bruce Turner (alt); Johnny Parker (p); Micky Ashman (bs); George Hopkinson (d).
 1952 & 1953
Travellin' Blues, Doctor Blues, Blue for Waterloo, Maryland My Maryland, Red for Piccadilly, Four's Company etc
 Dormouse DM11

A Tribute to Humph – Volume 8:
Collective personal includes Humphrey Lyttelton (tpt); John Picard (tbn); Bruce Turner (alt); Johnny Parker (p); Jim Bray (bs); Stan Greig, Eddie Taylor (d). 1955 & 1956
Slippery Horn, Handful of Keys, Lady in Red, Skeleton in the Cupboard, Bad Penny Blues, Looking for Turner, Christopher Columbus, That's My Home, Swing Out etc Dormouse DM14
(Note – up to the date of the preparation of these details the above LPs have been issued on the Dormouse label. It is the company's intention to complete the release of all of the Parlophone studio recordings made by Lyttelton.)

4 Traditionalism Rampant

Ken Colyer's Jazzmen – *The Decca Years*:
Ken Colyer (tpt, vcl); Mac Duncan (tbn); Ian Wheeler (clt); Ray Foxley (p); Johnny Bastable (bjo); Dick Smith, Ron Ward (bs); Stan Greig, Colin Bowden (d). 1955, 1956, 1958 & 1959
Dippermouth Blues, Beale Street Blues, Fig Leaf Rag, Gravier Street Blues, The Girls Go Crazy, The Entertainer, If I Ever Cease to Love, Kinklets etc Lake LA5001

Ken Colyer and His New Orleans Band:
Ken Colyer (cor, vcl); Harrison Brazlee (tbn); Emile Barnes (clt); Albert Gleny (bs) etc. New Orleans – 1953

Gravier Street Blues, Black Cat on the Fench, That's a Plenty, How Long Blues, Winter Wonderland, Frankie and Johnny, Panama Rag etc Dawn Club LP

Chris Barber's Jazz Band:
Pat Halcox (cor); Chris Barber (tbn); Monty Sunshine (clt); Lonnie Donegan (g); Jim Bray (bs); Ron Bowden (d). 1954
Bobby Shaftoe, Chimes Blues, The Martinique, Merrydown Rag, Skokiaan, Storyville Blues, Ice Cream etc Decca LK4246

Sandy Brown – Acker Bilk
Sandy Brown Jazz Band:
Al Fairweather (tpt); Sandy Brown (clt); Bob Craig (tbn); Stan Greig (d). 1953
Doctor Jazz, Four or Five Times, Wild Man Blues, King Porter Stomp

Acker Bilk:
Johnny Stainer (tpt); Johnny Skuse (tbn); Acker Bilk (clt); Dave Collett (p) etc 1955
Gettysberg Stomp, Milenberg Joys, Over in Gloryland, Gravier Street Blues Esquire (S)333

Sandy Brown – *McJazz*:
Al Fairweather (tpt); Jeremy French (tbn); Sandy Brown (clt); Ian Armit (p); Diz Disley (g, bjo); Tim Mahn (bs); Graham Burbidge (d). 1957
Go Ghana, Scales, The Card, Monochrome, Those Blues, Wild Life, Blues from Black Rock, Doctor Blues, Ognoliya, Saved by the Blues Dormouse DM6

Ken Colyer – *The Decca Skiffle Sessions 1954–1957*:
Ken Colyer (g, vcl); Alexis Korner (g, mand); Mickey Ashman, Ron Ward, Dick Smith (bs); Bill Colyer (washboard); etc
1954 to 1957
Midnight Special, Casey Jones, Take this Hammer, Down Bound Train, Stack-o-Lee Blues, House Rent Stomp, This Train, Go Down Sunshines, Ella Speed etc Lake LA5007

Mike Daniels's Delta Jazzmen:
Mike Daniels (tpt); Gordon Blundy (tbn); John Barnes (clt); Eddie

Smith (bjo); Des Bacon (p); Don Smith (b); Arthur Fryer (d).
September 1957/59
Milenberg Joys, You're Just My Type, At a Georgia Camp Meeting, Riverboat Shuffle, Weatherbird Rag, Baby Doll etc
Harlequin HQ3007

5 Bop on the Road

Johnny Dankworth Seven:
Jimmy Deuchar, Eddie Blair (tpt); Eddie Harvey (tbn); Johnny Dankworth (alt); Don Rendell (ten); Bill LeSage (p); Eric Dawson (bs); Tony Kinsey, Eddie Taylor (d); Cleo Laine (vcl)
1950, 1951 & 1952
Leon Bismarck, Get Happy, Lush Life, Cherokee, Seven Not Out, Stompin' at the Savoy, Strictly Confidential etc   Esquire (S)317

Vic Lewis and His Orchestra:
Hank Shaw, Johnny Shakespeare, Harold Luff (tpt); Don Lang, Stan Smith (tbn); Ronnie Chamberlain (alt); Vince Bovil, Kathy Stobart (ten); Dill Jones, Ken Thorne (p); Al Ferdman (g); Alan McDonald, Jack Honeyman (bs); Peter Coleman (d) etc   1949
West Indian Ritual, High on a Windy Hill, No Orchids, Harlem Holiday, Heir to a Chinese Maiden, Hammersmith Riff, Pepperpot, Love for Sale, Theme for Trombone etc
Big Band International LP2701

Jack Parnell and His Orchestra:
Collective personnel: Jimmy Deuchar, Jo Hunter, Hank Shaw, Jimmy Watson (tpt); Mac Minshull, Lad Busby, Ken Wray (tbn); Derek Humble, Bob Burns (alt); Ronnie Scott, Pete King, Joe Temperley, Ronnie Keene (ten); Harry Klein (bar); Max Harris (p); Sammy Stokes, Jack Fallon (bs); Jack Parnell, Allan Ganley, Phil Seamen (d).   1952 & 1953
Catherine Wheel, Summertime, The Hawk Talks, Carioca, Cotton Tail, Skin Deep, Sure Thing etc   Parlophone PMD1053

Ronnie Scott – *Live at the Jazz Club*:
Jimmy Deuchar (tpt); Ken Wray (tbn); Derek Humble (alt); Ronnie Scott, Pete King (ten); Benny Green (bar); Norman

Stenfalt (p); Lennie Bush (bs); Tony Crombie (d).   1953
Popo, Pantagrulian, Mullenium, Nearness of You, Nemo, All the Things You Are, The Champ, Day Dream, On the Alamo, What's New?, I May Be Wrong   Esquire (S)328

Kenny Graham Afro-Cubists *Volume 2*:
Collective personnel: Jo Hunter (tpt); Kenny Graham, Pete King, Joe Temperley, Derek Humble (ten); Oscar Birch (bar); Ralph Dollimore, Dill Jones (p); Roy Plummer (g); Joe Muddel, Sammy Stokes (bs); Phil Seamen (d); Donaldo (bongos).   1953
Jump for Joe, Night in Tunisia, Take the A Train, Flamingo, Mango Walk, Bongo Chant, Dance of the Zombies, Tempo Medio Lento, Beguine, Haitian Ritual etc   Esquire (S)329

Tubby Hayes and His Orchestra:
Collective personnel: Jimmy Deuchar, Dickie Hawdon, Dave Usden (tpt); Mike Senn (alt, bar); Tubby Hayes (ten); Jackie Sharpe (ten, bar); Harry South (p); Pete Blannin (bs); Lennie Breslow, Bill Eyden (d).   1955
Jor-du, Orient Line, May Ray, Monsoon   Tempo EXA14
I Let a Song Go out of My Heart, Sophisticated Lady, Fidelius, Tootsie Roll   Tempo EXA17

6 The Condon Connection, the Three Bs and Traddy-pop

The Condon Connection

Freddy Randall and His Band – *His Great Sixteen*:
Collective personnel: Freddy Randall (tpt, vcl); Geoff Sowden, Norman Cave (tbn); Bruce Turner, Archie Semple, Al Gay (clt); Stan Butcher, Lennie Felix, Eddie Thompson (p); Denny Wright (g); Lennie Hastings, Stan Bourke (d); Billy Banks (vcl).
                                                        1951 to 1956
That's a Plenty, Tishomingo Blues, Tight Lines, Dark Night Blues, Muskrat Ramble, Ja Da, Walkin' the Dog, If I Could Be with You etc   Dormouse DM5

Mick Mulligan's New Magnolia Jazz Band:
Mick Mulligan (tpt); Frank Parr (tbn); Ian Christie (clt); Ronald

Duff (p); Nigel Sinclair (g); Alan Duddington, Major Holley (bs);
Pete Appleby (d).   1956
Raver's Edge, Beale Street Blues, Sally Jane, Shimme-sha-wabble
                                              Tempo EXA52

Alex Welsh and His Dixielanders:
Alex Welsh (tpt); Roy Crimmins (tbn); Archie Semple (clt); Fred
Hunt (p); Chris Staunton (bs); Lennie Hastings (d).   1955
Smiles, Hard Hearted Hannah, What Can I Say Dear, Sugar
                                              Decca DFE6315

The Three Bs

Chris Barber and His Band:
Pat Halcox (tpt); Chris Barber (tbn); Monty Sunshine (clt); Lonnie
Donegan (g); Jim Bray, Mickey Ashman (bs); Colin Bowden (d);
Ottilie Patterson (vcl).   1955, 1956 & 1957
Petite Fleur, Wabash Blues, Old Rugged Cross, Thriller Rag,
When You and I were Young Maggie, Just a Closer Walk, Ugly
Child, Careless Love etc   PRT Records PYL6031

Acker Bilk's Paramount Jazz Band:
Ken Sims (tpt); Johnny Mortimer (tbn); Acker Bilk (clt); Roy
James, Jay Hawkins (bjo); Ernie Price (bs); Ron McKay (d)   1959
Old Comrades' March, The Gay Hussar, Summer Set, In a Persian
Market, Ory's Creole Trombone, Cushion Foot Stomp etc
                                              Columbia 33SX1205

Kenny Ball Jazz Band:
Kenny Ball (tpt, vcl); Johnny Bennett (tbn); Dave Jones (clt); Colin
Bates (p); Diz Disley (bjo, vcl); Vic Pitts (bs); Ron Bowden (d)
                                                       1960
Teddy Bears' Picnic, Hawaiian War Chant, I Got Plenty of
Nothin', 1919 March, South Rampart Street Parade, Waltzing
Matilda etc   Pye NJL24

Traddy-pop

Records by bands such as Bob Wallis and His Storyville Jazzmen,
Dick Charlesworth and His City Gents, Micky Ashman and His
Ragtime Band, etc, are not currently available.

7 Towards the Centre

Vic Dickenson Septet:
Collective personnel: Ruby Braff, Shad Collins (tpt); Vic Dickenson (tbn); Ed Hall (clt); Sir Charles Thompson (p); Steve Jordan (g); Walter Page (bs); Les Erskine, Jo Jones (d).
NYC – 1953 & 1954
Russian Lullaby, Jeepers Creepers, I Cover the Waterfront, Sir Charles at Home, Keepin' out of Mischief, Everybody Loves My Baby, When You and I were Young Maggie, You Brought a New Kind of Love to Me, Nice Work if You Can Get It, Suspension Blues, Runnin' Wild, Old Fashioned Love   Vanguard
(Note – these justly famous performances have been reissued many times on different labels.)

Humphrey Lyttelton and His Band:
Humphrey Lyttelton (tpt); John Picard (tbn); Tony Coe (clt, alt); Jimmy Skidmore (ten); Joe Temperley (bar); Ian Armit (p); Brian Brocklehurst (bs); Eddie Taylor (d).   1958
Trouble in Mind, Big Bill Blues, In Swinger, Unbooted Character, Out of the Gallion, Black Beauty etc   Parlophone PMC1070

Alex Welsh and His Band:
Alex Welsh (tpt); Roy Williams (tbn); John Barnes (alt, bar); Al Gay (ten); Fred Hunt (p); Ronnie Rae (bs); Jim Douglas (g); Lennie Hastings (d).   Edinburgh – 1967
It Don't Mean a Thing, I Got Rhythm, You've Changed, Just Squeeze Me, There Will Never be Another You etc
Dormouse DM16

Wally Fawkes and His Troglodytes:
Spike MacIntosh (tpt); Jeremy French (tbn); Wally Fawkes (clt); Colin Bates (p); Russ Allen (bs); Dave Pearson (d).   1959
Lucky Duck, Flook's Fancy, Just a Closer Walk, It's the Talk of the Town   Decca DFE6600

Bruce Turner's Jump Band:
John Chilton (tpt); John Mumford (tbn); Bruce Turner (clt, alt); Stan Greig (p); Tony Goffe (bs); Johnny Armitage (d).   1959
Accent on Swing, Opus Five, Don't Get Around Much Anymore,

Stop Look and Listen, Christopher Columbus, Good Queen Bess, Nuages, Blues for Lester etc   International Jazz Club AJZLP4

Acker Bilk and His Paramount Jazz Band:
Colin Smith (tpt); John Mortimer (tbn); Acker Bilk (clt); Bruce Turner (alt); Colin Bates (p); Tony Pitt (g); Tucker Finlayson (b); John Richardson (d)   19 March 1970
Drop Me Off at Harlem, Big Bill, Jazz Me Blues, The Whiffenpoof Song, Savoy Blues etc   Regal SRS5028

(Note – Dave Carey's band, while principally a revivalist unit, was another that frequently abandoned collective improvisation and the hackneyed traditionalist tunes in favour of 'swing' music material and loosely-strung solos against a banjoless rhythm team, excellent examples of which can be heard on their recordings of 'Special Delivery Stomp' and 'Feather Merchant', made in February and October 1956 respectively. So different is their sound from the usual run of their recordings that the listener could be forgiven for thinking that he/she is listening to a totally different band. Carey recorded for Tempo.)

8   The Ban is Breached

Jazz at the Philharmonic:
Charlie Shavers, Roy Eldridge (tpt); Bill Harris (tbn); Willie Smith, Benny Carter (alt); Lester Young, Flip Phillips, Ben Webster (ten); Oscar Peterson (p); Herb Ellis (g); Ray Brown (bs); J.C. Heard, Gene Krupa (d).   Carnegie Hall, New York City – 1953
Flying Home, Ballad Medley, The Challenges, The Drum Battle, One o'Clock Jump, Blues, Lester's Blues, I Cover the Waterfront, Lester Gambols   Verve JATP Volume 9

(Note – although obviously not recorded in Britain in March 1953 this album nevertheless is representative of the 'Flood Relief' concert and features many of the musicians who appeared in London.)

9 First of the Giants

Stan Kenton in Concert:
Ed Leddy, Vinnie Tano, Phil Gilbert, Lee Katzman, Sam Noto (tpt); Bob Fitzpatrick, Carl Fontana, Don Kelly, Kent Larsen (tbn); Lennie Niehaus (alt); Bill Perkins, Don Rendell (ten); Harry Klein (bar); Fred Fox, Irving Rosenthal (frh); Jay McAlluster (tu); Stan Kenton (p); Ralph Blaze (g); Curtis Counce (bs); Mel Lewis (d). West Berlin – 1956
Artistry in Rhythm, Stompin' at the Savoy, Collaboration, Love for Sale, Swing House, Yesterdays, Out of Nowhere, Royal Blue, Solitaire, 23°N, 82°W, Concerto to End All Concertos, Intermission Riff, Polka Dots and Moon Beams, Carl, Peanut Vendor, Stella by Starlight, Cherokee, Young Blood
Artistry Records AR2 100
(Note – this album is misleadingly labelled 'Live at the Festival Hall' and lists the names of Spencer Sinatra and Jack Nimitz in place of Don Rendell and Harry Klein. The above details are correct.)

Louis Armstrong and the All Stars:
Louis Armstrong (tpt, vcl); Trummy Young (tbn, vcl); Ed Hall (clt); Billy Kyle (p); Dale Jones (bs); Barrett Deems (d); Velma Middleton (vcl). Concert, Chicago – June 1956
Indiana, The Gypsy, Faithful Hussar, Rockin' Chair, Mack the Knife, Stompin' at the Savoy, Ko-ko-mo etc CBS 22106
(Note – the above is representative of the All Stars which played in Britain in May 1956.)

Lionel Hampton and His Orchestra:
Dave Gonzalves, Billy Brooks, Ed Mullens, Ed Preston (tpt); Al Hayes, Walter 'Phatz' Morris, Larry Wilson (tbn); Scoville Brown, Bobby Plater (clt, alt, f); Eddie Chamblee, Rickey Brauer (ten); Curtis Lowe (bar); Oscar Dennard, Robert Mosely (p); Lionel Hampton (vib, p, d, vcl); Billy Mackel (g); Peter Badie (bs); June Gardner (d).
(Note – the above personnel recorded an LP for RCA in Madrid in June 1956 and although the music is not typical of that played by the Hampton band in Britain later that year, the personnel is indicative of the men working with Lionel at the time.)

312   *A History of Jazz in Britain 1950–1970*

10   The Invasion Mounts

Eddie Condon and His Band:
Wild Bill Davison (cor); Cutty Cutshall (tbn); Bob Wilber (clt); Gene Schroeder (p); Eddie Condon (g); Leonard Gaskin (bs); George Wettling (d).   unknown location and date
At the Jazz Band Ball, Squeeze Me, High Society, Limehouse Blues, Gin Mill Blues, I ain't Gonna Give . . ., When the Saints, Mean to Me etc   Jazzology J–10
(Note – the fact that this LP features the precise personnel which toured Britain playing a very similar programme of music seems too much of a coincidence.)

Jack Teagarden – Earl Hines All Stars: *In England, 1957*:
Max Kaminsky (tpt); Jack Teagarden (tbn, vcl); Peanuts Hucko (clt); Earl Hines (p); Jack Lesberg (bs); Cosy Cole (d).
                                                              Manchester, 1957
Royal Garden Blues, Memphis Blues, Basin' Street Blues, Tea for Two, That's a Plenty, Original Dixieland One Step, Struttin' with Some Barbecue, Rosetta   Jazz Groove 001

Count Basie and His Orchestra – *The Atomic Basie*:
Wendell Culley, Thad Jones, Joe Newman, Snooky Young (tpt); Henry Coker, Al Grey, Benny Powell (tbn); Marshall Royal (alt); Frank Wess (alt, ten, f); Eddie Lockjaw Davis, Frank Foster (ten); Charlie Fowlkes (bar); Count Basie (p); Freddie Green (g); Eddie Jones (bs); Sonny Payne (d).   NYC – 1957
Flight of the Foo Birds, Li'l Darlin', Whirly Bird, Kid from Red Bank, Teddy the Toad etc   Roulette
(Note – this album has been reissued many times. It was recorded in America three days before the Basie band left to commence their tour of Britain.)

Modern Jazz Quartet:
John Lewis (p); Milt Jackson (vib); Percy Heath (bs); Connie Kay (d)   NYC – 1957
Venice, Cortege, The Rose Truc, One Never Knows, Three Windows, The Golden Striker   Atlantic LP(SD)1284

Dave Brubeck Quartet:
Paul Desmond (alt); Dave Brubeck (p); Gene Wright (bs); Joe Morello (d).   Copenhagen – March 1958
Tangerine, Wonderful Copenhagen, The Wright Groove, My One Bad Habit, Like Someone in Love, Watusi Drums
   Columbia CL1168

Duke Ellington and His Orchestra:
Clark Terry, Willie Cook, Cat Anderson, Shorty Baker (tpt); Ray Nance (tpt, vln); Britt Woodman, John Sanders, Quentin Jackson (tbn); Jimmy Hamilton (clt, ten); Russell Procope (alt, clt); Johnny Hodges (alt); Paul Gonsalves (ten); Harry Carney (bar, bs-clt, clt); Duke Ellington (p); Jimmy Woode (bs); Sam Woodyard (d); Ozzie Bailey (vcl).   NYC – July 1958
Jazz Festival Jazz, Princess Blue, El Gato, Multicoloured Blue, Hi Fi Fo Fun, Mr Gentle and Mr Cool, Juniflip, Happy Reunion
   Columbia CL1245

Woody Herman's Anglo-American Herd in England:
Nat Adderley, Reunald Jones, Les Condon, Kenny Wheeler, Bert Courtley (tpt); Bill Harris, Ken Wray, Eddie Harvey (tbn); Woody Herman (clt, alt, vcl); Don Rendell, Art Ellefson, Johnny Scott (ten); Ronnie Ross (bar); Vince Guaraldi (p); Charlie Byrd (g); Keeter Betts (bs); Jimmy Campbell (d).   Manchester – 1959
The Preacher, Like Some Blues Man, Like, From Pillar to Post, Four Brothers, Opus De Funk, Early Autumn, Playgirl Stroll, Woodchopper's Ball   Jazz Groove 004

Kid Ory's Creole Jazz Band – *Live in England, 1959*:
Red Allen (tpt); Kid Ory (tbn, vcl); Bob McCracken (clt); Cedric Haywood (p); Squire Gersh (bs); Alton Redd (d).
   Unknown location in England – 1959
Original Dixieland One Step, I Wish I were in Peoria, Careless Love, Bill Bailey, St James's Infirmary, That's a Plenty
   Queene Disc Q-052

11 Entry of the Soloists and Coals to Alabama

Tubby Hayes in New York:
Clark Terry (tpt); Tubby Hayes (ten); Horace Parlan (p); Eddie Costa (vib); George Duvivier (bs); Dave Bailey (d).
                                                    NYC – October 1961
You for Me, A Pint of Bitter, Airegin, Opus Ocean, Soon, Doxy
                                                           Fontana TFL5183

Red Allen – *Twenty Years Later*:
Red Allen (tpt, vcl); Lannie Scott, Sammy Price (p); Benny Moten (bs); George Reed (d).   NYC – June 1965
Canal Street Blues, Mack the Knife, Blue Spruce Boogie, Muskrat Ramble, Lover Come Back to Me, St Louis Blues, Caravan, Pleasing Paul, Hello Dolly, Memphis Blues, Never on Sunday etc.
                                                                    Meritt 27
(Note – this record is included as an example of Red Allen's playing from the period during which he toured England. It is not, of course, typical of the musical context he worked in while in the UK.)

Ted Heath at Carnegie Hall:
Personnel includes Bobby Pratt, Bert Ezzard, Duncan Campbell, Eddie Blair (tpt); Don Lusher (tbn); Les Gilbert, Ronnie Chamberlain (alt); Henry McKenzie (clt, ten); Red Price (ten); Frank Horrox (p); Johnny Hawksworth (bs); Ronnie Verrell (d).
                                      Carnegie Hall, NYC – May 1956
King's Cross Climax, Memories of You, Perdido, Autumn in New York, Just One of Those Things, Lulaby in Rhythm, I Remember You, Hawaiian War Chant etc   Memoir MO1R132

12 Jazz City

Tubby Hayes – *All Night Long*:
Collective personnel includes Bert Courtley (tpt); Keith Christie (tbn); Johnny Scott (f, alt); Tubby Hayes (f, ten); Ronnie Ross (bar); Colin Purbrook, Dave Brubeck (p); Ray Dempsey (g); Charlie Mingus, Kenny Napper (bs); Allan Ganley (d).   1961

Scott Free, Dedication to Johnny Hodges, Wingate's Spot,
Noodlin' etc Fontana TFL5179

Tubby Hayes and the Jazz Couriers:
Tubby Hayes (f, ten, vib); Ronnie Scott (ten); Terry Shannon (p);
Kenny Napper (bs); Phil Seamen (d). 1959
If This isn't Love, Easy to Love, Whisper Not, Autumn Leaves,
Too Close for Comfort, Yesterdays, Love Walked In
 Jazzland JLP34

Tony Crombie and His Orchestra:
Leon Calvert, Les Condon (tpt); Al Newman (clt, alt); Bobby
Wellins (ten); Harry Klein (bar); Stan Tracey (p); Kenny Napper
(bs); Tony Crombie (d). 1960
Caravan, Boo-bah, Lullaby, Reelin', Li'l Old Pottsville, Jamba, I
Let a Song Go out of My Heart, Summertime Tempo TAP30

Zoot Sims at Ronnie Scott's:
Zoot Sims (ten); Stan Tracey (p); Kenny Napper (bs); Jackie
Dougan (d). 1961
Blues in E Flat, Somebody Loves Me, Stompin' at the Savoy,
Autumn Leaves Fontana TL680982

Don Rendell Jazz Six:
Bert Courtley (tpt); Eddie Harvey (tbn, p); Ronnie Ross (alt, bar);
Don Rendell (ten); Pete Blannin (bs); Andy White (d). 1958
It's Playtime, Johnny Come Lately, Hit the Road to Dreamland,
The Lady is a Tramp, Packet of Blues, Dolly Mixture, My Friend
Tom, This Can't be Love, Bypass, Tickletoe Decca LK4265

Jazz at the Flamingo:
Jimmy Deuchar (tpt); Tommy Whittle, Don Rendell (ten); Benny
Green (bar); Bill LeSage (p); Sammy Stokes (bs); Tony Crombie
(d). 1953
Jump for Jeff, Tres Gai Decca DFE6253

Kenny Baker – *Date with the Dozen*:
Kenny Baker, Freddy Clayton (tpt); George Chisholm, Jackie
Armstrong (tbn); E.O. Pogson (reeds); Harry Klein (bar); Keith
Bird (clt, ten); Harry Hayes (clt, alt); Norman Stenfalt, Bill
McGuffie (p); Martin Slavin (vib); Joe Muddel, Lennie Bush (bs);

Eric Delaney, Phil Seamen (d) etc.   1955 & 1957
Baker's Boogie, Mean Dog Blues, Harlem Twist, Blues I Love to Sing, Whistle and I'll Come to You, Gal from Joe's Coquette, There Will Never be Another You etc   Dormouse DM9

Joe Harriott – John Meyer Double Quintet:
Eddie Blair (tpt); Joe Harriott (alt); John Meyer (vln, harpsichord); Chris Taylor (f); Pat Smythe (p); Diwan Motihar (sitar); Rick Laird (bs) etc.   1966
Overture, Contrasts, Raga Megha, Raga Gaud-Saranga
                                                       Columbia SCX6025

Instrumental Abbreviations

alt	alto saxophone
bar	baritone saxophone
bjo	banjo
bs	bass
bs-clt	bass clarinet
clt	clarinet
cor	cornet
d	drums
f	flute
frh	french horn
g	guitar
mand	mandolin
tbn	trombone
as	alto saxophone
ten	tenor saxophone
tpt	trumpet
tu	tuba
vcl	vocal
vib	vibraphone
vln	violin

Bibliography

Armstrong, Louis: *Satchmo* (London: Jazz Book Club, 1957)
Blesh, Rudi: *Shining Trumpets* (New York: Alfred Knopf, 1946, 1958, 1975)
Borneman, Ernest: *A Critic Looks at Jazz* (London: Jazz Music Books, 1946)
Boulton, David: *Jazz in Britain* (London: W.H. Allen, 1958)
Britt, Stan, with Brian Case and Chrissie Murray: *Illustrated Encyclopedia of Jazz* (London: Salamander Books, 1986)
Brown, Sandy, ed David Binns: *McJazz Manuscripts* (London: Faber and Faber, 1979)
Carey, Dave, with Albert McCarthy and Ralph Venables: *Jazz Directory Vols 1–6* (Hampshire: Delphic Press; London: Cassell, 1950–55)
Carr, Ian, with Digby Fairweather and Brian Priestley: *Jazz: The Essential Companion* (London: Paladin, 1989)
Chilton, John: *Who's Who of Jazz* (London: Macmillan, 1985)
—— (with Max Jones): *Louis* (London: Studio Vista, 1971)
Feather, Leonard: *The Encyclopedia of Jazz* (London: Arthur Barker, 1961)
Godbolt, Jim: *All This and 10%*, updated to *All This and Many a Dog* (London: Quartet, 1986)
—— *A History of Jazz in Britain 1919–50* (London: Quartet, 1984)
Grime, Kitty: *Jazz at Ronnie Scott's* (London: Robert Hale, 1979)
Harris, Rex: *Jazz* (Harmonsworth: Pelican, 1952)
Hughes, Spike: *Opening Bars* (London: Museum Press, 1946)
—— *Second Movement* (London: Museum Press, 1951)
Jepsen, Jorgan Grunnett: *Jazz Records 1942–65* (Holte, Denmark: 1960–65)
Kaminsky, Max: *My Life in Jazz* (London: Jazz Book Club, 1965)
Kernfeld, Barry (ed): *The New Grove Dictionary of Jazz* (London: Macmillan, 1988)
Larkin, Philip: *All What Jazz* (London: Faber and Faber, 1985)
Lewis, Vic: *Music and Maiden Overs* (London: Chatto and Windus, 1987)

Lomax: *Mister Jelly Roll* (London: Jazz Book Club, 1967)
Lyttelton, Humphrey: *I Play as I Please* (London: Pan Books, 1956)
—— *Second Chorus* (London: Jazz Book Club, 1958)
—— *Take It from the Top* (London: Robson Books, 1975)
McCarthy, Albert (ed): *PL Year Book of Jazz* (London: Editions Poetry, 1946)
Matthew, Brian: *Trad Mad* (London: Souvenir Press, 1962)
Meeker, David: *Jazz in the Movies* (London: Talisman Books, 1981)
Melly, George: *Owning Up* (London: Futura Publications, 1986)
Morum, William: *The Gabriel* (London: TV Boardman, 1951)
Nelson, Stanley: *All About Jazz* (London: Heath Cranton, 1934)
Ramsey, Frederic Jr and Charles Edward Smith: *Jazzmen* (New York: Harcourt Brace, 1939)
Rosenthal, George S. and Frank Zachary: *Jazzways* (New York: Greenberg, 1946)
Stewart, Jay Allison: *Call Him George* (London: Jazz Book Club, 1963)
Turner, Bruce: *Hot Air, Cool Music* (London: Quartet, 1984)
Wilber, Bob: *Music was not Enough* (London: Macmillan, 1987)

Specialist magazines

Jazz Express (ed Melissa Swanson) 29 Romilly Street, London W1 – monthly
Jazz Journal (ed Eddie Cook) 117 Farringdon Road, London EC2 – monthly
Jazz at Ronnie Scott's (ed Jim Godbolt) 47 Frith Street, London W1 – bi-monthly
Wire (ed Richard Cook) 115 Cleveland Street, London W1 – monthly
Storyville (ed Laurie Wright) 66 Fairview Drive, Chigwell, Essex – quarterly
Jazz News (ed Dara O'Lochlain) 28 Lansdowne Road, Dublin 4, Ireland – monthly

Jazz Rag (ed Jim Simpson) PO Box 944, Edgbaston, Birmingham — quarterly

Memory Lane (ed Ray Pallett) 40 Merryfield Approach, Leigh-on-Sea, Essex — quarterly

Jazz Record Shops (London)

James Asman's Jazz Centre, 23a New Row, St Martin's Lane, WC2 (01-240 1480)
Dobell's Jazz and Folk Record Shop, 21 Tower Street, WC2 (01-240 1354)
HMV Shop, 363 Oxford Street, W1 (01-629 1240)
John Kendall's Jazz Records, 28 Great Windmill Street, W1 (01-437 8100)
Mole Jazz, 291 Pentonville Road, N1 (01-278 8623)

Jazz Record Shops (suburbs and provinces)

Beckenham Record Centre, 64 Beckenham Road, Beckenham, Kent (01-658 3464)
Discovery Records, Stone Cottage, Broad Street, Beechingstoke, Pewsey, Wilts (Woodbrough — 067285 406)
Harvey's, 9 Station Road, Newington, Sittingbourne, Kent
Musicwise, 172 High Street, Egham, Surrey (Egham 33400)
Geoff Nichols, 13 Coatham Hill, Bristol (0272-731849)
Record Centre, 44 Loveday Street, Birmingham (021-7399)
Jed Williams, 16 Llwyn-y-Grant Terrace, Cardiff (0222-48422)
Peter Russell's Hot Record Shop, 58 New George Street, Plymouth, Devon (0752-669511)

Index

Abrams, Max, 66, 150
'Accordion Club', 33, 34, 39, 114
accordions, 33–4
Adderley, Julian 'Cannonball', 244, 298
Adderley, Nat, 228, 244
Adeane, Louis, 272
Afro-Cubists, 112–13, 250
agents, 120, 140
Ahrens, Edward, 73
Albemarle Jazz Band, 73
Albert, Don, 148
Alcorn, Alvin, 148, 232
Aldrich, Ronnie, 131
Aldridge, Don, 89
All Night Long, 266
Allandale, Eric, 138
Allen, Red, 127, 229, 232–7, 298
Allen, Russ, 34, 159
Allsopp, Ken, 138
Ambrose, 94–7, 98, 114
American Federation of Musicians (AFM), 72, 168, 170, 182–3, 186–7, 189, 231
American musicians, 166–87, 189–208, 209–30, 231–40
Anderson, Ernestine, 257, 261
Anderson, Ivie, 222

Anglo-American Band, 41
Anstey, Ted, 169–71, 187
Appleby, Pete, 89, 125
Archer Street, 26, 47, 48, 139, 247–8, 268–70
Archey, Jimmy, 148, 209
Armatage, John, 155
Armit, Ian, 151
Armstrong, Jack, 97
Armstrong, Lil, 224
Armstrong, Louis, 2, 3, 10–11, 42, 51, 52, 57, 77, 85, 93, 121, 122, 127, 152, 154, 168–9, 197–202, 206–8, 216, 229, 280–1, 283, 293
Arnold, Reg, 34, 40, 105
Ashman, Micky, 89, 138, 141, 142, 260, 278
Asman, James, 19, 20, 23, 82n., 104, 147, 182, 263, 273, 297
Aston, Martin, 94
Astor Club, 183
Atkins, Ronald, 277–8
Auger, Brian, 261
Austin High School Gang, 121–2
Australian Jazz Band,

6–7, 24, 45, 55, 85
Avon Cities Jazz Band, 10, 164
Ayling, Les, 98

Back o' Town Syncopators, 138
Backhouse, David, 135
Bacon, Max, 98, 181
Bailey, 222
Baker, Dorothy, 289
Baker, Ginger, 260
Baker, Kenny, 95, 97, 114, 183, 265
Baker, Shorty, 221
Baldry, Long John, 260, 261
Ball, Kenny, 2, 63n., 136–7, 142–3, 158, 164
Ball, Ronnie, 249
Bandbox, 250
Barbarin, Paul, 70–1
Barber, Chris, 2, 9, 10, 20, 73–4, 76–80, 90–1, 130–2, 136, 137, 140, 145, 158, 162, 164–5, 232, 245–6, 260, 262, 265, 288, 292
Bard, Ruby, 140
Barnehurst, 3–4
Barnes, Emile, 72, 76
Barnes, John, 84, 127, 163, 240

Barnet, Charlie, 97
Barriteau, Carl, 40
Barrow, Erroll, 119
Barton, Cliff, 261
Barton, Ken, 138
Basie, Count, 34, 51, 57, 81, 148, 158, 213–14, 223, 287, 298
Bassey, Shirley, 143
Bastable, John, 133, 215
Bates, Colin, 160
Bates, Collin, 155, 160
Bates, Peg Leg, 197, 199, 222
Bates, Phil, 116
Batty, Eric, 10
BBC, 18–19, 33, 34, 42, 45–7, 66, 74, 96, 101, 105, 106, 115, 137, 139, 146, 153, 157, 206, 217, 262, 266, 282
BBC Records, 147
Be-bop Preservation Society, 258
Beatles, 145
Beatty, Doreen, 86
Beaulieu Festival, 138
Beaumont, Father, 284
Beaverbrook, Lord, 25
bebop *see* bop
Bechet, Sidney, 13, 22, 51, 52, 56, 59, 81, 82, 100, 130–1, 168, 175, 192, 201–2, 208, 233, 238, 245
Becket, Harry, 120, 266, 267
Beiderbecke, Bix, 3, 52, 81, 150, 186, 289
Bell, Graeme (Australian Jazz Band), 6–7, 24, 45, 55, 85, 150
Bell, Ian, 138
Bell-Lyttelton Jazz Nine, 55
Bell-Lyttelton Jazz Twelve, 55
Bellerby, Vic, 223, 225
Beltona, 19
Bennett, Max, 221
Bennett, Tony, 118
Bentley, Jack, 48
Bernard, John, 73
Bernstein, Leonard, 207
Best, Skeeter, 228
Bexleyheath and District Rhythm Club, 4
Bier Bar, Dusseldorf, 126–7, 133
Big Ben Banjo Band, 262
Bigard, Barney, 221
Bilk, Acker, 2, 74, 128, 132–6, 138, 139, 140, 142, 143, 158, 164–5
Billboard, 281
Birch, Oscar, 37
Bird, Keith, 43, 116
Birmingham Town Hall, 59
Bishop, Dick, 130, 132
Bishop, Walter Jr, 231
Black, Cilla, 146
Black, Michael, 23
Black, Stanley, 98, 131, 189
Black Bottom Stompers, 87
Blain, Brian, 225
Blair, Eddie, 97, 102, 116
Blake, Cyril, 285
Blakey, Art, 261
Blannin, Pete, 115, 233
Blaze, Ralph, 190, 194
Blesh, Rudi, 55–6, 215–16, 285
Blue Flames, 261
Blue Jays, 260

Blue Room, 251
blues, 86, 91, 259–62
Blues Incorporated, 260, 261
Blues Syndicate, 261
Bobcats, 2
Bolden, Buddy, 55, 72, 227
Bonano, Sharkey, 183
Bond, Graham, 260, 261
books, 284–95
bop, 2–3, 27–47, 93–4, 96, 99, 233
Borneman, Ernest, 17–18, 22, 23, 144, 171, 173, 175, 274, 277, 285, 286–7, 293
Boston Jazz Band, 289
Botterill, Jack, 111
Boucarat, Norman, 58
Boud, Bert, 89
Boulton, David, 288–9, 292
Bowden, Colin, 215
Bowden, Ron, 15, 73, 74, 78, 130
Boyce, Denny, 250
Boyle, Gary, 261
Braff, Ruby, 127, 149, 232, 298
Bramwell, Bill, 123, 128
Brand, Pat, 171, 197–200, 211, 273–4
Branscombe, Alan, 102
Bray, Jim, 61, 73, 89, 155
Bray, Pete, 114
Brazlee, Harrison, 72
Breed, Perley, 264
Breen, Bobby, 115
Breslow, Lennie, 115
Briggs, Vic, 261
Brocklehurst, Brian, 151
Broonzy, Big Bill, 91, 164, 260

Brown, George, 58
Brown, Harry, 6, 52
Brown, Gerry, 138
Brown, Les, 97
Brown, Ray, 29, 179, 180
Brown, Sandy, 10, 23–4, 74, 81–4, 86, 89, 125, 136, 139, 143, 157–8, 229, 234, 265, 293
Brown, Terry, 31, 98, 113, 155
Brown, Tony, 179–81, 192–3, 218, 220
Brubeck, Dave, 219–20, 266
Bruce, Jack, 260
Brunies, George, 78, 122, 245
Brunskill, Bill, 9, 85
Brunswick label, 149
Bryant, Marie, 58
Bryce, Owen, 4, 10
Bryden, Beryl, 23, 78, 86, 91, 269
Bryning, Jimmy, 19
Buckley, Lord, 265
Buckner, Teddy, 148
Budd, Roy, 258
Bull's Head, Barnes, 258
Burbank, Al, 71
Burbridge, Graham, 82
Burdon, Eric, 260
Burke, Solomon, 145
Burley, Dan, 91
Burman, Maurice, 18–19, 37, 48, 95–6, 105, 106, 204
Burman, Peter, 117, 267–8
Burns, Norman, 45, 118, 179, 180
Burns, Tito, 33, 34, 38–9, 93, 106, 114, 115, 171, 179, 180
Burton, Dizzy, 10, 294n.
Burton, Richard, 132
Busby, Lad, 40, 41
Bush, Lennie, 35, 36–7, 109, 174, 206, 248
Butcher, Mike, 61–2, 110, 175, 190–1, 273
Byas, Don, 232, 266
Byrd, Charlie, 228

Caceres, Ernie, 209
Café de l'Europe, 6
Cairns, Forrie, 138, 139
Calloway, Cab, 191n., 192, 258
Calvert, Eddie, 130
Calvert, Leon, 167, 265
Campbell, Ambrose, 174
Campbell, Jimmy, 228
Candoli, Conte, 184, 193
Capitol Jazzmen, 10
Capitol label, 79, 99
Cardew, Phil, 41
Carey, Dave, 50, 53, 65, 85, 86, 263
Carey, Mutt, 11, 65
Caribbean Club, 118
Carnegie Hall, New York, 185
Carney, Harry, 136, 221, 225
Carr, Ian, 119, 261, 293
Carr, Pearl, 131
Carroll, Barbara, 102
Carter, Benny, 51, 59, 162, 167, 265, 286, 292
Catford Rhythm Club, 86
Catlett, Sid, 154
Caton, Lauderic, 118, 119, 147

Cave, Norman, 126
Caxton Hall, 171
Celestin, Papa, 71
Challenge, 22
Chaloff, Serge, 101
Chamberlain, Ronnie, 105
Chamblee, Eddie, 203–4
Charlesworth, Dick, 86, 138, 139, 140, 142, 259
Charters, Samuel, 12
Chessmen, 261
Chicago, 90, 121–2, 150
Chicagoans, 9, 122
Chilton, Charles, 34, 146
Chilton, John, 155, 156n., 232, 293
Chilver, Pete, 31, 33, 34, 40, 46
Chisholm, George, 40, 206, 292
Chocolate Dandies, 286
Christian, Charlie, 40–1
Christie, Ian, 9, 52, 53, 54, 68, 123, 125–6, 145, 156, 213
Christie, Keith, 21–2, 52, 53–4, 58, 61, 64, 65, 68, 88, 97, 102, 116, 193, 266, 292
Christie Brothers Stompers, 9, 53, 54, 68, 174, 176
Christy, June, 240, 243–4
Church Times, 284
City Gents (Dick Charlesworth's), 86
Claes, Johnny, 155, 196
Clambake Seven, 2
Clapton, Eric, 261
Clare, Alan, 258, 259
Clare, Kenny, 102

Clarke, Kenny, 27, 118, 248, 293
Clayre, Alasdair, 283
Clayton, Buck, 154, 158, 209, 213, 232, 235, 237, 266, 298
Clayton, Freddy, 23
Clayton, Peter, 264, 279, 281, 293
Cleall, Charles, 284, 295
Cleveland Rhythm Club, 17
Clooney, Rosemary, 118
Club Basie, 251
Club Eleven, 27, 31, 35–8, 41, 46–7, 93, 98, 249, 267, 297
clubs, 86–8, 247–59
Clyde Valley Stompers, 10, 138
Clyne, Jeff, 116
Codd, Johnny, 85
Coe, Tony, 158, 161, 233, 298
Coffee, Denny, 54
Cogan, Alma, 139
Cohn, Al, 184
Coker, Henry, 213
Cole, Nat King, 240
Coleman, Bill, 232
Coleman, Fitzroy, 58
Coleman, Ray, 274
Coliseum Theatre, Kingsway, 216–17
Collett, Dave, 133, 135
Colletts, 263
Collier, Jack, 40
Collier, Mike, 9, 23, 128
Collis, John, 90, 91
Coltrane, John, 261, 283
Columbia Records, 40–1, 80, 118, 135
Colyer, Bill, 13–17, 37, 67–8, 70–1, 82n., 90, 260, 263

Colyer, Ken, 2, 9, 14–15, 17, 54, 65, 67–78, 82, 84, 90, 91, 121, 123, 125, 130, 132–3, 136, 138, 143, 157, 158, 164, 186, 215, 231, 260, 292, 298
Commodore Jazz Band, 9
Commodore label, 43
Commodores, 175
Communist Party, 22, 24, 170
concerts, 262
Condon, Eddie, 2, 17, 54, 60, 68, 121–2, 125, 150, 209–13, 224, 229, 282
Condon, Les, 105, 118, 228
Connery, Sean, 81
Connor, Chris, 118
Conway, G., 179
Conway Hall, 60
Cook, Eddie, 281
Cook, Will Marion, 202
Cooke, Ann, 277–8
Cooke, Jack, 277–8
Cooper, Alan, 127
Cooper, George, 140, 142
Cooper, Reg, 276
Cooper, Roy, 10
Corrie, Ed, 138
Cottage Club, 87, 88, 213, 267
Cotton, Bill, 123
Cotton, Mike, 138, 145, 146
Counce, Curtis, 190–1, 194
Courtley, Bert, 105, 119, 218, 228, 266
Cox, John, 161

Coxhill, Lol, 261
Craig, Rob, 81
Cramp, Gerry, 88
Crane, Ray, 155
Crane River Jazz Band, 5, 9, 13–17, 18, 20, 23, 24, 68, 140, 143, 176, 248, 297
Crawford, Ralston, 72–3
Creole Jazz Band, 2, 10, 50, 52, 81, 87, 152, 233
Crescendo, 34
cricket, 88–9
Crimmins, Roy, 123, 125, 126–7, 163
Croker, Denis, 122
Crombie, Tony, 30–6, 109, 118, 174, 185–6, 262, 269
Crosby, Bing, 125, 126
Crosby, Bob, 2, 17
Croydon Rhythm Club, 85
Culley, Wendell, 213
Cummings, Jock, 40
Cunard, 29
Cundall, Tom, 279–80
Currie, Jimmy, 123
Curtis, Bix, 249, 267–8
Curtis, King, 261
Cutshall, Cutty, 209, 211, 212

Daily Express, 143, 192
Daily Herald, 192
Daily Mail, 138, 290
Daily Mirror, 192
Daily Sketch, 9, 192
Daily Telegraph, 281
Daily Worker, 16
Dameron, Tadd, 39, 101
Dance, Stanley, 148–9, 158, 205, 277–8, 281

Daniels, Joe, 24, 43, 101
Daniels, Mike, 9, 20, 84, 86, 138
Dankworth, Johnny, 29–30, 31, 32, 34, 35, 43, 46, 49, 53, 93, 95, 98–102, 155, 186, 204–5, 214, 217, 244, 250, 251, 259, 262, 266, 297
Dare, Reggie, 40, 269
Davies, John R.T., 13, 15, 82
Davies, Julian, 13, 15
Davis, Brian, 193–5
Davis, Cyril, 260
Davis, Kay, 167
Davis, Lew, 98
Davis, Miles, 62, 99, 233, 267
Davis, Wild Bill, 232
Davis Theatre, Croydon, 225
Davison, Harold, 140, 169, 183, 189–90, 199, 202, 257
Davison, Wild Bill, 122, 125, 126, 127, 209–12, 240
Dawbarn, Bob, 116–18, 123, 203–4, 220, 245, 274
Dawson, Eric, 102
De Barr, Will, 98
De Gray, Richard, 250
Decca, 19, 76, 79–80, 98, 118, 159, 264
Decca Band, 42
Decibel, 19
Deems, Barrett, 197, 199
Deitch, Gene, 18
Del Mar, Norman, 206–7
Delaney, Eric, 98, 137, 193, 214
Delaney, Jim, 144
Delmonte, Alfred, 288
Delta Jazz Band, 9, 20, 86, 138
Delta Jazz Club, 86, 87
Delta label, 19, 86
Delta Rhythm Kings, 10
Deniz, Frank, 40, 119, 181
Deniz, Joe, 119
Dennis, Denny, 23
Derby, 222
DeSanto, Sugar Pie, 145
Desmond, Paul, 219–20
Deuchar, Jimmy, 98, 107, 108, 109, 110, 116, 162, 232, 269, 298
Devere, Dickie, 38, 113, 174, 175, 249, 269
Dickenson, Vic, 209, 232
Dinnie, Wynne, 88
Disley, William 'Diz', 74, 269, 274
Dixieland style, 1–2, 7
Dixielanders (Alan Kirby), 9
Dixielanders (George Webb), 3, 4–6, 19, 22, 51, 59, 93, 99, 119, 140, 176, 236, 297
Dixon, Joe, 209
Dobell, Doug, 19, 135, 156, 263, 264
Dobell's, 263
Dodds, Baby, 3, 50, 150
Dodds, Johnny, 3, 10, 51, 81, 82, 83–4, 89, 121
Dodsworth, Norman, 123
Dollimore, Ralph, 113
Domnerus, Arne, 174
Donaldo, 58
Donegall, Marquis of, 6, 23, 24, 89, 183, 279
Donegan, Lonnie, 23, 73, 74, 78–80, 91, 132, 137, 176
Dorsey, Tommy, 2, 3, 97, 150
Dougan, Jackie, 231, 257, 265, 266
Douglas, Jim, 163
Dowling, Joan, 250
Down Beat, 26
Downbeat Big Band, 116
Downbeat Club, 116, 259
Driscoll, Julie, 261
drugs, 37–9
Dudley, Bessie, 222
Duff, Ronald 'Bix', 161
Duman, Steve, 165
Duncan, Fiona, 138
Duncan, Mac, 215
Dupree, Champion Jack, 91
Dusseldorf, 74, 127, 133
Dutton, Lyn, 54, 74, 88·9, 133, 140, 154, 164, 174, 292
Duvivier, George, 187
Dyani, Johnny, 120

East, Roy, 105
Eldridge, Roy, 158
Elizabeth II, Queen, 24, 89, 292
Elizalde, Fred, 33, 41
Ellefson, Art, 228
Ellington, Duke, 25, 34, 44, 52, 136, 148, 161, 166–7, 191–2, 203, 221, 222–7, 232, 266, 282, 284,

287–8, 298
Ellington, Ray, 33, 118, 262
Elliott, Bill, 274
Ellis, George, 263
Ellison, Jeff, 32, 36, 269
Elsdon, Alan, 138, 144, 145–6, 232, 238
EMI Studios, 40
Empire State, Kilburn, 225
Empress Hall, 197–9, 202, 203–4
The Encyclopedia of Jazz, 292
Erskine, Les, 149
Esquire label, 19, 30, 43, 101, 113, 135
Esquire Six, 43
Evans, Herschel, 213
Evans, Stomp, 57
Evening Star, 192
Everson, William, 272
Eyden, Bill, 115–16

Fairweather, Al, 81–3, 89, 139, 157–8, 164, 265
Fairweather, Digby, 33, 144, 293
Fairweather-Brown All Stars, 138, 157, 164
Fallon, Jack, 40, 58
Fame, Georgie, 252, 261
Fancy Free, 106–7
Farmer, Art, 231
Farnon, Bob, 171–3
Faubourg Club, 87
Faut, Volly de, 209
Fawkes, Wally, 4, 6, 13, 52, 53, 58, 60, 62–5, 82, 89, 138, 145, 158–9, 229, 290
Feather, Leonard, 12, 213, 216, 241–3,

247, 292, 293
Featherstonehaugh, Buddy, 42–3, 103, 265, 297
Fega, Mongegi, 120
Feldman, Joseph, 22, 31, 247–8
Feldman, Monty, 31
Feldman, Robert, 22, 31
Feldman, Victor, 31, 46, 66, 94, 298
Feldman Swing Club, 31
Felix, Lennie, 128, 159, 238
Felsted label, 149
Fenoulhet, Paul, 98
Fenton, Bernie, 35, 36–7
fiction, 293–5
Fielding, Harold, 178, 179, 185
Fierstone, George, 40, 41
Finch, Peter, 252
Firman, Bert, 264
Fishmongers Arms, Wood Green, 127
Fitzgerald, Ella, 27, 179, 180–1
Fitzgerald, Oscar, 185, 186
Fitzpatrick, Bob, 190, 193
Flamingo Club, 252, 254–5
Flood and Tempest Fund, 177–8
Fontana, Carl, 190, 193, 194
Ford, Brylo, 58
Foreman, John, 45–6
Foster, Frank, 213
Foster, Pop, 209
Foster, Teddy, 98, 267
Fountain, Pete, 217
Fowler, Billy, 286

Fowler, Harry, 250
Fox, Charles, 229n., 277–8, 279
Fox, Fred, 190
Fox, Roy, 94, 96, 105
Foxley, Ray, 10, 19, 176
Francis, Harry, 187
Frank, Aubrey, 37
Franzella, Sal, 209
Freeman, Alan, 138
Freeman, Bud, 60, 121, 127, 150, 232, 298
French, Jeremy, 128, 145, 159, 161
Fryer, Peter, 16
Fullado Club, 31–2, 35, 93, 249
Fuller, Bill, 183

Gaff club, 253
Galbraith, Charles, 9, 23, 137
Galleon Jazz Band, 23
Gammond, Peter, 264, 292, 293
Ganley, Allan, 102, 116, 193, 262, 266
Garbage Men, 17, 19, 98
Garber, Jan, 166
Garrat, Les, 196
Garrick, Michael, 119
Gaskell, Pip, 6, 233
Gaskin, Leonard, 209
Gates, Chuck, 174
Gatwood, Alan, 133
Gaucho Tango Orchestra, 28
Gay, Al, 127
Gehman, Dick, 210
Gelly, Dave, 293
George V, King, 24–5, 89
Geraldo, 28–30, 40, 42, 68, 94, 97, 105, 120,

189
Gershwin, George, 238
Getz, Stan, 221, 231
Gibbons, Tony, 85
Gilbert, Phil, 190
Gill, Mick, 10
Gillespie, Dizzy, 27, 32, 39, 44, 46, 47, 93, 97, 101–2, 103, 149, 221, 231, 233, 248, 249, 266, 293
Girsbach, Squire, 229
Gistal, Carlos, 243–4
Gleaves, Ronnie, 128
Glenny, Albert, 71–2
Godbolt, Jim, 173, 225
Gold, Harry, 43, 183
Gold, Jack, 156
Gold, Laurie, 23
Goldberg, Dave, 31, 37–8, 39, 40–1, 97, 167
Goldberg, Max, 48, 98
Golson, Benny, 231
Gonella, Nat, 42, 154, 201, 265
Gonsalves, Paul, 232, 298
Good Morning Blues, 162
Goode, Coleridge, 118, 119–20
Goodman, Benny, 3, 81, 119, 158, 167, 192, 203, 217
Goodwin, Henry, 209
Gordon, Dexter, 231
Grade, Lew, 169
Graham, Billy, 213
Graham, Kenny, 112–13, 154, 249, 250, 259, 268
Gramophone, 271, 272–3
Grant, Freddy, 58, 119
Grant, Jimmy, 153

Grant, Johnny, 109
Grant/Lyttelton Paseo Band, 58
Granz, Norman, 169–71, 177–80, 185–6, 220–1, 265
Grappelli, Stephane, 173n.
Gray, Johnny, 97
Gray, Wardell, 269
Greco, Buddy, 167
Green, Benny, 94, 109, 110, 111–12, 213, 247, 268–9, 292, 293
Green, Freddie, 213
Green, Hughie, 131
Green, Joe, 33n.
Green, Philip, 266
Greenwich Village club, 15
Greer, Sonny, 25
Greig, Stan, 61, 74, 81, 82, 150–1
Griffin, Johnny, 231
Grime, Kitty, 29, 279
Grimsby Jazz Club, 164
Grinyer, Ken, 10
Gross, Syd, 183
Guaraldi, Vince, 228
Gunnell, Rik, 250–2
Gypsy Larry, 267, 268

Haim, John, 9, 19, 68, 141, 143
Halcox, Pat, 73, 77, 132
Hale, Teddy, 269
Haley, Bill, 197, 200, 241, 243
Half Note club, New York, 231
Hall, Albert, 107
Hall, Edmond (Ed), 11, 131, 148, 149, 197, 208, 211, 229, 232, 238

Hall, Henry, 292
Hall, Tony, 30, 184, 250, 254–5, 273
Halperin, Daniel, 226–7, 255–6, 279
Hamburg, 74
Hamilton, Jimmy, 221
Hammond, John, 149, 160
Hampton, Lionel, 148, 158, 201, 203–5, 208, 217, 224, 232, 298
Harmonica Cats, 131
Harmony Inn, 108–9, 268–9, 270
Harold Davison Agency, 102
Harriott, Joe, 111, 112, 119, 120, 162, 175, 265, 267, 269
Harris, Bill, 228
Harris, Max, 107
Harris, Phil, 103, 105
Harris, Rex, 6, 22, 55, 56, 57, 239, 272, 285–8
Harrison, Len, 159
Harrison, Max, 277–8
Hartman, Johnny, 118
Harvey, Eddie, 4, 6, 13, 37, 88, 98, 99, 102, 105, 154, 228, 233, 235–6
Hastings, Lennie, 126, 127–8
Hathaway, Donny, 261
Hawdon, Dickie, 54, 82n., 88, 115, 119
Hawes, Pat, 6, 54, 85, 151n.
Hawkins, Coleman, 56, 57, 167, 168, 192, 221, 248, 287
Hawkins, Jay, 133

Hayes, Chris, 274
Hayes, Harry, 39, 40, 41–2, 44–5, 179, 180–1, 201
Hayes, Louis, 231
Hayes, Tubby, 38, 95, 105, 107, 114–18, 231, 232, 253, 259, 262, 266–7, 292, 298
Haywood, Cedric, 229
Heard, J.C., 179, 180
Heath, Percy, 218
Heath, Ted, 39, 97–8, 102, 103, 109, 181, 183, 185, 186–7, 189, 192, 214, 240–1, 242–3, 250, 262, 297
Heatley, Spike, 102, 161, 258
Heckstall–Smith, Dick, 260
Helm, Bob, 84
Henderson, Fletcher, 148, 222, 234, 287–8
Henebery, Terry, 266
Hennessey, Mike, 34, 281
Henshaw, Laurie, 250, 274
Herman, Woody, 81, 82, 185–6, 228, 266, 298
Heston and Isleworth Young Liberal Association, 16
Hibbs, Leonard, 277
Hideaway club, 253
Higginbotham, J.C., 154
Higgins, Jack, 140
Hill, Dr Ralph, 285
Hill, Teddy, 27, 167, 191n., 192, 221, 222
Hines, Earl, 148, 159, 216–17, 224, 232, 239, 240, 298
Hines/Teagarden All Stars, 216–17, 227
Hinton, Milt, 118
Hit Parade, 130–1, 136
HMV, 12, 42, 44
Hodges, Johnny, 57, 59, 161, 211, 221, 225, 265, 283
Hogg, Derek, 119, 161
Holiday, Billie, 153, 259
Holmes, Charlie, 59, 154
Honeyborne, Jack, 113
Hooper, Stix, 261
Hopkins, Claude, 11, 148, 149
Hopkinson, George, 54
Horne, Ellis, 84
Horne, Lena, 187
Horricks, Raymond, 277–8, 292
Horrox, Frank, 97
Horton, Molly, 259
Horton, Roger, 87, 128, 164
Hot Club of France, 167
Hot Club of London, 6, 22, 51, 77, 87
Hot Five and Seven, 2, 56, 87, 122, 152, 158, 229
Hot News, 271
Hotsy Totsy Gang, 34
Houston, Bob, 274
Howard, Darnell, 148
Howard, Kid, 71, 77, 227
Howell, Keith, 264
Hubbard, Freddie, 231
Hucko, Peanuts, 217, 229
Hughes, Bill, 213
Hughes, Glen, 261
Hughes, Spike, 42, 271, 290
Hull, Pete, 123
Humble, Derek, 105, 107, 108, 109, 112, 119
Humph at the Conway, 60
Humphanwally – It Seems Like Only Yesterday, 65
Humphrey, Percy, 72
Humphrey Lyttelton Club, 87, 160, 175, 248, 259
Hunt, Fred, 125, 126, 163
Hunter, Jo, 107, 113
Huntington, Billy, 72
Hutchinson, Leslie, 119–20
Hutton, Jack, 202, 274
Hyland, Vi, 249
Hylton, Jack, 66, 97, 108, 221, 284, 295
Hylton, Mrs Jack, 221

Imperial Jazz Band, 10
Indianola Jazz Band, 289
International Bookshop, 82, 263
IPC, 273
Isley Brothers, 146
It's Trad, Dad, 137–8

Jack, John, 82n.
Jackson, Edgar, 44–5, 101–2, 108, 271–3, 274, 276
Jackson, George, 10
Jackson, Lawrence, 42
Jackson, Milt, 29, 218–19
Jackson, Quentin 'Butter', 221

328 A History of Jazz in Britain 1950–1970

Jackson, Ray, 6
Jacobs, David, 138
Jagger, Mick, 260
James, Burnett, 278
James, Michael, 277–8
James, Roy, 135
Jaspar, Bobby, 231
Jazz (record company), 19
Jazz Aces (Dizzy Burton), 10
Jazz Aces (Eric Batty), 10
Jazz and Blues, 277
'Jazz at the Mapleton', 250
'Jazz at the Philharmonic' (JATP) concerts, 169–71, 177–82, 187, 192, 207–8, 265
Jazz Book Club, 288–9
Jazz Collector, 19
Jazz Couriers, 115–16, 262
Jazz Express, 277–8
Jazz Forum, 272
Jazz Illustrated, 52, 99, 104, 249, 276–7, 290
'Jazz Jamborees', 262
Jazz Journal, 15, 19, 20, 43, 55–7, 59, 68–71, 76, 83, 89, 126, 148, 163, 205, 234–5, 237, 238, 277, 279–81, 288, 291
Jazz Magazine, 20
Jazz Messengers, 261
Jazz Monthly, 277–9, 280
Jazz Music, 276, 285, 297
Jazz Music Books, 285
Jazz News, 75, 135, 142, 145, 161, 255–6, 279, 284
Jazz News and Review, 226
Jazz Record, 20, 297
Jazz Tête à Tête, 117, 267
Jazzshows Jazz Club, 87
Jelly Roll Kings, 9, 19, 68
Jesse, Kenyon, 276
Jig's Club Band, 285
John, Augustus, 258, 272
Johnson, Charlie, 234
Johnson, Gus, 221
Johnson, Ken, 159
Johnson, Laurie, 108
Johnson, Lonnie, 91, 174, 176
Johnson, Osie, 118
Johnson, Teddy, 131
Johnson, William 'Bunk', 11–13, 14, 16, 56, 60, 77, 100, 158, 216
Jones, Betty, 238
Jones, Dave, 137
Jones, Dill, 105, 119, 206, 221
Jones, Jo, 118, 149, 213
Jones, Jonah, 236
Jones, Max, 20, 63, 75, 89, 123–5, 132, 175–6, 178, 196, 197, 200, 210–11, 213, 217, 222–3, 225, 238, 239, 258, 264, 265, 272, 274, 276, 277–8, 284, 293, 297
Jones, Paul, 260
Jones, Reunald, 213, 228
Jones, Richard M., 224
Jones, Ronnie, 260, 261
Jones, Sam, 213, 231
Jones, Thad, 62, 213
Jordan, Dick, 252
Jordan, Louis, 232
Jordan, Steve, 149
Joyce, James, 282
Julies, Albert, 72

Kaminsky, Max, 119, 217, 289–90
Karas, Anton, 130
Katz, Dick, 118
Katzman, Lee, 190
Kaye, Cab, 174
Kaye, Danny, 105
Kaye, Robin, 111
Kaye, Trevor, 138
Keane, Shake, 120
Keeler, Christine, 252
Keene, Marion, 109
Keene, Ronnie, 109
Keir, Dave, 123, 126
Kelly, Bob, 215
Kelly, Don, 190
Kemel, Buglin' Sam, 71
Ken Colyer Club, 74, 86, 87, 250
Kendall, John, 263
Kenton, Stan, 31, 103–4, 183–5, 186, 189–96, 201, 208, 293
Kessel, Barney, 179, 180
Ketelbey, Albert, 34
King, Bertie, 57, 119, 265
King, Pete, 102, 106–7, 109, 111–12, 117, 119, 231, 248, 254, 256–8, 269
King, Peter (alto saxophone), 258
Kingswell, Don, 87, 267, 268
Kinn, Maurice, 23–4, 183, 190, 273
Kinnell, Bill, 19, 20, 297

Index

Kinsey, Tony, 98, 186, 249, 262, 269
Kirby, Alan, 9
Kirby, Kathy, 96
Kirchin, Basil, 98, 183, 192
Kirk, Andy, 221
Kirk, Roland, 231
Kirkwood, Pat, 106
Kit-Kat Band, 108
Klein, Harry, 37, 107, 181, 195, 196, 248–9, 261, 262
Klook's Kleek, 252
Knight, Tony, 261
Knightsbridge Strings, 131
Konitz, Lee, 59, 211
Korner, Alexis, 260, 261
Kozack, Ashley, 119
Krahmer, Carlo, 19, 29, 30–1, 36, 46, 49, 135
Kruger, Jeff, 115, 250
Kruger, Sam, 250
Krupa, Gene, 3, 44, 131, 179, 180–1
Kyle, Billy, 197, 199

La Rocca, Nick, 122, 147
Laine, Cleo, 266
Laine, Papa Jack, 71
Lake, Steve, 276
Lambert, G.E. 'Eddie', 234–6, 236–7, 238
Lambert, Hendricks and Ross, 118
Lane, Steve, 9, 85, 276
Lang, Eddie, 150
Lansdowne label, 265
Lansdowne Studios, 80, 265
Larkin, Philip, 281–3, 291
Larsen, Kent, 190

Lascelles, Gerald, 23, 24, 89, 226, 279, 280, 292
Lateef, Yusef, 231, 257
Laurie, Cy, 9, 61, 82, 83–4, 146, 245–6, 249, 267
Lavender, Johnny, 123
Lawson, Yank, 119
Layton, Teddy, 85
Le Sage, Bill, 98, 100–1, 258
Leader, 8
Ledbetter, Huddie 'Leadbelly', 79, 86
Leddy, Ed, 190
Lee, Dave, 102
Lee, Peggy, 298
Leicester Jazz Band, 10
Leicester Square Jazz Club, 6–8, 45
Lemon, Brian, 158, 298
Lennon, John, 283
Lesberg, Jack, 197, 199
Leslie, Peter, 23, 135, 175
Lester, Dick, 138
Levee Loungers, 10, 19
Levin, Tony, 116, 117
Lewington, Bill, 41
Lewis, Sir Edward, 80, 279
Lewis, George, 11–13, 14, 16, 56, 60, 72, 76, 81, 133, 136, 158, 182, 186, 215–16, 227–8, 229, 231, 232, 266, 283, 298
Lewis, John, 162, 218–19, 232
Lewis, Mel, 190, 193, 194
Lewis, Ted, 89
Lewis, Vic, 19n., 103–6, 114, 119, 181, 191, 192–3, 194, 197, 199, 242–3, 277, 297
Lightfoot, Paddy, 63n.
Lightfoot, Terry, 127, 135, 136, 137, 138, 140, 142, 146, 266, 278
Lindsay, Ken, 6, 23
Lipton, Sidney, 97
Lister, Eric, 86
Littlejohn, Alan, 85, 128, 144, 145
Living Jazz, 156
Logan, Ella, 197, 199, 222
Lomax, Alan, 229n.
Lombardo, Guy, 166
London City Stompers, 138
London Jazz Club, 8, 9, 50, 51–2, 54, 73, 87
London Jazz label, 50
London Palladium, 25, 107, 109, 138, 166, 167, 185, 192, 221
Loss, Joe, 183, 189
Lotis, Denis, 97
Lumby, Alf, 263
Lunceford, 288
Lusher, Don, 97, 116
Luter, Claude, 18, 84
Lyddiat, Don, 278
Lynn, Jackie, 86, 142
Lyttelton, Humphrey, 2, 6–9, 14, 18, 22, 23, 24, 42, 45, 48–66, 67, 71, 75, 80, 82–3, 105–6, 121, 130, 136, 138, 140, 143, 150–4, 156, 157, 165, 171–3, 175–6, 201, 202, 205, 207, 212, 217–19, 224–5, 232, 234–7, 244–5, 259, 262, 265, 274,

277, 286–8, 289, 290, 292, 293

Mac, Mrs, 291–2
Mac's Rehearsal Rooms, 8, 15, 27, 35, 83
McAllister, Jay, 190
McCarthy, Albert, 20, 85, 272, 274, 276, 277, 279, 297
McCracken, Bob, 229
Macey, Johnny, 133
McGarity, Lou, 54, 209
McGhee, Browning, 91
McGregor, Chris, 258
McJazz, 83
Mack, Bob, 85
McKay, Ron, 135
McKenzie, Henry, 97
McKenzie, Mike, 58
McKenzie, Red, 122
McKiernan, Paddy, 215
Mackintosh, Ian, 159–61
Mackintosh, Ken, 98
MacLean (bass player), 71
Maclean, Ian, 279
McNair, Harold, 120, 266, 267
McPartland, Jimmy, 119, 121, 150, 167, 186
McQuater, Tommy, 116
McRae, Carmen, 117
McShann, Jay, 27, 293
Maddock, Owen, 123
magazines, 20, 271–81, 297
Magee String Band, 13
Magnolia Jazz Band, 9, 24, 122, 220
mainstream jazz, 148–65
Mammoth Concerts, 23

Manchester Sports Guild, 164
Mann, Manfred, 252
Manone, Wingy, 2, 232
Mantovani, 143
Manzi, Bonny, 135
Mapleton Restaurant, 250, 252
Mardi Gras, Liverpool, 164
Margaret, Princess, 195, 213, 214
marijuana, 37–8
Markey, Joe, 196
Marquee Club, 162, 259–60
Marrero, Lawrence, 227
Marsh, Roy, 147
Marshall, Ben, 15, 54
Marshall, John, 260
Marshall, Joy, 117
Martin, John, 279
Martin, Pete, 6
Mary, Queen, 89
Mason, Pat, 137
Mason, Rod, 132
Massarik, Jack, 260–2
Mathewson, Ron, 116, 117
Mathison-Brooks, Percy, 273
Matthew, Brian, 137
Maxwell, Clinton, 119
Mayall, John, 261
Mayer, John, 265
Meeker, David, 266
Melly, George, 9, 23, 24, 65, 77–8, 81, 86, 123, 135, 138, 141, 146, 210, 251, 290–2, 293
Melodisc, 19, 239, 264
Melody Maker, 271–6, 296, *et passim*
Menzies, Malcolm, 278

Merrydown, John, 279
Merseysippi Jazz Band, 9, 10, 176, 278
Metrobopera, 35, 93, 249
Mezzrow, Mezz, 259
Mickleburgh, Bobby, 142, 155
Middleton, Tony, 263
Middleton, Velma, 197, 200
Miles, Lizzie, 71
Miley, Bubber, 282
Miller, Glenn, 217
Miller, Max, 221
Miller, Moe, 95
Millinder, Lucky, 148, 234
Milliner, Tony, 85, 234
Mills, Freddy, 218
Mills, Irving, 34
Milne, Geoff, 264
Mingus, Charles, 118, 162, 266–7
Ministry of Labour, 28, 166, 169, 174–8, 187, 197
Minshull, Mac, 37, 107, 111, 248
Minton's Playhouse, 27
Miranda, Jack, 66
Mirfield, Freddy, 17, 98
Mr Acker Bilk Requests, 135
modern jazz, 77–8, 103–20
Modern Jazz Quartet, 217–19, 266
Moholo, Louis, 120
Mole, Miff, 150
Monk, Laurie, 102
Monk, Sonny, 10
Monk, Thelonious, 27, 29, 244, 266
Monsbourgh, Ade, 7,

Index   331

55, 57
Montagu, Lord, 138, 226, 279
Montgomery, Wes, 261, 266
Moody, James, 231, 233
Mooney, Joe, 34
Moore, Dudley, 102
Moore, Gerry, 175
Moore, Henry, 282
Moore, Nicholas, 272
Morello, Joe, 219–20
Morgan, Alun, 277–8, 292
Morgan, Henry, 244–5
Morgan, Laurie, 29, 31, 32, 35, 36, 40, 47, 167, 249, 269
Morgan, Lee, 261
Morris, Harry, 35, 37, 267–8, 269
Morris, Rex, 102, 181
Morris, Sonny, 15, 68
Morrissey, Dick, 88
Mortimer, John, 86
Morton, Benny, 213
Morton, Jelly Roll, 2, 3, 11, 55, 56, 81, 93, 139, 158, 222, 229n., 238, 278
Morton, Ted, 87, 128, 259
Morum, William, 293–5
Moss, Danny, 102, 158
Moten, Bennie, 34
Moule, Ken, 118
Muddel, Joe, 33, 35, 98
Mulligan, Gerry, 217
Mulligan, Mick, 9, 23, 24, 81, 89, 122–5, 126, 138, 140, 161, 213, 220, 245–6, 251, 291
Mumford, John, 155, 159

Murad, Jerry, 131
Murray, Pete, 138
Murray, Ruby, 61
Murray Club Jazz Band, 288
Music Fare, 15
Musical Express, 273
Musicians' Benevolent Fund, 262
Musicians' Union, 20, 28, 52, 166–87, 200, 206, 214, 220–1, 231
My Kind of Jazz, 97–8
Mylne, Dave, 81

Nance, Ray, 29, 40, 167, 232, 239
Nanton, 'Tricky Sam', 221
Napper, Kenny, 116, 231, 257, 266–7
National Federation of Jazz Organizations (NFJO), 22–3, 24, 86, 174, 175, 176, 203, 215
National Jazz Federation, 125, 132, 204–5, 232, 259
Neagle, Anna, 66
Nelson, Ozzie, 222n.
Nelson, Stanley, 284, 295
Nevard, Mike, 36–7
Neville, Derek, 42, 248, 269
New Flamingo Club, 115
New Jazz Group, 262
New Jazz Society, 175
New Musical Express, 21–2, 54, 61–2, 68, 82–3, 110, 111–12, 120, 171–4, 182, 183–4, 189–90, 191–

2, 196, 243, 251, 273
New Orleans Item, 72–3
New Orleans jazz, 3–4, 11–17, 48–66, 67–85, 93, 121, 150, 186, 214–16
New Orleans Jazz Band, 9, 20, 140
New Orleans Jazz Club, 70
New Orleans Jazzmen, 138
New Orleans Joys, 78
New Orleans to London, 74
New Statesman, 156n.
New York, 29, 68
'New York' style, 150
New York Times, 246
Newman, Joe, 213
Newport Jazz Festival, 246
News Chronicle, 214
Nicholas, Albert, 11, 52, 68, 82, 123, 154, 209, 232, 238–9
Nicholls, Brian, 279, 292
Nicholls, Nick, 132
Nichols, Red, 150
Niehaus, Lennie, 190
Nimitz, Jack, 190, 195
Nixa, 135, 264
Nobes, Roger, 163
Noone, Jimmie, 121
Noto, Sam, 190, 194
novels, 293–5
No. 1 Rhythm Club, 247
Nuthouse club, 49

O'Brien, Shamus, 19
Observer, 290–1
October Song, 65
O'Day, Anita, 244
Odhams Press, 273

O'Donnell, Eddie, 74
Oliver, King, 2, 10–11, 56, 81, 93, 152, 158, 224, 233, 245, 278, 282
Oliver, Paul, 277–8, 279
Oliverie, Jack, 106
100 Club, 87, 128, 146, 249
100 Club News, 64
Original Dixieland Jazz Band, 1, 9, 10, 24–5, 55, 89, 122, 147, 238–9, 289
Original Varsity Sack Droppers, 10
Oriole Jazz Band, 138
Orpwood, Ray, 15
Ory, Kid, 3, 11, 56, 78, 228
Osborne, John, 132

Page, Hot Lips, 233
Page, Walter, 149, 213
Palmer, Stan, 111
Paramount Dance Hall, 248–9
Paramount Jazz Band, 133–6, 138
Paramour, Norrie, 262
Parenti, Tony, 27, 209
Paris, Sidney de, 148
Paris, Wilbur de, 131
Parker, Brian, 82
Parker, Charlie, 27, 29, 30, 39, 40–1, 47, 93, 103, 233, 282–3, 293
Parker, Johnny, 61, 132, 151
Parlophone, 19, 46, 52–3, 60, 61, 107, 265, 296
Parnell, Jack, 19n., 31, 39, 97, 102, 103, 106–9, 114, 206, 253, 262, 271, 297
Parnell, Val, 185
Parnes, Larry, 261
Parr, Frank, 89, 123, 213, 239, 278
Parry, Harry, 40, 42, 146–7, 297
Patchen, Kenneth, 272
Patterson, Ottilie, 132
Pavageau, Alcide, 13, 227
Paxton Records, 284
Payne, Jack, 74
Payne, Pete, 23, 86, 87
Payne, Sonny, 213
Pearson, Dave, 160
Pebberdy, Jack, 242
Peerless, Brian, 263
Pendleton, Harold, 23, 125, 279
Pepper, Art, 31, 298
Perez, Manuel, 227
Perkins, Bill, 190, 193, 194, 195
Perowne, Leslie, 288
Perrin, Les, 49, 84, 98, 273
Peter, Eric, 111
Peterson, Oscar, 179, 180–2, 185, 186, 221, 266
Petit, Buddy, 227
'Petite Fleur', 130–1, 245–6
Petrillo, James C., 182–3, 186–7
Pettiford, Oscar, 118
Phillips, Flip, 179, 180
Phillips, Sid, 23, 24, 43, 89, 98, 136, 183, 206
Phillips, Van, 33
Phillips, Woolf, 40
Picard, John, 61, 161
Picasso, Pablo, 78, 282
Piccadilly Club, 251
Picou, Alphonse, 71, 227
Pitterson, Pete, 37, 42, 248
PL Yearbook of Jazz 1946, 272
Plant, Robert, 260
Plomley, Roy, 34, 217
Pollack, Ben, 216
Pollard, Tommy, 31, 34, 35, 37–8, 42, 43, 46, 174
Polo, Danny, 98, 292
Pomeroy, Colin, 19
Postgate, John, 277–8, 288
Potter, John, 137
Pound, Ezra, 282
Powell, Benny, 213
Powell, Bud, 29
Pratt, Bobby, 97, 116
Premru, Ray, 116
Preston, Billy, 261
Preston, Denis, 58, 80, 136, 151, 208, 264–6
Preuss, Oscar, 52
Price, Ernie, 135
Priestley, Brian, 277–8, 293
Priestley, J.B., 295
Procope, Russell, 221–2
progressive jazz, 103–6
Pronk, Rob, 174
Prudence, Brian, 137
Pude, Charles, 173
Purbrook, Colin, 158, 161, 266
Purdie, Bernard 'Pretty', 261
Pye label, 135
Pyne, Chris, 161
Pyne, Mick, 116, 117, 161

R & B, 259–62

Rabin, Oscar, 262
Race, Steve, 23, 43, 70, 83, 104, 113, 171–3, 175, 181–2, 219–20, 274, 277
Radio Rhythm Club Sextet, 297
Radio Times, 90–1
Raeburn, Boyd, 29
Ramsey, Frederic, 12, 215–16
Randall, Freddy, 9, 17–18, 19, 20, 23, 98, 122, 125, 126, 140, 143, 155, 183, 197, 200–1, 241–3, 297
Raphaello, Neva, 86
Ratcliffe, Hardie, 169–70
Rattenbury, Ken, 10, 23
Ravers CC, 88–9
Rawlings, Les, 6
re-bop *see* bop
Record Changer, 18, 285
record companies, 19, 264–6
Red Hot Peppers, 2, 87
Redcar Jazz Club, 164
Redd, Alton, 229
Reddihough, John, 75
Redman, Don, 148, 221, 288
Reece, Dizzy, 118, 120, 174, 249, 269
Reece, Red, 261
Reinhardt, Django, 44
Rendell, Don, 29, 31–2, 34, 35, 36, 98, 119, 195, 218, 228
Rendell-Carr Quintet, 119
Revell, Alex, 84
Reweliotty, André, 202
Rex restaurant, 87, 108–9
Reynolds News, 61
Rhythm, 271, 273
rhythm and blues (R & B), 259–62
Rhythmic Eight, 264
Rice-Davies, Mandy, 252
Richard, Cliff, 132
Richards, Frank, 265
Richardson, Jack, 123
Richford, Dougie, 138
Ridley, Laurie, 127
Rigden, Reg, 4, 6
Riverside, 19
Roach, Max, 27, 29, 150
Roberts, Don 'Pixie', 55
Roberts, George, 58, 119, 248
Roberts, Joan, 86
Robeson, Paul, 262
Robichaux, Joseph, 227
Robinson, Damian, 119
Robinson, Dougie, 102, 111, 112
Robinson, Jim, 13, 54, 78, 227, 229
Robinson, John, 6
Robinson, Spike, 298
Roche, Harry, 95, 181
'Rock Island Line', 78–80, 90, 130, 245
Roderick, Stan, 116
Rogers, Johnny, 35, 42
Rolling Stones, 145, 259–60
Rollini, Adrian, 41
Rollins, Sonny, 261, 283
Ronnie Scott's Club, 253–8
Ros, Edmundo, 159, 262
Rosa, Lita, 97
Rose, Denis, 32–3, 34, 47, 119, 248, 249, 269–70
Rose, Pat, 122
Rosen, Harold, 168–9, 183, 201
Rosenthal, George S., 215
Rosenthal, Irving, 190
Ross, Annie, 118, 262
Ross, Ronnie, 116, 119, 261, 269
Rowden, Johnny, 85
Rowe, John, 263
Rowland, John, 261
Roy, Harry, 96, 118
Roy, Leon, 248–9
Royal, Marshall, 213
Royal Albert Hall, 23, 66, 187, 190–1, 194
Royal Festival Hall, 24, 57, 89, 111, 125, 132, 174, 183, 202–3, 204, 206–7, 208, 213, 216–23, 232, 298
Royal Philharmonic Orchestra, 206
Royal Theatre, Dublin, 185
Rugolo, Pete, 103, 104
Rushing, Jimmy, 237, 298
Russell, Bertrand, 265
Russell, Luis, 148, 154, 234, 237
Russell, Pee Wee, 122, 123, 127, 209, 232, 238, 283, 298
Russell, Rags, 88, 105
Russell, Tony, 277–8
Russell-Wickham Hot Six, 9
Rust, Brian, 43–4, 132, 264, 279

S and M label, 19, 125
St Andrew's Hall, Glasgow, 217
St Louis Four, 17
Saints Jazz Band, 10, 20, 24, 86
Salisbury, Gerry, 128, 132
Sampson, Tommy, 103
Saunders, Art, 87, 127
Saunders, Viv, 87, 127
Savoy label, 40
Saward, Bernard, 8, 53, 54, 66
Scala, Primo, 34
Schroeder, Gene, 209, 211
Scott, Johnny, 116, 228
Scott, Ronnie, 31–7, 40, 42, 43, 46, 93, 95, 97, 102, 105–12, 115–16, 119, 155, 157, 162, 179, 180, 184, 196, 241, 253–8, 262, 267, 269, 270
Scudder, Rosina, 86
Sculthorpe US Air Force base, 184, 185
Seamen, Phil, 37–8, 107, 111, 112, 116, 260, 261
Second City Jazzmen, 10
Sellers, John, 91
Semple, Archie, 10, 81, 123, 125, 126, 127, 240
Senn, Mike, 115, 259
Sergeant, Howard, 272
The Seven Ages of Acker, 135
'77' label, 19, 135, 264
Shadows, 132
Shalit, Emil, 19
Shannon, Terry, 115, 116
Shar, Hindu, 44
Sharon, Ralph, 21–2, 34, 40, 46, 118, 155
Sharpe, Jackie, 114–15, 259
Shavers, Charlie, 179, 180
Shaw, Hank, 31, 35, 36, 105, 107, 111, 258
Shearing, George, 40, 118, 147, 244
Shearing, Trixie, 243
Shepherd, Dave, 128, 221
Shields, Larry, 122
shops, 262–3
Short, Charlie, 39, 40, 41, 97
Short, Tony, 10
Shu, Eddie, 229
Sidwell, Roy, 265
Silk, Eric, 9, 23, 85
Silver, Horace, 261
Silvo, Johnny, 86
Simeon, Omer, 11, 82, 148
Simons, Judith, 142–3
Simpson, Paul, 123
Simpson, Ron, 175
Sims, Ken, 135, 139
Sims, Zoot, 184, 193, 231, 256–7, 267
Sims-Wheeler Vintage Jazz Band, 138
Sinatra, Frank, 143
Sinatra, Spencer, 190, 195
Singer, Harry, 44
Siptak, George, 268–9
Six Bells, 156, 157, 252–3
Skidmore, Alan, 260
Skidmore, Jimmy, 105, 119
skiffle, 90–1
Skivington, Pete, 163
Skrimshire, Nevil, 6, 8, 50, 65, 125
Skuse, Johnny, 133
Slim, Memphis, 91
Smallman, David, 269
Smeltzer, Cornell, 34
Smilby, 277
Smith, Bessie, 123, 282
Smith, Betty, 122
Smith, Brian, 261
Smith, Charles Edward, 12
Smith, Colin, 135–6, 144
Smith, Derek, 262
Smith, Dick, 74, 130
Smith, Elsie, 203–4
Smith, Jimmy, 261
Smith, Ray, 133, 263
Smith, Willie, 179, 180–1
Smith, Willie 'The Lion', 236, 266
Smoky City Stompers, 10, 19
Smythe, Pat, 259
Snow, Valaida, 167
Sollash, Don, 263
Sonin, Ray, 23, 171, 190, 194, 273
Soothill, Brian, 196
Souchon, Dr Edmond, 70, 71
South, Harry, 115, 118, 154
Southern Jazz Band, 9, 85
Southern Stompers, 9, 85
Southern Syncopated Orchestra, 25, 202
Sowden, Geoff, 132
Spanier, Muggsy, 17, 122, 239

Spike's Seven Pods of Pepper, 229
Spot, Jack, 270
Spring, Bryan, 258
Squadronaires, 98
Stainer, Johnny, 133
Stapleton, Cyril, 98, 131, 189, 192, 214
Star Club, 251
Starke, Tony, 276
Starr, Eric, 85
Steam Packet, 261
Stenfalt, Norman, 39, 40, 41, 43, 97, 109, 111, 269
Stephenson, Louis, 119
Stewart, Graham, 146, 229
Stewart, Jay Allison, 215, 227–8
Stewart, Rex, 85, 167, 232
Stewart, Rod, 261
Stobart, Kathy, 105, 118–19
Stokes, Sammy, 97, 107, 186, 262
Stone, Lew, 96
Storyville Jazz Band, 138, 142
Strange, Peter, 85, 155
'Stranger on the Shore', 136
Strayhorn, Billy, 226
Streatfield, Art, 4
Strict Tempo Ballroom Dancing Orchestra, 131
Stuart, Wally, 34
Studio Club, 258
Studio 51, 74, 86, 87, 249–50
Sullivan, Ed, 245
Sullivan, Joe, 3
Summers, Alf, 35

Sunday Club, 259
Sunday Telegraph, 156, 281
Sunshine, Monty, 15, 73, 89, 91, 130–2, 138, 245–6
Surman, John, 260
Sutton, Ralph, 174, 232
Swing Club, 247–8
Swing Music, 271, 277
Swing Shop, 263
Swinging Blue Jeans, 96
Swope, Earl, 102
Sylvester, Victor, 98, 131

Tailgate, 19
Tait, Dorothy, 215
Tally Ho pub, Kentish Town, 144
Tanner, Peter, 43
Tano, Vinnie, 190, 194
Tate, James, 140
Tatum, Art, 159, 167
Tauber, Richard, 128
Taylor, Eddie, 150–1, 154, 233
Teagarden, Charlie, 27
Teagarden, Jack, 27, 127, 216–17, 298
Teagarden-Earl Hines All Stars, 158
Tell, Billy, 289
Temperance Seven, 137–8
Temperley, Joe, 107, 118, 233, 236, 269
Tempo label, 19, 50, 85, 114, 118, 122, 264
Terry, Clark, 209
Terry, Sonny, 91
Teschemacher, Frank, 121
Thacker, Clive, 261
Tharpe, Rosetta, 91

Theatre Royal, Dublin, 183
Themen, Art, 260
Third World Festival of Youth and Students for Peace, East Berlin (1951), 16
Thomas, Alan, 82
Thompson, Barbara, 119
Thompson, Bill, 128
Thompson, Sir Charles, 149, 235
Thompson, Eddie, 46, 179, 180, 253
Thompson, Frank, 125
Thompson, Lucky, 231
Thorne, Ken, 103
Three Ts, 27
Tobbutt, Douggie, 232
Tollefson, 34
Tolley, Albert, 258
Topic, 268–9
Torme, Mel, 117, 118
Townshend, Cliff, 40
Tracey, Stan, 97, 231, 254, 257, 265, 298
trad jazz, 130–47
Trad Kings, 138
Traill, Sinclair, 19, 20–1, 22, 76, 89, 141–2, 274, 279–81, 292, 293
Trinder, Tommy, 106, 262
Tristano, Lenny, 244
Troglodytes (Wally Fawkes), 138, 159, 161
Troy, Doris, 145
Trumbauer, Frank, 27
Turner, Bruce, 58–61, 122, 127, 138, 150, 155–7, 161, 164–5, 211, 232, 234, 235,

242, 266, 292
Turner, Joe, 237, 298
Two-Way Club, 251
Tyndale, George, 119, 248

Umansky, Mo, 82
United States of America:
  British musicians in, 240–6
  musicians in Britain, 166–87, 189–208, 209–30, 231–40
Usden, Dave, 111, 112, 115, 248

Valentine, Dickie, 97
Vallis, Buddy, 4, 8
Van Rees, Lou, 171
Vanguard label, 149
Vaughan, Frankie, 139, 143
Vaughan, Roy, 9, 122
Vaughan, Sarah, 116, 258
Vedey, Georgette, 273
Vedey, Julian, 273
Venables, Ralph Goodwin Vaughan, 43, 85
Venuti, Joe, 150
Verrell, Ronnie, 97
Visiting Orchestras Appreciation Society, 178, 203, 204–5
Voce, Steve, 235, 238, 281, 291
Vogue label, 264
Voodoo Band, 146

Walker, Frank, 282
Walker, George, 58
Walker, Jimmy, 23, 24, 118

Walker, Junior, 261
Walker, Sammy, 118, 249
Wall City Jazz Band, 10
Waller, Fats, 51, 56, 159, 167
Wallis, Bob, 133, 137, 138, 139, 140, 142
Wallis, Shani, 248
Ward, Ron, 215
Warleigh, Ray, 161, 260
Warren, Earle, 213
Warwick, Dionne, 146
Washington, Jack, 213
Waters, Benny, 232
Waters, Muddy, 91, 132, 260
Watkins, Joe, 227
Watson, Jimmy, 106, 111
Watts, Charlie, 260
Wayne, Bruce, 174
Weatherburn, Ron, 85
Webb, Chick, 27, 148
Webb, George, 3, 4–6, 8–9, 10, 19, 22, 51, 52, 59, 64–5, 87, 93, 99, 119, 140, 143, 176, 236, 297
Webster, Ben, 232, 266
Weeks, Leslie, 58
Weir, Frank, 40, 98
Welch, Chris, 276
Welling, Johnny, 137
Wellins, Bobby, 43, 265
Wells, Dicky, 213, 232, 266, 298
Welsh, Alex, 125–7, 138, 139, 142, 162–3, 164, 232, 234, 238, 246, 266, 298
Wess, Frank, 213
West African Rhythm Band, 174
Westminster City

Council, 263
Wettling, George, 128, 209, 211
Whannell, Paddy, 156
Wheeler, Ian, 215
Wheeler, Kenny, 43, 228, 260, 265
White, Mark, 22
Whiteman, Paul, 166, 216, 284
Whittle, Tommy, 31, 39, 40, 97, 102, 119, 193, 195–6, 243, 249, 262
Whitton, Doug, 9, 19, 239
Who's Who of Jazz, 293
Whyte, Duncan, 31, 154
Wickham, Alan, 128
Wiggs, Johnny, 70–1
Wilber, Bob, 209–12, 229, 233
Wilcox, Bert, 8, 9, 22, 23, 54, 66, 73, 103–6, 202, 239, 276–7
Wilcox, Herbert, 66
Wilcox, Stan, 8, 22, 23, 54, 103–6, 239, 276–7
Wilcox Agency, 98, 102
Wilford, Charles, 272–3, 274, 277
Wilkins, Dave, 37, 40, 41, 97, 119, 147, 159
Williams, Jimmy, 232
Williams, Joe, 213
Williams, Mary Lou, 29, 258
Williams, Richard, 274–6, 283
Williams, Roy, 127, 163, 298
Williams, Sandy, 148
Wilson, John S., 246
Wilson, Teddy, 51, 151,

183, 185, 221, 232
Windmill Theatre, 269–70
Windsor, Duke of, 25, 95
Winstone, Cecil 'Flash', 23, 38
Winstone, Eric, 98, 112, 268
Winter Garden Theatre, 22
Wolverines, 10
Wood Green Jazz Club, 87, 249
Woodrow, Al, 88
Woods, Fred, 37
Wray, Ken, 88, 107, 109, 110, 228, 269
Wright, Denny, 58
Wright, Eugene, 219–20
Wykes, Roy, 4

Yerba Buena Band, 11
Yes, It's the Gents, 142
Yorkshire Jazz Band, 9, 23, 54, 74, 86
Young, Arthur, 173n.
Young, Leon, 136
Young, Lester, 30, 58, 179, 180, 213
Young, Trummy, 197, 232
Young Communist League, 22

Zachary, Frank, 215
Zan Zeba club, 249
Zenith Jazz Band, 84
Zenith Six, 10